*Norm and Context in Christian Ethics*

# *Norm and Context in Christian Ethics*

*edited by*
## GENE H. OUTKA
## PAUL RAMSEY

FREDERICK S. CARNEY • CHARLES E. CURRAN • DONALD EVANS
JOSEPH FLETCHER • JAMES M. GUSTAFSON • BERNARD HÄRING
DAVID LITTLE • EDWARD LEROY LONG, JR. • RICHARD A. MC CORMICK
JOHN G. MILHAVEN • BASIL MITCHELL • GENE H. OUTKA
PAUL RAMSEY • N. H. SØE

*CHARLES SCRIBNER'S SONS* • *NEW YORK*

Copyright © 1968 Charles Scribner's Sons

THIS BOOK PUBLISHED SIMULTANEOUSLY IN
THE UNITED STATES OF AMERICA AND IN CANADA—
COPYRIGHT UNDER THE BERNE CONVENTION

ALL RIGHTS RESERVED. NO PART OF THIS BOOK
MAY BE REPRODUCED IN ANY FORM WITHOUT
THE PERMISSION OF CHARLES SCRIBNER'S SONS.

A-6.68 (C)

PRINTED IN THE UNITED STATES OF AMERICA
*Library of Congress Catalog Card Number 68–17352*

# Contents

Preface ix

### Part One   Virtue, Principles, and Rules

1  *Deciding in the Situation: What Is Required?* 3
   FREDERICK S. CARNEY
2  *Moral Discernment in the Christian Life* 17
   JAMES M. GUSTAFSON
3  *Character, Conduct, and the Love Commandment* 37
   GENE H. OUTKA
4  *The Case of the Curious Exception* 67
   PAUL RAMSEY

### Part Two   Natural Law: A Reassessment of the Tradition

5  *Absolute Norms in Moral Theology* 139
   CHARLES E. CURRAN
6  *Calvin and the Prospects for a Christian Theory of Natural Law* 175
   DAVID LITTLE
7  *Dynamism and Continuity in a Personalistic Approach to Natural Law* 199
   BERNARD HÄRING
8  *Toward an Epistemology of Ethics* 219
   JOHN G. MILHAVEN
9  *Human Significance and Christian Significance* 233
   RICHARD A. MC CORMICK

Part Three  **Reformation Themes: The Uses of the Law**

10 *Soteriological Implications of Norm and Context* 265
EDWARD LEROY LONG, JR.
11 *The Three "Uses" of the Law* 297
N. H. SØE

Part Four  **Situation Ethics: Defense and Critique**

12 *What's in a Rule?: A Situationist's View* 325
JOSEPH FLETCHER
13 *Ideals, Roles, and Rules* 351
BASIL MITCHELL
14 *Love, Situations, and Rules* 367
DONALD EVANS

Index 415

# Contributors

FREDERICK S. CARNEY — Associate Professor of Christian Ethics
Perkins School of Theology
Southern Methodist University

CHARLES E. CURRAN — Associate Professor of Moral Theology
Catholic University of America

DONALD EVANS — Professor of Philosophy
University of Toronto

JOSEPH FLETCHER — Robert Treat Paine Professor of Social Ethics
Episcopal Theological School
Cambridge, Massachusetts

JAMES M. GUSTAFSON — Professor of Christian Ethics
Divinity School and Department of
Religious Studies, Yale University

BERNARD HÄRING — Professor of Systematic Moral Theology
and Pastoral Sociology
Lateran University in Rome

DAVID LITTLE — Assistant Professor of Christian Ethics
Divinity School, Yale University

EDWARD LEROY LONG, JR. — Professor of Religion
Oberlin College

RICHARD A. MC CORMICK — Professor of Moral and Pastoral Theology
Bellarmine School of Theology
Loyola University

JOHN G. MILHAVEN — Assistant Professor of Pastoral Theology
Woodstock College

| | |
|---|---|
| BASIL MITCHELL | Nolloth Professor of the Philosophy of the Christian Religion, Oxford University |
| GENE H. OUTKA | Assistant Professor of Religion Princeton University |
| PAUL RAMSEY | Harrington Spear Paine Professor of Religion Princeton University |
| N. H. SØE | Professor of Systematic Theology University of Copenhagen |

# *Preface*

There is currently a lively debate in the culture at large about a "new morality." The specific *occasion* for the essays in this volume is this contemporary discussion, especially as it has gone on in religious circles. The *substance* of the volume involves various efforts to assess the place of norms in religious ethics. Thus these essays are all roughly addressed in various ways to the question: What is the nature and authority of "norms," "principles," "rules," etc., in ethics and, more specifically, in Christian ethics? It is our hope that the essays included here are representative of, and in many cases an advance upon, previous treatments of these matters.

We believe they are representative of the contemporary discussion in at least three ways. First, no effort has been made to suppress the various kinds of discourse which do in fact characterize the present discussion at large. We have included, for example, essays representative of traditional Roman Catholic moral theology, the Protestant Reformation legacy on the "uses" of the law, and some of the formulations of a not dissimilar discussion in contemporary moral philosophy. The volume therefore has a healthy dose of both "ecumenical" and "philosophical" analyses. This sort of pluralism in the present discussion is at once a glory and a source of confusion. But it seems to us important that the volume reflect it if there is to be genuine representativeness. For we need no narrowing of the debate but, rather, engagement with a wide variety of representative views if our understanding of the questions is to be clarified and deepened. Second, there is a spectrum of the major alternative positions presented, both here and abroad. We have deliberately avoided a choice of contributors which would have resulted in a tacit consensus, either in the "contextual" or the "casuistical" direction. Various shades of "right" and "left" are included. Third, while it is the case that all of the contributions are in diverse ways related to the Christian tradition (this is where the "debate" has largely occurred thus far), it is our contention that many of the issues discussed and positions espoused involve overlaps and parallels with both "secular" ethics and other religious traditions (particularly Judaism—indeed, the frequent discussion of the Decalogue in the following pages is but one indication of how inseparable are the two traditions) and that therefore the contributions should prove broadly relevant and helpful.

We also hope that many of these essays will constitute an advance on the present discussion. There are a number of proposals for reform. The richness of the several traditions, both theological and philosophical, out of which these essays come, and the immediate importance of the issues addressed, may allow this volume to add substantially to the analysis of questions of ethics from a variety of points of view.

*Gene H. Outka*
*Paul Ramsey*

*Department of Religion*
*Princeton University*
*Princeton, New Jersey*
*July 25, 1967*

*Norm and Context in Christian Ethics*

*PART ONE*

# Virtue, Principles, and Rules

# 1

# *Deciding in the Situation: What Is Required?**

FREDERICK S. CARNEY

Whether consensus is a proper basis on which to run a government, as President Lyndon B. Johnson says it is, I venture no opinion. I can report, however, that neither the theory nor the practice of consensus has made much headway recently among those of us who make a profession of deciding how to decide in moral situations. Vigorous disagreements on fundamental questions prevail among moral theologians today, and are accepted by us as part of the hazards (and sometimes pleasures) of our occupation. Some of these disagreements illuminate basic issues. I plan to attempt my assignment in this symposium by suggesting in what sense each of three basic positions in Christian ethics has been arguing (sometimes inchoately) for something very important to the stucture of moral decision.

Position Alpha emphasizes an ultimate norm (or norms), or what I shall call *principle,* at the center of the Christian moral life. The distinguishing feature of principle is that it indicates what quality (such as love) should always be present in every moral act. Those who maintain Position Alpha believe that there are many (or at least some) situations in which the right decision can best be ascertained by examining the context and applying principle directly to it. Although they affirm that rules and virtue may be involved in decision-making, they deny that they are necessarily so. Thus Bishop J. A. T. Robinson has written that

* Reprinted from *McCormick Quarterly,* Vol. xx, No. 2 (January, 1967), pp. 3–15.

love alone, because, as it were, it has a built-in moral compass, enabling it to "home" intuitively upon the deepest need of the other, can allow itself to be directed completely by the situation. . . . It is able to embrace an ethic of radical responsiveness, meeting every situation on its own merits, with no prescriptive laws.[1]

Other proponents of Position Alpha include Joseph Fletcher,[2] H. A. Williams,[3] and the authors of *Towards a Quaker View of Sex*.[4]

Position Beta is centered largely around a defense of directional norms, or what I shall call *rules*, in Christian ethics. Rules differ from principle in that they are concrete standards for particular types of situations. Often, but not always, rules are understood to be expressions of principle, as a sexual rule may be thought to be an expression of love. Most supporters of Position Beta believe that some rules (but not all) are absolute (i.e., context-invariant). Thus Paul Ramsey has written of "generally valid rules of action that love itself implies" according to which some acts "are as unconditionally wrong as love is unconditionally right." [5] Other supporters of Position Beta would probably include V. A. Demant[6] and most Catholic moralists.

Position Gamma has been much confused with Alpha. This is because its supporters, like those of Alpha, have an antirule bias and often call themselves contextualists or situationalists. The difference is that while Position Alpha emphasizes principle in relation to context, Gamma focuses paramount attention on the relation of what I shall call *virtue* to context. What is here involved is not another kind of norm (in addition to principle and rule) for guiding the human agent to right decisions, but the forming of the character of the agent so that he is inwardly disposed to right decision in each situation. This is the historic problem of virtue, call it by whatever other name one wishes. It is man living and deciding in accord with the very essence of his manliness. Thus Paul Lehmann has written of decision as arising out of "the concrete ethical reality of a transformed human being and transformed humanity owing to the

---

[1] *Honest to God* (London: SCM Press, 1963), p. 115. See also Robinson's *Christian Morals Today* (Philadelphia: Westminster Press, 1964).

[2] *Situation Ethics: The New Morality* (Philadelphia: Westminster Press, 1966).

[3] "Theology and Self-Awareness," *Soundings: Essays Concerning Christian Understanding*, ed. A. R. Vidler (Cambridge, Eng.: Cambridge, 1962), pp. 69–101.

[4] London: Friends Home Service Committee, 1963.

[5] *Deeds and Rules in Christian Ethics* (New York: Charles Scribner's Sons, 1967), pp. 34–35.

[6] *Christian Sex Ethics* (New York: Harper & Row, 1963).

specific action of God in Jesus Christ." [7] Other ethicists who hold some version of this position include Dietrich Bonhoeffer ("formation in Christ")[8] and Joseph Sittler ("the believer's re-enactment of God's action").[9]

Each of these three positions points to an important feature of Christian decision-making. Position Alpha is concerned to lift morality above moral legalism, and proposes that this should be done by making all decisions responsible to an ultimate moral criterion. Position Beta wishes to avoid merely intuitional decisions in ethics, and proposes the employment of rules as objective standards for informing and judging particular decisions. Position Gamma holds that the basic disposition of the agent, an often neglected aspect of decision-making in the modern world, should actually be placed at the center of attention.

The remainder of this paper is designed to suggest how each of these features can be understood to function within a single theory of Christian moral decision. Its form will take shape around the notion of principle, rule, and virtue. A caveat, however, must be registered in advance. I do not propose to try putting these three positions together in any eclectic manner. These positions as currently affirmed by their advocates will not go together without conflict. Nor would such an eclecticism, even if possible, adequately present what is actually involved in Christian moral decisions. Rather, I propose to set forth each of these notions (principle, rule, and virtue) in a somewhat modified fashion from the manner in which they are found in these three positions, and thereby to demonstrate how each can play its role in one coherent theory of moral decision.

# I

Even though Christians may be willing to be known as "agapists," or love-oriented persons, it is not love alone, strictly speaking, that serves as the complete principle of Christian moral orientation. Rather, it is a unity of faith, love, and justice that performs this function. The principle begins in faith. It takes the form of love. And it extends to nothing short of justice.

I shall comment on each of these in turn, and attempt to make clear why the three together actually constitute one principle that

[7] *Ethics in a Christian Context* (New York: Harper & Row, 1963), p. 17.
[8] *Ethics* (New York: Macmillan Co., 1955), p. 18.
[9] *The Structure of Christian Ethics* (Baton Rouge: Louisiana State University Press, 1958), p. 57.

informs the whole of the Christian moral life. I shall begin with faith, which is man's response in trust and commitment initially to the world he encounters, but finally to the God who sustains and renews his world. No man lives without some kind of faith. For faith, generically speaking, is nothing other than man's response to life, the absence of which response is death. It is in this sense that man either "faiths" or dies. If he "faiths," he may do so more or less adequately. Most of us do so with considerable inadequacy. One expression of inadequacy is to respond to something less than the full range of our experience. By selecting out from our experience such objects as business success or sexual prowess or national loyalty for our exclusive (or at least disproportionate) attention, we live to these objects, but die to others. Thus we are, so to speak, partly living and partly dead. Another expression of inadequate faith is to respond to empirical objects as if existing in themselves, and not as subsisting in God. I may respond to my wife, for example, as if there were no dimension of her presence that does not transcend her presence. Thus I live to an immediate object who is indeed precious to me, but die to the transcending context that is finally the source of her existence, and indeed of her very preciousness to me. A third expression of inadequate faith is the responder's deficiency either of the passive movement of trust or of the active movement of commitment. The true believer is both passive and active. He receives in confidence; he acts in loyalty. Inadequate faith, on the other hand, is responding to one's world either in trust without commitment, or with commitment but not trust. It is accepting life as a gift from God without acknowledging its duties; or else it is a dutiful performing without confidence that we are finally sustained by grace. Either choice is deadly living.

When I affirm that the principle of Christian decision begins in faith, I do not mean thereby that our moral existence depends, as in *Alice in Wonderland,* on our believing five impossible things before breakfast. Rather, I mean to point to this responding activity, the absence of which is death, the imperfect presence of which is life (of sorts), and the perfect presence of which is the fullness of life (or life eternal).

I also mean to indicate thereby that faith is the fountain that nourishes love. For Christian love is not properly to be understood as a self-initiating activity, but as arising out of the Christian's response to his world, and ultimately out of his trust in and commitment to God. Although I have no argument with those who choose to define love as benevolence and beneficence toward valued objects, I do want to insist that *Christian* love values these objects from the standpoint of an already "faithing" activity. And thus the value of these objects depends not merely upon their instrumental importance to the person who loves, but also upon the importance with which they are held by other members of the world to which he is responding and, more profoundly, upon the preciousness with which they are cherished by God, in response to whom all other responses find their proper place. Thus we may say that Christian decision-making is "faith working through love."

It is important to underline that love is both benevolence (or the willing of good to the other) and beneficence (or the doing of those things that promote the good of the other). If while camping I were to fall over the side of a ravine, and someone up above were to say that he rejoices in my existence and intends me well, but were to take no action to throw me the end of his rope by which I might be helped out of my predicament, I should have some reason to doubt the adequacy of his love, even to doubt that he truly loves me at all. (And he, for his part, might eventually come to understand where the road that is paved with good intentions finally leads.) If, on the other hand, another man, seeing me in the same predicament and perhaps wishing to take advantage of my ill-fortune as the occasion by which to make off with my camping equipment, were accidentally to knock a rope over the side of the ravine by which I were able to extricate myself, are we to say that this unintended good result was an act of love? Hardly! The point is that both attitudes and actions —both benevolence and beneficence—are constitutive of what the Christian means by love.

In turning now to the dimension of justice in this three-dimensional principle of the Christian life, I want to call attention to the argument of some moral philosophers that standing at the base of the moral life are two principles, not one as I have affirmed.[10] These two principles are known to them as love (or some other term) and justice, and there are two principles rather than one because of their supposedly independent origins. By love they mean benevolence and beneficence toward valued objects. But they do not consider love to be adequate in itself because one could love, according to them, a limited range of objects which still (in a certain sense) could constitute a quantitative maximization of love by him who loves. They argue, on the other hand, that justice is precisely that moral sensitivity that

---

[10] See, for example, William K. Frankena, *Ethics* (Englewood Cliffs, N.J.: Prentice-Hall, 1963), pp. 35–45.

causes us to be dissatisfied with any manifestation of love that does not treat all potential objects with some sense of fairness. This is to say, it is justice that leads us to bring other objects we do not initially value, but which have characteristics comparable to those we do, into the same range of our moral consideration. Thus love is a teleological principle, or a general norm that looks to consequences, and causes us (if we act by it) to seek the welfare of what we value. Justice, on the other hand, is a deontological principle, or a general norm that calls attention to an immediately perceived duty (in this case, equal treatment of equal objects) without in itself considering consequences. It is in this sense, then, that the aforementioned philosophers believe that there is a duality at the very foundation of the moral life and its decision-making process.

It is to be noted that this supposed duality derives from the original definition of love. If love is merely benevolence and beneficence toward objects we value, then obviously something over and beyond love must be added to ensure that objects not initially valued are provided a standing in the court of our conscience, or, as it were, a right to make a claim upon us. It is not necessary, however, to define love in this manner. Indeed the Christian religion, if I understand it correctly, does not do so. For Christian love, by its very nature, is attitude and action that embraces *all* potential objects. This is to say that we are commanded (if I may put the matter this way) to love being as such. The reason for this is that Christian love roots in faith, as I have said, and faith in its fullness brings us into a vital concern for all of creation as part of our trust in and commitment to God. We cannot be loyal to God without being loyal to his cause. He who holds the whole world in his hands, metaphorically speaking, invites us to share in loving what he loves. This means that Christian love necessarily is love for all being, whether here or there, whether past, present, or future. It does not, therefore, require an independent principle of distribution (justice) over and beyond its principle of affection (love). Nevertheless, what these philosophers mean by justice is, I think, implied by the Christian notion of love.

If this is true, it is grossly inconsistent to call oneself a Christian while being unconcerned with what happens to the disadvantaged children born in underprivileged homes, or to tens of thousands of seemingly hopeless mental patients in our scandalously overcrowded and understaffed state institutions, or to the Communists and their allies with whom we are struggling in Vietnam, or to any part of God's creation, however distant or unpleasant it may seem to us. Indeed the Christian religion is so clear on this point—and so aware of the soothing rationalizations that we often offer—that it stacks the case with a bias in favor of those we are inclined to ignore. "Whatever you do to one of the least of these, my brothers, you do to me." This is the dimension of justice in the principle of Christian ethics.

So abideth faith, love, and justice—these three. And there is no greatest one among them. For none is truly great without the others, and each can be spoken of adequately only by invoking the others. It is in this sense that the principle of Christian ethics is a multidimensional unity.

## II

If this unity of faith, love, and justice is indeed the true principle of Christian ethics, it will then serve as the ultimate criterion of obligation to which all rules are subject. This is to say, a rule is a proper moral rule for a Christian only if it is an expression of faith, love, and justice. Moreover, it must be a fitting expression of this principle in the context in which it is to be employed. Thus the two points of reference for the validation of rules are principle and context. Since both are necessary for articulating Christian moral guidance, I warmly agree with James Gustafson's observation that the argument among some Christian ethicists today between principle and context is a misplaced debate.[11]

The issue is not whether Christians should be context-oriented. Faithful, loving, and just response to God's creating and redeeming activity requires that we be so. The issue is, rather, how we are to understand the context, and what are the implications of our contextual understanding for rule formulation and application. I submit that the context of moral action is to be characterized both by particularity and by generality. The context is particular in that there are no two societies exactly alike. Even within any given society there are no two persons or groups that do not exhibit some elements of differentiation from each other, nor do any two persons or groups confront therein exactly the same circumstances. Particularity is also characteristic of entities in time as well as in space. For persons, groups, and societies change in time and are thus further differentiated, as do the circumstances they confront.

It would be a mistake, however, to characterize the context of moral action entirely in terms of particularity and not also in terms of generality. For however much two societies may differ, there is

[11] "Context Versus Principle: A Misplaced Debate in Christian Ethics," *Harvard Theological Review*, Vol. 58 (1965), pp. 171–202.

always some measure of likeness in their basic features. Were this not so we should not be able to refer to them equally as human communities. Even more pronounced are the common elements present among persons and groups within any given society, as well as among the circumstances such persons and groups confront. Nor is generality to be denied because of the dimension of time and change. For some continuity amidst change is a basic characteristic of all existence, else we should have to reidentify every entity we encounter at the next moment in time. That we do not feel the need to do so is presumptive evidence that there is some degree of continuity in the encountered context.

The implication for Christian ethics of this characterization of the context as involving both particularity and generality is that moral rules are to be understood as having an "open texture." Let me explain. If the context of moral action were entirely one of particularity, rules would not be possible. This is because such a context would permit no classes of situations to which rules could be related. Rules have no applicability to whatever (if anything) is utterly unique, only to what can be classified. Thus a claim that the context is entirely particular implies that there can be "no texture" of moral rules. On the other hand, if the context of moral action were consistently so general as to exclude all except irrelevant particularity, moral rules not only would be possible, but could also be universal. This is because classes in the context that are entirely universal lend themselves, when joined with a moral principle, to universal rules. A claim that such is the case implies that there can be a "closed texture" of moral rules. In contrast to these two extremes, the position I am affirming is that the context is both general and particular. Because of contextual generality, moral rules are possible. Because of contextual particularity, such rules are relative rather than universal. Thus this position holds that there is a texture of moral rules, and that it is an "open texture."

This is not to say, however, that there is no absolute norm in Christian ethics. For the principle of faith, love, and justice is precisely such an absolute. It is binding in all situations in the sense that, assuming its acceptance, there is no moral occasion in which it ought not to be manifested. Although the principle does not direct us as to exactly what we are to do in any given situation (a function ordinarily performed by rules), it does indicate the general quality of moral response that is always incumbent upon us. And doing so, it provides one of the two poles—the other being context—within which rules are acknowledged both to exist and to be obligatory.

Thus Christian ethics is both absolute and relative. It is absolute in that its ultimate norm of obligation (principle) is context-invariant. It is relative in that its contingent norms of obligation (rules) are context-variant.

A mistake is often made in thinking that if rules are relative, then they are nonobjective (i.e., cannot be either valid or invalid). This mistake arises from an understandable confusion in the ordinary language employment of the term "relative." In some usages this term means "subjective" (i.e., varying with the personal preferences or vantage points of individuals). In the usage envisaged here, however, "relative" means context-variant (i.e., affected by contextual differentiation). Thus there is nothing to prevent a rule from being both relative and objective. It is relative if the determination of its meaning and force involves contextual consideration, and objective if there is logical sense in speaking of it as a right (or wrong) rule. Whether it is a right rule or not is ordinarily to be determined by inquiring empirically whether it can be judged the best rule expression of the principle of faith, love, and justice in the kind of context under consideration.

Not only can rules be objective in the sense just mentioned, but action according to rules can also be objective. To justify this claim I should like to discuss four types of decision procedure employing rules. The first pertains to what I shall call the *simple application of rule situation*. This occurs when a valid moral rule fits a case more or less precisely. It does this whenever its descriptive content, including whatever conditions of application are therein provided for, accords with the descriptive details of the case confronting it. In such a situation the right act is that which the rule indicates. And to justify our act we need only appeal to the rule itself. If, for example, it is a valid moral rule that we give crippled persons the right of way on entering passenger elevators, and we meet such a person in such a circumstance, then we simply apply the rule to our behavior and grant him the right of way. Most moral decisions would seem to be of this unheroic sort, so much so that they tend to become habitual to us, and to be overlooked when we think of instances of moral situations.

The second type of rule-employing procedure pertains to the *extension of rule situation*. In this kind of instance there is a valid rule that does not quite fit the case encountered, and there is no other rule that is more appropriate. Suppose, for example, there is a valid moral rule that we should truthfully answer inquiries put to us. Suppose further that I am in the process of selling a second-hand car the radiator of which I know to have an inadequately repaired hole in it that is not apparent to anyone except a carefully trained observer. I may well judge that although the content of the truth-telling rule does not literally apply here (my customer does not ask me about the radiator), the rule's fundamental purpose of proper representation among men certainly does. In such a situation I extend the coverage of the rule by adding to its content, and accordingly inform my customer about the defective radiator. By such a rule-extending decision I bind myself (I believe) to behave in a similar manner in any future case that is essentially like this one. Such future cases then become instances of simple application of rule procedure, not of extension of rule procedure as in the initial case of this sort.

The third way in which rules can be applied is in the *transformation of rule situation*. As in the second type, a change in the rule is called for. But whereas the former type of rule change was mere extension of content without denying the already existing requirements, in this kind of rule change the existing content itself is altered. Suppose, for example, that it was a valid rule at some time in the past to uphold limited forms of racial segregation. (If it were ever possible to justify such a rule, it would perhaps be on the basis that under the circumstances then prevailing segregation was required to preserve and enhance what human values for both Negroes and whites were possible.) Suppose further that it has now become apparent that the Negro is being placed in an increasingly disadvantageous position in society by the rapid development of technology (thus dispensing with many of his traditional sources of livelihood) coupled with the continuation of racial segregation (thus limiting him from entering into new sources of livelihood), and that this deplorable situation is amenable to moral change. Here, I suggest, we are bound by our commitment to the principle of faith, love, and justice, when confronted with these altered circumstances, to transform our moral rule on segregation to one of integration. When the rule has been transformed, its future employment, as in the extension of rule procedure, is likely to be in circumstances that approximate the simple application of rule procedure. Perhaps I should add in passing that other areas in which acute transformation of rule situations have arisen recently, largely because of rapid social change in our society, include sexual behavior and economic resource utilization.

# Virtue, Principles, and Rules

The fourth type of procedure pertains to the *conflict of rule situation*. What is envisaged here is the applicability to the same case of two valid rules both of which make *prima facie* demands upon us, and which are nevertheless in conflict as to what they require. For example, suppose there is a valid rule that I should not turn my back on my son when he especially needs help, and another that I should not enter the classroom as a teacher without being adequately prepared. It takes little imagination to conceive the details of a conflict between such obligations to family and vocation. The solution to this type of situation (and the one we quite naturally apply when confronted with such conflicts) is to elevate both rules into a new and more inclusive one in which we attempt to meet over the course of time our obligations in each area, and yet set forth the conditions under which our attention at any given time is to be granted primarily to one or to the other. Once this more inclusive rule has been determined, we thereafter normally confront simple application of rule procedure in its employment.

In the second, third, and fourth types of decision procedure, it is to be noted, reference is made both to principle and to context. In these procedures we are called upon not only to justify our acts by a rule, but also to justify the rule itself (or aspects of it). Thus a major concern of Position Alpha advocates is accommodated, namely, that there should be included within ethical thought and action a confrontation with both the ultimate norm of our existence and the varying circumstances in which this norm is to be applied. Furthermore, this concern is not accommodated at the price of denying criteria for the objective validation of particular acts. The consistent employment of rules enables us to say that particular acts are right or wrong, a matter of some considerable interest to supporters of Position Beta.

It is only in the first type of procedure that rules can be applied to contexts without necessarily thinking of principle. I consider that there is a decided advantage to being able to reduce a large part of our ethical existence to decisions of this sort. For it gives a dependable quality to our behavior in the many matters to which it pertains, while freeing our more creative energies for the ethical encounter with more complex issues that appear in the second, third, and fourth types of situations.

## III

There may seem to be good reason for discussing virtue prior to principle and rule. If virtue is the formation and disposition of character that underlies action, then it may be thought to be the starting point of all proper consideration of moral decision, even so far as to reduce the operation of principle and rule as norms of action to comparatively less (if any) importance. A number of advocates of Position Gamma apparently think this is the case. Nevertheless, if action according to norms is also, in some important sense, constitutive of virtue (as I think it is), then virtue can be sensibly discussed either before or after the discussion of norms. Perhaps it should be discussed at both points.

In order to develop further what I have in mind, I should like to make a brief excursion into history. At the time that the Protestant Reformation began in the sixteenth century, the dominant view of virtue was an unfortunate caricature from Thomas Aquinas' thought as propagated by a number of Catholic moralists. This view held that virtue is to be acquired, for the most part, by performing virtuous acts. The result is to make one's virtue (or the very essence of his manliness) dependent primarily upon his own achievement. This is so even though God is recognized as the ground and end of, and occasional intervener in, such development. Furthermore, each type of right action has its corresponding faculty in the human person, and each of these faculties needs disciplined development. So there are a number of virtues of which virtuousness is composed. Thus one's self-formation is also highly compartmentalized, and one "justifies" himself through the diligent performance of a great number of compartmentalized "good works." This is the less flattering version of what I shall call the *acquiremental* view of virtue.

This was not the authentic thought of Aquinas, but a late medieval trivialization of his thought. It was, however, the Thomistic teaching with which Martin Luther was presented, and against which he so dramatically rebelled. In place of self-justification through works, Luther affirmed God's gracious justification through faith. And instead of a compartmentalized man each faculty of whom needs justification, he proclaimed a potentially immediate unity of the human person. Thus Luther's doctrine of justification by faith can be understood as implying an alternative theory of virtue to that which was predominant in the pre-Reformation period. I shall call it the *relational* theory. Its distinctive feature is that man's virtue is understood to be a product not of his own achievement, but of his acceptance in faith of the justifying relation God freely offers him, and of his consequent acceptance in love of a servant relation with his fellow man.

These two theories of virtue have competed with each other for supremacy ever since in the modern world. In the eighteenth century the acquiremental view seemed to dominate again, even within Protestantism. But with the coming of the Neo-Reformation in the twentieth century, we have witnessed the revival of the relational view, at least in Protestant theological circles.

The supporters of Position Gamma are predominately relational, as distinguished from acquiremental, in their understanding of virtue. They can be thought of as wanting to recover a Lutheran Reformation motif in decided preference to a medieval Catholic (and eighteenth-century Protestant) one. They are open, however, to telling criticism, as are also their acquirementalist opponents. To the extent that relationalists deny objective criteria (e.g., rules) for determining the external rightness of an act (such as truth-telling or doing a kind deed) they are left with a mere internal criterion, namely, whether the act arises from a right disposition. Does any act performed in faith and love qualify as a right act? If so, is relational virtue simply *right disposition to action* regardless of the external aspects of action?

The acquiremental view of virtue, on the other hand, does entail criteria (e.g., rules) for judging the external rightness of an act. By employing these criteria it can indicate rather precisely what kinds of acts a man should be disposed to perform. One's manliness is thus constituted by the development of habitual tendencies to perform right acts. To this extent, acquiremental virtue appears to be *disposition to right action*. The problem is whether it may not involve a wrong disposition to right action that compromises the very rightness of the action. Many relationalists think it does, and are quick to accuse the acquirementalist view of involving self-seeking motivations even for acts that both groups might agree to be externally right, such as telling the truth or doing a good deed. If one does good to the fellow man out of egoistic desire for self-development, not out of faith-formed love for the fellow man, is the act itself corrupted and thus in some sense less than right? If it is, does acquiremental virtue, taken by itself, run the risk of becoming disposition to corrupted action?

The obvious way to meet these problems is to understand right action as involving both internal and external aspects, and to affirm a view of virtue that is both relational and acquiremental. This is precisely what the theory of Christian action here envisaged does. We cannot, however, simply add relational virtue to acquiremental. Such a procedure would make of relational virtue a caricature of what it fundamèntally is for Christian faith, namely, the ontological starting point of man's life, properly understood. Christians cannot add their basic orientation to God and fellow man to dispositions and actions determined apart from such orientation.

On the other hand, I believe that Christians can and should hold that acquiremental virtue is not something essentially separable from relational virtue, but is, rather, a necessity for the adequate expression of relational virtue. When a person is clear that the orientation and justification of his life is constituted by his general relation to God and fellow man, he may then recognize that faith and love demand the fullest possible development of his moral capacities for externally right acts. He will seek this development in order to serve God and fellow man with greater skill and dependability. In this sense, then, we can speak of an element of man's very being that is "acquired" through practice.

Granted that the source of man's virtue is both relational and acquiremental, what is the content? It is, I believe, a faithful, loving, and just character. It is a character predisposed to act consistently with the ultimate norm of all Christian decision, and to express itself through concrete norms of behavior as best they can be understood and applied in varying circumstances. Thus it is an integral part, together with principle and rule, of an adequate Christian understanding of what is required for deciding in the situation.

# 2

# *Moral Discernment in the Christian Life*

JAMES M. GUSTAFSON

## I. *The Notion of Discernment*

The practical moral question is asked in various ways. Sometimes it is, "What ought we to do?" Or, if one chooses to relax the imperative and accentuate the indicative, it is, "What are we to do?" When such ways of asking the question are scrutinized, it becomes clear that the words "ought" and "are" carry a heavy load of freight. There is not only the relative moral weight or authority implied by each, the degree of obligation that each suggests, but also an unexplored process of moral judgment-making. Indeed, the polemics out of which this book emerges have attended primarily to those processes. Most of the polemics in Christian ethics have been about *how Christians ought to make judgments*. They ought to use rules in a highly rational way, or they ought to exercise their graced imaginations, or they ought to obey the tradition of the Church, or they ought to respond to the situation of which they are a part. Not enough work has yet been done by either philosophers or theologians on just how people actually do make moral judgments, though the variously propagated "oughts" claim some validation on the basis that each is correlated with what people actually do.

In this chapter, I wish to suggest that the practical moral question of what we ought or are *to do* be held in abeyance in its strongest existential moral sense; and that it would be fruitful to look more carefully at how we *discern* what we ought to do, or are to do. Moral agents exercise some discrimination in making judgments, and it is this exercise of discrimination that I wish to explore. Such exploration is not done on the basis of a sampling of opinion; I have not approached a cross-section of men, not even a cross-section of Christians, with a schedule of questions to find out how they actually discern what to do. Nor does this exploration lead to a full-blown theory of the relations of motives, affections, rationality, and other aspects of moral selfhood as these have engaged the attention of moral philosophers in the past. I am not proposing that what seems to me to be involved in moral discernment is something that can be packaged, delivered, and taught to people who wish to become more moral. Nor am I suggesting the absence of wide variations in the ways in which people discern what they are to do; obviously some men are more emotive in their responses, some more intuitive, some more rational.

The intention of this chapter is more limited. It is based on the following rudimentary observations. Persons of moral seriousness do exercise discrimination in making judgments. They discern what they are or ought to do. Discrimination, or discernment, takes place not only in moral experiences but in other areas of human experience as well, such as esthetic experience. Common speech uses the adjective "discerning" with reference to persons who seem to be more perceptive, wiser, more discriminating than others are in judging, whether the object judged is a performance of a symphony, a person and his behavior, a political situation, or a novel. Thus by exploring the uses of the word "discern," we might be able to see what goes into moral judgments, and particularly into moral judgments that seem to have a quality of excellence.

In one usage, to discern something is simply to see that it is there; indeed, this kind of visual use of the word is the least qualitative, or value-laden. When I am driving in a fog, I might say to my companion, "I dimly discern the white line that divides the lanes." I do not see it with unusual accuracy; I am not making a qualitative judgment about what I see; I am using the word simply to indicate that I can see the line. Perhaps more commonly we use the verb "discern" to indicate a particular accuracy in perception or observation. Often we use it when we can locate a detail that misses the perception of others. Often we use it when some subtle shading or coloring registers on us. In accord with such use, we might call a person "discerning" who has an unusual capacity to isolate significant detail, to perceive subtleties, to be penetrating and accurate in his observations. While in one sense, to discern something is simply to notice it, to see it, in another sense we reserve the word for a quality of perception, of discrimination, of observation and judgment.

It is this quality of perception, discrimination, observation and

# Virtue, Principles, and Rules

judgment that is involved when we speak of a "discerning person" or of "discerning comments" in various realms of discourse. As one who has to read hundreds of letters of recommendations for admission to graduate school, and who has to live with admissions based upon such letters, I have come to regard certain persons who write letters regularly as being "discerning." I do not mean that they give the most detailed descriptions of the candidates, nor that they simply notice the most obvious things about them. I mean that they seem to be able to get at salient characteristics of the students that have great importance in assisting me to make my judgment about them. There is an accuracy to their descriptions and their judgments that is borne out over time; they have an eye for pertinent characteristics (pertinent to what it takes, for example, to be a good graduate student). They enable me to have some understanding of the student; I can begin to draw my own "portrait" of him. This is more than a picture of a man of twenty-four who achieved a high academic record at Princeton University, and is interested in further study of ethics. By the letter writer's discernment of the qualities of mind, spirit, and character of the man, I can grasp some of his significant features, what his strengths and weaknesses are. I rely on the discerning letters of discerning men to help me make my judgment of what I ought to do with reference to the admission of a student to graduate school.

The same sort of process occurs in other areas of experience. Good literary critics are the most "discerning" ones. The difference between the good schoolboy type of writer on literature, who does all his homework (research) and writes up accurate summaries of what he has read, and the writer who moves the discussion to another stage is one of a quality of discernment. The discerning critic helps the reader to "see" things in the literature that he might not see on his own; he helps the reader to perceive some of the subtlety of the writer's words, characters, or plots; he helps him to understand what the writer's intention is in the way in which he concretely organizes his details. The same would be involved in distinctions between types of people who go to art museums. There are the clods who pace through the rooms with nothing registering upon their consciousnesses other than the fact that at the museum they saw works by Rembrandt and Picasso, about whom everyone who reads the newspapers knows something. At the other extreme are the discerning students, who not only are open to the impressions that a painting makes upon them, but sense the significance of detail, of the arrangement of color patterns, of lines, and all other aspects of the work. The discerning observer can not only say, "I don't like that one," but he can give some reasons for his judgment that express more than his feelings, that have some objectivity to him.

By reading the works of discerning critics of art and literature my own capacities for making judgments are deepened and broadened. I begin to "see" what is involved in accurate observation so that my own perceptions of the text or the painting are altered. I learn to be more discriminating in my own judgments. Presumably my judgments will be "better," at least to the extent of being more informed. I will be less likely to miss salient points I had missed before; I will become more "sensitive" to nuances, to details and their suggestive meanings, to the structure and wholeness of the piece at hand.

What seems to be involved in the quality of discernment toward which the foregoing paragraphs point? This question might best be answered by indicating what seems not to be involved, indeed, what is excluded. First, a person who has a scheme for analysis that he woodenly and mechanically imposes on whatever he observes would probably not be called a "discerning" person. The tourist who visits art museums with one checklist of things that he ought to look at, and another of the things he ought to look for in what he looks at, would hardly at that stage of his life receive the appellation "discerning." Checklists and wooden schemes of analysis cannot attend to the subtle nuances that are involved in refined discriminations; they seem to stress the more universal elements found in all objects of a given class, rather than the particularities to be appreciated in a single representative of what might be a class. Although they may help the novice to avoid gross errors, such schemes seem to be "external," that is, imposed from the outside on both the observer and that which he observes. They do not in themselves have or require the qualities of empathy, appreciation, imagination, and sensitivity that seem to be involved in discerning perception and judgment.

Thus, also, in moral experience, someone might suggest that in making a judgment the agent ought to keep in mind a scheme that includes the following six things: the potential consequences, the variety of his motives, the moral maxims accepted by his community, the empirical data about the situation as he defines it, the love of God, and the moral order of the universe as understood by reason. A person who has to make a moral judgment might run his dilemma through such a scheme with several possible results. He might be more confused after than before. He might try to "add up" all these considerations and find that their sum is far from a judgment. Or he might find that the scheme usefully points him in a direction, and then simply follow the direction. But the critic would probably say that each of these ways of making a judgment is wooden, mechanical, external, and certainly not discerning.

Second, the person who has formulated a set of first principles, has refined his understanding of deductive logic so that he can move from the universal to the particular, and has consequently determined on a rational basis what conduct is right and good, might not be viewed as a man of moral discernment. He might be called a man of intellectual discernment on the grounds of his virtuosity in formulating the universal principles and by the authority of his deductive logic. But since moral judgments involve more than the arrangement of ideas to each other in a logical and orderly way, in actual practice such a person might not demonstrate the perceptiveness that helps one to be aware of the complexity of the details of a particular instance. Indeed, if he assumes that his intellectual virtuosity is sufficient for making a moral judgment, he has to classify the case at hand, that is, attend less to its unique elements and accentuate those it has in common with others, in order to proceed. Intellectual clarity and the use of critical reflection are involved in moral discernment, just as they are involved in discerning criticisms or discerning descriptions in response to works of art, but in themselves they are not sufficient to exhaust what we normally include in the notion of discernment.

Third, the person who is skilled in accumulating the relevant information pertaining to a subject is not necessarily a discerning judge. All teachers know instances of students who are admirably exhaustive in their bibliographical preparation, are assiduous in reading with comprehension the important treatises on the subject, and are even orderly in arranging this material and reasonably clear in writing it up, but who are not really discerning students of the subject. "Discernment" seems to be appropriate for pointing to the ability to distinguish the important from the unimportant information and the insightful interpretations from the uninsightful. It refers to the ability to perceive relationships between aspects of the information that enable one to see how it all fits together, or how it cannot fit together. It refers to the ability to suggest inferences that can be drawn from the information, and thus to an imaginative capacity. One can find sociological studies, for example, that seem to be exhaustive in the accumulation of the data pertinent to the topic under research but are of limited value because the researcher lacked discriminating judgment and imagination. So it is in the sphere of moral judgments. Accurate accumulation of relevant information about a matter that is the object of moral judgment is indispensable, but such accumulation in itself does not constitute a discerning moral decision.

The raw data for making judgments might be gathered, but the act of judgment itself involves more capacities than are required simply to pull relevant information together. Or, one can find biographies that are encyclopedic accumulations of objective data about the man involved, but do not enable the reader to penetrate in any way into the "character" of the subject, that do not give a coherent "picture" of the man so that he can be understood and not just known about.

Fourth, one might find persons who are articulate in giving their emotive and expressive reactions to a subject. By feeling deeply about something they are able to give an immediate reaction to its presence. But the reaction may be much more the expression of their indignation or their inordinate admiration than a discerning account of what was worthy of approval or disapproval, what was good or bad in the subject. The first hearing of music from India, for example, might evoke a judgment that it is unbearable, or that it is fascinating. Neither would be considered a discerning judgment, for neither would give reasons for the reaction. Whether it is the rhythm that either fascinates or repels, or the tonal qualities of the sitar, or the absence of Western style of harmony, would be matters that would be developed in a discerning judgment. Similarly in moral matters, the expressive ejaculation of approval or disapproval in itself is not a discerning moral judgment. Nor would response in action that was based only on the depth of one's sense of indignation or love necessarily be a discerning response. Some disinterestedness, some accuracy of knowledge, some reflective awareness of what the situation entailed beyond what is immediately present would be ingredients of a more discerning response. Some thoughtful discrimination between the values that compete for actualization, between the possible consequences of possible courses of action, would be likely to occur if the judgment were to be called "discerning."

Fifth, stubborn allegiance to a given basis for making a judgment hardly makes for discerning judgment. Moralistic critics of literature provide interesting examples here. All literature that uses profanity, that talks about sexual relations in four-letter words, or that details the accounts of homosexual or heterosexual relations has often been condemned as "bad." And the use of the word "bad" has seemed indiscriminately to include both moral and nonmoral (e.g., literary) values. The critic who makes such judgments may have a palpable consistency that gives him the appearance of integrity, of being a man who is clear about his principles of judgment. But such stubborn allegiance to such principles hardly enables him to have an appreciation for the varieties of values that might be present in a book, for the significance of the concrete and the detailed, for the cumulative effect of the character portrayals or the plot development. Discernment seems to require some sensitivity and flexibility, some pluralism of consideration that is *a priori* ruled out by dedicated allegiance to single principles of interpretation or criticism. Similarly, in moral experience, the person who has a highly visible integrity based upon stubborn dedication to one or two principles, values, or rules, is not likely to be discriminating in a complicated situation. His responses may be predictable, but they are not thereby discerning.

These remarks about what seems not to be part of "discerning" judgments all pertain to a quality of excellence in discrimination. By indicating what the discerning person (in a qualitative sense) may not be and do, perhaps we can get at the elements of a discernment both in a more descriptive sense of Everyman as a moral discerner, and in a more normative sense of what excellence in discernment is. Some of the same elements are involved in the discernment of the morally flat-footed clod and the moral virtuoso. When these can be enumerated, perhaps one can see what combinations and accents among them make for excellence.

Discernment of what one ought to do, even among the clods, no doubt involves a perception of what is morally fitting in the place and time of action. What is fitting is decided differently by different people: some attack a problem in a disinterested manner, with great objectivity involved in their collection of appropriate information, their use of generalized prescriptive principles or articulated values, and their careful assessments of possible consequences of alternative courses of action. Others are more passionate; they feel deeply about what the actual situation is, they trust their built-in compasses to guide them, and they express their courage and initiative in taking the risks involved in action. What is fitting is discerned with reference to some of the same things and some different things, and different valences are existentially placed on different things by different people. Some are more determined by emotions, and value their moral sensitivities highly; others distrust emotions, and value their moral reflection highly. But perhaps some of the same things are present in both flat-footed and virtuoso performances in each style.

What are the common elements in all moral discernment? Perhaps several. There is a "reading" of what actually is the case at hand. Sometimes this reading is simply a visual image of an event that evokes decision and action. Sometimes it is a highly researched reading. Sometimes it is checked against other readings; sometimes it is idiosyncratic. Sometimes there is a depth of interpretation: some will want to know how the case got to be what it is, what are the relations of various elements to each other, who among the participants is most important or has more at stake, what the pliable factors are, what patterns and structures are there, and how it differs from similar cases. Sometimes there is no desire to interpret in a sophisticated way; sometimes there is no time to do so. The reading is from a perspective; this is important. Because the perspectives of moral participants differ, some see certain aspects to which others are blind; different persons accent the importance of different aspects; and in some persons there is simply suppression of factual matters that are abrasive to the moral predispositions. We have seen the importance of perspectives in "factual" judgments in the arguments about what really is the case in Vietnam. Sometimes the case is read more complexly because the moral discerner understands the situation and its participants to be part of an extensive pattern of relationships to other situations and other persons; sometimes it is read more simply because the time and space box in which it is seen is limited. Even different "situationists" differ on what the situation is. But for clod and virtuoso alike moral discernment involves such a reading of the case, an assessment of pertinent facts.

It is persons who discern; and persons have histories that affect their discernment. Some have never been seriously challenged to examine the bases of their judgments; others are highly self-critical and introspective. Some have developed characters on the basis of critical evaluations of past experiences and of the exercise of their initiative in becoming what they are throughout their personal moral histories. Others have more or less bounced morally through life, accumulating the effects of one occasion or episode after the other without a sense of self-direction. Some have acute senses of justice and injustice by virtue of having been the victims of oppression, or by virtue of being members of groups that have histories of being oppressed. Others are blithely confident about the goodness of men and the world because the world and men have been blithely supportive to them. Some are committed to getting all that they can out of life for themselves, and will discern what they ought to do in the light of that commitment; others are committed to loving the neighbor and meeting his needs because they have a religious loyalty that makes them believe this is how life ought to be lived. Several things have thus been suggested about the persons who discern: they are persons of persistent moral dispositions, or the absence thereof, and some have different persistent dispositions from others. They are persons of certain moral sensitivities or sensibilities, or the absence thereof, and some have different "feelings" from others. They are persons of certain commitments or the absence thereof, and some have different commitments from others. Moral discernment in a particular occasion is determined in part by these aspects of the self. These other-than-rational aspects of selfhood partially determine perspective, partially determine what is seen and accented, partially determine what is judged to be right and wrong, and thus what one will do.

Most persons who make moral judgments live by some beliefs, rules, and moral principles that enter into their discernment. They are members of communities that have rules of conduct and some power of sanction in enforcing them. Thus, most people decide not to steal something from a store when they go shopping, for there are rules against this, and potential disruptive consequences if they should be caught stealing. Most people discern that they ought to assist someone who is suffering not merely because the observation of the suffering of others makes them feel bad, but because the "golden rule" or the principle of meeting the neighbor's need readily applies. There are not only principles, rules, and values to which men are committed that partially determine their moral discernment; there is also usually some rational reflection about how these function at least in the instances where the normal habituated responses seem not to apply readily. Both the moral clod and the virtuoso are likely to be able to give some principles that will justify their judgments, and are likely to be willing to show that they arrived at the judgment on the basis of some rational discrimination. Some men will give intellectually sophisticated justifications, indicating their reasons for selecting some principles and not others as applicable to the case at hand, and defending the principles that are applicable. Others might simply appeal to the generalized expectations of a given society of which they are a part, or appeal to the authority of an institution, such as the Church, which has taught them the principles by which they live, and supports them in their use of those principles.

Many other elements could be adumbrated either as extensions of those described, or in addition to them. At the minimum, however, discernment involves a reading of the case at hand, an expression of what constitutes the character and perspective of the person, and some appeals to reason and principles both to help one discern and to defend what one discerns. Excellence in moral discernment perhaps involves various combinations of these. There is a discriminating and accurate reading of the situation, and an understanding of the relations of elements of the situation to each other, and of its relations to other situations. There is a stipulation of the more and less important factors, and empathy for its "inner" character as well as a description of its external character. There is a refined moral sensitivity that registers subtle nuances not only of fact but of value, that is not just emotion or sentiment, but appears to contribute to the perception of what one ought to do. Moral sensitivity seems to contribute in the "discerning" moral man an intuitive element that leads to accuracy in moral aim, judiciousness in evaluation, and compelling authenticity in deed. Just as discerning critics of art know much about art, so the discerning moral man often knows much about morality. He can think clearly about potential consequences and applicable principles; he knows something of the range of values that might compete with or support each other, and he can discriminate between alternative courses of action. He is likely to have a clear head, to be able to argue with himself and others before a judgment is made, and give good reasons for it afterward.

The discerning act of moral discernment is impossible to program, and difficult to describe. It involves perceptivity, discrimination, subtlety, sensitivity, clarity, rationality, and accuracy. And while some men seem to have it as a "gift of the gods," others achieve it by experience and training, by learning and acting. It is probably more akin to the combination of elements that go into good literary criticism and good literary creativity than it is to the combination of elements that make a good mathematician or logician; it is both rational and affective. How we discern what we ought to do, whether we be morally flat-footed clods or moral vituosos, is a complex process indeed.

## II. *Moral Discernment in the Christian Life*

The human processes of discernment are no different among Christians than they are among other men. There are the moral clods and the moral vituosos among Christians; nothing can guarantee that because a man has faith in God whom he believes to have been disclosed in Jesus Christ he will be a man of excellence in moral discernment. Nor does the morally discerning Christian have different faculties or capacities that other men are deprived of because they happen not to be Christians. No special affective capacities, logic, or rational clarity can be claimed by Christians as possessions they have by virtue of their faith. Whatever the gifts of grace are, they function in and through the human capacities of discernment that are probably fairly evenly distributed throughout all mankind. Whatever "newness" there is in the Christian life is not a replacement of

# Virtue, Principles, and Rules

insufficient moral sensitivity with more sufficient, insufficient rational clarity with more sufficient. All this, however, is not to say that moral discernment in the Christian life ought not to be different, cannot be different, and sometimes is not different. Just what some of these differences ought to be, can be, and are is the subject matter of the remainder of this chapter.

There is a text from St. Paul's Letter to the Romans that makes a good starting point for discussion of this subject.

> I implore you by God's mercy to offer your
> very selves to him: a living sacrifice, dedi-
> cated and fit for his acceptance, the worship
> offered by mind and heart. Adapt yourselves
> no longer to the pattern of this present world,
> but let your minds be remade and your whole
> nature be transformed. Then you will be able
> to discern the will of God, and to know what
> is good, acceptable, and perfect.
> Romans 12:1–2 (NEW ENGLISH BIBLE)

Although this passage will not be exegeted in detail, it is suggestive not only of substantive themes of morality in the Christian life, but also of what changes might be registered in moral discernment. I shall use it at least as a starting point for further discussion.

We might characterize the Christian's obligation to answer the practical moral question, "What ought or are we to do?" in the following way. *Man is to discern what God enables and requires him to do.* Full explication of this sentence would require a book-length exposition of Christian ethics; here I merely suggest various lines that such exposition would take.

What is said about discerning what God enables and requires man to do is not presumed to be a description of how any one Christian does this, or how some "mean" or average Christian constructed out of a sample of all Christians does it. It is clearly said in a mode that suggests that something like it is appropriate normatively, and possible actually.

Christians have a particular stance, or perspective. They stand in a particular relationship which in turn affects their self-understandings, their perceptions and interpretations of the world, and they have certain norms by which they discriminate what is right and good. In St. Paul's language, they are a people who have offered themselves up to God; they are living sacrifices dedicated and fit for His acceptance; mind and heart are offered to God in devotion and in praise. This language suggests that something more is involved than the claim that Christians are people who hold certain ideas or propositions to be meaningful or true. It suggests that Christians are not people who are distinguished from others simply by their belief in a set of propositions about God, and by inferences they draw from those propositions about what man is and what his relationship to God and other men also is. Mind and heart are offered to God; their "very selves" are given to him. A particular relationship of man's personal existence to God is implored by the apostle. It is not only belief that certain things are worthy of acceptance intellectually, but conviction and trust that it is appropriate to rely upon God and to give oneself in this reliance and its consequent service. Christians are, by virtue of this faith, in a particular position; they have by virtue of this faith a particular perspective. Just as my sons are different from my neighbor's sons partly because of their filial relations to me that are different from the filial relations other sons have to their own fathers, so Christians are different because of the relationship in which they exist to God in whom they believe and trust. Just as the understandings which my sons have of themselves are partially determined by the relationship in which they exist to me, so Christians' understandings of themselves are partially determined by the relationship in which they exist to God. Just as the perspectives my sons have on the world of which they are a part is partially determined by their relationship to me, so also are the Christians' by their relationship to God. Just as my sons "see" and interpret life around them partially under this perspective determined by their relation to me, so Christians interpret the world around them from the perspective of their faith in God.

Thus one impact of Christian faith as it affects moral discernment involves the self-understanding that it evokes and directs. If I dedicate myself to be fit for the acceptance of God in whom I believe, I will consciously intend to live in such a way that my words and deeds are worthy of Him. If I frequently offer my mind and heart to Him worshipfully, I will be renewed in this self-understanding as one who depends upon Him, who is grateful to Him, who seeks to be consistent with what He gives and requires of me. The situation is parallel in structure to the self-understandings of others who have offered themselves, so to speak, to other objects of commitment. The devotee of the *Playboy* way of life has a self-understanding that is determined in part by his devotion to the symbols of that way of life, to the values that are pointed to by these symbols. He will see himself to be "sophisticated" and "cool"; he will value highly the gratification of his desires for a maximum of pleasure; he will intend to live in a way that is consistent with his self-understanding, which in turn is evoked and directed by *Playboy*. To put it simply, Christians will answer the question, "Who am I?" differently by virtue of their faith.

Just as one's interpretation of oneself is altered by Christian faith, so one's interpretation of the world around him is altered. Interpretations are informed by perspectives; indeed what one discerns to be important in his perception of the world around him is informed by his perspective. As I have indicated elsewhere,[1] the notion of perspective in matters of moral assessment is analogous to its use in matters of visual experience. Some things are seen clearly and some are shadowed by the perspective of the observer. Some are accented and others are diminished in the impressions that they register. Perspective and self-understanding both make one more sensitive to some things and less sensitive to others. The national leader whose obligation is clearly and primarily to the self-interest of his nation is likely to "read the situation" of Vietnam, or some other one, differently from the person who views his obligation to be primarily to a universal God of love who wills the well-being of all men. The former understands himself to be one who exercises power for the sake of the interests of the nation; the latter understands himself to be one who is the servant of Jesus Christ. (I shall not deal here with the nest of issues that are involved in such a case as one who in a position of political judgment seeks to exercise his power as both a member of a nation and a Christian. The two "selves" are not necessarily either in irresolvable conflict or in perfect harmony.) Certain "facts" have greater importance from one perspective than from the other. Both might observe the same human suffering, but interpret its significance differently because one is viewing things from the perspective of national interest and the other from the perspective of redeeming love. The significance of what is going on is determined by the perspectives of those who see it and participate in it.

Surely H. Richard Niebuhr was getting at this when he suggested that "interpretation" is part of "responsibility." Interpretation is "in the light of" some things that are particular and thus partially constitute the perspective of the interpreter. Thus Christians interpret what is going on in the light of their beliefs about God, and what men and the world are and are to be before Him. Differences of opinion among Christians in their moral discernment are not only affected by differences in the data that they might have available, but also

---

[1] In the last chapter of *Christ and the Moral Life* (New York: Harper & Row, 1968).

by differences in their understanding of what the "light" of the gospel is, and what it illuminates about the world and the self. (It is not our task in this chapter to enter into that technical theological realm where these differences of the latter sort are to be adjudicated.) In spite of differences, there are certain common elements. Christian affirmations about the goodness of God and the goodness of the world He created, the reign of God in the preservation of that which He created, the willful unfaith and disobedience of men, the redemptive purpose of God to reconcile the world to Himself, the hope of a consummation of all things in the coming Kingdom of God, the judgment of God on human disorder, and other affirmations, are part of the "light" that Christians bring to bear upon their interpretation of the world. At another level there are things believed about man: men are created to live together in order and in love, they are to seek each other's good, their lives are to be sustained and not oppressed or destroyed, they are to live in gratitude to God and to others for life and loving care, they are to respect each other, etc. Such assertions are related both to the gospel and to normal human experience; they become "lights" that help Christians understand both what is to be affirmed in the world and what is to be sought for the world.

The perspective of the Christian affects what he values; it gives direction to the moral ends that he seeks, to the longings and desires that he has, to the preferences that he articulates in word and deed. Valuations and preferences are by no means always the result of a conscious reflective process in which certain "values" are defined, judged, and determined to be worthy of acceptance, then in turn applied in rational discrimination to the interpretation of the world in which men live. Christians do not always first engage in a process of defining "love," which by tradition and experience they value highly, and then use this definition to engage in a rational process of interpretation of events in the world in the light of love. (It is clearly the task of the person whose vocation is theological and ethical thinking in the Christian community to engage in such deliberate, careful thinking, more than it is the task of every Christian.) Rather, Christians may have perspectives that are formed in their faith and belief in a God of love, who has demonstrated His love for man in creation, and in His forgiveness and renewal of life, who enables men to love one another as they have been loved, and who wills that men should love each other. This "loving" perspective is likely to color the things that Christians value and approve of in their perception, interpretation, and choices in the world. That which restores and brings life and joy is to be preferred to that which destroys and brings death and suffering and pain, for example. Not only in his rational discriminations, but in his moral sensitivities, the Christian is likely to be sensitive to oppression and injustice, to physical and mental suffering. Christians are likely to interpret not only what is the case, but what ought to be the case in the light of valuations that are determined by the perspective or posture of their faith.

The process of interpretation that is part of discernment is, as I have suggested, an expression of fundamental dispositions that are shaped in part by the faith and trust Christians have as they offer themselves up to God. Their sensibilities are colored by their faith and its perspective. But it is also, as has been suggested, a matter of using articulated and expressed beliefs. Both are part of the moral discernment of Christians. If Christians are to discern what God enables and requires them to do, they are involved in rational discrimination as well as sensible response. Just as I am more likely to do what is acceptable to my sons if I *know* what their needs and desires are, so I am more likely to do what is acceptable to God if I have some knowledge about what God seems to require and enable. Part of my response to my sons' needs is a matter of understanding based upon the human relationship that has been formed between us, with all the nuances of feeling and affection, of intuitive insight and perception. Part of it is a matter of thinking clearly and rationally about what they need in the light of who they are, the resources available to meet their needs, the ways in which they may not understand their needs any more clearly than I do, and the kind of order of life it takes for us to live together with some harmony and joy.

It is under this latter aspect of stipulated convictions and rational reflection that moral discernment in the Christian life uses dogma, moral principles formed in Scripture and the tradition, moral rules of the Christian community, and refined moral argumentation. If I am to discern what God enables and requires, I must be able to say some things about God. Thus the understanding and formed convictions that Christians have about God are important for the way in which they discern things morally, and what they actually discern to be morally appropriate. Variations are many, and changes both within the tradition and in the beliefs of an individual man occur through time. Some aspects of Christian belief are stressed on one occasion, others on another, and elements of belief are combined and recombined in particular times and places so that different themes are accented and muted. Sometimes we recall more cogently God as the awesome judge of human evil, sometimes God the redeemer of the world, sometimes God the restrainer of men who wills that order persist, sometimes God the just and merciful who wills a disruption of an unjust order.

Moral discernment, then, has reference to belief. It is the moral agent who discerns with reference to belief what he judges God to be enabling and requiring. This statement is important, for it precludes saying that Christians are "immediately sensitive" to what God is doing in the world (Lehmann), or that they hear in a clear and direct way what the command of God is to them (Barth). Discernment is a human act made with reference to human statements about God as these statements are forged from Scripture and from the theological tradition. Theologically, it might be said that God is enabling men to discern what God is enabling men to do; but the locus for the discernment is in the self as it relates beliefs about the God in whom it trusts to the situations in which it acts.

Moral rules and principles also play a part in the rational reflection that is part of discerning what one ought to do. Not all of them are rooted particularly in the Christian tradition, but certainly there are some that have historical origins in the Christian faith, and particular authority for Christians. Rules can be understood as having a social function and generally a social sanction in morality. They are determinations of what is definitely required and what is definitely prohibited in the community. As such they are ready and authoritative references for the man who is to discern what he ought to do in normal instances. He discerns clearly and quickly that the situation in which he is to act is one in which his behavior ought to be conformed to those rules that regulate the life of the community. Others before him have faced situations comparable to his own, and have interpreted them in such a way that it is clear that Christians ought to do very specific things on such occasions. There need be no ambiguity in discernment. Just as one need not engage in a unique process of discernment to judge that he ought to obey the traffic signals, so one need not engage in a unique process to judge that as a Christian he has the duty to respect another person as a human being. Elaborate reasons can be given for traffic rules and for the obligations that drivers and pedestrians have to obey them, but members of the civil community do not require that such reasons be given on each occasion. Elaborate theological and ethical reasons can be given for the rule that Christians must treat other persons with respect as human beings, but both because such a rule can be readily internalized and because its authority is clear and unambiguous, they can discern readily prohibited limits and required actions that are enabled and demanded of them. This is not to say that there are not situations in which re-

# Virtue, Principles, and Rules 33

flection and interpretation is not required pertaining to how the rules apply. But it is to say that often rules have immediate applicability, and even when they do not seem to apply readily, the agent can begin with the rule (and not a series of arguments for its validity) in his discerning. For example, in the realm of sexual behavior, there has been a commonly accepted rule, "Thou shalt not commit adultery." Reasons can be given for the authority of that rule, but the rule has relative autonomy by virtue of its long usage within the Christian community so that its members do not have to face every human relationship with a man or woman who is not their marriage partner as one that offers the moral possibility of adultery. Indeed, if for various reasons a relationship suggests that adultery might be committed, Christians begin with the rule. The weight of evidence and reflection clearly has to be such as to invalidate the application of the rule in that particular instance. Exceptions to such rules are not made lightly, and the existence of exceptions is hardly evidence for the invalidity of the rule.

Moral principles function in a similar way, though perhaps they can be distinguished in some instance from rules by the absence of social sanction. Nor are they so determined by what sociologists and anthropologists have called one's status and roles in the community. In different human situations moral principles function differently. Certainly such a principle as the commandment to love the neighbor as the self would be part of the "light" that Christians would bring to bear upon their interpretation of the general situation and also be part of their intention in acting within it. It would function to set the direction of their activity: what they do ought to be in accord with what love requires. To discern what the principle seems to enable and require places an obligation on Christians to interpret what love seems to mean, and how this meaning is applicable in the particular occasion. Moral reflection on such a general principle requires a great degree of sophistication on some occasions; on others its requirements seem to be self-evident. When sophistication is required, the Christian is involved in the process in which the situation must be defined (its proper time and space limits determined, its complex of relationships delineated, its data formulated and organized); in which other principles bearing on the case that might not be easily harmonized with the love commandment have to be stipulated and recalled, other theological reference-points that love remembered, other values than love designated, and the use of "love" itself carefully delineated so that it has some particularity and does not cover everything. He is involved in a process in which analogies from Scripture or from the moral experience of the community are rehearsed and brought to bear; in which moral sensibilities are recognized, judged, and affirmed or qualified by reflection; and in which finally a judgment is made about what God is enabling and requiring. This reflection will illumine the discernment of God's will; it will never have clear and unambiguous authority so that the reflecting man will equate his serious judgment with God's will itself. Indeed, careful reflection is necessary in discernment because of the partialities of men, and the tendency to discern what is fit and acceptable for one's own gratification or the gratification of one's own group rather than fit and acceptable to God. Reflection is necessary because Christians, like others, tend to be conformed to the expectations of their own desires and to the ethos of the time in which they live, rather than remembering that they are not to be conformed to this world.

Moral discernment always takes place within communities; the moral discernment of Christians takes place within the Christian community. The community is in part the present gathering of Christians, in a congregation or some other group, that engages in the moral discourse that informs the conscientiousness of its members through participation in moral deliberation.[2] Through moral discourse in the Christian community, both the minds and hearts of men can be trained to discernment; their capacities to make discerning moral judgments can be deepened, broadened, and extended. Such training is not an automatic accrual from hearing sermons or receiving the sacraments; if the Holy Spirit is at work in the community to make men better discerners of God's will he is present in and through the moral deliberations that occur, as well as the preached word and the bread and wine.

But the community is not only the present gathering at this time and place. Those presently gathered are part of a historical community that has lived the moral life as Christians in the past, that has reflected upon situations comparable to the present ones with references to the same gospel, and the same intention to discern God's will. This does not mean that an answer from the fourth century is the answer to the twentieth century, but it does mean that in present reflection the community does not have to begin *de novo* as if God's will for present and future had no consistency with God's will for the past. Certain values, or principles, or points for consideration that were arranged

[2] I have developed this theme in several other places, most concisely in "The Church: A Community of Moral Discourse," *The Crane Review*, Vol. 7, pp. 75–85, and in "The Voluntary Church: A Moral Appraisal," *Voluntary Associations*, ed. D. B. Robertson (Richmond, Va.: John Knox Press, 1966), especially pp. 313–322.

## Virtue, Principles, and Rules

in one combination with reference to a past situation might be rearranged and added to with reference to a present situation to the illumination and accuracy of the present community. John Noonan's *Contraception*,[3] the greatest book yet published on the history of an issue in Christian ethics, makes this point clear. Moral discernment is in continuity with the past, not discontinuity; it learns from, and is thus informed and directed without being determined by, the past. (The current celebration of the openness toward the future is proper insofar as it recognizes that the God whose will one seeks to discern for the future is the God who has willed in the past. Much of this celebration refers primarily to human *attitude* in any case, and as such is insufficient to determine what men ought to be doing in particular instances. Attitude alone does not determine act. To be open to the future is not to discern what one ought to do in it.)

Perhaps all that has been said about moral discernment in this chapter is only another way of talking about the virtue of prudence. Prudence is the virtue that is both intellectual and moral; it involves reason, sensibilities, and the will. It is a virtue: it is a lasting disposition of the self that comes into being not in the moment by some inspiration of the Spirit or by some visceral response to a narrowly defined situation, but by experience, training, reflection, and action. It does not exist independent from law, although it is the capacity to perceive what law might require in a particular case, and to perceive what might be required that is more than the law demands. It is open to the concrete situation, but not in such a way that the past is ignored, as if similar situations have never occurred before. It is an exercise of character that has been formed; the formation of character is important in the whole of the moral life of which a particular discernment is but a moment in time. It is formed and informed by love, trust, hope, and other gifts of the Spirit. But it is never simply an attitude; it is a capacity to discern that uses reason and intellectual discrimination.

Prudence in the Christian life refers to the fitting judgment, response, and act. But the fitting in turn refers to what God is enabling and requiring, not just what seems to be pleasing to men. Thus the exercise of prudence, of discernment, in the Christian life is intricate and complex; it can never be programed for all men, for some are gifted in different ways from others, and some have different roles from others. Its exercise is not only in moral discrimination; it is

---

[3] John T. Noonan, Jr., *Contraception* (Cambridge, Mass.: Harvard University Press, 1966).

itself offered to God in praise and devotion, in reliance upon the grace of God to empower and inform it. But it is human; man is the exerciser of prudence in reliance upon God, and in discernment of God's will.

At best, however, the Christian who is morally discerning, who has the capacity to be perceptive, discriminating, accurate, and sensitive, probably has to modify his acceptance of the words of St. Paul. He said with assurance, "Then you *will* be able to discern the will of God." I suspect that more modest claims would be more precise. By offering oneself up to God, and by formation in prudence informed by love and faith and hope, "Then you *might* discern the will of God."

# 3

# *Character, Conduct, and the Love Commandment*

## GENE H. OUTKA

A great deal of talk is heard today in many circles, both religious and nonreligious, about a "new morality." Sometimes such talk is seriously meant, though often it is only careless sloganeering. But there comes a point in any sustained discussion of a question of importance at which further complexities are acknowledged and more distinctions introduced. Such a point surely seems to be upon us in regard to the "new morality."

I want to try in a brief way to treat some of these complexities. Though what I shall say will pertain directly to the "debate" within religious circles and only indirectly to the cultural discussion at large, I hope to be dealing with questions of general moral interest. Essentially what I shall argue is that the discussion will remain more loquacious than clarifying until far more elucidative work has been done on a quite elementary matter: the possible *kinds* of things people may mean when they talk of "norms," "principles," "rules," and the like, and some of the connections between these things. The possibilities here are dazzling in their variety. What I propose to do is begin to sort out some of these things and to indicate my own sympathies as I go along.

I shall divide this complicated subject matter as follows. First of all, in Section I of this chapter, I shall consider a fairly comprehensive (though by no means exhaustive) list of the possible meanings of norm, principle, rule, and so forth. In attempting this, one must immediately reckon with a difficulty. There is no commonly accepted way of using "normative" terms, especially within theological ethics. Some writers indiscriminately lump together all such terms and repudiate them en bloc. Other writers posit more careful distinctions, but in such different ways that it is not always apparent what is accepted and what rejected in relation to other positions. In one treatment, "principles" may be affirmed as illuminative "maxims" and "rules" rejected as captious restrictions on authentic personal freedom. In another treatment, rules (or the "law") may have a far wider usage, encompassing what in the first treatment is meant by principles. This is not to say that genuine disputes are non-existent but merely to observe that they are frequently interspersed with definitional differences, all of which make precise assessments a peculiarly formidable undertaking. Thus it should be clear that any such list as the one I shall devise is not simply reportive of a consensus among ethicists, but that it is, at least to some extent, a "reforming proposal." In Section II there will be more extensive commentary on several items in the list which are of particular significance for present discussion. In Section III, as an illustration of these items, I shall examine one influential historical document, Luther's *Large Catechism* (specifically, his treatment of the Decalogue). Finally, in Section IV I shall conclude that the actual ways in which these matters have been understood is most complex (and often obscure) with many purposes served, and that it would be a serious mistake to draw up the alternatives in a simplistic fashion (such as shuttling back and forth between "love" and individual moral judgments without attending seriously to the host of intermediate considerations).

# I

1. Let us attempt some initial distinctions between the kinds of things people may mean when they talk of norms, principles, rules, and so on. It is a not infrequent practice to begin with principles which are judged to be essential to, or presuppositions of, morality as such.[1] These principles, it is often claimed, are logically involved in the possibility of moral judgments of any sort, irrespective of the "content" of such judgments. Perhaps the most familiar candidate for such a principle is "universalizability," which is associated with Kant and currently propounded by R. M. Hare. Hare nicely distinguishes between "universality" and "generality" (though he admits they are often used interchangeably). "The opposite of 'general' is 'specific';

[1] See, e.g., Dorothy Emmet, *Rules, Roles and Relations* (London: Macmillan & Co., 1966), pp. 56–88.

## Virtue, Principles, and Rules

the opposite of 'universal' is 'singular.' "[2] One cannot properly speak of singular moral judgments (because moral predicates must conform to "descriptive meaning-rules" which are necessarily universal), but one can speak of either general or specific moral rules, since all the terms employed are universal predicates. Universalizability in this sense means that in a particular situation of moral choice one logically commits himself or someone else to the same judgment in any other situation that is similar in the "morally relevant respects." According to Hare, "all the universalist is committed to in making a moral judgement is to saying that *if* there is another person in a similar situation, then the same judgement must be made about his case."[3] But the principle involved in such a judgment may be so complex that it is not verbally formulable at all. There is no stipulation that what is universalizable must be explicitly stated in every detail. Indeed, even parables and stories with a moral point may be regarded as universalizable. There are perfectly sound reasons for saying (*a*) that maturity in moral development "consists in the main in making our moral principles more and more specific, by writing into them exceptions and qualifications to cover kinds of cases of which we have had experience. In the case of most people they soon become too complicated to admit of formulation, and yet give tolerably clear guidance in familiar situations" and (*b*) that "since we cannot know everything about another actual person's concrete situation (including how it strikes him, which may make all the difference), it is nearly always presumptuous to suppose that another person's situation is exactly like one we have ourselves been in, or even like it in the relevant particulars."[4] Though Hare's argument is of extraordinary importance, our own concerns here are more largely with those kinds of principles and rules within theological ethics which are matters of degree and which have received actual formulation. Thus I shall concentrate on the "general" and "specific," endeavoring as I do so not to contravene the formal universalizability requirement.

The discussion I wish to pursue is not, therefore, directly concerned with such principles as universalizability and thus I shall bypass them here. I am concerned, rather, with principles and rules within morality as such, which provide substantive guidance for moral judgments.[5] The procedure in examining these will be to move from the more general to the more specific.

The starting point in much recent Christian ethical literature

---

[2] *Freedom and Reason* (New York: Oxford University Press, 1965), p. 39.
[3] *Ibid.*, pp. 48–49.   [4] *Ibid.*, pp. 40, 49.   [5] Cf. Emmet, *op. cit.*, p. 56.

has been "love," specifically the commandment, "You shall love your neighbor as yourself." [6] "Love" is a notoriously ambiguous word and this commandment has been taken in a multitude of ways. For our purposes here, I shall call this commandment an *unqualifiedly general ethical principle,* by which I mean that it is (a) applicable to everyone unrestrictedly, (b) and on every occasion so that it is always relevant, (c) and serves as the basis of subsidiary principles and rules, providing the fundamental justifying reason or warrant for their existence or the purpose or intent underlying them. Pleading guilty in advance to begging many questions (to say nothing of neglecting them), for the moment I shall simply make two observations about such a principle.

First, we are assuming that "You shall love your neighbor as yourself" is a distinctive moral posture to which there are alternatives and therefore that it is not a presupposition of morality in the sense just described.[7] Second, the principle is related (though in different ways)

---

[6] It seems that nearly all of the recent reflection on the general subject of love as a principle for conduct has been concerned not with love for God but for the neighbor. Very frequently the result has been to prescind from considering some of the more traditional issues connected with normative judgments, such as the "law" (including the love commandment) as the "accuser" of the easy conscience, as the means through which a man comes to know of his need for grace. Few would formally deny that there is a profound point to the recurrent Pauline protest (however inaccurate in relation to historical Jewish attitudes) against being haunted by unattainable obligations and against using external conformity to the "letter" of the law as a vehicle for self-justification. But the need for such an unqualified internal liberation at an "ultimate" level from all such legal millstones and temptations is only tacitly affirmed, if at all. Though there have been few explicit denials of the reality of such an experience, the tendency toward disavowal is itself significant, indicating at the very least a concentration on (to use the Reformation distinctions) the "moral law" as a societal requirement and as a guide for behavior but not as a goad to self-righteousness or a condemnatory force which drives men into despair. The religious ambiguity that may be in the law is not taken as exhaustive for construing it. In any event, I shall adhere to recent precedent in this chapter and confine myself largely to the "second great commandment."

[7] I. M. Crombie has an illuminating account of the way both the principle of benevolence (which he equates with loving one's neighbor as oneself) and what he calls the "quasi-Nietzschean" principle can legitimately appear before the bar of a principle constitutive of morality, in this case the "Golden Rule." The quasi-Nietzschean believes "in the effectiveness of competition and strife in producing the more valuable human qualities, which he takes to consist in strength, independence and the like. If this man concedes that the excellence of others is of equal importance with his own, and is prepared to allow that others may do to him what he believes he may do to them, then his outlook is a moral outlook, conforms to the golden rule, and is an alternative to the principle of benevolence. For he may well not at all concede that it is his business actively to concern him-

# Virtue, Principles, and Rules

to both character and conduct, i.e., to agent and action, traits and rules, goodness and rightness, being and doing. This general distinction is seemingly endemic to ethical reflection, whether philosophical or theological. William K. Frankena points out:

> In some of our moral judgments, we say that a certain action or kind of action is morally right, wrong, obligatory, a duty, or ought or ought not to be done. In others we talk, not about actions or kinds of action, but about persons, motives, intentions, traits of character, and the like, and we say of them that they are morally good, bad, virtuous, vicious, responsible, blameworthy, saintly, despicable, and so on. In these two kinds of judgment, the things talked about are different and what is said about them is different.[8]

Principles and rules subsidiary to love may be understood as attempts to specify its "implications" or "embodiments" in terms of traits of character to be fostered and courses of action to be pursued. How this is done and what authority such principles and rules have of course vary enormously. Moreover, there are doubtless profound connections between these two sorts of judgment. What we are to be and to do, though distinguishable, are not finally separable. I shall try to illustrate some of these connections as we proceed.

2. Though we have argued that "You shall love your neighbor as yourself" is a distinctive ethical principle, it is nonetheless so general as to be nearly truistic. There are problems, for one thing, with the meaning of "love," "neighbor," and "as yourself" which cannot be considered here.[9] If we say that the love commandment involves at least continuous regard for the welfare of others, then this initially rules out little beyond "ethical egoism" in its various forms. We must now examine possible kinds of further specification, beginning with general traits of character and moving toward externally perceptible behavior. Most of the sorts of things I shall distinguish will be "formal" (in the sense that there is allowance for a variety of kinds of moral content; an ethical egoist, for instance, might have his own traits

---

self either with gratifying the desires or even with furthering the excellence of others" ("Moral Principles," *Christian Ethics and Contemporary Philosophy*, ed. Ian T. Ramsey [London: SCM Press, 1966], p. 242).

[8] William K. Frankena, *Ethics* (Englewood Cliffs, N.J.: Prentice-Hall, 1963), pp. 8–9. Cf. John Laird, "Act-Ethics and Agent-Ethics," *Mind*, LV (April, 1946), pp. 113–132. There is a roughly equivalent distinction in German between *Seinsollen* and *Tunsollen*.

[9] For one effort to sort out some of these meanings, see my *The Characterization of Love in Contemporary Theological Ethics*, Ph.D. Dissertation, Yale University, 1967.

of character and moral rules), though the major examples I give will be "material" (i.e., about the love commandment and its relation to traits and rules) in that all reflect the current discussion in theological ethics.

When one attaches praise or blame, often he is engaged more in judgments of character than of conduct. Consider the following:

> (a) "To me he personifies goodness; his entire life consists in being devoted to others."
> (b) "I have seen him display patience with her when she has been insufferably irritating."
> (c) "I admit she is not very bright, but she is remarkably kind."
> (d) "I respect him because he is the most honest person I know."

"Principles," "norms," and "rules" are sometimes used to refer to the standards implicit in the above judgments. Let us scrutinize these judgments further. (a) really seems synonymous with the love commandment as such, with the pristine obligation to regard the welfare of others. It is the obligation *that* one is to care in this way rather than what, precisely, he must *do,* which is principally important. This has been appropriated, if we can believe the speaker, as a general frame of mind, an orientation or "life style" pervading the entire personality, a settled policy regarding how one should live which integrates various actions. One is here assessing the depth and permanence of this policy, the extent to which someone's conduct may be most accurately accounted for only by referring to it.

(b), (c), and (d) reflect perhaps slightly more specific enumerations, though of a rather platitudinous sort and still of extremely wide generality.[10] They seem to have a "qualitative affinity" with a general frame of mind. One can, if he wishes, call them "virtues," at least in a rough (i.e., not in an Aristotelian or Thomist) sense. "Trait" is in some respects preferable, especially because the notion of a "virtuous man" has become frequently a disparaging reference in our period. A welter of further questions could be considered at this point (e.g., the possibility of more precise characterizations of trait, virtue, motive, attitude, intention, disposition, etc.), but all of them would involve us in unwarranted digressions. We must limit ourselves to several very sketchy comments.

First, traits of character or virtues involve attitudes, intentions,

---

[10] These may be embodied in persons, stories, and parables which are sometimes notably successful in *inducing* people to regard the welfare of others (far more, very often, than precise rules governing conduct). In calling some of them platitudinous, I do not wish to deny that they may be edifying and important.

patterns of behavior, and the like, which are simply recurrent. They are expressed in our total "life-style" and deportment, sometimes with admittedly elaborate variations. This is the case even when it is acknowledged that, at least in part, such traits may acquire their meaning from conduct, that their content is established inductively *via* a pattern of actions. The evidence for whether they are present at all may be principally contained in the history of the self's past conduct. Yet there are still important differences. For traits of character persist through time. If, on the basis of past conduct, one says that a person is kind and patient, one is also referring to what might or will happen in other or future circumstances.

Second, though virtues or traits in the rough sense above constitute criteria for moral judgments of a sweeping kind, they do seem slightly more specific than the love commandment in itself. They are often applicable to all men unrestrictedly, but not necessarily on every occasion. At least this is so with some of their meanings. It seems more appropriate to argue that one need not act out of kindness on every occasion (one might say something like, for example, "Her problem was that she was too kind; for his own good she ought to have been more severe with him"), than it is to maintain that one ought not act out of love on every occasion (at least for the Christian).

Third, some words seem to imply further degrees of specificity in a way which others do not. In terms of the three illustrations we have been considering, such an implication is present in the case of honesty more than with kindness and patience. Honesty is a general trait of character in the sense that it may involve continual openness toward others, an abiding awareness of one's own guilt and failings, etc. But it often implies rather transparently further degrees of specificity, eventually pointing to definite actions (such as truth-telling in specific situations). Here then is a case where a trait of character is more closely correlated with a kind of conduct; the specific judgment typically connects the two in more than an *ad hoc* fashion. It is otherwise with kindness and patience which require conduct, but seem to be more relatively independent of any particular class of conduct. Being kind and patient assuredly signifies being disposed to act in kind and patient ways. But while many actions presumably enter into the judgments, no isolable kind of action is predictably present or determinative. Such "virtues" are expressed by actions which are often spontaneous; the connections appear to be more or less contingent. In this sense these latter virtues are extremely general.

3. Traits of character turn out to be staggeringly complex and I have not tried to do anything more than allude to them. There are

various possible elaborations, e.g., to intentions as more specific parts of a settled policy which is characterized only in very general terms. We must bypass such matters here and turn instead to another, more distinct level of specificity.

It is obvious that traits of character or virtues are relationally oriented (at least those which reflect the love commandment). Yet there is what might be called a relational factor in numerous moral judgments which is sometimes more definite than a trait of character and yet less specific than an externally perceptible act. Rather concise questions arise about how men ought to regard others in both "one-to-one" relations (e.g., within a family) and in more generalized social relations. Such questions lead to the formulation of certain definite principles or policies, or what I shall call *relational norms*. Relational norms in this sense serve to identify and delimit kinds of human relations and circumstances as morally significant and to express moral conclusions about them. There are many different kinds of identification possible, of which the following two are among the most important. (*a*) Such norms sometimes identify certain *states of affairs* and *circumstances* which are of primary and relatively specified moral significance, e.g., "One must not punish the innocent." [11] (*b*) Norms may also locate certain relatively definite sorts of *relations*, often involving roles and expressing generally what are taken to be fundamental rights and obligations. Examples include "Husbands and wives ought to be faithful to one another" and "Children ought to honor their parents." No doubt what counts as fulfilling them is usually subject to wide cultural variation and individual judgment. There are, for instance, conventional and symbolic agreements in a given society or among subcultures within it on what constitutes honoring one's parents (though these seem currently rather indistinct in American society).

Any extensive characterization of the different kinds of relational norms is beyond our purview. What I am concerned at the moment to emphasize is simply that there is an intermediate range of moral judgments which are in an important sense more precise than traits of character but more general than rules governing actions as such. On the one side, this is not to deny, as I have said, that traits of character involve being disposed to act in definite ways. "Dependability," for example, involves a fundamental disposition on the part of the individual to act in the appropriate ways in all relations which

---

[11] George Henrik von Wright, *Norm and Action* (London: Routledge and Kegan Paul, 1963), p. 11.

place a claim upon him. Moreover, it must be acknowledged that there is only a relative difference between traits of character and relational norms, that the connections between them are usually profound. What is a good man in a relation and what makes a relation good are difficult to distinguish or to perceive in practice. But relational norms often locate special relations and circumstances which affect how various claims are sorted out. Generally we may say that what is at stake in judgments about traits of character and virtues is the goodness or badness *of the agent* whereas relational norms involve judgments about the moral import of more definite relations and states. The latter kind of judgment contributes to the former without being equivalent to it.

This is also not to deny, on the other side, that such norms may be correlated with rules governing actions; that, for instance, certain relational bonds often provide the appropriate context for understanding and appraising rules governing conduct. They may in some cases lead quite self-evidently to, say, the prohibition of certain actions. If I accept the norm prohibiting punishment of the innocent, it would be odd, to say the least, if I then proceeded immediately to justify deliberately putting an innocent party into prison (though saying this seems invariably to prompt some to devote most of their time to thinking up just such unusual cases which it may be idle to deny but which in no way repudiate the persistent moral relevance for action of the relational norm). Yet here again, differences remain, primarily because relational norms are not subject in the same way as rules governing action to spatio-temporal delimitation. "We can ask 'When and where did David beget Solomon?' but not 'When and where was David the father of Solomon?' " [12] Though there are many actions which express and are correlated with relational norms, there are none with which such norms can be exhaustively identified.

However, there are perhaps some cases where no clear boundary at all separates relational norms from rules governing conduct, where the properties of both are present to some extent. This appears to be true, for example, with certain rights and obligations which are formally regulative for the entire society. These are not as directly relevant to personal (one-to-one) relations as are many relational norms (and as are basic moral rules). Yet they do reflect what are regarded as indefeasible moral considerations and claims *and* they are often more like broadly defined policies than rules pertaining to

---

[12] Anthony Kenny, *Action, Emotion and Will* (London: Routledge and Kegan Paul, 1964), p. 169. See also D. S. Shwayder, "Moral Rules and Moral Maxims," *Ethics*, LXVII (June, 1957), pp. 269–285.

individual acts. I shall call them *fundamental ground rules of the society*, though the phrase has its difficulties, since I am using "rule" here in a somewhat broader way than elsewhere. One instance of such rules would be the Bill of Rights in the Constitution of the United States. Though societal ground rules need not always be written down in, say, a constitution, they must be more or less explicitly recognized. They are usually promulgated by a definite authority with sanctions to assure effectiveness. Correlated to them are positive laws pertaining to their clarification, protection, and implementation.

4. I pass on now to conduct or action as such. "Conduct" here cannot refer to literally everything which people may be regarded as doing (e.g., crying) but to those things which are more or less deliberately done. "Rules" serve to locate classes of human conduct and typically indicate with respect to these "whether they are *required, forbidden,* or *permitted.*" [13] Rules in this sense do not include "regularities," i.e., those more or less uniform social patterns to be discovered more than obeyed (such as, in economics, the "marginal propensity to consume") and physical laws of nature (e.g., "the first law of thermodynamics").[14] But they still include a somewhat heterogeneous group of items, at any rate for our purposes. We shall not be concerned directly with (*a*) rules which are constitutive of an activity (e.g., a game of basketball) and (*b*) rules which are really "counsels of wisdom" for those developing certain skills (such as driving a golf ball without slicing).[15] While they are closer to the more usual meanings of moral rules, we shall also not consider (*c*) mores and customs in the sense of "the proprieties," which are neither promulgated nor abrogated by any single group but, rather, define standards of etiquette and "acceptable" behavior.[16]

This leaves us with at least two other meanings of "rule," though these overlap in multiple ways and degrees: (*d*) neutral rules, and (*e*) basic moral rules. There are what may be called *neutral rules,* where it is judged desirable or essential to adopt some rules, but which ones is often a matter of indifference.[17] Thus there are "regulations" which

---

[13] Max Black, *Models and Metaphors* (Ithaca: Cornell University Press, 1962), p. 108.

[14] Kurt Baier, *The Moral Point of View* (Ithaca: Cornell University Press, 1958), p. 125.

[15] *Ibid.,* pp. 125–126.  [16] *Ibid.,* p. 125.

[17] Cf. the use of "neutral norm" by Marcus George Singer, *Generalization in Ethics* (New York: Alfred A. Knopf, 1961), pp. 112–115. I am indebted generally to Singer for his discussion of "Moral Rules and Principles," pp. 96–138.

## Virtue, Principles, and Rules

are simply laid down and enforced, sometimes by certain groups (e.g., only the members of the Department of Physics are permitted to park their cars in lot 14) or by the community at large (such as rules governing automobile traffic generally). It is morally immaterial whether cars drive on the right or left side of the highway, so long as all members of the community adhere to one practice or the other. However, not all neutral rules are legally defined as such, though they may often have appreciable legal support. Virtually no society forgoes all regulations on sexual behavior, for example, but many people would argue that there is no set of regulations which ought to be regarded as invariant. Certain social needs and purposes must be served, but there is a variety of regulative means for doing so, none of which is "inherently" wrong.[18] For this view, it is necessary to adopt some rules, but which ones is dependent on a host of "local" factors (though it is usually wise to accept the regulations of one's own society).

The final meaning of rule that we shall consider concerns (e) *basic moral rules*. It is important to begin by seeing that such rules relate to certain acts which are judged to be of clear and irreducible moral significance and which must be taken into account in all situations in which they occur. These acts are always relevant considerations in characterizing a situation, whatever one may say about their decisiveness in one's final evaluation. As characterizations, they cannot be "elided" into words which refer to their consequences. "Case-terms" have been devised for placing such acts, e.g., "kill," "rape," "adultery," "theft," and "lying."[19] Some of these terms are clearly evaluative, e.g., "murder," while others may be more strictly reportive, e.g., "kill." The terms placing such acts may be called, following Eric D'Arcy, "species-terms" and they differ from many terms of more general applicability (often close to traits of character), which may be called "genus-terms."

> There are many terms of wider extension: for instance, "unchastity," "dishonesty," "justice," "charity," and so on. These frequently embrace a number of species. "Unchastity," for example, embraces "adultery," "rape," "incest," and so on. "Dishonesty" is of even wider extension; it includes "lying," with its sub-species such as "perjury," and "calumny," and "theft," with its sub-species such as "embezzlement" and "robbery"; "fraud," "forgery," and "cheating" may come under both "lying" and

[18] Crombie, *op. cit.*, p. 251.
[19] See the very incisive account by Eric D'Arcy, *Human Acts* (Oxford: Clarendon Press, 1963), especially pp. 2-39.

"theft," and "hypocrisy" not quite under either, though it will involve some sort of dishonesty.[20]

I shall regard basic moral rules as requiring, prohibiting, or permitting classes of human conduct (a) which are judged to be of irreducible ("nonelidable") moral significance, (b) which are relevant in both predominantly personal and social contexts, and (c) which are taken to be generally (rather than universally) right and wrong because, as actually formulated, they may conflict. Obvious examples here are the prohibitions against lying, killing, and stealing. There are, of course, many problems with such a cryptic definition, some of which we shall take up as we proceed.

## II

It is time now to offer some commentary on this list. I shall have in mind those issues of particular significance for the current debate within theological ethics, once again moving from the more general to the more specific.

1. There are at least two distinguishable ways in which the love commandment can be said to serve as the "basis" of subsidiary principles, norms, rules, etc. First, it is at any rate conceivable that love as such, i.e., "necessarily" or "intrinsically," is "constrained to cloak itself in principles not by anything outside of itself, but by its own nature or 'inner dialectic'. . . ." [21] The relationship is therefore essentially *deductive* (or at least love is held to be productive of them). Rules, for instance, may "be elicited by," "derive from," "be generated from," "comprise necessary determinations of," "be transcriptions of the demands of" love. Many of these kinds of claims can be found in the literature of theological ethics, but they frequently turn out to be painfully muddled. This is because the characterization of the content of love is normally not sufficiently full to allow one to say what counts as clear specification apart from at least some attention to "the nature and destiny of man" and thus to the things regarded as desirable features of human existence, the particularities of the context, and so on.

Perhaps the moral judgments which are closest to being "deductive" in the sense above, or to being immediately produced as obvious

---

[20] *Ibid.,* p. 25.
[21] William K. Frankena, "Love and Principle in Christian Ethics," *Faith and Philosophy,* ed. Alvin Plantinga (Grand Rapids: Wm. B. Eerdmans, 1964), p. 214.

"entailments" of love, are those pertaining to traits of character or virtues and ideals. For example, there would seem to be little serious dispute with Paul: "Love is patient and kind; love is not jealous or boastful; it is not arrogant or rude. Love does not insist on its own way; it is not irritable or resentful" (1 Cor. 13: 4–5). The point is simply that one can more readily envisage an elementary characterization of love (such as regarding the welfare of others) self-evidently and unexceptionably prohibiting attitudinal arrogance and rudeness than more tangible acts of theft and killing. There is often far more apparent and immediate expansiveness from love to traits of character than to rules of conduct. A major reason for this is that one has more freedom to decide *who* and *what* he will call arrogant or rude than what he can describe as theft or killing. This may make him more willing *always* to disapprove of arrogance and rudeness than of theft and killing. The search for ways in which love may sometimes justify qualifications, exemptions, exceptions, etc., to the latter becomes then much more understandable.[22] This is not to gainsay that there may be connections between love and rules prohibiting theft and killing, but only to question whether they are on the same level of transparency with certain very general traits of character which persist through time.

Usually, therefore, a second, more restricted way of affirming that the love commandment serves as a basis of subsidiary principles and rules is taken: love is the basis of rules "not by its own nature alone, but by its nature together with the facts about the world in which it is seeking to fulfill itself or reach its object." [23] A strong version of this way would retain for love the finally controlling center of gravity; rules, etc., are "subject always to reconsideration by," "revised in the light of," "transformed by," or "fulfilled only in" love. There is adoptive certification, selection, and transformation. A weaker version would regard love simply as the final reference point for judging the adequacy of past, existent, or emerging maxims, societal laws, etc., and for adjudicating between them in cases of conflict. Love is here the "ultimate perspective" which "ratifies," "confirms," "illuminates," "gives final coherence to" rules even as they "express," "are consistent with," and "implement" love. The connections of course may vary, depending on whether one has in mind a relational norm, a neutral rule, etc. In any event, this second, more restricted way of affirming that the love commandment serves as the basis of subsidiary principles and rules means that love can still be sovereign as the necessary

[22] Cf. Crombie, *op. cit.*, p. 249.    [23] Frankena, *op. cit.*, p. 213.

but not always the sufficient condition for their determination. They presuppose love's approbation without always self-evidently following from its dictates.

2. Traits of character often have an important broad connection with overt acts. The meaning or purpose or point of conduct in the mind of the agent may depend on certain virtues or life styles. As we have seen, overt acts may involve elements which are of such moral importance that "species-terms" are used in characterizing what the agent is doing. Yet a final assessment of an act often depends on particular attitudes and intentions of the agent which render possible descriptions of the act more or less appropriate or even true or false.[24] Suppose I demonstrate in a public place on behalf of racially integrated housing, intentionally disrupting traffic and interfering with the distribution of goods and services. I may view my action as simply a clear implicate of the love commandment, or as a condition for gaining political power in my constituency, or as the last peaceably coercive measure before resorting to violence, or as one expression of my wholesale alienation from the commonly accepted goals of my society. (Of course I might hold several of these simultaneously in view, ranking them in some sort of means-end fashion, or they may only have different weights.) How I perceive my action will have enormous ramifications for my entire style and deportment, for the arguments I offer and the reasons I find compelling, for my estimation of what future policies are morally permitted and politically viable. Such perception is affected by my own freedom from or bondage to anxiety about myself and my welfare, by my attitudes and intentions toward others which contribute to distinctive selectivity and evaluation, in short, by the content, intensity, and objects of my love. If one ignores these kinds of connections, he is sometimes unable to account for the subtle but often far-reaching differences between those who may agree to undertake the same specific action at a given moment in time.

3. Many would be disgruntled at least with some of the implications of the comments above. One can easily overemphasize, they might argue, the distinction between general traits of character and rules of conduct, with the former being platitudinously unexceptionable and the latter narrowly "external." Moreover, to say that a final evaluation of an act often depends on certain attitudes and intentions of the agent must not be taken to mean that moral appraisal is entirely a matter of

---

[24] D'Arcy, *op. cit.*, pp. 12–15.

character, with acts reduced to the status of "symptoms" of a loving frame of mind.

I would agree in general with both these statements. I have already indicated that there are connections between traits of character and rules of conduct and that certain moral species-terms (and the rules surrounding them or implied in them) are vital to the characterization of an act, if not always solely determinative for its evaluation. As is so often the case in moral questions, it seems that here we have to stay between two extremes. We must resist the collapsing of judgments of character into those of conduct if we are to avoid shallowness and legalism, if we are to care about the spirit as well as the letter. We cannot disavow the nuances of assessment and the subtleties of perception in any genuinely sensitive moral judgment. I have already noted one way in which traits of character often affect the meaning of conduct: many actions are susceptible to a variety of interpretations so that one's attitudes, motives, intentions, etc., put them in a particular light. But we also have to resist a bifurcation of character and conduct where moralists refuse to specify beyond motives and intentions or where all conduct is merely a matter of external "expressions" which may be left to take care of themselves. Without some public criteria connecting conduct to character, it is difficult to see how one prevents indistinctness and arbitrariness in moral judgments. We cannot here enter very far into what are finally some of the most perplexing and perennial problems in ethics. Generally we can say that character and conduct must remain in a state of reciprocal implication. It may in addition be instructive to examine briefly one example of what I regard as each distortion above.

A reader can find many instances where the distinctions between judgments of character and of conduct are not sufficiently acknowledged. There are sometimes cases, for instance, where a treatment ostensibly of the virtues turns out to refer to external conduct. Gérard Gilleman has written an impressive contemporary Roman Catholic work in ethics which draws deeply on the tradition but which is nonetheless critical of many of the older manuals in moral theology.[25] (Gilleman's book is an important piece and my criticism of one part of it is by no means intended as blanket detraction.) Formally, Gilleman denies any equivalence between love as such and "exterior con-

---

[25] Gérard Gilleman, S.J., *The Primacy of Charity in Moral Theology*, trans. William F. Ryan, S.J., and André Vachon, S.J. (Westminster: Newman Press, 1961). The French edition is *Le Primat de la Charité en Théologie Morale* (Bruxelles: Desclée de Brouwer, 1954).

formity" to rules governing conduct; he is explicitly wary of any concentration on external acts which implies independence from love's basic intention and directive presence. Love is profounder than "rules" and "law," in complexity and interior depth. Yet Gilleman also claims an almost self-evident congruency between virtues and some rules. He regards virtue as that which "inscribes in the faculty a presumption favorable to certain choices." [26] Love and charity are "incarnated" in various virtues in the constant movement from the level of basic indetermination within the self into the visible world of tangible acts. "Charity will elevate and give finality to our will, while the virtues will orient the diversity of our active powers." [27] Every virtue is a means or a specific end to the ultimate end of charity.

This signifies, on the one hand, that Gilleman is anxious to accentuate the controlling place of love in a way commonly ignored, he maintains, in far too many influential treatises of moral theology. Love, or charity, is the "radical dynamism" which penetrates into virtues and acts. Virtue effectively "participates" in charity; the latter is its origin, its animating power, its "sense." Charity is anything but an addendum to virtue.

On the other hand, Gilleman is aware of the potentially unorthodox implications of his interpretation and he deliberately draws back from them. Charity is indeed "eminently" every virtue, "just as sunlight is eminently red and violet." [28] But what if there is an apparent conflict between them? Is love then invariably victorious? To conclude so would be highly damaging to "objective morality" and would be tantamount to saying that the end justifies the means.

> For example, why can we not lie if by so doing we can save a soul incapable of bearing some necessary truth? Why is suicide forbidden even when it is the only means of not betraying friends who are in grave danger? Why not permit birth control where it is the only means of maintaining or restoring love in a home? Are we not, in fact, witnessing here the triumph of charity over the virtues of truthfulness, justice, and chastity? [29]

It is at this point that a critic might argue that Gilleman still "thing-a-fies" the virtues, i.e., that each is too much of an isolated and independent entity without sufficiently explicit connection with love. For he energetically denies that any of the questions above should be answered in the affirmative. Each virtue objectively manifests "true charity" and specifies its exigencies in a particular field or range of

[26] *Ibid.*, p. 163.  [27] *Ibid.*, p. 167.  [28] *Ibid.*, p. 174.  [29] *Ibid.*, p. 167.

activity. Gilleman thus become quite traditionalistic on these questions. One example he cites is of a prisoner-of-war who realizes that he will disclose information unconsciously and involuntarily under the control of drugs that will cost his friends their lives. Would it be morally preferable for him to commit suicide in order to save them? Gilleman denies that it would. Disclosure would be involuntary and hence nonmoral whereas suicide violates the "finality of man's being." [30] Virtues must remain in their particularity and be denominated as such. Their "objective" character prevents them from being expendable in any instance of supposed conflict with love; such conflict exists only when love is wrongly conceived. Love and the virtues are in point of fact always objectively congruent with one another.

In an ostensible consideration of the virtues, then, Gilleman moves rather specifically and without explicit acknowledgment into matters of conduct. Thus birth control appears to be unexceptionably and without qualification prohibited by the virtue of chastity. Gilleman asserts this more than he demonstrates it, though we can assume that he accepts the traditional "single-act analysis" about "what nature requires" in regard to sexual relations. Still, his argument seems a puzzlement. Chastity, a virtue effectively "participating" in love, unqualifiedly prohibits an *act* of birth control even when this destroys a definite *bond* of (familial) *love*. It is difficult to see why this does not involve a genuine conflict about "what love requires." My immediate point here, however, is simply that "chastity" as a virtue is a term of sufficiently wide extension that one is well advised not to be precipitous in regarding certain acts as transparently following from it or as equally praiseworthy. There frequently seems to be an increasing scale of relativity so that the more overt and circumscribed the act the more qualifications there are to rules placing and governing it. Furthermore, sometimes such qualifications delimit the number of cases falling under the rule in ways that Gilleman neglects to mention. It could be argued, for instance, that Gilleman's illustration of suicide is not really a case of suicide at all, at least as this term is precisely used. In any event, ethicists would often do well to attend more rigorously to the distinctions between judgments of character and conduct.

An opposite distortion is likewise possible. One can bifurcate character and conduct in a misleading way. Again one example, admittedly selective, must suffice. The subject of human sexuality and its relation to love has been considered perhaps more than any other as the classic instance of the questions involved in the dispute about

[30] *Ibid.*, pp. 176–177.

the new morality. Many contend that love refers to the entire quality of the relationship but not in any clear or obvious way to coitus itself. Coitus may or may not express genuine love; in and of itself or "objectively," it is too ambiguous to justify any claims about its "inherent" purposiveness beyond the biological level (which is much less fixedly understood than are, for example, most traditional Roman Catholic arguments). A statement by a group of British Quakers argues to a great extent along these lines.[31] There is no condoning of indiscriminate permissiveness and no belief that human beings can return to a state of primitive "innocence." But there is a clear distinction between attitudes defining an entire relationship and external acts.

> We condemn exploitation in any form. Exploitation is using the partner to satisfy a physical or an emotional need without considering the other as a person. . . .
> In seeking to find a truly Christian judgment of this problem, we have again and again been brought to the quality of human relationships as the only final criterion. To base our judgment on whether or not the sex-act has taken place is often to falsify that judgment fantastically. . . . *The Christian standard of chastity should not be measured by a physical act, but should be a standard of human relationship, applicable within marriage as well as outside it.*[32]

Coitus is *to be* integrated into the total relationship of love, but it is not defined in advance as necessarily constitutive *of* that relationship.

There is much in the Quaker statement as a whole with which I agree and the statement quoted above can be taken in more than one way. But it seems a serious oversimplification merely to say that there is one standard of human relationships applicable outside as well as inside marriage, for this may imply that in the morally relevant respects the standard is uniformly applicable. Certainly a general ethical principle such as "You shall love your neighbor as yourself" (which, it could well be argued, leads rather transparently to "nonexploitation") applies to all in a way previously explained. And whether the sex act has taken place is not in itself determinative of moral judgment; in some cases one may call it adultery or rape or marital love. Yet a principle such as "one ought never to exploit another person" implies more than simply a uniform standard of "chastity" as respect for the person. Nonexploitation is not simply a free-floating trait of character, applicable in the same ways inside or outside marriage. Again, as a trait of character, it involves being disposed to act in

[31] *Towards a Quaker View of Sex* (London: Friends Home Service Committee, 1964).
[32] *Ibid.*, p. 51.

definite ways in the particular relations and circumstances in which one is placed. Marriage includes such definite kinds of special relations and circumstances which are not without effect upon one's moral judgments; in part it determines the application. A husband and father has certain obligations and rights *qua* husband and father which are part of the meaning of nonexploitation in his case. Let us recall our characterization of relational norms at this point. They involve relational features which are more definite than traits of character and yet less specific than externally perceptible acts. They serve to identify and delimit kinds of human relationships and circumstances as morally significant and to express moral conclusions about them. They often serve in deciding what counts as exploitation in a given set of circumstances. A husband and father cannot lightly jeopardize or relinquish the relationships to which he has committed himself. His decision is different from someone who does not have these obligations and rights. The effects of his deeds are inevitably connected with such constituted relationships. The questions regarding sexual ethics are decidedly more complex than can be considered here. I do not mean to imply that relational norms are solely or in every case determinative. I have only been concerned to illustrate the connections between character and conduct. A great number of intermediary factors must be weighed which are less general than nonexploitation and less specific than the sex act as such and which comprise part of the criteria for moral assessment. It would be helpful if more of the disputants about the new morality would take such factors into detailed account.

4. What, more precisely, are the ways in which one attends to such intermediary factors? What, for example, are the senses in which one may be said to subscribe to relational norms and basic moral rules? How does one "violate" them, if at all?

Let us consider relational norms first, specifically the formulation, "Children ought to honor their parents." We have already observed that there are different cultural and symbolic agreements and individual judgments on what counts as honoring one's parents. But this very fact points to a critical distinction between the norm itself and the actions which meet the obligation expressed by the norm. I may care for my parents in their old age or send them a gift on their anniversary or spend Christmas vacation with them. To utilize the distinction as it has been formulated by A. I. Melden, these are "obligation-meeting actions" and are to be distinguished from "obligatory actions." [33] Suppose a close friend were seriously ill and wanted me to stay with

---

[33] A. I. Melden, *Rights and Right Conduct* (Oxford: Basil Blackwell, 1959).

him over Christmas vacation. I decide to do so, rather than return home to spend the time with my parents. I have not "broken" the norm of honoring my parents in the sense of repudiating it as a definite policy or setting it aside as not in this case a moral consideration. To say that on occasion I do not do what normally would count as honoring my parents is different from saying that I have decided not to honor them. To cite what has become a commonplace in ethics: I have not violated the relational norm in the sense of denying its *relevance;* I have only decided that it is not *decisive* in the particular case.[34]

This is far more than a pedantic distinction. A great deal of flippant talk about "exceptions" can be heard which is simply wrong. There is an important sense in which the norm to honor one's parents is unexceptionable. If I accept it seriously (however I construe the actions which meet it), I can never set it aside as something of no moral import. It is likely in most situations that there are no obstructions to my carrying out actions which meet my obligation to my parents. There may be certain occasions, as we have said, when carrying out such an action conflicts with another morally relevant consideration. Even on such occasions, however, I am not contemplating an exception to the norm, but to the action which customarily carries it out. "It is one thing to be justified in presenting the wishes of one's parents as a moral consideration; it is another to be justified in claiming on that account that the appropriate action is morally required. Exceptions may be taken to the latter, but never to the former." [35]

Subscription to the norm in this sense means that it is more than a convenient "rule of thumb" which I can set aside whenever I please. I may fail to do the action that meets the obligation in specific cases, but this is different from a moral justification for violating the norm as such. If regarding the welfare of the neighbor in the midst of the entire web of human relationships in which I am placed involves this norm as a way of identifying a certain set of these relationships as of particular moral significance, then I am saying that the norm is always morally relevant, if not in every case decisive.

Subscription to rules, as we have been using that term, involves additional considerations. For rules characteristically refer directly to specifiable actions (though there is not always a perfectly clear boundary between norms and basic moral rules just as it is sometimes difficult—and often a matter of debate—to distinguish the latter from neutral rules and customs). I shall confine myself here to *actually*

---

[34] See, e.g., J. D. Mabbott, "Moral Rules," *Proceedings of the British Academy,* XXXIX (London: Oxford University Press, 1953), especially pp. 96–99.

[35] Melden, *op. cit.,* p. 44.

## Virtue, Principles, and Rules 57

*formulated* rules. I do not wish to deny the logical requirement of the "universalizability" of moral judgments. But this requirement does not always entail actual formulations of the rule in all of its specifics, partly because in practice a point of diminishing returns may be reached where the rule becomes cumbersomely detailed. To specify further would in some cases take the formulated rule beyond the point of generally clear applicability. Often, too, any given formulation is subject to revision and qualification in the light of new circumstances and unanticipated consequences.

Various kinds of authority have been claimed for formulated rules. It is possible, of course, to deny them any authority, regarding them all as fatally legalistic or a matter of "bad faith." However, not even the animosity to rules of a self-styled "situationist" such as Joseph Fletcher extends to formal vindication of radical particularity. At least officially he wars against "antinomian unprincipledness" as well as legalism.[36] He regards rules as summaries of past experience or empirical generalizations, helpful only as rules of thumb, to be set aside when "love" requires. Doubtless there are many such summary rules, the chief function of which is more informative than censorious. Summary rules may suggest additional ways of assessing a situation, remind one of considerations he might otherwise neglect, and assist in the establishing of priorities among claims. They are "didactic" and "illuminative" rather than "dictatorial."

The principal question is whether there are more "general rules" as well and, if so, how they are to be construed. Many (including Fletcher) appear to lump what I have called a relational norm such as "Children ought to honor their parents" under "rule" and then carelessly speak of love "breaking" it or setting it aside or overruling it. I have already attempted to show in what sense this seems to me to be clearly a mistake.

I want now to consider one example of a basic moral rule: "You shall not kill." "Kill" is a more purely descriptive word than "steal" or, to a lesser extent, "lie," which often have a certain judgmental element built into them. One can more or less neutrally determine whether the destruction of human life has occurred. Moralists historically (especially in the Roman Catholic tradition) have recognized that a sweeping condemnation of all possible kinds of killing would not do. Qualifications were added very early.[37] The action prohibited could

---

[36] Joseph Fletcher, *Situation Ethics* (Philadelphia: Westminster Press, 1966), p. 31.

[37] For a brief but helpful account, see R. C. Mortimer, *The Elements of Moral Theology* (London: Adam and Charles Black, 1947), pp. 60–74.

not include what was sometimes done by the soldier or the executioner, if formal responsibility for the common good of the community is to be taken seriously. A qualification was supplied with the addition of the adjective "innocent"; prohibited killing was now regarded as the "destruction of innocent human life." But this was still too inexact. For if a man is guilty, this does not necessarily give any other man the right to kill him in reprisal. There is an obvious distinction between killing done by a soldier or an executioner and killing by a private citizen. The agent must be, as it were, authorized to kill. The prohibition is finally against *murder* as the "unauthorized killing of an innocent person."

Such a definition has had enormous consequences for moral deliberation in the West. There are many difficult cases to which it has been applied, e.g., abortion and warfare. In the case of abortion, if the fetus is judged to be a person, innocence is clear and killing thereby prohibited. But certain difficult borderline cases have resulted in further deliberation, particularly where there is conflict of life with life. There may be, for instance, the case of a normal uterine pregnancy where medical opinion is that there is no chance of saving either mother or fetus except by an operation which directly and intentionally kills the fetus. Such an operation has appeared to many to violate the most flexible application of the "rule of double effect," i.e., one may perform an act where one of the secondary though foreseen consequences will be bad *if* the primary consequence of the act can be characterized as right, if the intention of the agent is good, and if there is "adequate cause" so that the good secured exceeds the evil involved. Hence if not to bomb the enemy's factories prolongs the war, this may be regarded as a greater evil than killing some innocent civilians in the bombing mission. But direct and intentional killing of such civilians is still prohibited.

Several alternatives are possible regarding the conflict of mother and fetus. (*a*) One may simply say that the rule prohibiting murder applies without further qualification and that it would be preferable for both mother and fetus to die than that one should live by means of an act which by prior determination has been prohibited. (*b*) One may deny that the formulated rule applies. The fetus might be held, for example, not to be a "person." (*c*) One may reformulate the rule so it does not apply. The fetus may still be regarded as a person in the relevant respects, but one qualifies one's definition of murder so that, perhaps, its meaning does not include directly and intentionally taking the innocent life (of the fetus) if this innocent life will die in

## Virtue, Principles, and Rules

any case and another innocent life (the mother's) will be saved.[38] (*d*) One may say that the prohibition is always relevant and generally counts against abortion. But in some cases where it does apply, it comes into direct conflict with another rule (e.g., in certain situations of agonizing moral choice, one ought to save one innocent life rather than lose two) and is not necessarily decisive for one's final evaluation. Then one establishes a priority among formulated relational norms or moral rules; he does not elaborate a further meaning of one rule, perhaps because of the reasons of cumbersomeness, etc.

Once again it is not part of my purpose to give a detailed assessment of the specific question of abortion. I am only inquiring about some of the possible ways of subscribing to a basic moral rule. Of the ways noted immediately above, the following things may be said. (*a*) The first way involves allotting indefeasible priority to a particular formulation and application of the rule over all other considerations, such as conflict with other rules, arguments from consequences, and possible qualifications to the earlier formulation of the rule. In the particular case, such priority signifies, I would argue, genuine legalism. (*b*) The second way involves directly denying that the rule applies. The points at issue then are one's definition of "person," etc. (*c*) If one qualifies the meaning of the rule, a question may then arise (which is also applicable to the second way) whether in *another* case where even the qualified rule does apply, one at that point allots it indefeasible priority. Suppose one believes that the prohibition against murder as it has been qualified above applies also to warfare so that innocent (noncombatant) life can never be directly and intentionally killed. This would clearly seem to rule out "counter-city" as opposed to "counter-force" strategy (unless one argues, as I would not, that "modern technological civilization" has removed any viable distinction between combatants and noncombatants). Rather than conjure up some bizarre case to test this, let us consider an actual historical one (though we shall be highly selective in the way we do so). The dropping of atomic bombs on Hiroshima and Nagasaki unsettled the world. We shall ignore some of the controversies, e.g., whether the United States should have demanded unconditional surrender or whether representatives of the Japanese government should have been guaranteed safe conduct and given a prior "demonstration" in a remote part of the South Pacific. Suppose the choice was only (*i*)

---

[38] Cf. Paul Ramsey, *War and the Christian Conscience* (Durham: Duke University Press, 1961), pp. 171–191.

doing what was done to Hiroshima and Nagasaki, thereby shortening the war and thus saving many lives, or (*ii*) invading Japan with appreciably greater loss of combatant life on both the Japanese and American sides. It is hard to see how the qualified prohibition against murder could allow (*i*). It is also hard to imagine any *further* qualifications which would show that the United States did not "really" kill noncombatants directly and intentionally as the most effective way of achieving a termination of the war. (*d*) The final alternative involves saying that the rule is relevant but not invariably decisive for one's final evaluation. It will be recalled (and this obviously reflects my own sympathies) that I characterized a basic moral rule as requiring, prohibiting, or permitting a class of human conduct which is judged to be of irreducible or "nonelidable" moral significance, which is relevant in both predominantly personal and social contexts, and which is taken to be generally (rather than universally) right and wrong because, as actually formulated, it may conflict with another moral consideration, such as a relational norm, another moral rule, etc. I take the possibility of conflicts between formulated rules as a fact of our moral experience. There may be instances of choice between rules which as actually formulated both apply and conflict; our judgment states a priority, it does not extend the meaning of one of them. Any given priority is not, however, necessarily indefeasible. On this fourth alternative, the possibility of such conflicts in the case of Hiroshima and Nagasaki would be allowed.

Yet the number and significance of such conflicts can easily be overemphasized. An act for which the formulated relevant rule is not decisive is in special need of justification, whether by appeal to another rule, by qualifications to the rule itself, or by highly unique circumstances (which in effect may qualify the scope of the rule in question). There is always a presumption in favor of basic moral rules; they have a *prima facie* claim to acceptance.

## III

1. I want next to illustrate how some of the items in the foregoing list have been treated in at least one comparatively influential and untechnical historical document. I shall examine Luther's treatment of the "second table" of the Decalogue (i.e., "duties toward one's neighbor") in the *Large Catechism*.[39] It seems to me that his treatment

---

[39] Martin Luther, "The Large Catechism," *The Book of Concord*, ed. and trans. Theodore G. Tappert (Philadelphia: Fortress Press, 1959), pp. 379–407.

## Virtue, Principles, and Rules

is basically representative of many approaches to these matters in the tradition of Christian ethics.

I shall not consider the question whether there is a "functional" third use of the law present in his treatment or whether he is culpable of blatant eisegesis in his understanding of the text from Deuteronomy. What I am primarily concerned to examine is the way in which he connects judgments of character and conduct. Since for Luther there seem to be no external actions toward the neighbor which *qua* external actions indisputably distinguish the believer from the morally earnest nonbeliever, he often stresses the love which seeks the neighbor's welfare in highly mundane and immediate ways. I shall briefly explicate and comment on his treatment of each of the commandments.

2. "You shall honor your father and mother." There is an authoritarian strain in Luther's treatment which may sound somewhat strange to modern ears. Parents are to be the objects of reverence and deference, irrespective of their shortcomings and failures. It is out of parental authority that other kinds of authority are derived and unfolded, such as the authority of the civil government. In part such an authoritarian strain is due to the conviction that honoring one's parents is unequivocally the will of God. In this sense our use of the term "relational norm" can be misleading, if it is taken to mean a helpful rule of thumb (though I argued earlier that this is not the way in which it should be construed). For Luther, honoring one's parents is a divinely urgent matter; it is the opposite of human caprice.

Yet Luther does distinguish clearly in his own way between the obligation to honor one's parents and the actions which meet the obligation. He does not catalogue an entire series of specific duties which must be done, while at the same time he does adduce certain kinds of action which typically count as honoring them.

> You are to esteem and prize them as the most precious treasure on earth. In your words you are to behave respectfully toward them, and not address them discourteously, critically, and censoriously, but submit to them and hold your tongue, even if they go too far. You are also to honor them by your actions (that is, with your body and possessions), serving them, helping them, and caring for them when they are old, sick, feeble, or poor; all this you should do not only cheerfully, but with humility and reverence, as in God's sight. He who has the right attitude toward his parents will not allow them to suffer want or hunger, but will place them above himself and at his side and will share with them all he has to the best of his ability.[40]

[40] *Ibid.*, p. 380.

Luther seems confident that one honors one's parents in a creative myriad of definite ways, none of which need be fully predicted or described in advance.

3. "You shall not kill." Though this commandment is a basic moral rule rather than a relational norm as I have been using these terms, Luther is anything but preoccupied with questions of the definition, qualification, and application of a rule governing external acts. Certainly there are some acts which for him would be definitely prohibited. But he stresses broad behavioral policies and traits of character. The final meaning of the commandment for him is simply that "we should not harm anyone."

> This means, first, by hand or by deed; next, we should not use our tongue to advocate or advise harming anyone; again, we should neither use nor sanction any means or methods whereby anyone may be harmed; finally, our heart should harbor no hostility or malice toward anyone in a spirit of anger and hatred.[41]

The "kindness" which is enjoined here finally applies even to one's enemies. Luther moves away, then, from rules and toward virtues and relational norms. He is much less concerned with the precise "content" of harming than with the "consent"—verbal, actual, and motivational—to harm.

4. "You shall not commit adultery." Once more Luther moves immediately away from the external act technically denoted by adultery: "Not only is the external act forbidden, but also every kind of cause, motive, and means." [42] Adultery is particularly emphasized because, according to Luther, marriage was obligatory among the Jews of the time and it usually occurred at a young age. Virginity was not especially praised and public prostitution was not tolerated to the degree Luther thought it was in his own time. Adultery was then simply "the most common form of unchastity among them." [43]

He concentrates on the social context and set of relationships within which the commandment receives its intelligibility and significance: the institution of marriage and the family. Anything which threatens these special relational bonds, which undermines trust and commitment between the members, which jeopardizes its stability or the all-important rearing of children, is to be prohibited. Luther's praise of marriage is unbounded. It is "the most richly blessed" of all

---

[41] *Ibid.*, p. 390. There is also an emphasis on "the affections of the heart" in John Calvin's "Geneva Catechism," *The School of Faith*, ed. and trans. Thomas F. Torrance (London: James Clarke and Co., 1959), especially pp. 30–37.

[42] Luther, *op. cit.*, p. 392.   [43] *Ibid.*

particular human relationships. The commandment not only forbids unchastity but requires that the husband and wife love and cherish one another.

> For marital chastity it is above all things essential that husband and wife live together in love and harmony, cherishing each other wholeheartedly and with perfect fidelity. This is one of the chief ways to make chastity attractive and desirable. Under such conditions chastity always follows spontaneously without any command.[44]

The remaining commandments will be summarized briefly with a final comment at the end.

5. "You shall not steal." Luther defines stealing as "taking advantage of our neighbor in any sort of dealing that results in loss to him." [45] He is concerned to show how many actions fall under such an expansive definition. A much more precise definition of the "constitutive circumstances" of stealing than Luther gives would be as follows: "The theft of B's x is ascribed to A if, and only if, (1) A took x; (2) x did not belong to him, but to B; (3) he did not return it to B, but consumed, sold, or destroyed it; (4) B had not given A leave for the action." [46] Luther, on the other hand, seems often to identify stealing with more general acts of negligence and malice. Thus servants who are unfaithful in their duties or permit damage and waste are culpable under this commandment. "The same must be said of artisans, workmen, and day-laborers who act high-handedly and never know enough ways to overcharge people and yet are careless and unreliable in their work." [47] The situation is hardly better in the market-place. "Everyone misuses the market in his own willful, conceited, arrogant way, as if it were his right and privilege to sell his goods as dearly as he pleases without a word of criticism." [48] Lords and princes may often be the great "arch-thieves" who plunder cities and countries.

> Let everyone know, then, that it is his duty, at the risk of God's displeasure, not to harm his neighbor, take advantage of him, or defraud him by any faithless or underhanded business transaction. More than that, he is under obligation faithfully to protect his neighbor's property and further his interests, especially when he takes remuneration for such services.[49]

6. "You shall not bear false witness against your neighbor." The simplest meaning of this commandment, Luther believes, refers to public courts of justice. "They should let right remain right, not

---

[44] *Ibid.*, p. 394.
[45] *Ibid.*, p. 395.
[46] D'Arcy, *op. cit.*, p. 62.
[47] Luther, *op. cit.*, p. 395.
[48] *Ibid.*, p. 397.
[49] *Ibid.*, p. 396.

perverting or concealing or suppressing anything on account of anyone's money, property, honor, or power." [50] The widest meaning of the commandment refers to all injury and offense through speech. Luther does not appear concerned with issues of justifiable deception; he simply denounces "slander," "back-biting," and a general delight in stressing the neighbor's vices. One should not report what cannot be "adequately proved." Whenever possible, admonition should be a private affair. The "best construction" should be put upon the neighbor's motives.

> Now we have the sum and substance of this commandment: No one shall harm his neighbor, whether friend or foe, with his tongue. No one shall speak evil of him, whether truly or falsely, unless it is done with proper authority or for his improvement. A person should use his tongue to speak only good of everyone, to cover his neighbor's sins and infirmities, to overlook them, and to cloak and veil them with his own honor.[51]

7. "You shall not covet your neighbor's house." "You shall not covet his wife, man-servant, maid-servant, cattle, or anything that is his." Luther acknowledges that this is very close to the commandment which prohibits stealing. Here one "is also forbidden to entice anything away from your neighbor, even though in the eyes of the world you could do it honorably, without accusation or blame for fraudulent dealing." [52] Whatever the legal judgment, the neighbor must not be deprived of anything which is his. In short: "We are commanded not to desire harm to our neighbor, nor become accessory to it, nor give occasion for it; we are willingly to leave him what is his, and promote and protect whatever may be profitable and serviceable to him, as we wish that he would do to us." [53]

Luther is frequently more zealous than careful in his moral judgments and much of what he says in this document has an understandably homiletical tone. But it is clear that he is more preoccupied with traits of character and relatively definite policies of conduct than he is with careful criteria for determining whether and when a given act may be called a case of, say, theft or stealing. This is part of the reason why he transmutes each commandment from a negative prohibition to a positive injunction as well. I do not mean to imply that Luther ignores all connections between such policies and such acts or that the latter are not in his view prohibited. He is not, in this sense, a "situationist." But it is significant that he usually proceeds with some rapidity away from questions of strictly external behavior. If Luther

[50] *Ibid.*, p. 400.   [51] *Ibid.*, p. 403.   [52] *Ibid.*, p. 405.   [53] *Ibid.*, p. 407.

*Virtue, Principles, and Rules* 65

is at all representative in this regard, then it is seriously inaccurate to disparage the Decalogue and the importance which has been historically attached to it as an instance of "prefabricated" and "legalistic" morality.

## IV

Let us now return to the elementary point from which we began. I said that the discussion about the new morality will remain more loquacious than clarifying until more elucidative work has been done on the kinds of things people may mean when they talk about principles, rules, and the like. The list I have formulated is an attempt to distinguish several of these meanings. It is only one rough and tentative sketch of some of the possibilities.[54] Two final things may be said about this and other more expanded attempts at such formulation.

First, there is virtually no possibility of significantly opposing or defending "rules" unless that term is quite carefully delineated. The current penchant for attaching labels is at best provocative but too often faddish and fundamentally confused. It would be enormously helpful if there were at least some minimal agreements on *possible* meanings. Then the "debate" could proceed with less of the present number of pseudo-disagreements and sweeping defenses and denunciations. Such a "formal" requirement might bring great "material" benefits. Many of the questions in sexual ethics, to mention the most commonly discussed subject, might be importantly clarified in this way. One might contend, for instance, that there are no basic moral rules pertaining to sexual relations, that they are strictly a matter of neutral rules and/or customs. Alternatively, one might hold that it is essential to specify certain permanent relational norms and correlated moral rules. Whatever one proposed, there would at least be greater clarity about the precise character of the claims. Moreover, denying that pre-marital relations, say, should fall under a basic moral rule, would not be (as is frequently the case at present) tacitly generalized into a denial of the relational norm of marriage or the entire *class* of basic moral rules (such as the prohibitions against lying, stealing, and killing). There are dangers with such classificatory preoccupations, but these dangers are hardly pronounced at present.

---

[54] All I have attempted here is to suggest that moral judgments and the principles and rules governing them seem to exhibit different levels of generality and specificity. This is not the place to investigate any of these in detail or the kinds of connection between them.

Second, whatever may be said about the number and ways of subscribing to principles, rules, etc., there seems to be little doubt that in ethics generally and certainly in Christian ethics, one must attend seriously to the host of intermediate considerations between a general ethical principle such as the love commandment and the "situation." I would argue that this is especially the case with relational norms, roughly in the sense I have outlined. In Christian ethics, to say this is not to defend all the rules historically regarded as important but it is also to recognize that the genuine and permanent complexities of the ethical and moral life will not go away by simplistic fiat. If there is to be a moral *ethos* in any serious sense of that term, then matters such as relational norms simply cannot be ignored. The mind boggles at the extent of the difficulties in thinking about these intermediate considerations, but the ethicist, at least, has no responsible alternative.

# 4

# The Case of the Curious Exception

## PAUL RAMSEY

Is it possible to speak of justifiable violations of moral principles? Violations there are aplenty, of course. These are actions to which our principles discriminating between right and wrong apply, and in terms of which a particular action should be condemned. But the question to be raised here is whether there can be any such thing as a *justified* violation of moral principle—a commendable exception.

Today cases of the praiseworthy exception are supposed to be as frequent as cases of moral violation. In their nobility men act beyond and contrary to principles or moral rules, it is believed, as often as from sloth or wickedness they fail to abide by them. Since the tally of how many justifiable exceptional deeds there are, or how rare these are, is not the point, let it be granted that if in any given moral matter one such just deed is possible, some more or many are.

Ours will be an inquiry into *the conditions of the possibility* of a justifiable violation of moral principles or moral rules. This entails an inquiry into the nature of moral reasoning in its approach to the place where the case of the curious exception is likely to be found. Only then can we tell whether in the logic of moral reasoning and the nature of moral judgment there can possibly be any such thing as a justifiable exception. It may be that the so-called praiseworthy exception is ethically a homeless waif; that it can be located only where somebody stopped thinking morally. It might be the case that such an action is simply a contradiction in terms, and that it could be actualized only at the point where one simply failed to continue to think in ethical terms.

The question of a possible jutifiable exception is at the same time the question whether there are any unbreakable moral principles or any unbreakable moral rules. We shall ask whether there might be *any* moral matter governed by exceptionless rules; whether in *all* moral matters there could only be principles or rules having possible exception. (This allows, of course, that in some or many moral matters there are only exceptionable moral principles or exceptionable moral rules to guide behavior.)

It should be said here at the outset that this chapter is bifocal. As an advocate, I have in mind the current vogue of "exceptionism" in theological ethics and in religious circles, and I use the word "exception" in the sense given it by the proponents of this view. Some of these proponents mean by "exception" an *agapeic* quantification of expected beneficial results that obviously may be a given quantity for one action in its situation and another quantity for another action in its situation. This is a notion of a singular exceptional deed, no one exception like even one other exception except perchance in quantitative terms because neither can be characterized in any other way than by being "more" or "less" effective in loving. This is the more "rationalistic" or calculative view. Other proponents of theological "exceptionism" seem to speak in more intuitive terms of actions that are "unique" and in their uniqueness "creative" of new moral departures. They seem to regard moral action as an unrepeatable spiritual venture that alone can be truly sensitive to the demands of the hour and fully open to the needs of other persons. Any regularity would mean a cloture upon the inspiration that is a resource for action in a Christian context, and this would be less than responsive and less than responsible. This view also alleges that there are singular exceptions befalling moral action, this time with uncalculating originality.

On either view the claim must be that there is such a thing as a qualitatively featureless action that is justifiable. This is surely a curious proposal in ethics, since "whatever ethics is about, it simply is not about unique situations";[1] and to justify any action one must be able to characterize it as a *sort* of action that should be done by anyone who is in a similar situation.

---

[1] Helen Oppenheimer: Moral Choice and Divine Authority," *Christian Ethics and Contemporary Philosophy*, ed. Ian T. Ramsey (New York: Macmillan Co., 1966), p. 225.

We should mention a third type of theological "exceptionism"—if the word "exception" is a proper translation of what Karl Barth calls the *Grenzfall*, or the action men may be commanded and permitted to do in a "borderline-situation." Generally, such a situation consists of a mortal conflict between two human lives, each of whom has equal claim upon respect and protection because of the "holy awe" that alone is fitting in the presence of someone with whom God has pledged covenant from all eternity. Barth's "exception" means choosing to save one rather than the other life, or to kill one to save the other, in the medically rather dated cases he supposes of "justifiable abortion." Where there is no such conflict of equal ultimates—in, for example, abortion for the sake of the child or "fetal euthanasia" because the unborn child has a probability of being seriously defective mentally or physically—Barth allows no "exception" to men's duty to respect, protect and preserve life. He is much less certain that "suicide" would always be a case of abandonment. It follows from the "Thou-I" structure of Christian ethics, Barth seems to be saying, that to destroy oneself is not so certainly to suppress a life's share in charity than, unless there is mortal conflict, to destroy nascent life. But he thinks it sufficient to allow for the possibility of self-destruction, without saying what would be the justifying features of such an action. Still less does he enter upon the question of what constitutes the meaning of the forbidden "suicide" in contrast to a justified sacrifice of one's life. Also, Barth speaks in mortal conflict-situations of a divine permission to do such an astonishing thing as to take life with such theological verve that even in case of conflict between equal ultimates he neglects to say what features of these situations would be relevant to deciding *which life to save* (and often, of course, there is only one that can be saved).[2]

Thus, *beyond* the rules specifying the protection and preservation of life, Barth speaks of cases in which one's duty and freedom is to do seemingly the opposite at God's call, permission, or command. This would entail that there can be an action which we would be morally justified in doing but which has in its unusualness few if any general features that could count as justifications.

This I take to be the meaning of "exception" in some current discussions of theological ethics. I adopt this usage in the first part of this chapter, and bring against it the nature and logic of good moral reasoning in justifying anything, whether from a theological or any

[2] *Church Dogmatics*, III/4, §55.

other final norm. The pursuit of this curious exception is one of our main concerns.

Such, however, is not the notion of an "exception" as the word is currently used among philosophers, who do not imagine one could claim to justify a nondescript action, or that the quantifiable *agapeic* or utilitarian force of actions are unarguably the only morally relevant features. For a complete grappling with the question of the "exception," we must therefore turn our attention to the general understanding of this in philosophical ethics today. We propose to ask: Must all principles and moral rules have exceptions, either in the conception of an "exception" in some theological ethics or in some of the conceptions of it in philosophical ethics today? The latter is a second concern of this chapter.

Turning to some philosophical conceptions of seemingly limitless future possible significant moral exceptions, I seek in the end to bring to bear upon this question, among other things, some of the insights of Christian ethics. It ought not to be surprising if there are philosophical analyses that are useful in repairing some of the worst aspects of theological ethics, and Christian ethical understanding that may improve some of the best philosophy. This is what I mean by saying that this chapter is bifocal in its outlook.

In dealing with either sort of "exception," there is another consideration to be taken into account in the following pages. Generally speaking, our quest for the justifiable exception is a *formal* matter; it rests on the nature of good moral reasoning on any subject and from whatever ultimate norm. But there may be differences to be taken into account because of the ultimate norms in different systems of ethics. It is also the case that our conclusion in regard to whether there can be exceptionless principles or moral rules will vary according to the moral matter or relation we are talking about or which our ultimate norm has marked off as most important. We may come to one conclusion on this question if the *content* of ethics, or the matter or relation in question, is judged primarily to depend on the *consequence*-features; another, if on *fairness-* or *justice*-features; another, if, as I shall argue must be the case in Christian ethics, on *canons of loyalty* or *canons of faithfulness*. At least these three variables must be considered in attempting to answer the question this chapter poses. I do not say that these three matters to be evaluated exhaust the list; only that these are important.

It should also be said here at the beginning that, even as there are differing conceptions of the exception, so also there are differing

*Virtue, Principles, and Rules*  71

conceptions about what happens to principles or moral rules if there are any exceptions to them.

Among theological exceptionists—with the notable exception of Karl Barth, if he is to be called one—and also among some of their opponents, I should say that the view is that if there are justifiable exceptions the principles or moral rules are somehow defeated, or at least weakened. Some are jubilant over this result, others are alarmed; but they are generally agreed, for example, that if exceptions are rare the principles or rules remain strong, while if exceptions are allowed more frequently then principles or rules are correspondingly weaker.[3]

Philosophers generally disagree that principles or moral rules are threatened by exceptions. This is correlated with their conception that an exception is no random, individually unique, featureless thing, but something that can be *thought about* and brought within the range of moral deliberation—or else it is not to be justified. Philosophers reason soberly about exceptions, and the *definition* of the *sorts* of things warranting them. Theologians, whether in fear or jubilation, seem to outdo feverish gamblers at Las Vegas. The latter sometimes extrapolate from the probabilities of winning to a particular case, the next throw; we go further and extrapolate from the probabilities to the perilously particular conclusion that there are bound to be exceptions in all or many or most cases. They loose their shirts; we, our wits.

Yet it may be argued, and philosophers do so argue, that there can be no exception to a rule that does not apply; that, if anything, a justifiable exception fixes the application of a principle or rule more firmly and definitely in all cases to which it continues to apply; that, as it were, a moral rule does not become habituated to having exceptions; it does not become measurably more unreliable if it admits exceptions; that *justifying* an exception is "not like making a breech in a dike"; that "nothing unfortunate" happens to a moral rule if it admits exceptions; that a resolution of conflicts among moral rules

[3] The British philosopher, George Woods, seemed also to imply that exceptions *could* have a calamitous effect on principles and moral rules when he wrote: "What is rejected is the conception of any universal moral law to which there are no exceptions but the number of exceptions is taken to be very small indeed. *The exceptions are wholly exceptional.* The matter for discussion, therefore, is the moral justification of rare exceptions" ("Situational Ethics," in Ian T. Ramsey (ed.), *op. cit.*, p. 336, italics added). This is also the view of Karl Barth, who brings the entire force of theological warrants to bear on preventing "exceptions" from becoming the rule, or at all greatly affecting the weighty requirements to which they are borderline.

to the subordination of one of them still leaves that rule sovereign over the activity in question in situations of no moral conflict. When two people are arguing about a moral matter, one may argue for an exception. In doing so he is not objecting to the rule, which is admitted to apply. He is objecting, rather, to a judgment supported by citing the rule. Another person argues against that judgment. One of these judgments will be defeated in the debate, not the principle or rule. If the claimant to an exception loses after deliberation, an action observing the rule is then not *probably* justified; it *is* justified. If the claimant wins, the rule wins also; it is established more firmly as applicable to cases not having like reasons or as good or better reasons.[4] A principle or moral rule cannot be challenged without confirming its validity—*"except . . ."*—then must follow good moral reasons for the exception. Without these, no exception; with these, a class of right actions will have been defined within or beside the rule. No dike is opened; nor need any be plugged. There is no increased probability of unprincipled or ruleless behavior, if one thinks about it.

These are some of the considerations to be brought against theological "exceptionism," before turning to the case for the exception in some contemporary philosophical ethics.

In taking up these issues we shall distinguish between *principles* and *rules*. This will allow for the possibility that there are exceptions to morally relevant rules but no exceptions to morally relevant principles (only applications of them). It will allow that there may be unbreakable moral principles even if there are no unbreakable moral rules. On the other hand, the upshot of unhurried consideration of these questions could yield the conclusion that there may be some unexceptionable morally relevant rules of conduct (or "definite-action rules") as well as certain unexceptionable morally relevant principles.[5]

---

[4] See Leonard G. Miller: "Rules and Exceptions," in *Ethics*, Vol. LXVI (July 1956), pp. 262–270.

[5] Also, different answers may have to be given to these questions according to whether *consequences*-features, *fairness* or *justice* claims, or *canons of loyalty* or *faithfulness* are judged to be decisive in a given act, relation, or situation (the "moral matter" to which our formal reasoning is being applied). Traditional moral theology should receive a salutary reminder from H. L. A. Hart's warning to his fellow philosophers: ". . . There is undoubtedly a standing temptation in philosophy to assimilate all types of moral judgment to a single type" ("Legal and Moral Obligation," in *Essays in Moral Philosophy*, ed. A. I. Melden, [Seattle and London: University of Washington Press, 1958], p. 120). We need to keep this warning in mind in the question of the justifiable exception, and at least be

## Virtue, Principles, and Rules

To take the step of distinguishing, for purposes of this discussion, between *principles* and *rules* is a move not yet made by the present writer in any of his writings in the vicinity of these questions. This may be worth pointing out. Heretofore, when treating the methods and the options for adducing or elaborating the full contents of a normative ethics upon the basis of the ultimate norm in Christian ethics (*agapé,* or whatever is a more adequate or fruitful name for our basic Christian perspective upon the moral life), I have used the word "rule" as shorthand for "principle," "orders," "ordinances," "ideal," "direction," "directives," "guidance," the "structures" of *agapé* or of *koinonia* life, the "style" of the Christian life, the "anatomy" or "pattern" of Christian responsibility—as well as for "rules" strictly so-called. My undertaking has been to ask whether *agapé* may not lead to principles (i.e., "rules") no less than to singular acts; and whether these relevant moral principles need be summary-principles only and not general principles also.

This has not been an unusual use of the word "rule." In fact, in the sense in which most philosophers use the word today, a "rule" is implied, writes R. W. Hepburn, "by any universalizable judgment (even though to state it might require many words), whether or not it exists as a fundamental copy-book maxim. In this sense, any judgment that could be called 'feature-dependent' may be called the expression of a rule or principle—the same features, the same judgment." [6]

However, it is now necessary to distinguish between *principles* and *rules*. Principles are *directions* of action; and I have elsewhere

---

open to answering it in a different fashion for matters in which the *consequences* are decisive, or in the matter of *fairness* or *justice,* or in regard to those relations in which *fidelity* may be overriding.

[6] "Vision and Choice in Morality" in Ian T. Ramsey (ed.), *op. cit.,* p. 192. Hepburn continues: "[In this sense of 'rule'] a judgment expressed in fable [or] parable is just as inescapably a 'decision of principle,' the endorsing of a rule, the expression of a resolution, as any other moral judgment. . . . If the 'rule model' does no more than affirm the feature-dependent nature of any moral judgment, then the 'parable model' cannot displace it, cannot even conflict with it; for it *assumes* it. The parable-obeyer need not formulate his rule as rule. . . . [Still his is a] specification, through fable, or a way of life" (*ibid.,* pp. 192–193). The discussion of these matters by R. W. Hepburn, Iris Murdoch, and Helen Oppenheimer in the volume edited by Ian T. Ramsey is enough to show how little support will be found among contemporary philosophers for the view that there can be an ethical system composed of or a moral life directed by a single high-flying principle (*agapé,* utility, self-realization, etc.) with no further *specifications* in morality.

undertaken to show that these elements subordinate to *agapé* and comprising the texture of the moral life may be general principles, and need not be summary principles only. In contrast to principles governing or regulating conduct, rules would be particular *directives* of an action, prescribing or proscribing a *definite* action. We shall ask, What is the meaning of the most *definite*-action rules ethics can afford? Since heretofore the present writer has been dealing with principles = rules, and not with rules in distinction from principles or styles of life, I judge I have not altogether committed myself to the conclusion that there are *rules* to which there are no exceptions. At least I have not earned the right to the latter opinion, since the argument for unexceptionable rules in the broad sense of that term may have lent false strength to the conclusion that there are such rules in the more restricted meaning of the word.

Situationists themselves seem to give evidence that there are such rules by the definite-action prohibitions or approvals which they endorse while failing methodologically to accredit these judgments within their systems of ethics. There is no Christian contextualist who finds there are only breakable principles or rules who is not also open to dialectical refutation on account of his failure to begin *ab initio* with all the sorts of actions he himself always expressly condemns in his writings because such actions could not conceivably be compatible with *agapé*. But then his (or my own) unearned or seeming endorsement of definite-action incriminations or commendations may only be the result of thoughtlessness.

These are the questions now to be directly addressed, by distinguishing between *principles* and *rules:* Can there be exceptions to morally relevant principles? and, Can there be exceptions to morally relevant rules? Must or should every principle or every moral rule have possible exceptions?

## I. *Action within Principles or within the Rules Miscalled "Exceptions"*

Admittedly, "principles" and "rules" are only the extremes on a spectrum of specificity or "particularity." The distinction between principles and rules is only a relative one. There are principles having the greatest generality, such as the principle of universalizability, the principle of reversability, the principle of benevolence, etc. In the following discussion I shall leave these behind and take up instead substantive principles concerning which there is greater controversy. I propose to use the expression *"defined*-action principles" (or moral-

*genus*-terms) for those principles that have already been elaborated a considerable distance along the spectrum toward specificity—in contrast to those more general principles just mentioned, on the one hand, and, on the other, "moral-*species*-terms" or "*definite*-action rules" (to be discussed in the following section).

Our model of the component stages in moral reasoning can, therefore, be stated as follows: ultimate norm (*agapé,* utility, self-realization, etc.); general principles; *defined*-action principles, or *generic* terms of approval and *generic* offense-terms; *definite*-action rules, or moral-*species*-terms; then the *subsumption* of cases.

I here connect "moral-*genus*-terms" with "*defined*-action principles" and "moral-*species*-terms" with "*definite*-action rules." Perhaps it would be better simply to say "*defined*-action principles" and "*definite*-action rules." I do not mean to settle the question whether orderly reasoning concerning moral matters does not have significant differences from reasoning that in other connections locates *species* within *genera.* This is very likely the case. Still this usage is suggested when we speak of more "specific" principles or rules; and a subordinate use of this language will enforce the point that in ethics we are talking about *sorts* or *kinds* of action. As we shall see, the most "*definite*-action rule" must still be, in this sense, a *species* or a sort of action. Whether the sorts of actions we talk about in ethics always fall *within* a *genus,* etc., are different questions. This usage also helps to suggest that the movement of moral reflection toward increasing specificity in its verdicts is along a spectrum on which only relative distinctions can be made. For this reason I shall not attempt to be always consistent in connecting "*genus*-term" with "*defined*-action principle" or "*species*-term" with "*definite*-action rule." The latter expression in each of these pairs might be thought to embrace more of the spectrum from generality to specificity in moral judgment; and we might be thought to embrace less of the distance when we speak of the moral *species* of a *genus* immediately "above" it in the direction of greater generality, and which itself is a *genus* to (sub)classifications "below" it in the direction of greater specificity. The offense-term "murder" is a *species* of "killing a man" ("homicide"), and at the same time it is a *genus*-term having morally significant classes of action within it, e.g., "murder with malice aforethought," "first-degree" murder, "second degree," etc. Here *genus-species* language seems exact enough. But I ask that it be remembered that this may not always be so, in every moral matter; and that this language is adopted mainly as a heuristic device for keeping it quite clear that in ethics we are talking about *definable sorts* of actions, which may have great "specificity."

Of course, practically no one runs through such a sequence as we will be supposing. Indeed, a "style of life," or living by some "parable model," may be said to be having the moral sensibility to recognize how to do the ethical thing and to see the relevant moral considerations very early in the game laid out by the above "rule model," or any other. Still an "artist" of a moral agent could give his reasons, or these could be adduced for him, if he did a fitting thing. He senses the wise and good thing to do without much elaboration of why; he cuts across moral reasoning; he soon "subsumes" cases without stating what their rightness consists of. This may be perfectly proper. But it is not a very good model for what we should be doing in ethics.

While it is a relative one, there is a *significant* distinction to be made between more general principles and more specific principles or rules. Not least in importance is the fact that to distinguish between principles and rules and to see that there are these gradations from the general to the specific is to see at once that in some moral matters there may very well be exceptionless principles.

The question, Can there be unbreakable principles (i.e., principles that have only applications falling under them)? is almost a self-answering question. It is self-answering by virtue of the fact that moving from greater generality to greater specificity may at least be compared to moving along a spectrum of moral-*genera*-terms to moral-*species*-terms. These more *specific* designations of what should be done or not done serve then as *genera* that themselves may be thought of as having *species* which express further elaboration, qualifications, explanations, or limitations upon the meaning of right or wrong conduct. No matter how narrowly defined may be the multiple terms or qualifications of the meaning of a moral permission or prohibition that has been elaborated or stated as fully as possible, these terms falling within the principle always remain *specific*. That is to say, one *describes* a *sort* of action to be done or not done.

Such specification of action is never a *particular*. The production of a particular deed is always a matter of the subsumption of a case, because of its features or because of the claims discerned in some situation, under the last *specific* to which moral reasoning had led us, for which there is some statable moral warrant. The latter must always be in terms of repeatable *kinds* of cases. One can say, of course, that one is moving along a spectrum of increasing "particularity"; but that is only a manner of speaking. Moral reasoning is always a matter of surrounding the particulars of actions by increasingly specific general terms—i.e., increasing illumination—for the direction of concrete actions.

## Virtue, Principles, and Rules

The logic of the increasing *specification* of actions to be done or not done has not only the consequence that one must answer in the affirmative the question, Can there be unbreakable relevant moral principles? It may also be sufficient to place the burden of proof on anyone who says that there cannot possibly be any relevant moral "rules" (as distinct from "principles") to which there are no exceptions. One wonders what could be more definite than some of these *defined*-action principles except the definite action itself! And the most *definite*-action rule, we shall see, must still be a specific sort or class of actions.

In any case it seems clear that there may be *principles* to which there can be no exceptions in any proper meaning of the word. The reason this is so is that a *justifiable* exception to any existing principle (or rule?) must be proposed in terms of some objective *feature* of the action, or of some claim the action answers, correlated with objective features in the situation in which it is said to be the right thing to do. As R. W. Hepburn said, an exception would have to be "feature-dependent." This means that it would be repeatable: "the same features, the same judgment," the same *sort* of justifiable exception. To call this (in theological ethics) an "exception" would be a misnomer. Instead, one's general moral wisdom was deepened or enlarged before ever that deed was justified. The action violated a former principle, no doubt; but it did not violate a better principle. Instead it may have been an instance of that principle more correctly apprehended and understood. Therefore, if we rightly grasp the course of moral reasoning through which we have to move toward the location of a justifiable exception, it becomes evident that actions may be miscalled exceptions when the correct description of what took place would be simply that someone stopped giving his feature-dependent reasons for the actions he rightly puts forth.

If an act's uniqueness, if its individuality consists in its *thatness* alone, then there is no way to justify such an action as an exception: it falls under already existing principles or rules governing the *sort* of action it is. An act that differed from another only in numerical particularity could not *qualify* as an exception to the principles in terms of which such actions have to be assessed. If, on the other hand, the alleged uniqueness of an action, if its individuality is constituted by its *whatness*, by its characteristics, or by certain unusual features not confronted heretofore or yet taken into account, neither is this the genuine exception for which we are searching: if such an act is justified it falls under reformed or reformulated morally relevant principles of some sort.

The case of the curious exception is a case of a most elusive thing: by grasping for the features relevant to justifying it morally, one grasps nothing at all or else he grasps nothing exceptional. The so-called exception disappears in the very process of trying to find warrants for it. If there are relevant moral warrants for it, then the action can only be miscalled an "exception" (in the theologians' sense of the word). It is an action falling within moral principles by whatever ultimate norm, not an action located beyond or outside principles. The effort to locate a *justifiable* exception can only have the effect of utterly destroying its exceptional character. The deed is found to be morally do-able, it is repeatable, it is one of a *kind*. How rare or frequent is of no consequence to the moral verdicts we render. The same justifying features, the same verdict, the same general judgment upon this sort of conduct should again be forthcoming. This judgment falls upon the alleged exception, if it is justified; and so that act falls within our deepened or broadened moral principles.

A genuine exception to moral principles (meaning the unique, singular "exception" some theologians think it proper to pronounce possible) would be an action that differed from some already specified acts in no relevant moral respects. It would be an unspecifiable particular; then, on what grounds could it be justified?

At this point, we simply have to come to clarity about the fact that ordinarily practical reason proceeds in quite another way in the course of accumulating wisdom about the moral life. Suppose it is held that "picking someone else's apples without his permission" would on the whole be undesirable. But for a man who himself and whose children are starving, and who has no other recourse, to pick someone else's apples without his permission might well be desirable. "Picking someone else's apples without his permission" is and *remains* a wrong-making condition. But "when one is starving and there is no other recourse" is, within this, a right-making condition sufficient to override it. If it does so, it does so not only in this instance. This determination of right from wrong is correct for all other morally similar instances. If there is a feature-relevant extension of defined-action principles to one single case (miscalled an exception), this is in principle true for other similarly justifiable cases—even if none ever occurs, or many occur. In fact, it can be said that not-to-pick-someone-else's-apples-without-permission-when-one-and-one's-children-are-starving-and-there-is-no-other-recourse would be *wrong*. This would hypothetically be a valid further specification of moral principle in the matter of "stealing" even in Utopia where there is no starvation. Although *there* it is hard to imagine how one would get to know the defined-

# Virtue, Principles, and Rules

action principle which we have just formulated, this is in any case the nature of possible further specification of the moral life that is at issue. The question is not the incidence of situations believed to be uniquely unusual before ethical reflection lights upon their morally relevant features in rendering a verdict upon the fitness or unfitness of a proposed action.

If only there are morally relevant features of any sort, this serves to justify the "exception," to bring it within the principles appropriate to the moral matter—and destroys its "exceptional" character. It does not matter whether in the steps prolonging principle into life's situations one's ultimate resort or test for all intervening principles is *agapé* or utility or self-realization or some other final norm. And it does not matter whether these are *fairness*-features or *consequence*-features or "canons of loyalty." The justification of an action always depends on some feature or features in that act's proper description.

Of course, the features of the proposed action, its characteristics or description, correlated with features in the situation allegedly requiring this action, have to be *morally relevant* features, qualities, or characters. If the general principle is: "Other things being equal, it is wrong to tell a lie," no one would think of proposing: ". . . unless one is asked to tell a lie on a Tuesday by a red-headed man with one eye, with a wart on his right cheek and a mermaid tattooed on his left forearm." [7] Of course, there might conceivably be argument over this point. Most people would say that locating a lie in the class of actions performed on Tuesday, etc., does not change the wrongfulness of lying because the class of actions performed on Tuesday, etc., is indifferent. Others might deny this. Of these some might say that because of some hitherto unknown causal efficacy all acts performed on a Tuesday have more serious consequences than those performed on other days of the week: deceitful acts on Tuesday, self-sacrificial actions on Tuesday, or revengeful acts on Tuesday would all be more effective; and such a person might conclude that lies told on Tuesday would, because of this characteristic, be more undesirable than lies told on other days. Others might say to the contrary that to establish the reservation that lies may be told on a Tuesday when asked by a man with a wart, etc., would be "better, or at least no worse than" if lies are told every day of the week, and probably no more calamitous than for one *never* to be able to tell a lie. On the other hand, *fairness*-features of the situation and of the proposed action may prove decisive,

[7] Cf. Jonathan Harrison, "Utilitarianism, Universalism, and Our Duty to be Just," *Proceeding of the Aristotelian Society*, LIII (1952–1953), p. 114.

and not only the causal efficacy of such acts. It is conceivable that, for example, public policy requiring certain acts to be performed on a Tuesday would be wrong—because unfair to members of the society who belong to a religious sect which celebrates that day of the week as their Sabbath. While some such arguments might be advanced for the *moral relevance* (pro or con) of the characteristic "performed on Tuesday, etc.," I presume the reader will agree that such features as these are to be excluded when we say that the justification of any particular action depends on its *morally relevant* features. Ordinarily, "we do not regard 'performed on Tuesday' as a legitimate candidate for inclusion in the relevant specification of an action from a moral point of view." [8]

This nevertheless affords us a good example of the way in which *features* of acts, situations and relations (not logically excepting knowledge into the *humanum* of man or revealed knowledge into the nature of man and the good for him) are the foundation of moral reasoning about principles and cases. It is noteworthy, by contrast, that a situationist in order to preserve his exception inviolate and to keep that singular deed from being included under moral principles would have to justify it because of its featurelessness, because of its *thisness*, or because of quite indifferent features such as "performed on Tuesday." That would be to try to justify something that is affirmed to be without any quality to justify it.

Ordinarily we can tell the difference between morally relevant and morally irrelevant features of acts and situations; and we avoid getting into esoteric discussions of such probably indifferent, factual characterizations as "performed on Tuesday, etc." Beginning with a general prohibition of lying (which is judged to be warranted by one or another ultimate normative test), we confront in thought or in actual life a situation that seems to require that this be set aside. If it is right to set aside or violate this defined-action principle in this instance, our act is not *gratuitous*. It is not gratuitous either because of God's *arbitrary* will or because of ours. There is some relevant reason for it. The reason may be feature-dependent. This means that this action requires, for *its* justification, a further specification of principle, of *kinds* of things to be done or not done, of the meaning of right and wrong. So we qualify the verdict "it would be wrong for anyone to lie" by the verdict "except to save life." This judgment is applicable to other cases, and not in this special instance alone. In

[8] David Lyons, *Forms and Limits of Utilitarianism* (Oxford: Clarendon Press, 1965), pp. 53, 57.

fact, we may affirm that it would be wrong not-to-lie-in-order-to-save-another's-life. We justify *this* particular action and at the same time other hypothetical or actual particular actions by reference to this further specification of right and wrong, by this *more definite "defined-action* principle" or "moral-*species*-term" and not by the former one under which, however, our present principle in some sense falls. The right-making, feature-dependent condition "in order to save life" is sufficient to rebut the wrong-making, also feature-dependent but more general, condition, "no lying." Some argue that the word "rebut" is too strong. Instead, it can be contended, as we shall see, that we have arrived by this qualification at a more adequate definition of the forbidden lie.

The problem in passing from the most general material principles to defined-action principles and to definite-action rules that more closely specify what is to be done or not done is ordinarily not how to avoid lighting upon morally irrelevant or indifferent features of acts and situations. A greater difficulty is posed by how hard it is to pay attention to *all* of their morally relevant features. This difficulty in turn does not flow from myopia or simply from habitual inattentiveness or occasional unresponsiveness in the decisions we make. It flows, rather, from the fact that the agent's moral "onlook," his ultimate norm or operational "system" of ethics *selects in* the features of acts and situations that will appear morally *relevant* to him while *selecting out* characteristics that may, on a larger view, be not only relevant but necessary in order to comprehend all the moral wisdom needed for the direction of conduct. Thus, *fairness*-features or *justice*-features of acts, relations, and situations may be overlooked by someone whose *gestalt* in perceiving relevance or perspective in judging importance or whose ultimate norm leads him always only to *consequence*-features. Therefore it had better be said that sound moral reasoning "requires . . . consideration of *all* relevant features of the act in question, whether relevant for the given principle or not";[9] or, if "all relevant features" seems apt to lead us again to "actions performed on a Tuesday," we should, rather, say all *possibly* morally relevant features. It is in uncovering all the morally relevant features, all the claims that may not be feature-dependent, it is in giving decisive importance to personal faithfulness-claims establishing "canons of loyalty" both in the moral life and in the organization of an ethical system that a Christian outlook makes its special contribution to moral reasoning.

These latter considerations have brought us to the place where, it

---

[9] Lyons, *op. cit.*, p. 48.

has to be acknowledged, conflicts of principles, or of moral relations, dimensions, realms, roles, or duties may arise. Some people seem to miscall any resolution of such conflicts, e.g., a judgment whether, for example, fairness or good consequences or personal fidelity should be the more commanding, by the name of "exception," meaning by this an unprincipled or ruleless deed. *That* would be *another* misnomer. At least, nothing "happens" to "defeat" or "weaken" a principle or moral rule in regard to the moral matter or relation it governs when in cases of conflict it is judged for good reason to be subordinated to another dimension or relation or activity in the moral life.[10]

At the moment, however, we are following out the nature and the logic of moral reasoning along a single line from a single general principle in the direction of more and more specific defined-actions (moral *genera* and *species*). In the nature of the case, we have said, to *justify* any statistically unusual action or even an allegedly unique one requires that this be done because of some morally relevant, possibly feature-dependent, good reason characterizing that act and the situation or the moral relation to which it is judged to be fitting. Such an action is a deed falling within our deepened or broadened or more specific principles. It is a *sort* of thing, if justifiable. It is no unique or singular exception.

Moral reasoning which discriminates or defines right or wrong action by what we are calling *genera* and *species,* David Lyons terms reasoning by "*exempting*-conditions." [11] While that expression is not incorrect, it is too narrow in its denotation; it suggests only the formulation of more specific, feature-dependent conditions by which one justifiably *escapes* or is *released* from the observance of a former principle, *sorts* of things to which the original principle no longer applies. "Stealing" is still "stealing," "lying" is still "lying" as first defined; only now we know that "saving life" is a condition that rebuts those prohibitions and defines a smaller class of situations in which the act of *stealing* or *lying* is justified. That would not be to discover a particular action exempt from all definable principle; it

---

[10] There is a humorous illustration of this that can be taken from the statement of Alphonsus de Liguori (quoted by Bernard Häring. C.SS.R., p. 213 below) that "It is lawful to interrupt intercourse, provided there is a just cause for interrupting, e.g. if danger of illness, or death from an enemy should result from the continuation of the act. . . ." One has only to know when the activity of coition should no longer be engaged in and when the activity of self-defense and the "laws of war" have supervened. One could say this without altering his judgment that morally relevant features in the nature of coition require that *coition* be completed, so long as *coition* is the activity that is going on—not *war.*

[11] *Op. cit.,* p. 127.

would not be, morally, a nondescript deed. Still that *sort* of thing would be exempt from the prohibition of stealing or of lying; in cases falling under this class of action it would be *right* to *steal* or to *lie*.

This may be illustrated by an analysis of Joseph Fletcher's case of "sacrificial adultery."[12] This was the case of Mrs. Bergmeier confined by the Russians in a concentration camp in the Ukraine. She more than anyone was needed by her husband and their three children to reknit them as a family in that dire situation of "hunger, chaos, and fear" caused by the collapse of Nazi Germany before the Allied forces from west and from east. The regulations provided that if a woman inmate was pregnant or became pregnant "she would be returned to Germany as a liability." There was no other way she could rejoin her family. She asked a friendly camp guard to impregnate her, and was released to rejoin her family in Berlin, who received her with rejoicing "even when she told them how she had managed it." When little Dietrich was born, "they loved him more than all the rest, on the view that little Dietrich had done more for them than anybody else" (unless as much gratitude was owed the camp guard.) "Did Mrs. Bergmeier do a good and right thing?"

Here there are morally relevant features aplenty. At this point I propose to outline three different ways in which that woman's action might be justified, the first as an act falling *without* principle and the second and third as an act falling in some sense *within* defined principles. We can state these possibilities for justifying this case of "sacrificial adultery" without committing ourselves to the conclusion that in fact it was done with positive ethical warrants.[13]

Each of these three views would hold that in some sense there is a principle or principles specifying the good for the marriage relation. (1) The first holds that the marriage-principle is a "maxim" or "guideline" to which there are singular exceptional cases justified in each case by direct appeal from the marriage-principle to one's ultimate norm, and that Mrs. Bergmeier's is one of these exceptions. The second and third modes of reasoning also agree that her act was

[12] *Situation Ethics* (Philadelphia: Westminster Press, 1966), pp. 164–165.

[13] There is something to be said in behalf of holding that in the order of ethical justification Mrs. Bergmeier's *act* was *wrong*, that the *blame* for this rested elsewhere or upon others or the evil system of regulations, and that *she* was *excusable*. Christian ethics would seem to be able to keep clear these two meanings of "justification": the logic of ethical justification from the "logic" of forgiveness. Precisely because of the latter recourse, there need be no hurry to collapse or deflect the former. Both "judgments," we believe, are powerful to reach and encompass ourselves and all our acts.

justified, but as a case falling under further specific principles connected in some morally relevant way with the marriage-principle or practice itself. These further specifying principles or closer definitions of the appropriateness of her action may be (2) a class of actions *exempted* from the rules that have up to now been known to govern the marriage-practice, or they may be (3) further stipulations or explanations of the faithfulness-claims of marriage itself.

But first, let it be understood that all three ethical justifications presuppose that there are content-full principles expressing the meaning of marital *fidelity* and governing the marital relation. These can be stated more exactly than by a generalized "faithfulness" which (like *agapé* or utility or self-realization or self-preservation or any other norm) might lead to almost anything "counting for fidelity." Such a more closely defined-principle would be: "We shall not commit adultery." This may be only (1) a guideline capable of being set aside by an "exception" falling *outside* it or (2 and 3) a principle capable only of qualification by another principle yet to be stated. Still, the prohibition of adultery in some sense belongs among the meanings of the responsibilities and commitments of marriage. If not the essence, it is of the essence of this moral relation, which is violated by any breach of it. A more expanded version of this defined-meaning of the faithfulness specifically pertaining to and constituting the bond of marriage would be the traditional one: Marriage is the mutual and exclusive exchange of rights to acts which of themselves tend to the transmission of life and to the strengthening of conjugal love. Or this might be stated as the pledge that each partner's love-making and life-giving powers be held together in unity of life, and keeping himself or herself in these morally relevant respects only for the other so long as they both shall live. This would seem to prohibit love-making or baby-making with any other person; and that is to say far more than "generally be faithful."

1. The first possible justification of Mrs. Bergmeier's action attaches an individual-act *exception*-making or exception-*generating* criterion to every statement of the marriage-principle. This turns that principle into a maxim or guideline or summary of its past observances; a principle whose observance or whose violation has equally to be validated afresh in each case by appeal to one's ultimate norm. The *exception-making* criterion states:

> We should not commit adultery, except when it would do more good on the whole to do so.
> We ought to hold our love-making and live-giving powers together in the unity of our married life together, except when to communicate

# Virtue, Principles, and Rules

love or to communicate life with someone else would accomplish a greater good.

The justification of an act of adultery in this manner—by virtue of an exception-making criterion—could, of course, be claimed to be feature-relevant and feature-dependent. This is true, however, only in the sense that one would be bound in each case to quantify the tendency or force of each action in "making for good on the whole." A unique congeries of objective circumstances and consequences would be said to warrant the act. The so-called "features" of the proposed action and its situation would simply, as a set of particulars, be brought directly before one's final court of normative appeal for the verdict to be rendered upon them. This would still be the case if one added as a formal condition the test of universalizability, that anyone should do *the same*. The *same* would still be defined only by *agapeic* quantification of the tendencies to good on the whole. Whether there are other than making-for-good-on-the-whole features in this particular case that are needed to justify it and that also have implications beyond this allegedly unique case is not a question raised. In this sense, the particular case is "constructively" unique.

This is not what philosophers usually mean, or not all they mean, by an "exception" or by the morally relevant features of acts, relations, and situations that are right-making or wrong-making. It is, however, the notion of "exception" that has gained some currency among theologians and in religious circles. Indeed, it must be said that theological exceptionists ordinarily do not even stress formal universalizability, in their quest for a uniquely creative deed.

The attachment of an exception-making criterion to the marriage-principle has already destroyed that principle and set it aside, whether the decision in a present instance is to abide by it or actually to depart from it for the sake of doing good. This is the case whether, in determining the "good" to be done, one's final and immediate court of appeal is to a generalized faithfulness, *agapé*, utility, self-realization, saving life, continuing the human race on the earth, or to some other principle of exception-making. In every case and all along the course of life one is free to decide whether to abide by or depart from this merely "maxim"-meaning of marital fidelity, by reference to "good on the whole." In this manner of moral reasoning, one does not proceed *through* the marriage-principle to the features of situations that (as the following lines of reasoning assert) establish *specific sorts* of cases (2) exempting from or (3) qualifications within the marriage-principle which remains as binding as before, even though, so these views assert, there may be morally relevant features requiring further defined-principles or moral-*species*-terms expressing a justification of Mrs. Bergmeier's action. These other modes of moral reasoning, we shall see, treat one's ultimate norm as a principle of principles and as a principle in the elaboration of further principles, not as a principle of exception-making.

The fact is that if one attaches an exception-making criterion at any point along a line of reasoning from the more general to the more specific principles, all the moral insight that went before on the scale is immediately suspended. If one adds to the verdict: "Never tell a lie or steal except to save life . . ." the exception-generating criterion: ". . . unless not-to-lie-or-steal-in-order-to-save-life would accomplish greater good on the whole," this promptly undercuts one's grounds for saying that not-to-lie-or-steal-in-order-to-save-life would be wrong or one's grounds for saying that to-lie-or-steal-in-order-to-save-life would be right. One had not learned that defined-action principle, after all. Moreover, if an exception-making criterion had been attached earlier: "Do not lie or steal, unless to do so would accomplish greater good on the whole" that would not only have put the prohibition of lying and stealing out of commission. It would also have prevented our learning from serious reflection upon these principles and upon the morally relevant features of cases in question this further determination of right from wrong: "To 'lie' or 'steal' *to save life* is right."

Similarly, let us suppose that our reflection concerning the moral matter of marriage has begun with the principle: "We shall not commit adultery." Suppose then that the characteristics of the instant case leads us to attach to this prohibition an *exempting* moral judgment: ". . . unless the woman is in a camp whose regulations are that only pregnant women are let go, when her family imperatively needs her, and there is no other recourse." Then if anyone thought to add to *that* the generalized *escape*-clause of an exception-*making* criterion: ". . . except when not to do so would accomplish greater good on the whole," would this not weaken the general justification of Mrs. Bergmeier's action at which we had arrived upon the basis of important, morally relevant characteristics of her situation and the claims of her family upon her? We could say with less assurance that "adultery" would be *right* on condition that "the woman-is-in-a-camp, etc., etc." Mrs. Bergmeier would have acted less decisively had she to calculate all the ultimate good to come. Instead, consciously or unconsciously, she acted upon the premise that she already knew enough to say how any woman should act who should do *the same* as she; and "the same" or the permitted *sort* of thing anyone else should do can be described by using these words in a class-designation: "being

# Virtue, Principles, and Rules

a woman in a concentration camp whose regulations are that only pregnant women are let go, her family imperatively needing her, and there being no other recourse."

2. We have already bordered upon the second distinct mode of moral reasoning to be set in contrast to mere escape-clauses and exception-making, namely, exempting moral classification of actions according to their completed or relatively complete and morally relevant descriptions.

In the face of the morally relevant, indeed the important, features of this case, one may be impelled to formulate, and we may suppose the woman was impelled to act upon, an *exempting*-condition (like "saving life" in the case of lying or theft). The *sort* of case warranting adultery we can express as: "unless a woman is in a concentration camp whose regulations are that only pregnant women are let go, when her family imperatively needs her, and there is no other recourse." That may be a right-making condition sufficient to set aside in this defined-sort of case the wrong-making conditions still pertaining to the marriage bond. Shall we hold firm the stricter concept of marital fidelity (prohibiting adultery as a physiological *definite*-action rule) and say that the woman's violation of it was justified because of this *exempting*-condition; that hers was neither a *featureless* action claiming gratuitous uniqueness, nor an allegedly *unique* unrepeatable act claiming justification beyond all definable principles or rules by direct reference to one's final norm, but was instead a kind of action theoretically repeatable and perhaps actually repeated, having features which warrant all deeds falling under that kind? This seems to be Lyons' mode of moral reasoning, or that of the utilitarian philosophies he brings under scrutiny.

3. Alternatively, we might say that this kind of situation and action enables us to make explicit certain meanings and stipulations that were all along *implicit* in the meaning of *marital fidelity*. We might say that when the morally relevant and gravely important features of this situation are taken into account we have not so much stated an *exemption* from the meaning as we have deepened or clarified the very conception of what marital fidelity can require. This would be to begin with a very definite conception of the meaning of this particular fidelity among humankind, and to find *qualifications* within this, not exemptions warranting a violation of it. Like exempting-conditions, this too would mean no direct reference at every point to doing good on the whole, or to what *that* might allow. It was, after all, the restoration of a rather specific thing, namely, the bond between love-giving and the transmission of fully human lives in the

unity of that family, which was the whole justification of Mrs. Bergmeier's action. No appeal was made to some vast or undefined calculus of faithfulness or good consequences in general, considered in independence of the marriage-principle. We might suppose that she held firmly in mind the defined-meaning of marital fidelity, that she did not attempt to go behind or around this to make immediate appeal to *agapé* or utility or her own survival or self-realization or any other ultimate norm to justify her action. Instead, she may have appealed only to the requirements of marital fidelity; then she extended into practice in a critical situation what *this* entailed, expanding the meaning of (in that situation) a denial of it. The extraordinary situation she faced brought to light certain stipulations or understandings that were implicit in the requirement of this specific fidelity. Her action was a case of it.

In the first of these variations (*exempting*-conditions) the prohibition "We should not commit adultery" is held to be a "*definite-*action rule" having precise, literal, physiological meaning; and the *adultery* is said to be justified because of feature-dependent exempting conditions characterizing that critical situation and the woman's action. In the second of the variants (*qualifying*-conditions), the prohibition of any violation of *marital fidelity* is held to be a "*defined-*action principle" specifying general faithfulness more closely in terms of the meaning this should have for the marriage relation but yet not so definitely that (as this case shows) every literal, physiological case of intercourse-impregnation would necessarily be a violation of it. In this case also the woman did a right and good thing, but *she did not commit "adultery"* if that means a fundamental violation of the marriage-principle. In the one case, her action was adultery but it was justified by the stated exemption; in the other case, her action was justified as a qualification within the meaning of marriage-fidelity. What she did was right because appropriate to the faithfulness-claims of marriage upon her. This was not the meaning of the forbidden adultery.

It may be questionable whether the latter line of reasoning can be carried through in the matter of "adultery." Yet certainly, against the proposal that moral reasoning proceeds exclusively by exempting features, it can be argued in the matter of picking someone else's apples when one's children are starving and there is no other recourse, that this is *not* "theft"; and in the matter of lack of verbal integrity in order to save life that this is *not* "lying." Such sorts of action, it can be contended, are warranted by qualifications within these prohibitions by which we come to apprehend more adequately the meaning of the forbidden stealing and the forbidden lying.

In the bourgeois period property rights have been regarded as an absolute, definite-action rule; and therefore picking those apples could be justified only by an exempting-type justifying *theft*. In the Christian ages private proprietorship was a right, of course; but also property had in *usus* an orientation to the common good and the needs of all men. These were the ingredients of the *defined*-action principles governing ownership and use of property. Taking someone else's property in case of dire distress when the titular owner withheld it from its destined service and there was no other recourse was readily justified, of course, but *not as a case of "theft."* This was justified constructively as a stipulation within the meaning of the defined-action principles governing the relation of property and persons, and person to person —a qualification brought to light by the features and claims in the situation of starving men. In fact, Christian ethics did not wait for such situations to bring this meaning to light. Instead, the "anatomy" of Christian moral reasoning was that *first private property had to be warranted* as a rule of practice and as a human right *within* the commonality of all things. This move was required even to sustain a narrower definition of theft—and in order for philosophers then to discuss exemptions from that strict definition!

Suppose "lying" is regarded as a violation of a *definite*-action rule requiring literal, verbal veracity; this so understood, if held firm, permits a breach of verbal integrity to save life only by the logic of feature-dependent *exempting*-conditions. This then means that it is *lying* that was justified—by "saving life." The latter class of actions, because of its right-making features, sets aside the wrong-making features warranting the prohibition of lying. This assumes the strictly verbal meaning of "lying." Our reasoning about men's responsibilities in telling the truth in the sort of situation in which verbal veracity would gravely endanger or kill has brought out no other meaning within the concept "lying." Suppose, however, the definition of the principle prohibiting lying is taken to mean "withholding the truth from someone to whom the truth is due." Then cases of lack of verbal veracity when answering questions of the Gestapo if one had a Jewish fellow man hidden in one's house whom they were after, and dissimulation or even plain false statements to Nazi interrogators while swearing on the Bible that one was telling the truth, would be justified, of course; but as implied species of acts within the meaning of truth-telling, not as instances of "lying." [14]

---

[14] Helmut Thielicke, *Theological Ethics:* Vol. I: *Foundations* (Philadelphia: Fortress Press, 1966), contains a remarkable chapter (27) on truth-telling that makes extensive use of the above argument.

We may be disposed to see some sense to this limited and morally significant expansion or deepening of the meaning of the forbidden theft or the forbidden lie. Still few of us are likely to be as readily persuaded of the cogency of this same line of reasoning in regard to Mrs. Bergmeier's "adultery." It is an interesting question why in sexual morality we tend to judge that *if* there are no physiologically unbreakable *definite*-action rules, then there can be no *defined* marital fidelity that is always binding, only a generalized "candor" or "caring" in love which anything can mean. In the case of the "exceptions" we *apprehend,* the one unbreakable maxim seems to be *Cherchez la femme!*

This, however, is enough to show that in *some* moral matters there may be defined-action principles to which there are no exceptions in any proper use of that language. Whether by *exempting*-conditions *beside* the extant principles or by *qualifying*-conditions *within* the extant principles, ordinary moral reasoning often or usually or sometimes if not always proceeds by principles and through principles, by *genera* and moral-*species*-terms.

It remains to be pointed out that the expression "qualifying-conditions" is not a fully adequate expression for the considerations introduced in the foregoing to correct and supplement the limited meaning which Lyons' term "exempting-conditions" seems to suggest. While the latter refers to kinds or sorts of things which are right-making beyond the extant principles and the former refers to the further specification of right-making qualifications falling within the extant principles, that difference is not enough. Both of these procedures or modes of moral reasoning entail that all significant distinctions among the principles guiding conduct are to be made in *dependence* on situational features; all, in Kant's meaning, "arise from" experience. To say that alone would be a great disservice to morality. This would not be to acknowledge the power of morality itself to make an imprint upon human life, the capacity of moral principle to mold and shape our lives and to specify out of its own nature the moral terrain. We who do Christian ethics, at least, need have no prejudice in favor of the view that only the terrain supplies the conditions for discriminating right from wrong. For Christian ethics means living in thought the sort of human life which God is shaping into the divine righteousness, or prolonging the meaning of God's righteousness in life's situations and searching out all of the requirements of this for human behavior. The closer qualifications of the meaning of this cannot all be derived from the material behavior that is subject to this judgment and reformation.

While our ethical judgments are doubtless all "feature-*relevant*," not all need be feature-*dependent*. Not all need arise from "conditions," whether these are exempting-conditions beside the extant defined-principles, or qualifications and closer specifications within these principles that are also quite dependent on the features of situations. Granted, this is to a large extent the way we proceed in broadening and deepening our moral wisdom.

Still it is also the case that there are meanings or stipulations or explanations or qualifications implicit within the moral law or within moral principles themselves. These meanings or explanations—of, for example, the forbidden lie or the forbidden theft, or of the meaning of truth-telling—arise from moral principle itself. While no doubt this better understanding of a defined-principle is feature-relevant, it as such does not simply adjust to a condition. Nor is it simply a reflection of features. Nor is this only a meta-rule. It, rather, states a further meaning of the defined-principle or rule. This may be brought to light by experience; it certainly "arises with" experience. But it does not "arise from" conditioning experiences. It "arises from" the implied meaning of principles as stipulations within these principles or terms.

In Christian ethics, at least, *agapé* works by many a principle through principle and to defined-principles in its ceaseless endeavor to unfold the meaning of the life of charity. These are always feature-relevant specifications of love. There may be exempting sorts of things or qualifying sorts of things dependent on those features and arising from them. Still love itself continues to enter into all the specifications of the moral life. There are faithfulness-claims upon us to which we are alerted by the ultimate norm shaping every principle or moral rule, conscience or pattern of behavior. Christian love in alignment with God's gracious acts has the power to direct attention to the requirements of faithfulness and to make these and "canons of loyalty" primary in the moral life and our ethical system. This means that if we use the analogy of reasoning by *genus* and *species*, this is not a matter of mere classification or derivation. A better analogy would be an evolutionary one, if biological *species* are thought to arise from some thrust forward or ahead. In some such way principles of faithfulness are unfolded from the elevating and directing power of divine charity. This and our intervening principles are capable of producing from within Christian morality itself deeper meanings, clarifying explanations or stipulations for the "upbuilding" of the actions and the moral agency going on ordinarily. Thus, there could be no good charitable reason for saying that picking someone else's apples to save life belongs among the meanings of "theft," or for saying that mere verbal inaccuracies of speech to save life belongs among the meanings of "lying." These were extensions and explanatory principles "conditioned" by principle itself. There may be a good many such insights or defined-principles and a number of further stipulations needed and relevant to our decisions and to our actual behavior and situations that arise from Christian morality itself and not from the conditions or merely from general features of situations, much less from the situational variables.

We now border on some very complex questions which cannot be explored here. But at a minimum it should be said that in addition to "exempting-conditions" and "qualifying-conditions" we need such designations as "explaining-principles" or "explanatory-qualifications" in order to comprise all the elements within the nature and the "logic" by which we move along the spectrum from the most general ethical principles to more specific ones. There are *faithfulness*-claims, and a Christian evaluative outlook upon these claims, calling upon us to deepen the meaning of moral requirements, and not only *feature*-dependent judgments. And "explanatory qualifications" in the matter of canons of loyalty are something more than logical rules governing the rules or stipulations concerning their derivation. Such qualifications draw forth the fuller meaning itself of fidelity between man and man in the covenants of life. There are more ways than one in which normative ethics elaborates an understanding of the moral life in the direction of defined-principles, even perhaps definite-action rules; and by which we can know how our moral behavior should be built up into righteousness. These subtle and variable and fecund alternatives are not apt to find entrance into the typically modern mind which has lost all sense of "the range of moral reason."

Such a mind has replaced good moral reasoning by what Paul Tillich called "technical reason"—the quantifying reasoning baptized by *agapeic* exceptionism. This explains our contemporary penchant for escape-clauses or exception-generating criteria as the only way to introduce creativity and sensitivity into the moral life. If the breadth and depth and flexibility of good moral reason is lost from view, then all that once passed for rationality is bound to seem a cruel master. Anyone antecedently persuaded that rationality entails a "managerial" spirit will dismiss the logic of good moral reasoning as a straitjacket, or anyway a "legalism." Anyone antecedently persuaded that orderly moral reasoning means only an external technical reason or that this must inevitably result in forcing flesh-and-blood human decisions into prearranged categories is bound to reject ra-

# Virtue, Principles, and Rules

tionality as such and to replace it by some form of voluntarism. Such a mind has simply lost touch with the full range of moral reason.

Our contemporary penchant for escape-clauses and exception-making criteria to free the human spirit can only be compared with the displacement of sound political reason and statesmanship in the contemporary period by "crisis-managers" with their "rationality of irrationality" policies. Political agency in our day is also said to be required to respond to allegedly unique particular situations in its "compromises," with no relevant political doctrine governing state actions. In the absence of good *political* reasoning, responsibility in the encounters within the international system is reduced to the play of will upon will having no limits. In the absence of good *moral* reasoning, responsibility in moral action is reduced also to singular acts of the will. Except, of course, in both cases, *agapé* on one side and quantifying reason on the other. Among men living in this hour the range of political reason and the range of moral reason is considerably contracted. This explains why so many discover principle-less exceptions, both in personal morality and in social and political ethics.

## II. *Definite-Action Rules*

We now take up, and shall criticize, some of the philosophical answers to the question of the justifiable exception. These quite rightly make use of the logic of moral reasoning which in the previous section was brought against theological "exceptionism." An exception would be a *sort* of thing. A justifiable exception to one principle or rule would be the observance of better principles or rules, as yet not adduced. Then the question is whether or not all principles and moral rules need have exceptions in *this* sense. *Must* (or *should*) all principles and moral rules be believed to have exceptions in *this* sense?

There seem to me to be two points of view that should be brought under scrutiny at this point. One is the view that while there may well be exceptionless *principles* there cannot be any exceptionless moral *rules* because, so far as human moral judgment alone is concerned, we cannot know and we cannot formulate rules of conduct that are *both* certain in their determination of wrongfulness or praiseworthiness and certain as to the description of the actions to which these verdicts apply. This point of view holds that if we are certain that a sort of action is wrong we are uncertain about the actions to which to apply this judgment, and if we are certain about the action we are talking about we remain uncertain whether it should be judged to be wrong or praiseworthy. Thus, while there are exceptionless principles there are no exceptionless moral rules in any moral matter. This position will be taken up in the present section of this chapter. Then in the following section we shall examine the argument that any and all principles or moral rules must or ought to be held open to possible future exceptions, in the sense in which philosophers generally use this term, i.e., open to further morally significant expansion or qualification.

Our own argument has already mixed "principles" and "rules" together again. Our first question was: Are there any exceptionless moral *principles?* In searching for an answer to this question we found that the more general principles shape themselves and are shaped for the direction of behavior in the increasing specificity of *defined*-action principles and in *genus* or moral-*species*-terms. It was at this point that we unavoidably found ourselves discussing the question: Are there any exceptionless moral *rules?* Why this was so should by now be quite clear. There is only a relative distinction between *defined*-action *principles* and *definite*-action *rules*.

The latter is still a definition of a sort or kind or class of actions. However definitely a *rule* discriminates right from wrong, it cannot tell us "*This* is right or wrong." Definite-action rules are therefore only the more specific from among defined-action moral principles. Because this is the logic of good moral reasoning, it should at once be clear that anyone who allows that there are significant, informative, and closely defining principles in some moral matters or moral relations cannot then likely deny that there may be some moral rules that are without *significant* exception. He may already have said in effect that in some moral matters or relations there may be no *"justifiable"* exceptions to the moral rules. If he demands more of a definite-action rule than a term defining right action as closely as possible and discriminating this from the sort of thing that is wrong, he asks too much. His failure to discover the possibility of definite-action rules may be because the question was wrongly put. It may be that he asked for a contradiction in terms; he asked that *the particular* be produced.

Still it is encumbent upon us now to begin at the other end of the spectrum and ask: Can there be exceptions to all morally relevant rules? Are there any, or is it possible for there to be any, unexceptionable morally relevant rules? Can there be any definite-action rules?

## Virtue, Principles, and Rules

We shall approach these issues through an analysis of I. M. Crombie's discussion of "Moral Principles."[15]

Crombie argues that (unless God has revealed them) there can be no moral principles which are "both such that they must never be broken and also such that it is theoretically possible to say with certainty in a given situation that it is this or that action which would constitute a breach of them."[16] In other words, he denies that there are any "definite action-rules," on an understanding of the meaning of such rules which we may have to call in question. Crombie does not deny that there are significant moral principles. Perhaps, indeed, there are a number of such principles, together comprising the texture of the moral life and moral judgment, in addition to the ultimate norm or norms which warrant them. It is only that all such principles remain somewhat general in reference to the final act of choice, i.e., when we come, I shall argue, to what is called in classical casuistry "the subsumption of cases."

Crombie's contention is simply that a principle which always applies will turn out to be sufficiently *elastic in meaning* that we do not always know what we must do in order to conform to it; and, conversely, a principle whose demands upon action are always more or less unambiguous will turn out to be one that is *elastic in application*, so that this will be a principle concerning which we are unwilling to say quite categorically that it ought to be obeyed in all conceivable circumstances.[17]

Principles of the first sort vary greatly in the elasticity of the particular interpretations that may be drawn from them in determining action. Such moral principles *which always apply* range from the more general to the more specific. ". . . The golden rule leaves us almost totally uncommitted on the question how to behave"; an upholder of jungle law or of benevolence may equally adhere to it.[18] Yet Crombie believes that the Golden Rule is in fact the fundamental moral principle; it is expressive of our moral constitution: "The man who does not conform to the golden rule in trying to decide what to do does not reflect on what men in general ought to do."[19] Less open and elastic than the Golden Rule is the principle of benevolence which says that a man ought always to love his neighbor as himself. Nevertheless, from the principle of benevolence

---

[15] In a chapter bearing this title, in *Christian Ethics and Contemporary Philosophy*, ed. Ian T. Ramsey (New York: Macmillan Co., 1966).
[16] *Ibid.*, p. 235.   [17] *Ibid.*, p. 236.
[18] *Ibid.*, pp. 241–242.   [19] *Ibid.*, pp. 240–241.

we cannot always know what we must do in order to conform to it. Then there are more qualifying ways of spelling out the material meaning of benevolence (for example, that my neighbor's higher aspirations and welfare should be served, and not his happiness only) which are less open than merely formal benevolence. Still, all this does not tell us unambiguously how to behave; it yields no "definite action-rule."

The prohibition of murder or of cruelty are examples of moral rules that have the greatest degree of specificity while still belonging to the class of "principles" that always apply. Yet membership in the class of cruel acts remains "indefinite"; and whether this was or was not a murderous action is what the argument is all about, as Socrates knew, in courts of law. "Cruel acts" and "murderous acts" do not constitute a "definite kind." [20] Instead, Crombie says, these are "indefinite action-rules" (cf. our "defined-action principles").

It is important to note that Crombie believes that there must be these indefinite action-rules, else we could not begin to know how to practice benevolence. Not only principles like benevolence but also indefinite action-rules prohibiting murder or enjoining virtuous conduct are the kinds of things we should always be applying in practice. In common with a number of other philosophers, Crombie does not deny (in casting logical doubt upon the possibility of "*definite* action-rules") that there are these morally significant, closely defined, although still indefinite action-rules *which always apply*. Notably, when a number of theologians doing Christian ethics get hold of the idea that a defined-action rule is still indefinite as to the particular action this calls for, or when they grasp the fact that a moral offense-term is still a *species*-term, they promptly conclude that all principles discriminating among actions which should always be observed must necessarily be purely formal ones, empty of meaning, or else that a moral judgment using such terms must be circular. Murder is only *wrongful* killing (or even unlawful killing) and therefore to say that one should never do murder is true but uninformative. Crombie does not so conclude; in fact he says the opposite concerning such indefinite action-rules, in the course of saying that men cannot establish that there are any "*definite* action-rules."

It is sometimes said that "Doing X is always wrong" is only useful in decision-making if "doing X" describes a kind of action which one can identify without having judged already that it is always wrong. That would seem to be an apt description of what goes on in courts

---

[20] *Ibid.*, p. 248.

## Virtue, Principles, and Rules

of law where the trial is always to see whether one can describe a kind of action—the lethal act, *mens rea*, malice of forethought in varying degrees, feature-relevant qualifications—which one can identify as one *species* among all other sorts of killings. *The law* may not have waited for the completion of the description of that definite kind of action under which this particular case falls before saying that *that sort* of thing is always, say, first- or second-degree murder and always wrong. But nothing prevents the completion of the description of the kind of thing this was *while* completing the statement of the *offense*-term or moral-*species*-term used in the verdict upon that *sort* of thing and in subsuming this *particular* case under the moral and the criminal category. An act does not have to be wrong *before* being that sort of thing. The wrongfulness of it does not infect or inhibit its being of a fairly definite sort. There is no circularity here, and certainly not emptiness. One is simply accumulating the feature-relevant meaning of the offense-term and out of the relevant and ruling moral principles themselves elaborating more narrowly defined discriminations of right from wrong killings. The fact that the greatest possible specification remains a "universal" means only that one is rightly employing the constitutive moral principle of "universalizability"; it does not mean that the category of moral or legal offense is formal, empty, or morally uninstructive. This is simply the course of good moral reasoning. This is the case even if the last specification remains somewhat "indefinite" as to the particular actions falling under it.

Were this not so the whole of civilized life would have long since perished. Judgments within the ethico-legal system and within the ethico-political system and within the moral constitution are always of this order. For example, the whole history of Anglo-American liberties can be written as a history of the meaning of one verdict contained in Magna Carta: "No freeman shall . . . ." That is, the history of our liberties can be written as the history of the deepening and broadening of the meaning of being a "freeman," its qualification, extension, application, the defined-features relevant to a judgment falling under it, etc. If at any point anyone had been so foolish as to say that since being a "freeman" was always taken in some sense to be a right-making and a rights-making condition all these subsequent claims and struggles were formal, empty, and circular (because one already knew that to wrong a freeman was analytically wrongful)— and if he had been able to make this stick—at that moment our civil tradition would have perished from the earth.

There are, then, for Crombie, a number of action-rules which while "indefinite," are still rather well defined, and which may always apply in directing proper behavior. The prohibition of murder and of deliberate cruelty are among these.

Still such necessary action-rules only confirm Crombie's main thesis, which at this point he restates "When a description [of a *kind* of action] is such that we retain freedom of manoeuvre over the question whether to apply it in a particular instance, there we have no qualms over allowing that we shall approve (or condemn) everything to which we decide to apply it. When however we have no freedom of manoeuvre in the matter of application, there we naturally want to retain freedom to approve or disapprove, as may seem best to us, of some action to which, as we have to concede, the description certainly applies." [21]

A man who came into the possession of a *definite action-rule* of behavior would, presumably, renounce both freedoms of maneuver. He would no longer be free to debate about the meaning of the moral rule in the application to be made of it in this instance, and no longer free to doubt whether the rule applies. ". . . The man who subscribes to a definite action-rule is apparently willing to forego both the liberties of which we have just spoken" [22]—both the liberty to question (and to continue to enlarge or deepen his understanding of) the meaning of an action-rule he should certainly apply and the liberty not to apply an action-rule he unambiguously knows the meaning of.

On the face of it, this looks like a program for squeezing out the role of prudence in the subsumption of cases or, rather, of supplanting the function of practical wisdom by some "definite action-rule." This would seem to require *per impossibile* a *principle* or *rule* governing the *application* of one's last specification to particular cases, as the only way of showing that particular choice should always accord with some definite rule or principle or moral-*species*-term. There may be within our principles or moral rules some significant rule-governing-rules or stipulations. These are usually called meta-rules, or second-order rules in an ethical system. But in the nature of the case there can be no definite *application*-governing-rule beyond one's last specification of definable right- or wrong-actions. Crombie has so framed his objection to "definite action-rules" that his objection could be answered only by proof that the prudent subsumption of cases or the application of principles to them is the same thing as logical deduction, or that the subsumption of cases is itself rule-governed.

[21] *Ibid.*, p. 249.   [22] *Ibid.*

# Virtue, Principles, and Rules

To test whether this is the case or not, we must inquire more fully of Crombie what would be the nature of a "definite action-rule"? This will be to reverse the direction of the exposition we so far have followed. So far we have been coming down Crombie's mountain, from principles that are always valid but whose meaning for action ranges from greater to lesser elasticity without ever reaching entire certainty on the question how to behave. Can we not begin at the foot of the mountain, and ask what sort of statement, principle, or rule it would be by which we could say with certainty in a given situation that it is this or that action which would constitute a breach of the rule? It is necessary to examine carefully what a "definite action-rule" would be like in order to tell whether from the fact that such rules are impossible it follows that we must necessarily believe that there are always conceivable or actual circumstances in which any rule should be broken. We need to ask what, according to Crombie, would be a rule that leaves us no freedom of maneuver in the matter of application before we can decide whether it is the case that in regard to all principles and rules we retain the freedom to approve or disapprove, as may seem best to us, of some action to which, we concede, our relevant moral characterization certainly applies. These questions are not to be settled by references to men's "qualms" over lost "freedoms of maneuver" or to what they "naturally want."

A *definite action-rule* would be a rule proscribing or approving "actions of a definite kind," according to specific factual descriptions of these separate kinds of actions which leave no remainder of doubt (i.e. doubt not corrigible by more adequate description) whether an individual action belongs to the kind specifically described. There are, indeed, these action-descriptions which leave no invincible doubt whether the description certainly applies to a particular action; but, according to Crombie, these are all *neutral action-descriptions*.[23] I suggest the following as examples of neutral action-descriptions which convey certainty as to the actions falling under them: homicide, writing a name other than one's own, actions that cause pain to others, lying = verbal statements that do not correctly express the mind's apprehension, obeying one's father. But while these are the names of definite actions, it is also clear that sometimes we approve and at other times we disapprove of actions to which, we concede, these descriptions certainly apply.

A *definite action-rule* would have to be a *non-neutral* action-

[23] *Ibid.*, p. 247.

description. Offense-terms and terms of approbation are certainly non-neutral action-descriptions. The crucial test therefore is not that there would have to be incriminating or approving characterization of kinds of action, but one that left *no uncertainty* concerning what should be done or not done. A "definite action-rule" in Crombie's sense would have to leave no uncertainty as to how we should act in a particular instance, no more than the foregoing neutral characterizations left it an open question what we were talking about.

Suppose we reformulate the foregoing list of neutral descriptions as incriminations or recommendations. Instead of homicide (which may be justifiable or not), suppose we say "murder," plus further morally relevant specifications of this category. Instead of writing a name other than one's own, "forgery." Instead of actions that cause pain to others, "cruelty" (or, if the latter may possibly be justified, "*wanton* cruelty"). Instead of lying as lack of verbal veracity, lying as "dissimulation" or withholding the verbal truth from someone to whom that truth was due. Instead of obeying one's father, "honoring" one's father. These now are offense-terms or terms of moral approbation. And the most notable thing that has happened, according to Crombie, in the course of formulating these offense-terms or commendatory terms is that, while we have no qualms over allowing that we should approve (or condemn) any action to which we decide to apply them, it remains uncertain whether these terms should be applied in a number of particular instances. Therefore, again, there are no *definite action-rules* within the compass of human moral verdicts.

We may interject here some comment on Crombie's treatment of "forgery." This offense term obviously means more than the neutral action description "writing someone else's name." Yet to forbid forgery has greater definiteness than to forbid "cruelty." The latter certainly "implies moral condemnation" (and allows us greater freedom to say what does or does not constitute cruelty), while " 'forgery' at most suggests" moral condemnation (and allows us less freedom in determining the cases of the forbidden "forgery").[24] It is a more definite action-rule. In fact, I should say that in ordinary moral discourse the forbidden forgery may be compared with the forbidden lie because of the personal betrayal men usually mean by these offenses, in contrast to a stricter meaning. If anyone proposed as an *exempting* condition that it would be right to commit a "forgery" if by signing someone else's name to an official document he could

---

[24] Cf. *ibid.*, pp. 247–248.

# Virtue, Principles, and Rules

save a large number of Jews from extermination in Hitler's "final solution," would not a proper reply be that this was not what was meant by forgery; that forgery *means* to do the physical action for selfish personal gain, etc.? This occasion only drew our attention to what was meant by forbidding forgery.

We ordinarily would proceed another way if we subscribed to the *definite*-action rule, "Never torture your wife to death while giving her to believe that you hate her." That rule encompasses a very definite sort of action, and forbids it. If there is any escape it must be by future further exempting conditions.

Crombie does not deny that there are these definite-action rules in the sense that men subscribe to them. His point seems to be, however, that a proper subscription to them should acknowledge the fact that the most definite-action rule we can imagine still allows *either* future possible exceptions (a question we will consider in the sequel) *or* in the moment of present action, such latitude in meaning or in application that we cannot know both the *definite* action and that it is *wrong*.

Along this line of discourse today one comes sooner than later to sexual intercourse. If by "adultery" as a neutral action-description we mean sexual relations with someone other than one's marriage partner or with the marriage partner of another, that is a definite enough description; and then we naturally want freedom of maneuver to approve or disapprove, as may seem best to us, of some action to which, we gladly concede, the foregoing description certainly applies. If, however, by adultery as an offense-term we mean "unloving sexual intercourse," or even "marital infidelity" with a meaning not including the specific prohibition of physiologically definite acts of extramarital intercourse, then we retain an alternative freedom of maneuver, this time over the question whether to apply this verdict in a particular instance; and we have no qualms over allowing that we shall condemn everything to which (inside or outside "the marriage line" or of *this* sort of "fidelity") we decide to apply it.

This I take to be the argument Crombie mounts against the possibility that there are any *definite action-rules*, against the proposition that there may be unbreakable principles or rules of conduct. It is a formidable argument. Crombie has another argument against the possibility of unbreakable rules, by no means so weighty, which we must take up in a moment. However, we must introduce here decisive objection to his argument so far. Our objection, like his argument, has to do with the logic of moral reasoning. Crombie has simply asked too much or the wrong thing of "definite action-rules."

He wants them to be at the same time "universals" (however limited in their specification) and particulars. It is not surprising that this is a demand impossible of fulfillment. Crombie's case is not so much a case "not proven" (to use the language of the Scottish legal verdict). It is, rather, that the indictment was falsely drawn.

As Aristotle said, in moral science no more exactitude is to be expected than the subject allows. The clarity with which one can subsume cases under neutral action-descriptions may not be the same degree of clarity with which one is able to subsume particular cases under offense or commendatory terms. Theoretical (objective) reason is not the same as practical (moral) reason. As Richard McCormick, S.J., writes in his chapter in the present volume, ". . . We do not *prove* that an individual act (and all like it—a category, therefore) contains an attack on value, if by proof we mean a type of logical argumentation which all but traps the mind into assent" (see below, p. 246).

Still, the judgments and *defined*-action rules or moral *species*-terms which Crombie admits to be ingredients of a systematic normative ethics are quite definite ones. If, for example, a person believes he has good and sufficient moral reason for saying "it is wrong ever to kill a man," the kind of actions this forbids would be rather clear, e.g., all killing in war, capital punishment. As yet the meaning of the rule would, of course, be elastic as to whether nascent life is human; and if there is any uncertainty about the proper clinical meaning of "death" there would be question in regard to medical practice in treating terminal cases as to whether a particular action would be "killing a man." On the other hand, if the offense-term is "murder," this can be given a narrower meaning which, for example, allows that killing in war or capital punishment *may* be justified, and the meaning of the forbidden murder would admit of degrees, etc. If one has, upon proper moral warrants, established that just conduct in war is governed by the principle of discrimination and the principle of proportion, one then has only to get to know the meaning of these principles or "laws of war" and get to know certain stipulations governing the relation between them—that discrimination is the primary of the two, the fact that only proportion admits the possibility of significant reference to consequences while discrimination does not, etc. This can all be made pretty clear in its bearing upon conduct, although this clarity in ethical judgments does *not* remove the question; What then is required in *this* case? and certainly no specification within the meaning of these principles takes the place of many a "policy-decision."

# Virtue, Principles, and Rules

Or to take another illustration, if a person believes there are good and sufficient moral reasons for saying that "we shall not commit adultery," meaning the *definite* act, belongs to the obligations of marriage, it would be fairly clear how to go about observing this claim, or violating it. Of course, there remains some uncertainty as to whether a particular action falls under it or not. An unmarried man might in all seriousness undertake to perform simple fornication and find that his act was adultery, because the woman was married. Then there would be question whether his was a perfect case of adultery, since he did not know this.

All that Crombie has shown is that the most definite-action rule must logically be a *defined*-action rule. After that comes prudence in the subsumption of cases. The issue between Crombie and the present writer comes to focus, in fact, in where respectively each of us places the *hyphen* in the expressions we are using. I write: "defined-action" or "definite-action" rules; while Crombie always writes definite "action-rules." "Defined-action" and "definite-action" rules suggest the logic of moral reasoning by *genus* and moral-*species*-terms whose increasing specificity cannot in the nature of the case ever lead to anything other than verdicts incriminating or approving *sorts* of things. This Crombie does not deny; in fact his argument depends on it. Yet Crombie's quest is for a definite "action-rule."

What on earth would an "action-rule" be? This could only be a second-order rule governing the subsumption of cases under our first-order moral-*species*-terms. It could only be an *application*-governing rule. There are these second-order stipulations among the principles and rules of any normative ethics, of course. But these can only be *rule*-governing-rules. An *application*-governing-rule would be a project for putting out of commission the actual production of particular deeds by absorbing them utterly into the principles. There would have to be a logically infallible way to tell in *this* case and *that* case that *this* is a case of the sort of thing we with good reason approve while *that* is a case of the sort of thing we with good reason disapprove. That was ever the work of prudence or practical wisdom in subsuming cases under non-neutral judgments like "No drinking while driving" no less than under neutral descriptions like "key" and "stairs" in order *properly* to find one's way home at night. This practical wisdom, Plato said, even a philosopher needs and, after all his moral reasoning, may lack.

There can be no *subsumption-ruling* rules; and this means, of course, that there can be no such thing as Crombie's definite "action-rule," hyphenating principles and practice together so that there is no wise practice of life within moral principles and rules, but only infallible moral reasoning going on in the world, a casuistry which *deduces the particular.* It cannot be denied, of course, that there may be some few suggestions made in the direction of how to be prudent. But this is a moral virtue no one has yet been able to *teach.* Still less could there be a *principle* governing infallibly the prudent subsumption of its own cases. A particular-decision-rule or "action-rule" would be to "program" *the particular.*

The fact that Crombie fails to discover the possibility of any "definite action-rules" in his sense in no way establishes that there cannot be morally exceptionless "definite-action" rules; nor does he everywhere consistently say that it does. If even God revealed one of Crombie's definite "action-rules," that would be an edict, "Do *this.*" It would not be that He has revealed to us His moral will.

Indeed, if Crombie's quest for "definite action-rules" had succeeded, he would have established the possibility of that caricature of "casuistry" which too often is in the mind of those who under this heading attack the traditional way or any other way of relating a range of moral reason to the actualities of the moral life.

Many learned men make the common mistake of supposing that a telling objection can be brought against casuistry by pointing out the distinction between the articulation of moral principles and the application of these principles to concrete cases. Thus Helmut Thielicke writes:

> Whereas conclusions diminish in certainty the further removed they are from the original basic norms, the loss of certainty takes on gigantic proportions and becomes all but complete the moment individual cases are subsumed. This is because the transition from conclusion to subsumption involves a complete change in the manner of cognition. Conclusions arise by a process of deduction, whereas subsumption proceeds from that which is inductively apprehended. . . . Consequently, subsumption lies in the sphere where deduction and empiricism intersect.[25]

Whether or not "conclusion" or "deduction" are apt words to designate that prior moral reasoning, it has to be stressed that "subsumption" was always the great work of "prudence" or "practical wisdom," which as Plato says even a philosopher needs in order to

---

[25] *Theological Ethics:* Vol. I: *Foundations* (Philadelphia: Fortress Press, 1966), p. 411. If subsumption or the prudent application of moral rules to particular cases were not a "complete change in the manner of cognition," and subject to an entirely different kind of "error," one wonders what was ever the meaning, in both ecclesiastical practice and secular marriage-law, of the provision "nullity" on grounds of "mistaken identity."

# Virtue, Principles, and Rules 105

be able to find his way home at night. He would have to know the meaning of "housekey" and "going up one flight (and not down to the basement)" (these are neutral action descriptions) and of "no drinking while driving" (this is a non-neutral action description, an offense-term). If he pretty well knows the *sort* of thing this prohibits, then he would have to subsume his own case under it. It looks as if there are only *defined*-action rules, and that to ask for something more definite than this is to ask for the action itself. What Crombie has proved the impossibility of falls outside *ethical reasoning* and beyond the play of principles and rules. It is the actual practice of morality.

Thus also Karl Barth opposes a "practical casuistry" to "theoretical and systematic casuistry," and describes the latter as "an undertaking in which man, even though he calls upon God's grace, would like to win clear of the occurrence, the freedom and the peril of this event, to reach dry land, as it were, and to stand there like God, knowing good and evil." [26] I presume this means free from the perils of exercising a just and charitable prudence (if justice and charity are among our prior principles), and in the possession of knowledge of good and evil in *definite action-rules* (which Crombie does not deny God may have laid down for His creatures).

Only very rarely was this the undertaking of casuistry. But what of the *prohibitiva* in natural law ethics? This, indeed, seems to be the locus in any system of ethics of the problem Crombie raises in regard to definite action-rules. Moreover, both Thielicke and Barth also have their *prohibitiva* (as do, too, our contemporary situationalists) even after claiming a too easy victory over traditional casuistry largely misunderstood, and marking off its procedures too sharply from their own. Still, the *prohibitiva* in any normative ethics are stated and can be stated only in *genus* and *species*-terms. The fact that Crombie fails to find any definite action-rules has nothing to do with whether there are these *prohibitiva* or not. It does not prove that all moral rules have elasticity of such a sort that there can always be exceptions to them. It only shows that prudent men have still their work to do in getting to know the meaning of moral principles and rules and in deciding the application these require.

There is a final move by which one could show that there are *definite action-rules*. Crombie discusses this under the heading of "*factitious* action-rules or principles." [27] Other philosophers speak rather of *practice*-rules or rule-utilitarian rules. The rule that drivers

---

[26] *Church Dogmatics*, III/4, ¶52, p. 11.   [27] *Op. cit.*, pp. 250 ff.

of motor vehicles keep to the right (or left), that medical doctors do not advertise, and the societal practice of monogamy or polygamy are *rules of practice*. They also seem to be *"definite-*action rules." [28]

Do we not have in practice-rules a way of escape from Crombie's quandary? Are not at least *some* rules of practice (with the "definite-action rules" falling under them) "both such that they should never be broken and also such that it is theoretically possible to say with certainty in a given situation that it is this or that action which would constitute a breach of them"? That would seem to be the nature of a practice. The possibility that some practice-rules may also be *definite-*action rules can scarcely be excluded in any argument from the nature or the "logic" of practices.

This may be the reason Crombie shifts ground at this point in his argument; and this may also be the reason his significant shift was prepared for by the term he uses for practice-rules, namely, *factitious* action-rules or principles, and by the fact that the model for this kind of rule seems to be "rules of the road" which are factitious and entirely *non*moral prescriptions of definite actions. The stipulation upon the "definite-action rule" for which we are searching is no longer simply that it provides us with inelastic definition of *what sort* of action is wrong and clear and certain specification that *this* is the action prohibited. The requirement placed upon a definite-action rule (if there are any) is now that (1) every single infringement of it would be a wrong response to the situation in which it was done, i.e., that every infringement of it would be, on its own merits, and apart from its being a valuable rule, an independently wrongful act;[29] and that (2) every *good reason* for its being a "valuable rule" must be a good *moral* reason, even as the reason for the "independent wrongfulness" of the single infringement must be an *inherent moral* wrongfulness of the act when singly done, and indeed the universal and certainly known inherent moral wrongfulness of the *direct* consequences of that action taken alone.

This is simply not to prosecute seriously the search for the *possibility* that there are definite-action rules falling under rules of practice. Crombie is no longer asking simply whether there are any good reasons for rules or principles in terms of which we know both *what* is wrong and that *this* is wrong. He is no longer asking whether the elasticity of the *meaning* of principles or offense-terms can be narrowed without increasing our elasticity in judging that this

---

[28] From this point on I consistently adopt my usage in regard to the hyphen, since a class of "definite-actions" is all that ethics can afford, not "action-rules."

[29] Crombie, *op. cit.*, pp. 260–261.

### Virtue, Principles, and Rules

particular action to which, we concede, the principle or term applies nevertheless is *not* wrong.

Moreover, it is of the very nature of practice-rules that (1) a single infringement need not be *independently* wrongful to be still prohibited, and that (2) the *good* reasons for the principle or rule *may* not always be restricted to *moral* reasons, or the infringement be prohibited only because it is *inherently* immoral—least of all when only or mainly the *direct* consequences of the action are taken into account (these being certainly known to be universally, independently, inherently wrong). Crombie's argument at this point does not prove that practice-rules may not afford us definite-action principles or action rules in answer to his original quandary. It, rather, has the effect of *setting aside* practice-rules as by their very nature having no bearing on that question.

Yet under this heading Crombie comes closest to his "goal," and what he says in this connection is worth examination.

Suppose it is said that one should never torture his wife to death, giving her to believe that he hated her. That is a moral-*genus*-term (no torture) qualified by several moral-*species*-terms. When so qualified, have we then arrived at certainty that actions so described would be wrong and *also* at certainty concerning this rule's application, concerning *every* possible case subsumable under it and prohibited as wrong, so that there *could* be no "exception"? Not quite, says Crombie; some might invent a "case," admittedly remote from actual life, concerning which we would have to say that it is not clear that our principle or rule prohibited *that*. This being so, we have not yet located the possibility of a "definite-action rule" that *might* not on occasion enjoin the wrong action. Since the "situation" invented to yield this limitation upon the rule just stated was a *factitious* one, Crombie concludes that "if I uphold some definite action-rule as binding in absolutely every situation, then I must do so factitiously."[30] (From the case we are talking about, it is clear that we now are a long distance from the meaning of "factitious" applicable to "rules of the road"; we are in the midst of genuine *moral* questions and we have a moral rule that always holds. Therefore now we must "make up" the exception in order to have one.)

The justification for upholding "factitiously" the rule against torturing one's wife to death while giving her to believe one hates her, Crombie writes, is because "it is better so." That is to say, the probability that one will make a wrong decision if he acts on the

---

[30] *Ibid.*, p. 258.

policy that this rule *can* be set aside far outweighs the likelihood of occasions—indeed, all of them fictitious situations—in which one would probably make a wrong choice if he felt that one should always observe this rule. This does *not* bring into consideration the slight degree of possibility clinging to the singular rightfulness of a possible violation of that rule in some *future* imaginary situation (which we might call an exceptionalism based entirely on agnosticism with regard to future improbable cases). The argument invokes instead the degree of probability of *now* making a moral error if a person believes the rule could be set aside. We shall consider this argument for future possible exceptions in the next section. However, a present calculation of probability may well conclude that the rule is quite inviolate. This is a necessary ingredient in the nature and "logic" of rules of practice. Given the acceptance of the force of this argument, one has concluded to a *definite-action rule.* This is a *good reason,* although some may hold it not to deserve description as a good *moral* reason.

Crombie immediately passes to yet another aspect of rules of practice when he notes that a person may believe he should uphold the rule against taking innocent life (without claiming that the act of doing so would be "independently wrongful" in a case in which this might save lives by, for example, preventing a dangerous riot) on the grounds that "the greater danger is that people *should come to think* that innocent lives can be taken in situations which in no sense justify such action." [31] That is *another* justification of rules of practice, and definite action-rules falling under them. Some there are who will call this a *good reason,* some a good *moral* reason for the rule in question. In any case, few would call this the immediate, *direct* consequence of taking an innocent life in the situation supposed. The indirect consequences of such an action upon the habits of peoples and the values of society had to be taken into account by anyone who wanted to act rightfully, or wanted to avoid acting wrongfully. Again, some there are who will regard these considerations as *good reasons,* some as good *moral* reasons in determining their actions. In any case, in the language of traditional moral theology, ever to inculcate the habit of taking innocent life should be a matter of the "indirectly voluntary" and only as such an aspect of the total moral decision to do so even on the part of someone who justified doing this as collateral to the immediate, direct consequences of his

---

[31] *Ibid.,* p. 258 (italics added). These are the rule-strengthening and rule-assuring stipulations stated below, p. 114.

action. This, too, has always been among the justifications of rules of practice; and one should not be as surprised as Crombie is that this threatens to yield "definite action-rules," or at least "definite-action rules."

It may or may not be the case that one should uphold a definite-action rule because of the inherent wrongness of the action which it forbids. If, because of the likelihood of human error on the part of moral agents or because a single infringement will tend to inculcate serious wrongdoing generally, it is morally *expedient* that a definite-action rule be upheld, it is *morally* expedient that it be so upheld. Or, as we might say in the terms of Christian ethics, there are practice-oriented ways as well as person-centered ways of being compassionate to people. In face of these considerations, one would have to demonstrate weighty *purely moral* reasons why there *should not* be definite-action rules, in order to avoid the conclusion that there may be among these mixed or prudential reasons sufficient grounds for some such rules or principles among the foundations of human civilization.

In the end Crombie concedes that, having himself found no warrant for the possibility of unbreakable moral rules or principles, he does not find "the notion that it [the Christian revelation] does contain them so unplausible as some writers seem to find it." This is not really because of any appeal to God's commanding what he wills—contrary to the best moral reasoning of which man is capable. Such definite-action rules would not be *arbitrary* requirements. In fact, such definite-action rules Crombie (with no claims to divinity) has himself put forward as the verdicts of reasonable men. "We have already seen that a man might come to think it morally expedient that some rule should be upheld universally, and in that case it might presumably *be* morally expedient that it should be so upheld." "This," he adds, "might be the reason why universal obedience was a divine command." [32] Surely, Crombie means in this instance to claim that ideally human moral judgment cannot be denied this same possible verdict. Revelation might plausibly contain such requirements because it is, after all, not so implausible that human moral reasoning also so conclude.

Yet Crombie proposes less than he might have proposed as among the competencies of human moral judgment. When talking about "inherent wrongness," he formally can think of only two explanations of such wrongness. These "must consist either in the badness of what

[32] *Ibid.*, p. 259.

the action brings about or in the badness of what the action comes from." [33] Between these, between future consequences and the past motive, the moral agent and the action and its nature might rightfully protest that they have been squeezed out. Crombie himself knows better than to reduce all moral considerations to what actions lead to or came from—unless we are to extend past motive so far as to include in that category the nature of every present moral relation and the entire moral meaning of present actions and action-systems. The fact that the wrongfulness or rightfulness of these things can and must be estimated by reference to things other than what they arose from or led to, Crombie makes clear in all that he materially says about slavery. Because of the adaptability of human beings, it is "probably a little naive to suppose that slave-owning societies will always contain more unhappiness or more wickedness [slave-owning aside] than societies in which all men are free." Therefore Crombie writes that it is doubtful "whether those who object to slavery ought to object to it for what it leads to rather than for what it *is*." [34]

And, of course, what slavery as an action-system *is*, is not the same as what it came from. ". . . The institution is inherently wrong because it distorts the true relationship between human beings" and "nobody who saw that a slave is a fellow-human would want to retain the institution if he could get rid of it." Similarly, "respect for truth is something that any right-minded man will have." And in general, "what is in accord with human nature is what it is fitting that we, being the kind of creatures that we are, should think and do; and *fitting* is of course an evaluative notion." [35]

The point at the moment is not whether any of these evaluations qualify as definite-action rules. (The prohibition of slavery may meet the tests Crombie laid down in the beginning, while respect for truth may have too elastic a meaning.) The point is, rather, to establish the fact that in addressing the question whether there may be definite-action rules to be found among practice-rules, Crombie now sets up formal tests for the rightfulness or wrongfulness of definite-actions or action-systems which, on his own showing, are at least not adequately formulated. He does write, when first introducing these tests, that the options are that there may be "rules that we deem it wise to uphold and conform to because we think that the overall consequences of such conformity are morally beneficial" and there may be "rules which we deem it, not wise, but necessary to uphold on the ground that the actions which they forbid are actions which are inherently

[33] *Ibid.*, p. 260.   [34] *Ibid.*, p. 255 (italics in original).   [35] *Ibid.*, p. 256.

# Virtue, Principles, and Rules 111

wrong, and will be felt to be *objectionable* by any morally sensitive man." [36] Definite "action-rules" of unqualified universality can hardly be derived from considerations of the first sort, Crombie asserts, because it seems impossible to find some kind of direct consequence so objectionable that it could *never* be right to choose that consequence." Notice here the insertion of the restriction that the consequence be a "direct" one only, in contrast to "the *overall* consequences" in the statement of this general method of reasoning from consequences which is in the "logic" of practice-rules of a utilitarian sort. Here plainly Crombie has not simply failed to find definite-action rules to be a possibility afforded by practice-rules. Instead he has set such rules aside by the requirement that a given *direct* consequence must be found which by itself would be so objectionable that we would know from this alone that the action should never be done. That is to abandon the practice or the *rule*-utilitarian conception of rules.

As for the possibility that there may be rules which we deem it necessary to uphold on the ground that the actions they forbid are inherently wrong (which was at issue in the question of slavery), Crombie immediately proceeds to measure that possible "inherent wrongness" or "moral objectionableness" by either the direct consequence of such actions or the "frame of mind from which they would normally proceed" (or both). But slavery was judged to be a violation neither because of its consequences nor because of the frame of mind from which it proceeds, but because of what it *is* as an action-system or system of relations.

Therefore I do not see how we can take with uttermost seriousness Crombie's statement in the end that "to say that *any* action of *some kind* is *wrong*" (which is a nice statement of what a definite enough defined-action rule would be) is "to say something which is not primarily about the action considered as a member of some definite kind." [37] And why not? Because Crombie is predisposed (which is to say prejudiced) to regard any statement about an action considered as a member of some definite kind as necessarily only a *neutral* definite action *description*. Also because (in the immediately preceding sentence) he has arbitrarily limited the meaning of offense-terms or "what inherent wrongness might be thought to consist in" to "the badness of what the action directly brings about" and "the badness of what the action comes from." [38] There may be "generalizations" about the good or evil that any action is likely to produce, or about "the state of mind" from which it is likely to result; but "it hardly seems

[36] *Ibid.*, p. 257.   [37] *Ibid.*, p. 260 (italics added).   [38] *Loc. cit.*

reasonable to expect such generalizations to hold universally." [39] This may be granted Crombie—always with the reservation that by limiting "results" to *direct* consequences alone, not considering the over-all and the indirect consequences and not pressing the point about likelihood of human error in departing from some rule or principle sustained by men's moral experience generally, Crombie has thrown roadblocks in the way of his own employment of the rule-utilitarian sort of practice-rules. Still the badness of what an action brings about or of the state of mind from which it comes was not all that Crombie had to say about the inherent wrongness of action-systems such as slavery.

I conclude, therefore, that there is no rational moral argument that can exclude the possibility that there are exceptionless moral rules, in some moral matters. The case for this seems especially strong in regard to *rules of practice,* whether these are warranted by *agapeic* or rule-utilitarian or other normative appeals. But not only so, as we shall see in the final section of this chapter where we take up the question of the exception in regard to person-centered (not practice-oriented) ways of being faithful to fellow man. There we will be discussing "canons of loyalty," and not practice-rules only. But first we must take up the question whether or not in the philosophical sense of an "exception" there must always be possible future further justifiable exceptions to any principle or moral rule.

In any case we have not yet apprehended *the exception,* if that means there must necessarily be one. We have not yet been shown that there can be no exceptionless principles or rules, or that an exception is logically possible or morally required in regard to every human moral concern. Ours is a more serious plight than that of Euthyphro in his attempt to get the general idea of "piety." When we try to comprehend the "general idea" of a "justifiable exception," "somehow or other our arguments, on whatever ground we rest them, seem to turn round and walk away from us."

## III. *Exceptions in Our Future*

For completeness' sake, there is a final possibility that should be brought under scrutiny. Having in mind the "general idea" of a justifiable exception which philosophers generally employ, someone may say that every principle or moral rule, however firmly established, may for good reason which the future will bring forth have further

---

[39] *Ibid.,* p. 261.

## Virtue, Principles, and Rules

possible significant qualifications or exceptions. Whether there must be these exceptions in our future in regard to every sort of moral claim or relation is the question now to be raised. That would seem to be a sort of exception any Socrates should allow Euthyphro to turn around and walk away with—provided not too much is claimed for it. There may even be very good moral reasons why some or most principles and moral rules should be held open to future further possible exceptions in this sense. Our question is only whether this must always be so, in every moral matter. In conceding (indeed, insisting on) the possibility of future further possible justifiable exceptions, I shall argue that (1) there may be ethical counterarguments and other good reasons for holding principles or moral rules significantly closed, and (2) that one should accent the improbability and near inconceivability of such further expansion in the case of a number of moral rules ("Never torture your wife while giving her to believe you hate her"). These are the two provisos Euthyphro must grant if he is going to take away that general idea of a justifiable exception.

In taking up this question we need to remind ourselves how utterly different the "exception" now under consideration is from the "exception" which has lately gained a great reputation for agility in the dance of the theologians, for its penetrating power among advisers to youth, and for its cash rewards to those who point to it and praise it in the popular press.

We left *that* exception behind long, long ago in this chapter. Or, rather, we found it to be lacking in substantive reality, like the man who wasn't there or the smile on no Cheshire cat. This was simply the airy notion of an exception that can be located only at the point where someone ceases to think in ethical terms and instead attaches at that point a sweeping exception-generating stipulation. One is not apt to get written up in *Playboy* or to publish in the *Ladies' Home Journal* by becoming a proponent of the universalizability of the kind of exception we have now traced down, i.e. a proponent of good reasons for future further sorts of right-making qualifications.

However, this quite new form of the question is before us: Is it possible that *some* moral principles or rules are "exceptionless" in the sense that no further significant right-making *sorts* are expected, no further *specifying* exemptions, qualifications, reversing refinements, explanations, stipulations? Why may not *any* moral principles or moral rules be significantly closed? Must we *always* in *every* moral matter expect further exception-*species* to put in their appearance?

In the nature of the case it would be impossible to prove a universal negative proposition to the effect that there *can* be *no* principles or rules to which there are no further specifying exceptions. It is not impossible, it is logically conceivable that there might be some principles or rules governing some moral matters or relations of which it could be said that any differentiating features not yet taken into account would be morally irrelevant, or not sufficiently relevant to call for a further *morally significant* discrimination of right from wrong.

Still there might be good moral reasons in support of the judgment that in any moral matter the relevant principles and rules ought to be held open to further specification or qualification. If this is so—and I do not doubt that it is in a great many moral matters—there may also be moral counterarguments. We need not deny that ordinarily this is how ethical reasoning should proceed, by admitting further admissible permissions or requirements. Still, this rule-governing-rule or stipulation may itself be subject to further morally relevant qualification. There may be exceptions to be written into that rule when expressing or exhibiting its meaning for a given moral relation. We might begin with the rule-governing-rule that "There ought to be no moral principle or rule that is not open to further significant qualification" and then be morally impelled to add to this the further qualification, ". . . unless in a given grave moral matter one is more liable to make a mistake by adopting the policy of being always open to morally significant, future permissions than by acting in accord with the extant principles and specifications based as these are on quite important features of the moral relation in question." Or one might add: ". . . unless the direct and indirect effects of openness to further exceptions that might have some warrant would tend seriously to impair the social observance of an extant important moral practice."

This is only to suggest that if in many moral matters it holds true that morally we should not act from a conviction that ethical principles have in them all admissible moral qualifications, this may not always be the case. If we begin with the general claim that no rules can contain or be based on all the morally significant specifications, then perhaps this openness of all rules to further revision ought not itself to be held to be exceptionless for all future time. In some moral matters, is not that rule-governing-rule open to further admissible qualification? Two such exempting qualifications have just been proposed, stating in specific terms the warrants or the relevant and significant features that might be adduced for saying that some principle or moral rule *ought* to be regarded as closed to further

## Virtue, Principles, and Rules

morally significant alteration. These, then, are rule-*strengthening* or practice-*upholding* rules; and it is difficult to see how it could be established that these are "classes without any members," or that no known *faithfulness*-requirement pertaining to any moral relation fits these specifications.

On the question whether all principles and moral rules should be or should not be open to morally significant additional exceptional classes, a discriminating judgment is to be commended. Some should be, some should not be, depending on the moral matter or moral relation or ethical principle in question. A great many moral rules may be such that exceptions are always additionally possible; some might be significantly closed.

G. E. Moore formulated the above rule-strengthening rules in a quite rigorous, *status quo* fashion:

> . . . With regard to any rule which is generally useful, we may assert that it ought *always* to be observed, not on the ground that in *every* particular case it will be useful, but on the ground that in *any* particular case the probability of its being so is greater than that of our being likely to decide rightly that we have before us an instance of its disutility. In short, though we may be sure that there are cases where the rule should be broken, we can never know which these cases are, and ought, therefore, never to break it. . . . The individual can therefore be confidently recommended *always* to conform to rules which are both generally useful and generally practiced. . . .[40]

Moore even says that the utility of abstinence on the part of a single individual from certain kinds of theft, in a society where these kinds of theft are the common rule, "becomes exceedingly doubtful."

No such presumption of probable rightness should be attached to any rule or *de facto* practice, nor should a generalized ignorance be attributed to men in that they can *never* know when generally useful rules should be broken. Let this be clearly understood. The rule-assuring warrants stated in the text above in no sense do this. They are, rather, morally relevant counterarguments based on some feature in the moral matter itself or in faithfulness-claims, which in some moral matters or relations could outweigh the moral reasons that can correctly be adduced for holding moral rules open to future significant revision.

One reason Moore invoked, namely, that "our judgment will

---

[40] *Principia Ethica* (Cambridge, Eng.: Cambridge University Press, 1929), pp. 163–164.

generally be biassed by the fact that we strongly desire one of the results which we hope to attain by breaking the rule," [41] is surely often a stronger consideration than any appeal to "general ignorance" to prove that any and every claim to an exception has in it greater probability of error than there is probability that observance of a generally useful social practice will lead to the right individual act. Our strong desire for one of the results which we hope to attain is, I judge, depending on the content of morality or the moral matter in question, a stronger rule-strengthening consideration than Marcus Singer believes it is.[42] To assume otherwise would be to assume that a person has an equal power to sustain good moral reasoning and to make the proper choice in every one of his sorts of desires for one of the results of making for his action an exception. That would not be to take human nature into account. It would replace Moore's generalized ignorance by a generalized rationality.

The proposed rule-assuring rules have in them only the wisdom that led Aristotle to say that in the practice of virtue a man should in the case of one sort of human appetite or fear lean more to the side of the "excess," in another he will lean more to the side of the "defect," in order to locate the "mean" of right conduct. In other words, he will lean against what he can know to be the force of specific human desires or fears biasing him and most or all men one way, and not in another.

I will give only one illustration. Suppose it can be argued that, because of the claims of the persons upon one another and because of the gravely serious responsibility to see that all children are born to parents when they can be cared for, our moral rule should be *premarital chastity*. Then suppose it is said that not every case of premarital intercourse can itself be shown to be inherently uncaring, really damaging to persons; that this moral rule ought not to be held to have already written into it all possible feature-relevant exceptions; that we ought to be open at least to future sorts of situations in which for unforseen but conceivable reasons premarital intercourse might be said to be responsible—in which case it would then be said that *anyone* considering the question in situations having the same morally relevant features could responsibly do the same. In the case of *this* moral relation, the counterarguments would be as follows: Human sexuality has deep connections with human self-assurance or

[41] *Ibid.*, p. 162.
[42] *Generalization in Ethics* (New York: Alfred A. Knopf, 1961), pp. 130–133, especially p. 130, n. 6.

# Virtue, Principles, and Rules

lack of assurance. A young man or young woman should know that there is very great likelihood that, in the midst of the sincerity of their loves, deeply felt needs and weaknesses may very likely bias them toward one of the results of justifying an exception. These self-needs may weaken their sensitivity to or may even obliterate from view many of the faithfulness-claims upon one another which they wish to acknowledge and do not *mean* to renounce. Indeed, they may only be unknowingly conducting an emotional *blitz* on one another, the man on the woman's love or the woman, perhaps more subtly, proving herself. In particular, it is very, very unlikely that they could have adequately considered their awesome responsibility for an unborn child—not enough to know that this faithfulness-claim upon men and women ought not to be thrown into a probability-calculus, however minimal the "chances." Such a couple might ask whether, biased as they are toward one result of making an exception from the rule prescribing premarital chastity, whether they can likely estimate whether among the direct effects of their own present action there may not be carry-over into later *marital* infidelity which they do not mean to endorse; and finally, whether, because of understandable bias one way, they can have given proper weight to the destructive indirect effects of their action upon the general *practice* of such exceptions and upon marriage as a whole, which, we are supposing, they still mean to cherish.[43]

Thus, it cannot be denied that there may be good reasons for the rule-governing-rule that principles and moral rules should be regarded as open to further morally important revision. On the other hand, there may be good reason for saying, in some moral matters, that such a rule-governing-rule should be replaced by a

---

[43] In a symposium of articles in the *New York State Journal of Medicine* (reported in the *New York Times,* July 15, 1967), Dr. Graham B. Blaine, chief of psychiatry at Harvard University Health Services, states that one out of eighteen babies born in the United States today is born out of wedlock, despite widespread use of contraceptives, and that "the correlation between premarital intercourse and post-marital affairs at least suggests that one influences the other." He opposed the trend toward greater promiscuity. In seeming to disapprove of the decline in the influence of the Church's and other moral teachings which, he said, accounts in part for the rise of these evils, Dr. Blaine would seem to be offering not a reason why every case of premarital intercourse is necessarily wrong but reasons for saying that there is grave likelihood that it may be; and that for this reason the practice of premarital chastity should be upheld by anyone. This would then be an instance of the validity in this case of the counterarguments to holding all moral rules open to present or future further possible justifiable exceptions.

rule-strengthening one. In this as in other moral concerns a discriminating judgment is the better one. We ought not to rule out the possibility that there are exceptionless moral rules which, because of the significance of the faithfulness-claims in a given moral relation and because of the propensities of human nature in that matter, ought in the time-span of our moral lives, and in civilized life if we are not to bring the whole house down, to be regarded as rules of the highest human loyalty that should not be expected to be subject to significant future revision. This may be the only wise way, either in ourselves or in social practices, to hit the "mean" of excellence in the face of forseeable human propensities one way or another. If any part of the function of imperative moral rules is to "sit on ourselves" lest we make false exceptions in our favor,[44] it is difficult to see how that virtue in them, enabling us to do the right, could be maintained if it is said that every rule concerning any moral matter must on principle be open to further exceptions. It is not enough that this means "for good reason." That would only replace G. E. Moore's assumption of "general ignorance" in support of received practices by an assumption of general rationality. The latter is a needed premise, if it is to be argued that in every moral matter men should always expect the good they know to be always open to morally significant alteration.

Man's competence to know the good is, of course, not to be denied. Our capacity to reason morally is the only means by which we can, from whatever ultimate norm, articulate ethical principles or order the moral life, or improve our practices. But we can also grasp the fact there is another law in our members, and we can anticipate the consequences of this even in metaethics (in rule-strengthening rules of moral reasoning that allow this to be taken realistically into account). At least, this is a part of Christian theological *normative* metaethics—not only to call good the fidelities to be done but also to exhibit the fact that faithlessness in ourselves needs governing by ordinances ever to ensure that we keep covenant.

However, it should be said that the case for exceptions in our future is especially strong in all cases where *consequence*-features are overriding. Perhaps in regard to all *purely* societal *rules of practice,* or rule-utilitarian-rules, these should never be held closed against future further morally significant exceptions. This would hold open progressive refinements and future admissible alterations in the accepted practice, and hold open also the possibility that in certain sorts of cases unforseen consequences of the practice upon individual

---

[44] A. Boyce Gibson, in Ian T. Ramsey (ed.), *op. cit.,* p. 115.

# Virtue, Principles, and Rules

persons can be taken significantly into account as a reason for violating societal rules.

Still there is overlap and perhaps conflict between acknowledging the moral impact of consequences not now known and other bases of our present verdicts in social ethics. There are in any case grounds of our moral judgments concerning *fairness* and *justice* and concerning *faithfulness*-claims that are not decisively consequentialist in character. While the formal logic of good moral reasoning remains the same in all cases, we may have more moral matters or moral relations to think about than those that are governed by practice- or rule-utilitarian rules. While we can and may and must always think about the meaning of right and wrong in terms of the *sorts* of things that are right-making or wrong-making, it may be that this leads to different verdicts when we are thinking materially about behavior or practices that are primarily rooted in moral or in personal relations and not in generalized utility. It might even be that in some respects our quest for the justifiable exception would reach a different conclusion if we acknowledge that not all moral practices have only utilitarian warrant. A complete canvass of this matter would require us to investigate any difference there may be in this regard between the relevant *fairness*-features or *justice*-features of actions, situations and relations, and their *consequence*-features alone. Some verdicts as to fairness or justice might be now known to be never possibly dispensable by significant exceptions in our future, while moral matters that put judgments as to consequences really to work would require new stipulations or qualifications indicating the sort of thing that further experience justifies us in saying is right-making and in which anyone should do the same.

It would be difficult to demonstrate that all principles or moral rules in regard to *justice* and *fairness* or that every canon of loyalty among men ought to be expected to have *morally significant* exceptions in the future. To say this as a general policy governing all principles and rules in every moral matter would be to submit, even now, every moral judgment to imaginable future consequences. That would reduce every present claim to rebuttability by those consequences. In morality, the priorities may in some matters be quite the reverse.

This is of considerable importance in Christian theological ethics which marks off faithfulness-claims in the covenants of life with life as a moral matter to be given primary significance, both in actual conduct and in an ethical system. In fact, faithfulness-claims and canons of covenant-loyalty may be the profoundest way to understand all our concepts of fairness and justice. To the question of future possible further exceptions to canons of loyalty, Christianly viewed, we now turn.[45]

## IV. Canons of Loyalty

I shall first introduce at this point some fundamental considerations in regard to the enterprise of Christian ethics. Above and beyond the analysis of questions in *normative ethics,* Christian theological ethics is a "metaethics," and the Christian community in all ages is a standing "metaethical" community of discourse about substantive moral matters. By this is meant a *"normative* metaethics," of which Professor W. K. Frankena has written, in distinction from a simply descriptive, elucidatory or reportive type of metaethics.[46] The latter analyzes the meaning that "right," "good," and other ethical terms have in ordinary moral discourse, how they function in the or in *an* extant moral language. This attempts "to lay bare what we actually mean when we judge that something is good or right." [47] But behind every descriptive or elucidatory metaethics, Frankena contends, there is a *normative* metaethics, i.e., a proposal for how ethical terms *should* be used. This may be hidden from view, because the *normative* metaethics behind a number of elucidatory analyses of moral discourse is a *conservative* one, that is, a proposal that moral terms should continue to be used in the way and with the meaning described as being the case. It is only when someone or some community of men comes forward with a *revisionary* proposal, a reforming normative metaethics, that the distinction between normative and descriptive metaethics becomes quite evident.

The sharpness of this distinction itself may have to be qualified

---

[45] This would be to correct my *Deeds and Rules in Christian Ethics* (New York: Charles Scribner's Sons, 1967) in that I there allowed (pp. 137–142) that principles and rules expressive of the loyalty governing covenants such as marriage and promise-making, might be entirely comprehended as "rules of the game"-*practices.* We must now *distinguish significantly,* if not entirely separate, "canons of loyalty" from rules of practice having primary utilitarian justification. In fact, there is need for more elaboration than I will here undertake. There is need throughout our Christian ethical reflection to distinguish a merely *practice* conception of the promising-game or the marriage-game and all the other covenants of life with life in which men are engaged from a thoroughly *performative* conception of all these faithfulness-claims upon men.

[46] "On Saying the Ethical Thing," Presidential address delivered before the Sixty-fourth Annual Meeting of the Western Division of American Philosophical Association in Minneapolis, Minnesota, May 5–7, 1966. *Proceedings and Address of the American Philosophical Association, 1965–1966,* Vol. 39 (Yellow Springs, Ohio: Antioch Press, 1966), pp. 21–42.

[47] *Ibid.,* p. 22.

# Virtue, Principles, and Rules

when we remember that there are a plurality of universes of moral discourse. A descriptive account that attempts to lay bare what "we" actually mean when "we" judge that something is good and right may too readily be taken to be an account of what "men" mean when they judge that something is good and right, which has already the force of a *normative* metaethical statement, i.e., what men *should* mean. Among these normative metaethical communities is one that would *reduce* the meaning of ethical terms to nonmoral meanings, whether by shouting silence in a loud metaethical voice or by recommending that the terms continue to be used but henceforth with, for example, the meaning some science might give to them. ("An 'onlook which rejects onlooks,'" Donald Evans writes, "is perhaps what some people have called 'the scientific attitude.'"[48]) Most contemporary philosophers do not subscribe to such a normative metaethics.

Still, it is logically necessary for there to be a *normative* metaethics, and the issues this raises should be debated. We should not simply take an account of our actual use of language (its use in a given community, or cultural epoch) as a recommendation for the future. Frankena also argues that a good reason in support of a normative metaethics may be either a good *moral* reason or a good reason of some other sort. ". . . An inquiry into the meaning and logic of moral discourse may be normative without being moral. Normative judgments and proposals [in metaethics] are not necessarily moral."[49] The judgment, for example, that we should in normative metaethics presume that revisions are not to be advocated unless necessary (which goes to support our continuing to use ethical terms with the meaning they currently have) may not itself be a *moral* reason.

It is at this point that Frankena formulates the place in normative metaethics that Christian theological ethics faithful to its task must occupy. There are statements at the heart of any theological ethics that refer for the meaning of "good" or "right" to "the will of God" or to "how God brought us up out of the house of bondage" or "how God first loved us." In general, these religious acknowledgments or faith-commitments refer the "correlative performative force" of man's obligation to a "divine performance."[50] These statements are usually

---

[48] *The Language of Self-Involvement* (London: SCM Press, 1963), p. 254.
[49] Presidential address, *op. cit.*, p. 23.
[50] Donald Evans, *The Language of Self-Involvement*, p. 77: "[A] human utterance concerning this divine performative is a self-involving acknowledgment which has correlative performative force." These words will be invoked several times in the text below.

objected to in ordinary language analysis on the ground that one cannot derive an Ought from an Is. This reply takes classically the form of "the open question" argument. That is to say, the rejoinder will be in the case of any alleged theological ultimate, "But is 'the will of God' *good,* or that divine performative action *right-*making?" Frankena contends, and I think rightly, that the objector can only riposte a *like* normative metaethical statement: "surely this is not a desirable use of words," [51] or the meaning that should be *assigned* the terms "good" or "right" or "obligatory." It is perfectly proper for a normative metaethics (i.e., Christian theological ethics) to appeal to reasons that are not themselves intrinsically moral (that do not themselves fall within the system of Christian normative ethics, nor are drawn from *another* normative metaethics with its *prescriptions* as to how moral terms must mean and be used). It may indeed be perfectly proper for someone or some community of men to assert that all our going moral language is "too poor to say the ethical or normative thing." [52] There is no need for us—either in normative ethics or in normative metaethics—to be "frightened out of our wits by the relativists, subjectivists, and sceptics" [53] when we are only explaining the reasons we affirm to be good ones. Frankena concludes (in language that itself shows, verbally at least, the influence of Christianity functioning as a standing metaethical community going beyond laying bare the meaning of ordinary morality and undertaking to affect what men shall mean by "good," etc.): ". . . Perhaps we may now roll away the stone from before the tomb in which naturalism [and also what is called "super-naturalism"] has lain ever since that day when the earth trembled under the naturalistic fallacy and the rocks were rent by the open question." [54] Those objections to Christian theological ethics (even in the mind of a philosopher who himself does not undertake our task) fall before the simple realization that "No metaethical Ought can logically be derived from any metaethical Is alone." [55] It is perfectly proper for the Christian Church throughout history to have proposed the meanings it intends to assign to certain primary ethical terms, and to have tried to influence men to come and do likewise, on grounds not all of which are already intrinsically moral, i.e., falling within a Christian system of ethics or borrowed from some other.

So much is at stake in saying that Our Father in Heaven is the

[51] Presidential address, *op. cit.,* p. 25.
[52] *Ibid.,* p. 30.   [53] *Ibid.,* p. 32.   [54] *Ibid.,* p. 33.   [55] *Ibid.,* p. 25.

## Virtue, Principles, and Rules 123

Name from whom the meaning of all performatives (like all fatherhood) in heaven or in earth is taken. This I suppose can be more simply stated by saying that Christian ethics makes ultimate appeal to a divine performance, making proto-typical use of something that is also said in the analysis of human performatives, namely, that it is not only one's own committing action that creates an obligation; one can also be put under obligation to someone by *their* conduct rather than one's own,[56] as when a beggar asks us for help or in claims upon our hospitality or in the so-called "Good Samaritan" principle in our law. This does not mean that God is good because He is a father; but that from the measure of His steadfastness we know something of the meaning to assign to "good" fatherhood. It does not mean that God's performative actions are to be acknowledged because they have the quality we know from men's committals, but rather that from the nature of His self-involvement with us in our history we know something of the self-involvement men should display in their elected and their nonelected covenants of life with life. If, as Helen Oppenheimer writes, "to marry, to become a parent, to make friends, is to put oneself morally into a distinct situation," then ". . . *a fortiori*, to be made God's children by adoption and grace can be understood as a change of status capable of transforming one's elementary categories." [57]

When we go about these demonstrations that Christian ethics is a *eucharistic* ethics,[58] that ours is an ethics of gratitude, that we should joyfully abide by God's ordinances, forgiving as we have been forgiven, etc., it is not at all necessary to prove first by a general or autonomous ethical investigation the correctness of such normative ethical statements as that we should be thankful to all who benefit us or that we should forgive because others have forgiven us, or that one should obey God's ordinances because it is "right" to do so or that God's will is "good" according to tests for this that have arisen in some other community of discourse or according to an elucidatory metaethics that describes the meanings and logic and what men mean by good in some other "ordinary language." This is not necessary even though there are good reasons for some or many of these statements in a good many systems of normative ethics. It is not necessary because all these are statements of *normative* Christian metaethics. They express

---

[56] John Lemmon, "Moral Dilemmas," in Ian T. Ramsey (ed.), *op. cit.,* p. 264.
[57] "Moral Choice and Divine Authority," in Ian T. Ramsey (ed.), *op. cit.,* p. 231.
[58] Joseph Fletcher, *Situation Ethics,* p. 156.

what we mean and are resolved to mean by the right and the good among men. Christianity proposes to inculcate an entire "symbolic form," "type of discourse," or "realm of meaning." [59]

Whether this means a *revisionist* or a *conservative* normative metaethics can scarcely be decided. It is conservative in the sense that there is this standing metaethical community whose moral discourse can simply be elucidated or described in these terms, plus the recommendation that these moral meanings and this logic of ethics continue to be fostered and used. It is *revisionist* in the sense that, amid the pluralism of discourse about ethics, this understanding of the elements of ethics would cut athwart many an all-too-ordinary language or rival normative metaethics—so much so that the Christian language and logic of ethics is hardly understandable today to a good many notable intelligences, including some who are by denomination "Christian."

In any case, we mean and should mean in Christian ethics to say that there are correlative performative understandings of moral acts, relations and situations that arise from our faith-commitment or acknowledgment of God's performatives and his mandates. This we mean to say in some sense also of all men and their good always. This we express when we say "I look on all men as brothers whom God made to be one" or "I look on each man as a brother for whom Christ died." [60] In these primary "norms" which are controlling in a Christian ethical system there is appeal to the performative force of God's "Verdictives"; and then there follows for the Christian ethicist the task of living the meaning of this in all his rational reflection, and of elaborating and deepening every one of its requirements. This, I suppose, is not far from Frankena's meaning when he speaks of adopting an "appropriate mode of expressing oneself when one is taking a conative point of view and meaning to be rational within it"; or when he writes that in making a normative ethical judgment, we mean to suggest "that there are good reasons for a certain action or attitude, and we usually have in mind more or less clearly a certain type of reason, that is, we are taking a certain point of view and claiming that one who is rational from that point of view would or would not have that attitude or perform that action." [61]

---

[59] Cf. W. K. Frankena, Presidential address, *op. cit.*, p. 26.

[60] Cf. Donald Evans, *The Language of Self-Involvement,* p. 129; and the entire section on "Onlooks," pp. 124 ff.

[61] W. K. Frankena, Presidential address, *op. cit.*, pp. 39, 37. As for the claim that, among the rivalry of *normative* metaethics, the Christian outlook and consequent ethical onlook may in some sense be true for all men, the reader might

If one *begins* in Christian *normative ethics* with some such statement as "Look on all men as brothers for whom Christ died" or "Be grateful to the Lord who made us His covenant people," and if all moral reasoning is then reasoning from these "premises," then the ultimate warrant of them must be an appeal to what the Lord of heaven and earth is believed to have been doing and to be doing in enacting and establishing His covenant with us and all mankind, in all the estates and orders and relations of life to which we have been called. These performative actions, the final warrant of all our ethics, are celebrated in the action and worship of the Christian community through all ages. This is what makes it a standing normative metaethical community. We propose to show our children's children (if not our children) what should be the meaning of "righteousness" and "faithfulness" among men.

It is now time for us to resume our chase of the "exception"—so elusive because curiously called "justifiable." The trail may now be a little cold. Still, in the meantime we have acquired some new resources for criminal investigation that may enable us to close the file on this case.

If it is true that in Christian ethics we are mainly concerned about the requirements of loyalty to covenants among men, about the meaning of God's ordinances and mandates, about the estates and moral relations among men acknowledged to follow from His governing and righteous will, about steadfastness and faithfulness, then it follows that in Christian ethics we can and may and must be enormously disinterested in any exception, or openness to exceptions, that would have to be justified primarily by future consequence-features, and indeed, consequences imagined in extreme, fictitious cases. Instead, in the Christian life we are driven deeper and deeper into the meaning of covenant obligations, to specify as aptly as possible the meaning of the faithfulness to other men required by the particular covenants or causes between us. The relevant moral features which this understanding of the moral law uncovers in every action, moral relation, or situation are primarily the claims and occasions of faithfulness. We are therefore driven ever deeper into the meaning of the bonds of life with life. The relevant moral features are not primarily *"exempting* condi-

---

ponder Frankena's remark on p. 41: "At any rate, so long as the case against the absolutist claim is not better established than it is, we may still make that claim; it may take some temerity, but it is not unreasonable. As for me and my house, therefore, we will continue to serve the Lord—or, as others may prefer to say, the Ideal Observer."

tions," and they are certainly not oriented mainly upon consequences. They are, rather, perceptions of claims upon us already aptly comprised in appropriate principles or canons expressive of specifiable loyalties. What we have to expect is further sensitivity to what the moral law so understood requires of us, driving us ever deeper into the meaning of the fidelities of life with fellow man and forming conscience and behavior in these terms.

The consequences of individual or of joint action are, of course, not unimportant; but what holds us together in the communications of life with life does not consist of ways to secure certain consequences. Bad consequences could rebut the justification for putting forth a certain action, but in the first place it is the criteria governing our involvements with other men, it is what makes for fidelity, which permits or calls for actions that embody righteousness in the relations of man to man and which define the essence of practices that are genuinely human.

One cannot, of course, deny that the *consequence*-features of acts, relations, and situations are morally relevant in articulating what we Christians are required to do, but the *faithfulness*-exhibiting features of these same acts, relations, and situations are the primary considerations to be taken into account in determining the patterns of behavior that are justifiable. There is moral behavior whose justification is not dependent on consequences, even if not independent of consequences. One has to unpack the relation between the morally relevant consequence-features and the morally relevant faithfulness-claims. This is no simple matter. Nevertheless it is enough to establish a presumption that good Christian ethical reasoning may not lead us always in every moral matter in the direction of the conclusion that there is nothing we know about the Christian moral life that *ought* not to be open to future *further* morally significant revision—especially not if the appeal is merely to consequences made to seem overriding in extreme examples.

This is a conclusion that can and must be drawn were it only the case that moral practices have, all of them, *both* a consequence justification *and* a performative or a faithfulness justification. If even the practice conception of promise-making or of marriage has also the meaning of personal self-commitment, if indeed a performative conception of the promise-practice or of marriage is a more correct way to understand these relations, if fairness and justice have independent weight in moral judgments, and if finally some of the *practices* into which we are born are also covenants into which we are called and in which we are called to be true, then surely we may have

## Virtue, Principles, and Rules

discerned the meaning and the requirements of some of these particular relations that place faithfulness-claims upon us well enough to presume that there *ought* not to be further morally significant, universalizable exceptions that could in principle be written into the principles or moral rules governing our moral behavior in these particular regards. These will be, if there are any, moral relations in which faithfulness-claims have by far the greater weight. To open every canon of loyalty to morally significant further qualification by consequences would be to place fidelity in peril.

This does not mean that further experience counts for nothing. It means instead that further experience could only disclose deeper meanings as to how faithfulness within these relations should shape our behavior and our very *being* in them, our being married, for example, or provide us new occasions for caring for childhood within exceptionless limits we now know to specify what should never be done to children. Within a proper Christian ethics it will be quite impossible to show that every principle or moral rule must always be such that by them we are never in any moral matter committed to refraining from further "exceptional" qualifications of any significance.

We need not strain our far-fetching imaginations in manufacturing future possible exceptions to rules such as that one should never murder his wife while giving her to believe that he loves her, or the prohibition of rape. One needs a little wisdom, of course, in order to know how to apply these moral rules. One would have to know something of the meaning of "murder" and "wife" and "love" and "giving her to believe," and the meaning of "forced sexual intercourse." Future experience may provide us deeper insight into the faithfulness claimed of us by a holy awe in regard to human life, by more particularly the duty in being a husband; or we may gain a fuller realization of the heinousness of unwilling sexual intercourse because we come to see more clearly the obligations created in relation to all men by a woman-being who, simply by being, claims at least this faithfulness of us.

These are surely exceptionless moral rules in the sense that the moral presumption should be that no future eventuality and none of the consequence-features of future situations are going to require morally significant revision of them. Someone may say at this point (seizing the less articulated one of these rules), *suppose* that as an inmate of a concentration camp you are *commanded* by a sadistic camp guard *to rape* a woman inmate, under the threat that unless you do so he will kill *her* (not you!), would not this be a case of "justifiable rape," and at long last our "justifiable exception"? If this objection is made, the reply surely should be in kind: that anyone doing such a thing to save another's life would be obliged at least to whisper in the woman's ear or otherwise signal what he is really doing, thus transforming his action into a case of willing sexual intercourse on the woman's part. Such a reply, of course, opens other questions; but this is a fairly good answer to the proposal that there are good moral reasons for holding the prohibition against rape open to future morally significant qualification by "exceptions" that might have yet to be made in which we would say any man ought to do *the same.* Granting, let us suppose, that *this* right-making "exception" should be allowed for, how could it be shown that not even *then* and not ever can we get to know the meaning of freedom in the exercise of a person's sexuality, and the claims upon us in this regard, well enough to conclude that we now are committed to refrain hereafter from future morally significant qualifications?

It is a better answer, however, to reply as does J. G. Milhaven, S.J.: "Even when extreme exceptions are conceivable, no sane man decides his actions . . . on the basis of the remotely possible exception" (see below p. 229). Therefore some moral rules, in their actual bearing on conduct, are significantly closed. This is important to note, because it is not the logical impossibility of exceptionless rules that is generally asserted, but some moral inappropriateness attaching to *holding* any moral rules to be completed in all their morally significant respects.

Insofar as consequence-features are the ones that are the morally relevant considerations, we might agree, indeed, with Jonathan Bennett that "in proportion as a situation gives real work to the rider '. . . whatever the consequences of not doing so,' in proportion as it puts pressure on this rider, in proportion as the 'consequences of not doing so' give some moral reason for doing so" [62]—to that extent moral principles and rules should always be open to future further significant revision. But when, as now in the argument, the substantive moral considerations are *faithfulness*-claims upon our performances, the presumption must fall on the other side. At least this would have to be the presumption in Christian ethics, from seeing with Christ into the heart of man and into our own hearts and into the meaning of the fidelity and righteousness to be practiced so far as may be in particular covenants. The burden of proof would have to be upon anyone who said that Christians ought always to hold the principles

---

[62] "Whatever the Consequences," in *Analysis* (January, 1966), p. 102.

# Virtue, Principles, and Rules

and specific requirements of being faithful to another in every moral matter and every moral bond of life with life open to further morally significant "exception." To say otherwise, and especially to rest the case against the possibility of exceptionless moral rules on supposable future consequences would be, in giving that answer to this single question, to shift the whole foundation of Christian ethics from covenants and promises to consequences. Moral practices would in their morally significant revision be made virtually dependent on consequences. To say only that obligations are not independent of consequences, is to say at once that we can possibly know enough about the meaning of the "right" to be done among men, at least in some matters, to know that presently unforseeable consequences are not going to qualify in morally significant respects the meaning of the faithfulness we now apprehend.

In medical ethics there is a rule governing experimentation involving human subjects that this should be done only when an informed consent has been secured. There are enormous problems, of course, in knowing how to subsume cases under this moral regulation expressive of the meaning of medical *care*. What is and what is not a mature or informed consent is a preciously subtle thing to determine. Then there are questions about how to apply this rule arising from those sorts of medical research in which the patient's knowing too much may alter the findings sought, and there is debate about whether the use of prisoners in medical experimentation or paying the participants or using one's own medical students would not put them under too much duress for them to be said to consent even if fully informed. Despite these ambiguities, however, in this matter we are dealing with an obligation in a relation and a practice in which men are committed to men in definable respects. The *faithfulness*-claims which every man, simply by being a man, places upon the researcher are the morally relevant considerations. This is the ground of this rule of medical practice, though obviously the practice has also its consequence-features.

Indeed, precisely because there are these unknown future consequences and precisely because the results of the experimentation may be believed to be so important as to be overriding, this rule governing medical experimentation upon human beings is needed to ensure that for the sake of those consequences no man shall be degraded and treated as a thing or an animal in order that good may come of it. These would in fact be precisely the morally relevant considerations sufficient to bring into play those rule-strengthening rules we dealt with in the previous section, *even if* we were not quite sure that every particular case of medical experimentation using human subjects without their informed consent would in itself always be inherently wrong. In this age of research medicine it is not only that medical benefits are attained only by research but also that a man rises to the top in medicine by the success and significance of his research. The likelihood that a researcher would make a mistake in departing from a generally valuable rule of medical practice because he is biased toward one result of justifying an exception is exceedingly great; in such a seriously important moral matter, this could rebut a policy of being open to future possible exceptions to this canon of medical ethics. Surely we would say, however, on grounds of the faithfulness-claims alone, that future experience will provide no morally significant exception to the requirement of an informed consent, although doubtless we may learn a great deal more about the meaning of this particular canon of loyalty, and how to apply it in new situations with greater sensitivity and refinement—or we may learn more and more how to practice violations of it.[63]

From that rule of medical practice it follows that children (who cannot give a mature or fully informed consent) should not be made the subjects of perilous medical experimentation unless, other remedies having failed to relieve a child's grave illness, it is reasonable to believe that the administration of a drug as yet untested or insufficiently tested on human beings or the performance of an untried operation may further *the child's own recovery*. Now, that is not a

[63] Jonathan Bennett mounts an impressive argument against the verdict of the strictest traditional moral theology that, in obstetrical cases, the mother should be "allowed to die" rather than her life saved by direcly killing her unborn child ("Whatever the Consequences," in *Analysis* [January, 1966], pp. 83–102). Yet in the course of this he observes: " 'Is the woman a potential murderess or the child a mongol?'—the answers are probably unobtainable. 'In what way would the woman's death represent a real loss to others?'—the answer, even if discoverable, could be so complex as to elude a manageable rule. . . . 'Would the child, if delivered alive, be especially helpful to students of hydrocephalus?'— asking that would be the first step on a downward path: by allowing one woman to die partly because her child will be medically interesting if alive, even an uncorrupt man may ease the way towards allowing some other woman to die because *she* will be medically interesting when dead" (p. 100). I should say that these observations give independent place to canons of loyalty to fellow humanity; and that Bennett's other argument was concerning what *is* the relevant canon of loyalty and what *does* fidelity to two lives in conflict require in obstetrical cases. His argument did not crucially depend on consequences other than those marked out by the faithfulness-claim upon us to save life rather than allow to die. This removed from decisive consideration the question whether the woman was going to prove to be a murderess. (See my "The Sanctity of Life— in the First of It," in the *Dublin Review* [Spring, 1967], especially pp. 13–17.)

very elaborate moral rule governing medical practice in the matter of experiments involving human subjects; and it is a good example of a specification of the claims childhood places upon medical care and research. Again, one has to be a prudent man (which does not mean an overcautious or scrupulous man) in order to know how to care for child patients in this way. The degree of possible relation to the child's own recovery would have to be known, and this undeniably may be proportioned to a calculation of the likelihood of the benefits that could flow from the experiment for many other children. Still the limits this rule imposes on practice are essentially clear: where there is *no* possible relation to the child's own recovery, a child is not to be made a mere object of medical experimentation for the sake of supposable good to come. The child is to be tended in his dying, he constructively not being able to donate his dying to be studied and worked upon for the advancement of medicine. Again, future experience may tell us more about the meaning of this particular rule expressive of loyalty to a human child in its dying, and we may learn a great deal more about how to apply it in new situations with greater sensitivity and refinement—or we may learn more and more how to practice violations of it. But we are committed to refrain from morally significant exceptions to this rule defining impermissible medical experimentation upon children.

Notice that to say this is not to invoke any "thin edge of the wedge" argument. It is not to say that to begin to use children in medical experimentation having no relation to their own possible recovery will wind up in the barbarism of the Nazi experiments on human beings. The wedge-argument is, however, a good reason, a good rule-strengthening-rule, even if it be not in itself a good *moral* reason. It is too often carelessly dismissed as men go about finding justifiable exceptions to moral practices. But this need *not* be invoked here, or not alone. The argument is rather that to begin to experiment on children in ways that are not related to *them* as subjects is already a sanitized form of barbarism; it already removes them from view and pays no attention to the faithfulness-claim which a child, simply by being a sick or dying child, places upon us and upon medical care. We should expect no morally significant exceptions to this canon of faithfulness to the child. To expect future justifiable exceptions is, in some sense, already to have forgotten the child.

In the criminal law and the administration of justice we say that there are "cruel and unusual" forms of punishment that ought never to be used upon any man—no matter how much deterrence of crime may follow from it. The word "unusual" may refer to purely conventional understandings, but the word "cruel" refers to more substantively moral matters. Where to place "whipping" may be uncertain. It is now unusual. It may also be cruelly degrading to a human being. Our belief, with all our contemporaries, that it is, may, however, be mistaken. That sort of punishment may be respectful of the manhood of an offender as much as any other form of punishment. The prohibition of whipping may not be an exceptionless rule governing the administration of justice. But what are we to say of castration as a form of punishment? If it is said that, given certain (false) findings of fact about gross sex-offenders, castration might be legitimated as a punishment, or as a condition of release from incarceration, what of castration as a purely punitive measure for other than sexual offenses? Or as a threat or torture? Or sterilization required of women on relief, or conditioning their continuing to receive welfare assistance for their dependent children? Are there here no exceptionless moral rules? Does not civilized life, rather, proceed by the identification of those cruel and inhumane punishments that no unmentioned consequences in the administration of justice could justify? These questions, I judge, are rhetorical ones having an obvious answer that cannot be set aside by the fabrication of remote conceivable cases claiming warrant by consequences alone. That would be to forget the claims of humanity as such; it would be to deny the primacy of that sacredness in the temporal order who is a man although a criminal or on relief, and the respect due to be given him as a fellow man and as a creature called with us into being by God's performative acts, or as a brother for whom Christ also died.

If in the encounters between the political communities of mankind there is to be and sometimes there should be that barely human activity that bears the name of "war," there are two moral principles governing this activity. These are rules of the practice of warfare, the principle of discrimination and the principle of proportionately lesser evil. The latter refers to the consequence-aspect of the practice of war, while the former states the moral rule exhibiting the fact that even in war men are men and brothers under God's ordinances and not fighters only or all fighters. The principle of discrimination states what is never permissible (as have our foregoing illustrations). One has only to get to know the meaning of this, and how to apply it to concrete conditions of warfare, in order to know that there are no justifiable exceptions to it, that only violations are possible—when men conduct war on the supposition that its objective may legitimately include the direct intention to kill a fellow human being and not only to incapacitate or stop him as a combatant and when they suppose it ever to be legitimate to direct acts of war upon populations or to "aim indiscriminately." There is a weighty burden of proof on anyone who says that in regard to the principle of discrimination as a moral rule of warfare this should be held open to future possible exceptions that may provide us reason in consequences for saying that any man in such-and-such a war situation should do the same. The present writer has yet to hear even a fabricated, remote case that is at all persuasive.

It should be noted also in this illustration, as in the foregoing, that it is incorrect to say that the defender of exceptionless rules is the one who places collective or societal values first, and is insufficiently compassionate or open to exceptional action that may take the individual's good more into account. The reverse is the case. It is the defender of exceptionless rules who would build a floor under the individual fellow man by minimum faithfulness-rules or canons of loyalty to him that are unexceptionable, while it is the proponent of future possible exceptions who may be placing societal and gross consequence-values uppermost.

It must be said, of course, that anyone who proceeds in this way to elaborate an understanding of "correlative performative obligations," to which we Christians are committed in and by our acknowledgment of the "divine performatives," will make and must and does make certain assumptions concerning the moral universe and this our history which God governs. The primary assumption or conviction is that the *ultimate* consequences cannot be such as to render his performance of fidelity obligations *wrong*. This is, I suppose, a sort of Kantian "postulate" which we Christians make when spelling out in thought and life the meaning of fidelity in all covenants. It is a postulate (not a mere supposition) that the grain of things cannot ultimately prove unsupportive of the doing of our fidelities under the moral constitution God makes known in His word-deeds toward us. But that is far and away different from supposing that the final worldly consequences of faithful deeds will show the success of the good (or that from taking account of that, one gets to know the meaning of the right and the good in any morally significant measure). As Professor Lon Fuller has written in explicating the good he finds to be the good at the heart of our network of legal covenants, "communication is something more than a means of staying alive. It is a way of being alive." [64] It is the survival of the communication of one to another that is at stake in covenantal morality, and

---

[64] *Morality of Law* (New Haven: Yale University Press, 1965), pp. 185–186.

one has to get to know the meaning of this in order to know those substantive moral relations which to survive must shape the future and not be shaped indefinitely by an expectation of future further morally significant revision of our fidelities by consequences to come. (A man who subscribes to the latter viewpoint, I recognize, adopts a comparable "postulate," namely, that in the nature of the moral order this will not lead him to Auschwitz.)

We must now conclude that whether one searches for the justifiable exception which in the main was our pursuit in the earlier parts of this chapter from the point of view of societal practices which for the general good an individual should perform or, as in the present section, from the point of view of answering with our lives the faithfulness-claims placed upon us by a particular individual in a specifiable sort of moral relation, it cannot be shown that Christians or just men should never say Never.

Some Christian ethicist may affirm that the Bible provides us with a "divinely-approved content" of *agapé,* a "particularization of the moral life," "God's inscripturated will" of which Christ was the "original autograph." [65] Another may say, with Bernard Häring in the present volume, that marriage is a lifelong partnership, and then proceed to deal "pastorally" and with a considerable measure of the divine liberality, in the small coin of excusability, with the *wrongs* men and women do and continue to do in this our pilgrimage from faith through faithlessness to faithfulness (see below, pp. 217–218). A third may say that, because our covenants have all been touched by the divine covenant, the searching claims of Christian love cannot be withheld from being productive of commitments to present and future patterns of more than attitudinal behavior, and that the behavior required of us in some specifiable moral relations should *not* be held to be subject to further morally significant revision. A fourth may organize theological ethics in terms of ordinances, mandates, or the orders of creation, governance, and redemption. There is no way in the logic of moral reasoning or by adducing good moral reasons to place any of these positions *ab initio* under constraint never to say in regard to any moral matter that there are only principles or moral rules having possible exceptions to guide us. We ought, rather, to get on with the tasks of an ecumenical Christian ethics without any such proscription upon us in probing the meaning of every particular covenant of life with life. At least we ought not to call by the name

---

[65] Carl F. H. Henry, *Christian Personal Ethics* (Grand Rapids: Wm. B. Eerdmans, 1957).

of ecumenical or Christian a constraint that is demonstrably only one of the chief presuppositions of the present age, and moreover its most uncivilizing unexceptionable principle, namely, that there is nothing men should never do.

The case of the curious exception concerns only the matter of *prohibitiva*. This is only a small part of morality having to do with the permitted and the impermissible. There are far better parts. But it does not help to clarify the Christian moral life for ethicists to have *prohibitiva* in place in their own lives as Christian men which they have not taken up into rational reflection and found the good reason for in Christian ethics.[66] Nor does it advance the cause of ecumenical ethics for a Protestant ethicist to locate such *prohibitiva* in his own system of ethics while castigating a misunderstood traditional casuistry and rejecting out of hand the ethical reasoning of contemporary philosophers who serve the *sympathetic* Ideal Observer.

---

[66] The man who thought that Christian existence "suspends" the "ethical" said one of the best things about the range and depth of moral reason: "To become sober is: to come so close to oneself in one's understanding, one's knowing, that all one's understanding becomes action" (Søren Kierkegaard, *Judge for Yourselves!* in *For Self-Examination and Judge for Yourselves!* trans. Walter Lowrie [Princeton, N. J.: Princeton University Press, 1944], p. 130).

PART TWO

# Natural Law:
# A Reassessment of the Tradition

## 5

# *Absolute Norms in Moral Theology*

## CHARLES E. CURRAN

Catholic moral theology generally defends the existence of absolute and universally valid norms for Christian ethical behavior. In the last few years a renewal of moral theology has taken place, but the renewal has merely accepted the existence of certain absolute norms. The *aggiornamento* in moral theology stresses that, within the boundary lines marked off by absolute norms binding on all, there exists a large area of moral conduct which is not governed by the application of general norms to particular cases. Bernard Häring has emphasized the concept of *kairos*.[1] Karl Rahner has spoken about a formal existentialist ethic.[2] Contemporary moral thology realizes that all men are called to perfection in the reign of God and that theology can no longer be content to discover the dividing line between sin and no sin, or with locating the floor between the permissible and the prohibited. The biblical, liturgical, and catechetical renewals in the Catholic Church have influenced the outlook and scope of moral theology. Personalism and an emphasis on conscience characterize the recent developments in moral theology. Contemporary Catholic moral theology can no longer be accused of legalism and negativism on a wide scale.

However, there still remains the question about universal, absolute, negative norms of Christian conduct (e.g., divorce, direct abor-

---

[1] *The Law of Christ*, Vol. I (Westminster, Md.: Newman Press, 1961), pp. 501 ff.; Häring, *This Time of Salvation* (New York: Herder and Herder, 1966).

[2] *Theological Investigations*, Vol. II (Baltimore: Helicon, 1963), pp. 212–234.

tion, euthanasia, sterilization, artificial insemination, etc.). Even in this area there may have been an inflation of absolutes. Is Roman Catholic theology irreparably committed to the existence of such absolute norms in moral theology? What is the reason that explains the existence of absolutes in Catholic theology? The purpose of the present chapter is to show that Roman Catholic theology is not unalterably committed to a generic insistence on absolute norms in ethical conduct. The first section of the chapter will examine the two alleged sources of absolutism in Roman Catholic theology—the natural law and the teaching authority of the Church.[3] The second section will propose two other factors that have contributed to the existence of absolutes in Catholic moral thought.

## I. *The Natural Law in Catholic Theology*

Both Protestant and Catholic theologians agree that the Roman Catholic teaching on natural law is one of the prime factors for the existence of universal, absolute norms.[4] I shall try to show that the theory of the natural law and the teaching of such a theory in the Catholic Church does not necessarily mean that Catholic theology must always insist upon universal norms of behavior which are true in all cases. First I will attempt to show that the term "natural law" does not designate a coherent philosophical system with an agreed-upon body of content which has been accepted by the Catholic Church from the beginning. Second, I do not think that in what is by far the larger part of its moral teaching the Catholic Church has used natural law as a vehicle in determining the morality of a particular action.

A historical investigation is necessary to show that natural law does not designate a monolithic philosophical system with an agreed-upon code of ethical conduct which has existed throughout the history of the Catholic Church. Although Aristotle made many contributions to the Thomistic concept of natural law, Aristotle never explicitly formulated a natural law doctrine.[5] Aristotle maintains that every

---

[3] John C. Bennett, *Christian Ethics and Social Policy* (New York: Charles Scribner's Sons, 1950), pp. 33–41; Paul L. Lehmann, *Ethics in a Christian Context* (New York: Harper & Row, 1963), p. 317.

[4] E.g., Joseph Fletcher, *Situation Ethics: The New Morality* (Philadelphia: Westminster Press, 1966), pp. 18–22; Josef Fuchs, S.J., *Natural Law* (New York: Sheed and Ward, 1965), pp. 123–162; also Bennett and Rahner.

[5] John L. Russell, S.J., "The Concept of Natural Law," *The Heythrop Journal*, Vol. 6 (1965), pp. 434–438. My historical investigation of the natural law does not pretend to be an original study of the primary sources. I am merely trying to gather together some of the conclusions reached by more recent studies of

living organism has its own nature which is teleological, dynamic, and specific. The growth toward which it tends is the perfection of the organism itself, but this perfection is specific and not individual. For example, each dog tends to develop into the ideal exemplar of the species of dog except insofar as it is impeded by extrinsic circumstances (disease, other killing animals, etc.). However, with regard to man Aristotle did not accept any intrinsic dynamism which alone propels man toward his goal of rational perfection. Although Aristotle describes man as having a desire for happiness and self-realization, man has no intrinsic principle of operation which necessarily leads him to this goal. Man's success in obtaining his goal depends more on favorable extrinsic circumstances (such as health, wealth, friends, etc.) than upon an intrinsic, dynamic tendency to perfection.

Commentators often point to the Stoic period as one of the high points in natural law development.[6] However, even among the Stoics natural law was not monolithic. In general, the Stoics, like Aristotle, shared a rational view of reality. But whereas Aristotle stressed the individual substance as the principle of intelligibility, the Stoics looked upon the universe as the unit of intelligibility. Happiness or virtue then consisted in having a right relationship with the universe, the cosmos.[7] The Stoic philosophers employed the term "natural law," but natural law did not designate a coherent philosophical system. According to one Catholic scholar, natural law for the Stoics was a generic term much like the term "morality" in our day. Stoic philosophers believed that right and wrong can be predicated of human actions just as true and false can be predicated of claims to human knowledge; but they disagreed among themselves on the ethical goodness or evil of particular actions.[8] Some Stoics held that the wise man at times can find sufficient reasons to justify the taking of his own life. Zeno definitely maintained that among the wise there should be a community of wives with a free choice of partners. Chrysippus is

---

the historical development of the natural law. For more complete historical studies see Odon Lottin, *Le Droit Naturel chez Saint Thomas d'Aquin et ses Prédécesseurs*, 2nd ed. (Bruges: Charles Beyaert, 1931); Philippe Delhaye, *Permanence du Droit Naturel* (Louvain: Éditions Nauwelaerts, 1960); Yves R. Simon, *The Tradition of Natural Law* (New York: Fordham U. Press, 1965), pp. 16–40; Heinrich A. Rommen, *The Natural Law* (St. Louis: B. Herder, 1947). I have followed Lottin very closely in the exposition of the thinking of St. Thomas.

[6] Joseph Arntz, O.P., "Natural Law and its History," *Concilium: Moral Theology*, Vol. 5, No. 1 (May, 1965), p. 23.

[7] Russell, *op. cit.*, pp. 438–440.

[8] Gerard Watson, "The Early History of Natural Law," *The Irish Theological Quarterly*, Vol. 33 (1966), p. 74.

quoted by Sextus Empiricus as approving those practices in which the mother has children by her son and the father has children by his daughter. Some of the Stoic philosophers were accused of permitting masturbation, homosexuality, and prostitution. Perhaps these accusations against the Stoic philosophers are polemical and exaggerated, but they at least indicate that the natural law for the Stoics did not include an agreed-upon code of ethical conduct. Although a general agreement in thinking about morality existed among the Stoics, the agreement did not always extend to the morality of particular actions.[9]

Roman law adopted and used the notion of natural law, but in Roman law there were also different ways of understanding natural law. Gaius (about A.D. 160) distinguished two types of law: the *ius civile* which is proper to each country; and the *ius gentium,* the common heritage of all humanity which is known through natural reason.[10] Gaius meant by *ius gentium* what philosophers today mean by natural law. Ulpian (A.D. 228) proposed a threefold division of law. The *ius civile* is again the proper law of the given community, but Ulpian divides the more universal law into two parts. The *ius naturale* is the rule of actions common to man and all the animals, such as the union of the sexes and the procreation and education of offspring. Ulpian uses the term *ius naturale* to designate the work of nature apart from every rational intervention. The *ius gentium,* as the common heritage of all the people, is the work of human reason. For example, before any human intervention men were born free; but then wars occurred, and *de iure gentium* slavery arose.[11] Among the Roman jurists the *ius gentium* was to some extent a human institution, but not in the same sense as the *ius civile*. Man's reason establishes the *ius gentium* by conforming to the natural order of things through the human instinct which is common to all when it comes to the necessities of human existence.

In the development of the concept of natural law, the Scholastic period, and in particular Thomas Aquinas, have greatly influenced Catholic moral teaching. Thomas did not invent the natural law, but he found the concept existing among the theologians, philosophers,

---

[9] These remarks summarize some of Watson's conclusions and are documented by him, *op. cit.,* pp. 72–73.

[10] *Digesta* 1, I, tit. 1, 9. The *Corpus Iuris Civilis,* the codification of Roman Law of Justinian, is divided into *Institutiones, Digesta, Codex,* and *Novellae Constitutiones.*

[11] *Digesta* 1, I, tit. 1, 1, 4.

and jurists who lived before him. In fact, in his writings, Thomas cites four different definitions of the natural law from older authorities, and all these definitions are different! Certainly before Thomas Aquinas there was no monolithic philosophical system called the natural law. Thomas cites the definition proposed by Cicero (*ius naturae est quod non opinio genuit sed quaedam innata vis inseruit*).[12] Thomas also refers to Ulpian's definition of the nautral law as that which is common to man and all the animals apart from any intervention of reason.[13] Perhaps many of the problems in contemporary Catholic explanations of the natural law stem from Ulpian's definition, which tends to identify the natural law with brute natural facticity. Man must respect the laws of nature and cannot interfere with them.

But does not man's rationality demand that at times he interfere with the laws of nature so that he might live a more human existence? Particularly in the area of marital ethics Ulpian's concept of the natural law has created problems. Nature teaches both man and the animals that sexual union exists for the procreation and education of offspring. Animals know nothing about the love-union aspect of sexuality. Consequently, traditional Catholic thought stresses procreation as the primary end of marriage with the love-union aspect of sexuality as the secondary end added on to what is primary and fundamental. Thus Ulpian's definition seems to favor a dichotomy between nature and reason and gives primary importance to what is natural before any interference from reason.

Thomas also cites the definition of natural law proposed by Isidore of Seville: *ius naturale est commune omnium nationum*.[14] Although Isidore accepted the threefold division of law proposed by Ulpian, he modified the concept of *ius naturale*. The *ius naturale* is that which is common to all nations because it results not from any positive human institution but from the inclination and instinct of human nature itself. Isidore thus seems to avoid the dichotomy of separating in man the rational element from that which is common to man and all the animals. The notion of *ius gentium* for Isidore corresponds to the modern concept of international law and includes such things as wars and treaties.[15]

Thomas also quotes the definition of natural law proposed by

---

[12] *In IV Sent.*, d.33, q.1, a.1, ad 4um.
[13] *Ibid.*; also *I–II*, q.94, a.2.   [14] *I–II*, q.94, a.4 and 5.
[15] *Sancti Isidori Hispalensis Episcopi Etymologiarum*, lib. 5, c. 5 and 6; in Migne, *P.L.*, Vol. 82, col. 199, 200.

Gratian, the monk who codified the laws of the Church in the twelfth century.¹⁶ Gratian approvingly cites a text from Isidore to show that the human race is ruled by two things, natural law and customs (*moribus*). The natural law comprises two fundamental norms: Do unto others what you would want them to do unto you; and do not do to others what you would not want them to do to you. However, Gratian then introduces some confusion into the matter by saying that the natural law as found in these two norms is what is contained in the law and the gospel.¹⁷

The Decretists who commented upon the *Decree* of Gratian are not in accord about accepting Ulpian's definition. Among theologians, Albert the Great categorically rejects the definition of Ulpian, while St. Bonaventure espouses it. St. Thomas on this point follows the Franciscan master rather than his own teacher. The Decretists and theologians of the twelfth and thirteenth centuries were also influenced by the school of Anselm of Laon. According to Anselm, the natural law as the primitive law of humanity, which existed even before the detailed prescriptions of the Decalogue, can be reduced to the obligation to do good to others and to avoid evil. The natural law reduced to such immediately evident principles is an innate law written on the hearts of man by God, the Author of all nature.¹⁸

In his *Commentary on the Sentences* (1254–1256), Thomas cites the definitions proposed by Cicero, Ulpian, and Gratian. Thomas here accepts the definition proposed by Ulpian, but tries to modify its brute facticity by interpreting it as what natural reason says about those things which are common to man and all animals.¹⁹ In his *Commentary on the Ethics of Aristotle,* Thomas accepts the Greek philosopher's twofold division of *iustum naturale* and *iustum legale,* but he reconciles such a division with the threefold division of Ulpian. Ulpian's *ius civile* is Aristotle's *iustum legale.* Ulpian divides Aristotle's *iustum naturale* into that which is common to man and all the animals (*ius naturale* in the strictest sense) and that which is rational in man (*ius gentium*). Thomas thus attempts to reconcile the Aristotelian and Ulpian formulations.²⁰

Thomas begins his treatise on the division of human law in the *Summa Theologiae* by citing Isidore, who divided all laws into divine and human laws. Isidore put natural law under the divine law, but human law embraced both the *ius civile* and the *ius gentium.* How

---

[16] *I–II*, q.94, a.4, ad 1um; *In IV Sent.*, d.33, q.1, a.1, ad 4um.
[17] *Decretum*, pars I, d.1.    [18] Lottin, 28–57.
[19] *In IV Sent.*, d.33, q.1., a.1., ad 4um.
[20] *In X Libros Ethicorum ad Nicomachum*, lib. 5, lectio 12.

can the *ius gentium* be placed under human law while the natural law is placed under divine law? Did not Thomas himself in his *Commentary* say that the *ius gentium* is the rational part of the natural law? As usual, Thomas shows his respect for a famous predecessor by accepting Isidore's definition and divisions; but then Thomas goes on to explain the matter in his own way. All human law is derived from the natural law. *Ius gentium* is human law derived from the natural law by way of deductions; whereas *ius civile* is a further specification and determination of the natural law. Since the *ius gentium* is derived from the natural law by rational deduction, one might truly say that the *ius gentium* is the specifically human or rational natural law.[21] Thomas was definitely acquainted with the writings of the older canonists and theologians and frequently tried to reconcile their seemingly opposed views. Thus, even in St. Thomas' writings, there appears some confusion about the definition of natural law and its relationship to other laws.

In general, Thomas' teaching on the natural law is clear. The natural law consists in certain very fundamental judgments acquired intuitively and not by deductive reasoning. These are *principia per se nota*, which can be reduced to the general principle that good is to be done and evil is to be avoided. The natural law is innate because man learns its first principles from a natural inclination and not from a reasoning process. Thomas compares the first principles of the moral order, which are *per se* known, to the first principles of the speculative order. From the first principles of the moral order man then derives other rules of moral conduct just as other truths are derived from the first principles of the speculative order.[22]

Thomas as well as his predecessors struggled with the problem of the characteristics of the natural law: universality, immutability, and indispensability. I grant that such terminology smacks of legalism, but Thomas was the product of his own times, which had been discussing the question in these terms. At least Thomas was aware of the problem concerning the existence of absolute and universal laws of human conduct and in his own way was willing to face up to it. Perhaps the present-day discussion about situation ethics is coming to grips with the same problem created by the tensions of universal norms and the demands of the concrete situation. Thomas also was aware of some of these problems. The Old Testament itself contained many such difficulties: Abraham was commanded by God to kill his son; polygamy was allowed; Israelites were told to steal from the Egyptians;

---

[21] *I–II*, q.95, a.4.   [22] *I–II*, q.94.

Abraham lied to the Egyptians about Sarah his wife. In addition, the canonists and theologians with their respect for authority had to reconcile the practice of private property with the opinion of Isidore, who maintained that according to the natural law all property should be held in common.[23]

Thomas' concept of universality appears to be much more restricted than the idea of universality often proposed today in the name of Thomas. In nature some things like the sunrise always occur, but other things which usually happen can be impeded by external circumstances and accidents. So in human moral laws some are absolutely universal, such as the primary law of acting according to right reason. Other laws, however, admit of exceptions because of accidental circumstances. It is true that what is owed must be returned, but not if the rightful owner will use the thing to harm others. Since the moral matter is changeable such general laws oblige only *ut in pluribus*.[24] In the *Summa* Thomas delves a little more into the question. He speaks of a twofold universality: a universality concerning the precepts themselves and a universality concerning the knowledge of the precepts. Once man leaves the first principles even in the speculative order, error easily enters into reasoning. In the speculative order the derived principles are always true, even though a particular individual might not realize the truth of such a derived principle. In the practical and moral order, however, as one descends from the first principles, the principles themselves do not always oblige because of the defectibility of the matter and the other circumstances which may enter into the picture. Thus, Thomas admits that the conclusions of the common principles oblige *ut in pluribus,* but *in paucioribus* they can be defective. Thomas gives two examples: acting according to reason as an illustration of the common principle, and returning what is owed as a conclusion from first principles. Thomas indicates that whenever deductions occur there is the possibility of an exception; and the more one descends to particulars, the greater the possibility of defections becomes.[25]

In discussing the question of the immutability of the natural law Thomas falls back on the same distinction between the first principles and the conclusions of the natural law. The law of nature is completely immutable with regard to the first principles. But the second precepts of the natural law, which are the close conclusions from first principles, admit some exceptions because of obstacles and impedi-

---

[23] *Etymologiarum*, lib. 5, c.4. (*P.L.*, Vol. 82, col. 199). Thomas treats the objection from Isidore in *I–II*, q.94, a.5, ob.3.

[24] *In III Sent.*, d.37, q.1, a.3, in corp.     [25] *I–II*, q.94, a.4.

ments.²⁶ Thomas proposed different solutions to explain the various dispensations granted by God in the Old Testament. An act can be opposed to God in two ways: either directly as hatred of God; or indirectly insofar as it affects other creatures and the harmony existing among creatures. By a miracle God can intervene so that what affects other creatures does not affect Himself. Consequently, God can intervene and dispense with the obligations of the second table of the Decalogue, since they do not affect Him immediately.²⁷ But Thomas also gives another explanation in the *Sentences* which denies the possibility of a dispensation from the Decalogue. The statements of the Decalogue are somewhat general so that when they are properly understood they do not admit of exceptions.²⁸ Thomas merely follows the two possibilities that are open in such considerations. If the commandments of the Decalogue are understood in a general sense, they do not admit exceptions. If the commandments are understood more specifically, they do admit exceptions. In the *Summa*, Thomas flatly states that the precepts of the Decalogue do not allow the possibility of a dispensation. The biblical exceptions are not really exceptions because God, the Author of life and the Supreme Master of all things, is able to dispose of these as He sees fit.²⁹

This brief historical survey indicates that before the time of St. Thomas there was not a coherent philosophical system with an agreed-upon ethical content which was called the natural law. In Thomas' own synthesis of natural law, he expressly denies that the natural law is a written code. In fact, Thomas admits as a principle that once one descends from the first principles of the natural law which are known by inclination and not deduction, then the possibility of defectibility in particular cases becomes a reality. Thomas' own understanding of the natural law does not seem to justify the insistence on universally valid, absolute norms of human behavior in Catholic moral theology. Catholic thinkers following St. Thomas chronologically did not follow his thinking systematically. A voluntaristic and nominalistic philosophy put much more stress on the will. Outside the limits of Catholic thought, natural law was explained in different ways and used to justify both the divine right of kings and the French Revolution.

The Thomistic revival in the present century has produced some distinguished scholars. The better Thomists take pains to point out that the natural law is not a unified and minute code governing ethical actions. Jacques Maritain, for instance, claims that the metaphor of the natural law written on the heart of man has been responsible for

²⁶ *I–II*, q.94, a.5.
²⁷ *In I. Sent.*, d.47, a.4.
²⁸ *In III Sent.*, d.37, a.4, ad 3um.
²⁹ *I–II*, q.100, a.8.

the impression that the natural law is a ready-made code rolled up within the conscience of each one of us, which we have only to unroll, and of which all men should naturally have an equal knowledge.[30] John Courtney Murray, S.J., likewise attacks a legalistic, overrationalistic concept of the natural law.[31] Yves Simon admits that what is wrong by nature can never be rendered right, but he wants to be very cautious before declaring that a particular act is wrong by nature.[32] Speaking of divorce, Simon says:

> One thing is sure: complete instability, no restrictions on instability, divorce at will, divorce granted as soon as one partner feels like terminating the marriage is certainly contrary to natural law. Too great a human good would be destroyed by unrestricted instability in the relation of husband and wife. Between some restrictions, enough to give children a chance to be brought up in better than completely casual circumstances, and indissoluble marriage the difference is that between the more necessary and the less necessary.[33]

Columba Ryan, O.P., says about the natural law that its primary injunctions are purely formal and amount to little more than the discrimination between good and evil. According to Ryan, the derivative precepts of the natural law are either so general as to provide little guidance to conduct or else so disputable as to win no general consent.[34]

Other Catholic thinkers today are calling for a more radical revision of the whole concept of natural law. Karl Rahner, S.J., has observed that natural law should be approached through a transcendental methodology.[35] Kenneth J. Schmitz has called for the primacy of actual, personal existence over essential, natured individuality and for a consequent relocation and subordination of the natural law.[36] Joseph Arntz, O.P., maintains that we must realize that natural law is nothing but the truth of living together. "Natural law is itself the primary evidence which unfolds itself constantly, and constantly de-

---

[30] *The Rights of Man and Natural Law* (New York: Charles Scribner's Sons, 1943), p. 62.

[31] *We Hold These Truths* (New York: Sheed and Ward, 1960), pp. 295–336.

[32] *The Tradition of Natural Law*, p. 148.

[33] *Ibid.*, p. 157.

[34] "The Traditional Concept of Natural Law: An Investigation," in *Light on the Natural Law*, ed. Illtud Evans, O.P. (Baltimore: Helicon, 1965), p. 33.

[35] "Naturrecht," *Lexicon für Theologie und Kirche*, Vol. 7 (Freiburg: Herder, 1962), col. 827–828.

[36] "The New Freedom and the Integrity of the Profane," *Proceedings of the Society of Catholic College Teachers of Sacred Doctrine*, Vol. 11 (1965), p. 33.

mands to be translated into concrete human relationships." [37] Robert O. Johann, S.J., sees natural law in terms of the responsibility of man as a person, open to the Absolute, and called to promote being.[38] John G. Milhaven, S.J., calls for an epistemology of ethics which gives more importance to empirical evidence.[39] Edward Schillebeeckx, O.P., admits that modern life accentuates the gap that has always existed between abstract norms and concrete reality. It is the creative function of conscience to close that gap.[40]

In the future, Catholic philosophers and theologians will probably propose more radical explanations of the natural law and even advocate other philosophical systems. Catholic theology, now encouraged by the clear calls for dialogue with modern man made by Vatican Council II, is just beginning to break out of its intellectual ghetto. The textbooks of moral theology in use in seminaries before Vatican II derived their content, purpose, and format from the *Institutiones Theologiae Moralis* of the seventeenth century. They contain, for all practical purposes, no references to other Christian thinkers and to the ethics of contemporary philosophers. The very fact that Catholic life survived for over ten centuries without the benefit of Scholastic philosophy shows that Catholic thought is not indissolubly wedded to such a philosophy. The greatness of St. Thomas was his attempt to understand Christianity in the terms that were known in his contemporary society. A true following of St. Thomas demands that contemporary thinkers do for Catholic theology today what Thomas did for it in his day.

The conclusion of this brief historical summary is this: The natural law cannot be an adequate explanation of the generic insistence on universally valid, absolute norms of conduct in Catholic moral theology. The very obvious reason is that for the greater part if not all of the Church's existence the natural law has not been a coherent philosophical system with an agreed-upon content of ethical norms. Those who espouse the natural law as a method in forming moral judgments are quick to point out that the natural law does not

---

[37] *Concilium: Moral Theology*, Vol. 5, No. 1 (May, 1965), p. 31.

[38] "Responsible Parenthood: A Philosophical View," *Proceedings of the Twentieth Annual Convention of the Catholic Theological Society of America*, pp. 115–128.

[39] "Towards an Epistemology of Ethics," *Theological Studies*, Vol. 27 (1966), pp. 228–241. Reprinted in the present volume as Chapter 8.

[40] *Approches Théologiques II: Dieu et L'Homme* (Bruxelles: Éditions du Cep, 1965), pp. 262–269.

imply the existence of always valid, universal norms of conduct once one descends from the first principles.

One more point must be made: The Catholic Church and Catholic theology are not irreparably committed to accept the natural law as a coherent system for the understanding of moral conduct. The assertion that the Catholic Church is not wedded to the natural law theory follows from the fact that the natural law has not been a monolithic ethical theory with agreed-upon ethical norms throughout the entire history of the Church. A further historical reflection will buttress the assertion. How did the Catholic Church arrive at its moral teaching on most issues, such as abortion, birth control, divorce, fornication? I am sure that Clement of Alexandria did not sit down with a team of natural law theoreticians to examine the question of the use of contraception in marital intercourse.[41] The Thomistic natural law synthesis was not even in existence when the Church first formulated its moral teachings in most areas. The natural law theory like any other theory tries to be an explanation of the reality that man knows and experiences. The reality comes first, and the theory has value only to the extent that it corresponds to the reality. Since the term "natural law" was known to both Greek philosophy and Roman law, it is only natural that theologians would use such a concept in trying to explain the teachings of the Church. The vast majority of the moral teachings of the Catholic Church on particular moral problems are not the result of the application of natural law theory to the particular moral point in question.

In the last hundred years moralists within the Catholic Church have begun generally to use the natural law theory in their approach to contemporary moral problems. This usage corresponds with the magisterium's own re-emphasis of Thomistic thought.[42] The Church

---

[41] John T. Noonan, Jr., *Contraception: A History of Its Treatment by the Catholic Theologians and Canonists* (Cambridge, Mass.: Harvard University Press, 1965), pp. 57–106.

[42] Leo XIII in his encyclical letter, *Aeterni Patris* of Aug. 4, 1879, *Acta Sanctae Sedis*, Vol. 11 (1878–9), pp. 98 ff., prescribed the restoration in Catholic schools of Christian philosophy in the spirit of St. Thomas Aquinas. For subsequent papal directives on following the philosophy and theology of St. Thomas, see Pius X, *Doctoris Angelici (Motu Proprio), Acta Apostolicae Sedis*, Vol. 6 (1914), pp. 384 ff.; Pius XI, *Officiorum Omnium* (Encyclical Letter), *A.A.S.*, Vol. 14 (1922), pp. 449 ff.; Pius XI, *Studiorum Ducem* (Encyclical Letter), *A.A.S.*, Vol. 15 (1923), pp. 323 ff.; various allocutions of Pius XII, *A.A.S.*, Vol. 31 (1939), pp. 246 ff.; Vol. 38 (1946), pp. 387 ff.; Vol. 45 (1953), pp. 684 ff. According to Canon 1366 of the Code of Canon Law promulgated in 1917, rational philosophy and theology should be taught "*ad Angelici Doctoris rationem, doctrina, et principia. . . .*"

magisterium frequently talks about natural law in its approach to problems of social morality. However, since many non-natural law theoreticians have accepted much of the Catholic teaching on social principles, I do not think that there exists here a rigorous application of natural law theory but, rather, a general argumentation based on the rights of man and the human person. One might expect many references to the term "natural law" in the *Pastoral Constitution on the Church in the Modern World* (*Gaudium et Spes*). In reality, the Constitution uses the term "natural law" very sparingly.[43] Perhaps during the present century the one area in which the Church has applied a strict natural law theory to particular moral problems is the area of modern marriage problems and medical ethics (e.g., contraception, sterilization, masturbation for seminal analysis, transplantation, etc.). However, precisely in this area of medical ethics Catholic theologians are questioning some of the conclusions arrived at by the natural law theory as interpreted in the magisterium of the Church.[44] The Catholic Church has never irrevocably committed itself in principle to the natural law theory as the sole means of approaching the solution of moral problems. In practice the vast majority of the Catholic Church's moral teachings have not arisen from the application of natural law to particular questions.

The same question can be considered from a more theoretical viewpoint: Can the Catholic Church ever commit itself irrevocably to any philosophical system and understanding of man? The sovereign freedom of the Word of God cannot be tied to any one philosophical understanding of man and reality. Every philosophical theory must be constantly rejudged in the light of the living Word of God. As mentioned earlier, Catholic theology is emerging from an intellectual ghetto. The conciliar stress on the need for dialogue with Christians, non-Christians, and the whole world shows that Catholic thinking can no longer claim a monopoly on the truth. The contemporary emphasis on the pilgrim Church and the increasing awareness of an evolving human existence have made Catholic theology realize that truth is never totally possessed. The Church was able to exist for the greater part of its history without Scholastic thinking, so there can be no absolutely necessary tie between Catholic theology and Scholastic

---

[43] One writer maintains that the term natural law never appears in the Constitution. Cf. J. Jullien, "Nature et culture: Droit naturel ou droit culturel?" *Supplément de la Vie Spirituelle*, Vol. 78 (1966), p. 449. However, there is significant use of the expression in paragraphs 74 and 79.

[44] Archbishop Denis E. Hurley, "A New Moral Principle," *The Furrow*, Vol. 17 (1966), pp. 619–622.

thought patterns. Thomas and Scholasticism certainly deserve a high place in the history of thought, but in no sense can they constitute the last word in Catholic theological thinking. *De facto,* the Catholic Church has not in the majority of cases used the natural law theory as a method of arriving at a moral judgment about a particular question. *De iure,* the Catholic Church can never irreparably commit itself to the natural law theory or any other specific theory as a method for the understanding of Christian behavior. This has to be said, while granting that some philosophical theories lend themselves more easily to an interpretation of Catholic thinking, and some theories may be incompatible with the Catholic understanding of the Word of God.

The investigation of the relationship between the natural law theory and the way in which the Catholic Church has arrived at its moral teachings seem to prove the assertion that the natural law theory cannot be the adequate explanation of the emphasis on absolute norms of behavior which is present in Catholic moral theology.

## II. *The Teaching Authority of the Catholic Church*

Does the magisterium or teaching authority of the Roman Catholic Church account for the insistence on absolute norms in moral theology? Obviously there is a connection between the existence of a teaching authority and a more authoritarian teaching on particular issues. Catholic moral theology does believe that the Church helps to interpret what is right and wrong. In the past, the impression has definitely been given that the teaching authority of the Church tends to operate in an *a priori* and absolutistic way. But Catholic theology today must begin to reflect more on the way in which the magisterium forms its moral teaching. The recent discussion in the Catholic Church on birth control forces theologians to ask about the way the magisterium or teaching authority functions. The possibility of a change in Church teaching naturally calls for an examination of the way in which the Church actually forms its moral teaching.

What role does Sacred Scripture play in the formation of Catholic moral teaching? Sacred Scripture is an important guide for the teaching Church. Unfortunately, in the past Catholic moral theology has not had a scriptural basis and dimension. Vatican Council II, however, has reminded theologians that the Scriptures are the soul of all theology.[45] The Scriptures certainly show the over-all context of Christian morality—the covenant of love between God and his people.

---

[45] *Dogmatic Constitution on Divine Revelation (Dei Verbum),* n. 24.

Man's life and activity must be seen in the light of his existence in the covenant community of salvation. The written Word of God insists on the basic attitudes that should characterize Christian life. Faith is the openness to the saving Word of God in Christ, and love of neighbor is openness to others. Love of neighbor becomes the infallible sign of Christian existence and is manifested above all in love of enemies and a willingness to forgive. Many important themes of the moral life are treated in the Scriptures—law, conscience, sin, hope, etc. Some moral questions such as divorce are mentioned in Scripture, but the teaching of Scripture on these points is not absolutely clear. Many other moral problems confronting the Christian today are not even mentioned in Scripture—racial justice, world peace, poverty, euthanasia, questions connected with genetics. The Church even seems to go against the express words of Scripture by approving the taking of oaths and the receiving of interest on loans. The teaching authority of the Church must judge all things in the light of the Word of God, but the Scriptures themselves do not furnish concrete answers to all the moral problems facing modern man.[46] The limits of the moral knowledge derived from Scripture are apparent, for the Scriptures record just one experience of the Christian life in a particular time of history.[47] The teaching authority of the Church must always judge in the light of the Word of God, but the Scriptures are not the sole determining element in the teaching authority of the Church.

Catholic theology has always stressed tradition and the role it plays in forming the teaching of the Church on a particular issue. Theologians today are seeing tradition not as opposed to the Scriptures but, rather, as the living Word of God in time and space. Tradition is most important in forming the moral teaching of the Church, but history teaches that the Church has changed its traditional teaching on certain points. Usury presents a good example of a change in the teaching of the Church. The prohibition of usury as it existed in 1450 condemned the making of profit from a loan. Certain extrinsic titles would justify compensation; but interest could never be lawfully sought on a loan, nor could the mere risk involved in lending be a just title for compensation or interest. The prohibition of usury was based on random biblical texts and strongly upheld by such influential Fathers of the Church as Ambrose, Jerome, Augustine, and the more influential of the Greek Fathers. In 1139 the Second Lateran Council

---

[46] E. Hamel, S.J., "L'usage de l'Écrite Sainte en théologie morale," *Gregorianum*, Vol. 47 (1966), pp. 53–85.

[47] For the use of Scripture as a source of knowledge, see Eugene Fontinell, "Reflections on Faith and Metaphysics," *Cross Currents*, Vol. 16 (1966), pp. 37–39.

condemned "rapacious usury" as detestable and repugnant to divine and human laws. The Third Council of the Lateran (1179) denied Christian burial to manifest usurers. According to the Council of Vienne (1311–1312), a person affirming that the practice of usury is not a sin is to be treated as a heretic. Also a long list of Popes condemned usury. Today, however, Catholic teaching permits the taking of interest on loans and forbids only exorbitant interest.[48]

The question of religious liberty again illustrates the possibility of change in a traditional teaching of the Church. Greogry XVI's encyclical, *Mirari Vos*, of August 15, 1832, condemned

> the false and absurd maxim, or rather madness, that every individual should be given and guaranteed freedom of conscience, that most contagious of errors, the way to which is opened by the absolute and unfettered freedom of opinion which, to the ruin of Church and State, is spreading everywhere, and which some men, with excessive impudence, have the temerity to describe as beneficial to religion.[49]

The encyclical *Quanta Cura* of Pius IX states:

> As a result of this utterly false idea of the government of society, they do not hesitate to support the erroneous opinion, than which none is more fatal to the Catholic Church and the salvation of souls, and which our predecessor of happy memory Gregory XVI called a madness, to wit, that freedom of conscience and worship is every man's proper right; that it should be proclaimed and ensured in every well ordered state; and that the citizens have a right and perfect liberty, to voice their opinions, whatever they may be loudly and publicly, in words or through the press, without any limitation by the civil or ecclesiastical authorities.[50]

Among the condemned propositions in the Syllabus of Errors joined to Pius IX's encyclical is the following: "Every man is free to embrace and profess the religion he considers to be the true one by the light of reason." [51] Leo XIII's encyclical *Libertas* condemns religious liberty and the separation of Church and State.

> And, first, let us examine that liberty in individuals which is so opposed to the virtue of religion; namely, the liberty of worship, as it is called.

---

[48] John T. Noonan, Jr., *The Scholastic Analysis of Usury* (Cambridge, Mass.: Harvard University Press, 1957). For a brief summary of the teaching of the magisterium on usury and interest, see Noonan, "Authority, Usury, and Contraception," *Cross Currents*, Vol. 16 (1966), pp. 55–79.

[49] *Acta Gregorii XVI*, Vol. 1, p. 172.

[50] *Acta Sanctae Sedis*, Vol. 3 (1867), p. 162.

[51] *Ibid.*, p. 170, n. 15.

... Justice therefore forbids, and reason itself forbids, the State to be godless; or to adopt a line of action that would end in godlessness; namely, to treat the various religions (as they call them) alike, and to bestow upon them promiscuously equal rights and privileges.[52]

All these statements must be understood in the light of the historical circumstances of the times, especially the opposition of the Roman Catholic Church to the liberalism of the day. However, there is a great discontinuity between these documents of the official magisterium of the Church and the teaching of the *Declaration on Religious Liberty* (*Dignitatis Humanae Personae*) promulgated by Vatican Council II. Since the Church has changed its teaching on religious liberty, the mere repetition of the past teaching of the Church is not a sufficient guide for the present teaching Church.

Another example of a change in the traditional teaching of the magisterium concerns the question of the defendant's right to silence. Patrick Granfield has examined the documents of the magisterium and concluded that the privilege against self-incrimination by the defendant was first recognized by the magisterium in the Code of Canon Law (canon 1743), which was promulgated in 1917. Granfield maintains there was no organic development in the magisterium, for as late as 1910 no provision was made for the right to silence. Although the documents involved (a response, a papal bull, a catechism approved by a general council, a statement from a provincial council, a series of papal constitutions, and some procedural norms for the Roman Rota) do not possess the highest magisterial authority, nevertheless, they do form the traditional teaching of the magisterium. However, as early as the seventeenth century English law admitted the right to silence. Obviously, the magisterium changed its traditional teaching in the light of the new developments in civil law and greater awareness of human dignity and rights.[53]

Another topic of discussion among Catholic theologians today is the obligation of the Catholic spouse to raise the children of a mixed marriage in the Catholic faith. Ladislaus Örsy has collected thirteen papal documents, nine documents from the Holy Office, and eight other documents from the Roman Curia which teach the divine law obligation of the Catholic spouse to raise the children of a mixed

---

[52] *Acta Leonis XIII*, 8 (1888), 229, 231. An English translation may be found in *The Church Speaks to the Modern World: The Social Teaching of Leo XIII*, ed. Étienne Gilson (Garden City: Image Books, 1954), pp. 70–71, nn. 19, 21. The English translations are from Gilson.

[53] Patrick Granfield, O.S.B., "The Right to Silence: Magisterial Development," *Theological Studies*, Vol. 27 (1966), pp. 401–420.

marriage in the Catholic faith. From these documents Örsy concludes that the divine law obligation for the Catholic spouse to care for the Catholic upbringing of the children is a true and immutable Catholic teaching.[54] While Örsy himself only allows for certain nuances of this conclusion, other theologians even deny the divine law obligation to raise the children of mixed marriages in the Catholic faith.[55]

The Catholic Church always lives in continuity with its past. The Church has learned much in its development, and tradition may well be called the memory of the Church. The Church, like every living body or individual, must confront the present situation armed with the experience and the knowledge gained from its development. However, the fact that something was taught at an earlier time in the Church is not a guarantee that the same teaching holds true today. Tradition and Scripture are both most important in the formation of the decision of the teaching Church, but they are not adequate criteria in themselves.

What about the use of reason and man's rational faculties in arguing to a particular moral decision? The teaching Church must use all human means to investigate the world and its problems and to apply the gospel message to present-day problems. However, history shows that reason alone can come to very different conclusions about particular issues. Theologians cannot always agree on the reasons behind a specific teaching of the magisterium. For example, the teaching magisterium of the Church proposes that masturbation is wrong, but Catholic theologians in history have not been in agreement on the precise reason for the malice of masturbation.[56] The first part of this chapter tried to show that the Catholic Church cannot be committed to any one rational system or explanation of the world. Reason does play an important part in the formulation of the teachings of the magisterium, but reason alone is not an absolute and self-sufficient norm for the teaching Church in considering specific moral problems.

How, then, does the teaching authority of the Church form its moral judgments? Scriptures, tradition, and reason all play a definite part, but neither singly nor together do they constitute an adequate

---

[54] Ladislaus Örsy, S.I., "Documenta selecta de educatione religiosa prolis ex matrimonio mixto natae," *Periodica de Re Morali, Canonica, Liturgica,* Vol. 53 (1964), pp. 267–284.

[55] *Ibid.,* "The Religious Education of Children Born from Mixed Marriages," *Gregorianum,* Vol. 45 (1964), pp. 739–760; Charles E. Curran, "The Mixed Marriage Promises—Arguments for Suppressing the Cautiones," *The Jurist,* Vol. 25 (1965), pp. 83–91.

[56] V. Vangheluwe, "De Intrinseca et Gravi Malitia Pollutionis," *Collationes Brugenses,* Vol. 48 (1952), pp. 108–115.

# Natural Law

explanation of the way in which the Church formulates its moral teaching. All Catholics would admit the help of the Holy Spirit in guiding the Church magisterium, but the Spirit does not produce ready-made answers out of a vacuum. I propose that a very important additional factor in the teaching of the Church is the experience of Christian people. The teaching Church definitely learns from the experience of the living Church.

The areas in which the Church has changed its moral teachings highlight the importance of the role played by the experience of Christian people. Different circumstances and a new understanding of money influenced the change in the teaching of the magisterium on interest. But how did the Church become aware of these changing circumstances? I believe that the Church learned from the experience of Christian people and then could look back and rationally justify such a change because of changing circumstances. Any realistic interpretation must admit that the taking of interest did not become right the moment the Church said it was allowed. No, the Church authority was rightly following the experience of Christian people. On the question of religious liberty, Vatican Council II expressly admits that the teaching authority of the Church has learned from the experience of Christian people.

> A sense of the dignity of the human person has been impressing itself more and more deeply on the consciousness of contemporary man. And the demand is increasingly made that men should act on their own judgment, enjoying and making use of a responsible freedom, not driven by coercion but motivated by a sense of duty. The demand is also made that constitutional limits should be set to the powers of government. . . . This Vatican Synod takes careful note of these desires in the minds of men. It proposed to declare them to be greatly in accord with truth and justice. To this end, it searches into the sacred tradition and doctrine of the Church—the treasury out of which the Church continually brings forth new things which are in harmony with the things that are old.[57]

The twentieth-century development in the Church's teaching on religious liberty illustrates the truth of the role of experience in the formation of Catholic teaching. The acknowledged architect of the *Declaration on Religious Freedom* is Father John Courtney Murray, S.J. Murray did not come to his conclusions by an abstract consideration of the nature of Church and State and the dignity of the human person. Murray reflected and rationalized, in the good sense of that term, the experience of the Christian people as found in the American

---

[57] *Declaration on Religious Freedom,* n. 1.

experiment of Church-State relations.[58] Murray shows clearly that moral theology is a reflection on life; but life and experience came first. The present debate in the Catholic Church on birth control has arisen precisely because of the experience of Christian people. Theologians would never have begun to rethink the whole question unless they had been prodded by the problems raised in the living of marriage in this world. The agonizing reappraisal that the Pope is undertaking illustrates the tension created by a changing experience in the Church. Many Catholic couples have grappled with the same problem of conscience in coming to their own personal solutions in the area of responsible parenthood.

Some Catholic theologians might object that the emphasis on the experience of Christian people would destroy the very concept of the Roman Catholic Church and its teaching authority. I do not think so. The renewed Catholic theology of the Church is stressing the fact that the Church is not just the hierarchy and the magisterium but the whole people of God. If the Church is the people of God, then the experience of Christian people would have a part to play in the teaching of the Church. The primary ruler and teacher in the Church is the Holy Spirit, but no one person in the Church has a monopoly on the Holy Spirit. The office of hierarchy is a gift of the Spirit, but the Spirit dwells in the hearts of all the just. The Spirit can also speak in the lives of Christian people. The teaching Church must always be attuned to the living Word of God and the Spirit no matter where they are found.

Is there truly any need for a teaching authority in the Church if the experience of Christian people is such an important element? Yes, there still remains the need for a teaching authority. One individual can very easily be led astray by his own limitations, prejudice, blindness, or sinful egoism. Since the Church is a community, a *koinonia,* the teaching authority of the Church represents the experience of the total community. Only within the total community can one discern the call of the Spirit. The teaching authority of the Church must be willing to test the experience of individuals against the background of the whole community. Is the teaching authority of the Church reduced to the status of an ecclesiastical George Gallup? No, the teaching authority of the Church does not just count noses on a particular subject. As the community of salvation, the Church

---

[58] John Courtney Murray, S.J., *The Problem of Religious Freedom* (Westminster, Md.: Newman Press, 1965). This monograph originally appeared in *Theological Studies,* Vol. 25 (1964), pp. 503-575. Also Murray, "The Declaration on Religious Liberty," *Concilium: Moral Theology,* Vol. 5, No. 2 (May, 1966), p. 310.

owes its existence to the Word of God. During the course of its continued existence the Church has learned much from the accumulated experience of the years. The teaching authority of the Church tests the experience of Christian people in the light of the living Word of God and the memory (tradition) of the Church itself. Consequently, the teaching authority does not function merely by taking a poll of the attitudes of a particular group at a particular time.

The experience of Christian people is not the only element that enters into the way in which the teaching Church comes to its conclusions on particular points. The primary teacher in the Church is the Holy Spirit who speaks in many and diverse ways, one of which is the experience of Christian people. The Church must always teach the central values and attitudes of the Christian life as they are proclaimed in the good news of salvation. The Church at times must also speak about particular issues and problems, but teaching on such matters must be somewhat tentative. The wisdom of the teaching authority of the Church in the past is evident in the fact that the Church has never made an infallible pronouncement on an absolute moral norm as such. Even in speaking about particular problems the Church does not depend totally on the experience of Christian people. History, even contemporary history, shows that in some areas, such as racial equality, peace, and questions of sexuality, the teaching Church must lead the individual Christians. There is a reciprocity between the living and the teaching Church which defies neat categories or analysis. However, the experience of sincere Christian people trying to conform to the Spirit remains an important element to be considered by the teaching authority in the Church.

Roman Catholic theology needs to reconsider the place and meaning of the magisterium and the teaching authority of the Catholic Church. Just as the Church is no longer identified with the hierarchy, so the teaching of the Church can no longer be identified completely with the teaching of the hierarchical magisterium. There are many ways in which the Church teaches. The hierarchical magisterium is just one of the ways in which the total Church teaches. The concept of the magisterium of the Church is wider and more inclusive than the concept of the hierarchical magisterium.

A proper understanding of the hierarchical magisterium with its dependence on the experience of Christian people indicates that the teaching authority of the Church as such cannot be the adequate explanation of the generic insistence on absolute norms in Catholic moral theology. The hierarchical magisterium cannot function merely in an *a priori* way, but the teaching Church also learns from the experience of Christians and all men. We have also seen that this insistence on absolutes in moral theology is not logically the result of an insistence on the natural law as such. There may be some absolute moral norms governing particular moral actions, but our concern has been the over-all insistence on absolute norms in moral theology. Neither the natural law nor the hierarchical teaching authority of the Church is an adequate explanation of the prevalent insistence on absolutes in moral theology.

What, then, is the explanation for the insistence on absolutes in Catholic moral theology? It would be an impossible task to explain adequately the insistence in Catholic theology on universal norms of conduct which are always binding. In the next section I will indicate two factors that I believe have played an important role in the emphasis on absolute norms in moral theology. Since the Catholic Church is not in principle committed to a generic insistence on absolutes in moral theology, and since some of the factors influencing such an emphasis are now changing, the conclusion reached in this chapter is that in the future Catholic moral theology will have to question many of the moral absolutes which heretofore have been upheld.

## III. *Changing Theological and Sociological Understandings of Life in the Church*

An inadequate understanding of the Church, which has characterized Catholic theology since the Reformation, has led to an undue insistence on authority and absolute norms in the life of the Catholic. Reacting against the Protestant concept, Catholic theology stressed the visible aspect of the Church and especially the visible authority in the Church. Pre-Vatican Council II textbooks on ecclesiology devoted most of their space to the Roman Pontiff.[59] Even the role of the bishops and the whole hierarchy did not receive a developed consideration. Only with Vatican II has the notion of the collegiality of the bishops assumed again its proper role in the understanding of ecclesiology.[60] There were nineteenth-century renewals in a better understanding of ecclesiology, but even after the encyclical *Mystici Corporis* in 1943, the textbooks still gave a rather one-sided picture of ecclesiology.[61] The

[59] E.g., Ioachim Salaverri, S.I., *Sacrae Theologiae Summa I: De Ecclesia Christi* (Madrid: Biblioteca de Autores Christianos, 1955), pp. 497–988.

[60] *Dogmatic Constitution on the Church (Lumen Gentium)*, Chapter III.

[61] Peter Riga, "The Ecclesiology of Johann Adam Möhler," *Theological Studies*, Vol. 22 (1961), pp. 563–587.

*Dogmatic Constitution on the Church* (*Lumen Gentium*) promulgated by Vatican II now views the Church primarily as the people of God in the covenant community of salvation.

The manuals of moral theology reflected the concept of life within a very authoritarian society that was structured entirely from the top down. Moral theology became a separate branch of learning apart from dogmatic and ascetical theology. Moral theology then assumed a much closer relationship with the science of canon law, so that many considerations in the manuals of moral theology today belong, rather, to canon law. All morality took on the perspective of relationship to law, for law was seen as the guiding and directing force of all life. The fact that the manuals of moral theology had the primary purpose of training confessors to distinguish between mortal sin and no sin only heightened the attention given to drawing clear and certain boundary lines between sin and no sin. Moral theology as separated from spiritual theology paid practically no attention to the growth and development of the Christian life beyond the floor of the permissible. Moral theology considered the Christian life primarily in terms of obedience to an elaborate system of laws. The tract on law became one of the primary considerations in moral theology textbooks.[62]

The pre-Vatican II concepts of life, authority, and law in the Church do not reflect either the current theological understanding of the Church or the circumstances of life in modern secular society. The proliferation of recent studies on law and authority in the Church indicates the changes that are occurring.[63] The Church is no longer equated with its hierarchical structure. Theologians now speak of authority in terms of service of the people of God. Papal infallibility is being discussed, and infallibility is viewed as belonging to the Church itself and exercised in one way through the Roman Pontiff. The Vatican Council renewed the idea of episcopal collegiality and indicated that such collegiality and communitarianism must be found on all levels of life in the Church. The Church no longer appears as an authoritative society completely structured from the top down. The

---

[62] E.g., H. Noldin, S.J., A. Schmitt, S.J., G. Heinzel, S.J., *Summa Theologiae Moralis I: De Principibus*, 33rd ed. (Oeniponte: Rauch, 1960), contains six different "books"—the last end of man, human actions, laws, conscience, virtues, sins. The longest of the six books is the one on law.

[63] *Problems of Authority*, ed. John T. Todd (Baltimore: Helicon, 1962); Yves Congar, O.P., *Power and Poverty in the Church* (Baltimore: Helicon, 1964); John L. McKenzie, S.J., *Authority in the Church* (New York: Sheed and Ward, 1966).

changing concept of the theology of the Church and authority in the Church also calls for a change in the role of law in the Church.[64] Law in the Church has only an ancillary function. The source of all life in the Church remains the Holy Spirit who dwells in the hearts of all. Law in the Church does not direct all activity but merely serves to create the climate and order in which the community may live under the primary guiding force of the Holy Spirit. Individual responsibility, creativity, and initiative are much more important than mere conformity to an elaborate system of law. The realization of the secondary role of law in the life of the Church will necessarily have repercussions on the emphasis on law in moral theology.

The concept of the Church and its life which was so familiar in Catholic thought before Vatican II resembled very closely the life of the secular society in medieval Europe and in the later period of the monarchies. Such societies were structured from the top down and were relatively static. The life and even the attitudes of the people were completely dependent on the authorities. The famous axiom, *Cuius regio eius religio,* indicates that the ruling prince even determined the religion of his subjects. The people were truly subjects and serfs who contributed very little in the way of initiative and creativity.

Catholic teaching on Church and State in the nineteenth century shows the very authoritarian view of society which has pervaded Catholic thinking even to the present times. Pope Leo XIII referred to the people as the untutored multitude.[65] Such people could not decide anything for themselves but had to be led by their rulers. Since the State directed almost all life in the society, the State had to look out for the religious beliefs of its subjects. The nineteenth-century popes with their understanding of society naturally rejected the notion of religious liberty. Only in the last few decades has the Catholic Church accepted a view that realizes the very limited role of government in society. Law, consequently, is not the primary and most important force contributing to the common good of society. Modern society promotes the creativity and initiative of individuals and other groups within society. Law and the State government have the rather limited function of preserving the public order, i.e., of making it possible for

[64] See *Law for Liberty: The Role of Law in the Church Today,* ed. James E. Biechler (Baltimore: Helicon, 1967). This volume contains the papers originally presented at a seminar on the role of law in the Church sponsored by the Canon Law Society of America.

[65] *Libertas Praestantissimum,* n. 23. Earlier (n. 19) the Pope spoke of freedom of worship as being opposed to the virtue of religion. *Acta Leonis XIII,* Vol. 8 (1888), p. 233.

the other forces in society to contribute to the common good. Individuals in modern states are citizens and not subjects. Contemporary society is not structured from the top down in an authoritarian way. Men and institutions are given the freedom to develop as best they can for their own good and the good of society.

Catholic moral theology's teaching on probabilism is a good illustration of a teaching that reflects a life situation which is no longer present in the life of the contemporary Catholic Church. The birth-control controversy in the Church has highlighted the inadequacy of the concept of extrinsic probabilism. According to that theory, if a sufficient number of authorities maintain that an opinion favoring freedom from a particular obligation is probable, an individual may follow such an opinion in good conscience. Theologians in the past have debated about how many authorities constitute a probable opinion.[66] In the matter of birth control, the primary question pondered by priests in the active ministry was whether or not the opinion which says the pill or contraception may be used is probable. One theologian maintained that if the Pope made no authoritative statement within a few months, then the opinion favoring the use of contraception would be probable and could be followed in practice.[67] However, how can a certain number of authorities or a certain number of months make something practically right which was wrong a few months before? (I grant that probabilism does not speak in terms of what is speculatively true but only in terms of practice.)

Probabilism fails precisely because it tries to give a legalistic solution to what should be a prudential decision of conscience made by the individual. Probabilism has a meaning in a society in which people are always looking to the authorities for what they should do. Where people are the unlettered masses with no education and no creative role, a theory appealing to the decision of authorities has intelligibility. But today the situation has changed; conscience must assume its true role in such cases. Conscience must do for the twentieth-century Christian what probabilism did for the Catholic in the seventeenth and eighteenth centuries. The prudent Christian will naturally investigate the problem and see what other prudent Christians and experts have to say, but the final decision will rest with the conscience of the individual. Extrinsic probabilism saved the individual from taking the risk involved in a personal decision whenever some doubt

---

[66] Noldin, n. 238.
[67] Richard A. McCormick, S.J., "Notes on Moral Theology," *Theological Studies*, 26 (1965), p. 646.

existed. Like all legalistic solutions, it is clear, precise, and somewhat easy to apply; but it does not come to grips with the reality of the situation. This is just one example of an inadequacy in moral theology because of an understanding of life and society which no longer corresponds to the reality of life in the Church.

In general, the authorities in the Catholic Church thought they had to direct the entire life of the sheep who were committed to their care. The very word "sheep" connotes the passive and docile characteristics of the faithful. Even today the hierarchy will frequently talk about the need to protect the simple faithful from the dangers that might beset them. Moral theology has reflected the same concern in its consideration of the scandal of the weak. The scandal of the weak is a reality, but moral theology and the authorities in the Church frequently do not mention the scandal of the strong. Some people today are repulsed by the Catholic Church because its life does not reflect all the demands of human dignity and freedom. The unfreedom in the Church is a scandal to many people of good will. Today people are speaking of a crisis in obedience and authority in the Catholic Church. The tensions existing about authority in the Church mirror the changing circumstances in which individual responsibility assumes a greater role and authority assumes a lesser role in the life patterns of individual Catholics. Moral theology must also reflect the changing circumstances by placing more emphasis on individual conscience and responsibility with a corresponding de-emphasis on the role of laws in the life of the Christian. Moral theology is being forced to reconsider the existence of absolute, universal laws of behavior which are obliging in all circumstances.

An older theology pictured the Church as a perfect society having all the answers, which were handed down by the authorities of the Church. Triumphalism was one of the most frequent charges made during the Vatican Council. The Church had become smug and triumphal precisely because it thought it had all the answers and did not have to go through the doubts and anxieties of human existence. On the contrary, Vatican Council II in the *Dogmatic Constitution on the Church* has reiterated time and time again the pilgrim nature of the Church. The Church here on earth is not the Church triumphal; it has not yet reached its eschatological perfection, but is striving like Christ to grow in wisdom and age and grace before God and man. Life in the pilgrim Church is not all structured from the top down. The concept of the Church as the people of God emphasizes the role that belongs to all Christians in the Church by reason of their baptism. The Vatican Council has renewed the concept of the prophetic office in the Church.⁶⁸ In his dealings with his chosen people, God has always raised up prophets to guide his people. The history of renewal in the life of the Church reminds us that renewal frequently comes from underneath and not from the top down.⁶⁹ Look at the renewal in the Church that has taken place as a result of the Council. Yes, we are most grateful for Pope John and the Fathers of Vatican II. But there would have been no renewal in the Catholic Church had it not been for the prophets of the biblical, liturgical, catechetical, and ecumenical movements. Many of these theologians were at one time under a cloud of suspicion, and yet they prepared the way for Vatican II.⁷⁰ Like all prophets, they needed the twofold gift which the Lord constantly gives to his prophets: knowledge and the courage to proclaim their message in the face of the established order.

In many other ways the Church has admitted that it does not possess all the answers. The Vatican Council has spoken of the need for dialogue with other Christians, non-Christians, and the world itself. Dialogue by its very definition assumes that the Church does not have all the answers but is earnestly searching for the truth in collaboration with all men of good will. History again records that Roman Catholic theology has relearned many truths in its dialogue with Protestants: the importance of Scripture, the insistence on personal commitment, the Church as the people of God, the ministry as service, etc. The Church has also learned from the world. The *Declaration on Religious Freedom* admits that this desire has already been existing in the hearts of men (n. 1). Humanists and others have been spending themselves even more than the Church in the interest of racial justice and world peace. The Roman Catholic Church may rightly be proud of the teaching in the social encyclicals from Pope Leo XIII to the present day, but we can never forget that Karl Marx was there first. Marx realized the injustices involved and tried to do something constructive for the workers before the Catholic Church was commensurately sensitive to the problem. The Vatican Council has sounded the death knell for the picture of the Church as primarily an authoritarian society structured from the top down in which the hierarchy, with the protection of the Holy Spirit, led their children or sheep to eternal perfection. The Catholic Church will never deny the need and function of the hierarchy, but for too long the Church was identified with

---

⁶⁸ *Constitution on the Church,* n. 12.

⁶⁹ Karl Rahner, S.J., *The Dynamic Element in the Church* (New York: Herder and Herder, 1964).

⁷⁰ Yves M. J. Congar, O.P., "The Need for Patience," *Continium,* Vol. 2 (1965), pp. 684–693.

the hierarchy and little or no role was given to the people of God. As the newer theology of the Church makes its impact on moral theology, more stress will be given to the creativity and initiative of the Christian people. Christian life will no longer be seen primarily as obedience to laws and norms. It would certainly seem that the older view of the Church and the life of the individual Christian within the Church has contributed somewhat to the emphasis on absolute norms in moral theology.

## IV. *Changing Theological Methodology*

A second factor, a question of theological methodology, has influenced the tendency toward absolutes in moral theology. Catholic theologians today speak of a transition from a classicist methodology to a more historically conscious methodology.[71] A classicist methodology tends to be abstract, *a priori*, deductive, and a-historical. The classicist world-view attempts to cut through the accidents of time and history to arrive at the eternal, universal, and unchanging. The universal abstract norms are then applied to the particular situation. The classicist methodology is definitely connected with a Greek way of knowing and thinking. The Platonic notion of a pre-existing world of ideas well exemplifies such a methodology. Primary attention is given to substances and essences, while the contingent, the particular, and the historical are regarded merely as accidents which modify the already constituted reality. The personal, historical, and existential do not receive as much emphasis as they do in modern thought.

A historically conscious methodology proceeds in a different manner. More attention is given to the historical, the contingent, the personal, and the existential (without necessarily denying the other aspects of reality). Bernard Lonergan argues for a methodology which "can apprehend mankind as a concrete aggregate developing over time where the locus of development and, so to speak, the synthetic bond is the emergence, expansion, differentiation, dialectic of meaning and of meaningful performance." [72] For Lonergan, meaning is not something fixed, static, and immutable; but shifting, developing, going astray, and capable of redemption. However, the defenders of the new methodology are quick to point out that such a methodology will not

---

[71] Murray, *Concilium: Moral Theology*, Vol. 5, No. 2 (May, 1966), pp. 7–10; Bernard Lonergan, S.J., "The Transition from a Classicist World-View to Historical Mindedness," in *Law for Liberty*, pp. 126–133.

[72] "The Transition from a Classicist World-View to Historical Mindedness," p. 130.

result in a purely subjective ethic since they, too, base ethics on reality. However, the concept of reality is more historical and less abstract. The manuals of moral theology definitely reflect a classicist world-view. As Catholic theologians begin to employ a more historically minded methodology, questions will naturally be raised about abstract, universal norms of behavior. Perhaps a few illustrations will clarify the use and understanding of a more historically conscious methodology in Catholic moral theology.

John Courtney Murray, S.J., maintains that the change in the Catholic Church's teaching on religious liberty reflects a change in theological methodology from a classicist to a more historically conscious methodology.[73] The older view of Church-State relations and religious liberty in Catholic theology well illustrates the use of a classicist methodology. The older view started with an abstract view of the perfect society. Then the notion of perfect society was applied to both Church and State. The theory then deduced the relationship which should exist between the two. However, there were situations where it was impossible to apply the general principle that the State should recognize and actively support the Catholic Church at the expense of all other churches. The older theory then distinguished between thesis and hypothesis. The thesis or the ideal always maintains that the State must support the true Church of Christ; but in certain situations the Church may tolerate a system in which the State does not support the Catholic Church but admits a general policy of freedom of conscience and religious liberty. Notice the emphasis on abstract, universal norms which should apply in all circumstances. Even when the historical situation does not permit the application of the general norm, the contrary situation is only tolerated.[74]

The newer view of Church-State does not begin with an *a priori* notion of a perfect society. Murray began from the concept of the limited State as verified in existing governments today and from the contemporary consciousness of human dignity and the freedom of conscience in religious matters. The historical methodology does not demand the distinction between thesis and hypothesis, between the ideal and the real.[75] The differing conclusions stem from the different methodologies employed.

The question of the promises in mixed marriages, which was mentioned above, also illustrates the two different methodologies. Most theologians defend a divine law obligation of the Catholic partner to

---

[73] *Concilium: Moral Theology,* Vol. 5, No. 2 (May, 1966), p. 7.
[74] Murray, *The Problem of Religious Freedom,* pp. 7–17.
[75] *Ibid.,* pp. 17–45.

raise all the children of a mixed marriage in the Catholic faith. The argument is based on the truth of the Catholic Church as the one, true Church of Christ and the obligation of the Catholic to pass his faith on to all his children. In particular situations the fact that the children will not be raised in the Catholic faith may be tolerated.[76] The argument is based on abstract, general truths and obligations. However, the opinion affirming such an obligation seems to neglect the very important historical reality of political and even ecclesiological pluralism as well as the freedom of conscience. In the light of religious liberty and the reality of ecumenism it seems difficult to accept a divine law obligation to raise all the children of mixed marriages in the Catholic faith. Notice that the affirmative opinion would be true in every possible historical situation. It would make no difference if all people freely embraced Catholicism or only a small minority. The reality of ecumenical ecclesiology today would make no difference. The freedom of conscience and religious liberty do not even enter into the principles upon which the whole solution is based. The defects of a classicist methodology are present in the view affirming a divine law obligation to raise all the children of mixed marriages in the Catholic faith.

A classicist methodology tends to favor the existence of absolute, abstract, universal norms in moral theology. The various criticisms recently directed against traditional moral theology seem to center on the fundamental problem of methodology.[77] The classicist methodology tends to be a-historical, but modern man is very conscious of the importance of history and time. The historical aspect of reality has been submerged in the past. The deductive character of the older methodology tends to emphasize conformity and not creativity. A static world-view gives little or no place to growth, development, and change. A Hellenistic view of the universe and nature has a difficulty in explaining the discontinuities in life. Aristotelian and Thomistic thought do not pay sufficient attention to the individual. For Thomas, the principle of individuation in man is not something positive but negative. Aristotelian philosophy looks to the good of the species and considers the individual good primarily in relationship to the good of the species. Traditional Catholic thought has not given as much place to the individual and the contingent as have more modern philosophies. Catholic moral theology has been accused of naturalism and biologism because it views reality in terms of narrow biological laws. Scholastic

[76] See notes 54 and 55.
[77] Charles E. Curran, *Christian Morality Today: The Renewal of Moral Theology* (Notre Dame, Ind.: Fides Publishers, 1966), pp. 127–133.

philosophy has concentrated on substances and essences; whereas modern thought often views reality in terms of the existential and the historical. Modern thought also gives more emphasis to the personal while Scholastic philosophy concentrates more on nature. Absolute certitude is the goal of the classicist methodology, and such certitude is achieved through the knowledge of abstract universals which are always true. Modern sciences do not really seek such certitude, but only a working certitude until they can discover something better. A more historically conscious methodology will not be able to seek the absolute certitude of unchanging universal essences. A change in methodology will have to reflect the best aspects of both approaches, but the greater importance attached to a historically conscious methodology will necessarily mean less emphasis on the existence of absolute norms which are binding in all circumstances.

The traditional Catholic insistence on an intrinsic morality would still be present in a more historically conscious methodology. The understanding of the terms, intrinsically good or intrinsically evil, has frequently been interpreted as actions in the abstract which are either good or bad. However, John Coventry has recently criticized such an understanding of intrinsic morality.[78] Coventry claims that the understanding of intrinsic morality as referring to particular actions in the abstract has resulted from a confusion with the Scholastic debate about the possibility of indifferent actions. Intrinsic morality merely means that the act in its total complexity is right or wrong and not right or wrong just because of something extrinsic such as the will of the legislator. In the context of intrinsic morality the object of the human action is not something abstract, but the entire moral complex, the situation, as it is presented to the will. Consequently, such an understanding of the intrinsically evil is most compatible with a more historically minded methodology.

All Catholic theology, but especially moral theology, has been at a low point in the past few centuries. The manuals of moral theology merely present the same basic matter as the *Institutiones Theologiae Moralis* of the seventeenth century which came into existence after the Council of Trent to train confessors as judges in the confessional. For the most part, moral theology has been content to cite the opinions of authorities in the past and only occasionally does it venture a new application. Notice how infrequently, if at all, the manuals of moral theology ever cite an author who is not a Catholic or even a Catholic

---

[78] John Coventry, S.J., "Christian Conscience," *The Heythrop Journal,* Vol. 7 (1966), pp. 152–153.

dogmatic theologian. Moral theology has been divorced not only from the mainstream of secular thinking but even from Catholic dogmatic and ascetical theology.[79] A defensive and ghetto mentality has prevented moral theology from conducting a dialogue with the thought and life of the modern world. Historical circumstances of the last few centuries have intensified the defensive and isolated posture of moral theology. The thinking of the modern world was looked upon with suspicion by the Catholic Church, for it seemed to question teachings of the Church. Notice the opposition to Galileo, Darwin, etc. The liberalism of the nineteenth century appeared as a threat to the Church not only in the intellectual sphere but also in the political.[80] When some Catholics in the past century were beginning to speak of a dialogue or accommodation with modern thought, the Church responded by calling for a renewal of the theology and philosophy of St. Thomas. Döllinger in Germany was trying to break away from older thought patterns, but at that time the Church authorities looked suspiciously upon such moves.[81] The encyclical, *Aeterni Patris* of Leo XIII in 1879, called for a return to the teachings of St. Thomas.[82] Succeeding popes and the Code of Canon Law itself prescribed that philosophy and theology in Catholic schools should be taught according to the reason, doctrine, and principles of the Angelic Doctor.[83] Excesses in the modernist crisis at the beginning of the present century again emphasized the need to avoid the contemporary thought of the times.[84] Now, however, the Church is talking about the need for dialogue with the modern world and modern thought. In the future, Catholic moral theology will be much more open to the philosophical methodologies and thought patterns of the modern world. The emphasis will be away from the classicist world view with its stress on abstract universals.

An excessive rationalism in Catholic theology in the last century has compounded the problems arising from a classicist world-view. Other areas of Catholic theology have also experienced an over-

[79] Bernard Häring, C.SS.R., *The Law of Christ*, Vol. 1 (Westminster, Md.: Newman Press, 1961), pp. 3–33.

[80] R. Aubert, *Le pontificat de Pie IX* (Paris: Blond & Gay, 1952), pp. 224–261.

[81] *Ibid.*, pp. 240–242; 259–260.

[82] H. Denzinger, S.J., A. Schönmetzer, S.J., *Enchiridion Symbolorum Definitionum et Declarationum de Rebus Fidei et Morum*, 32nd ed. (Freiburg im Breisgau: Herder, 1963), n. 3135–3140.

[83] The pertinent references are given in note 42.

[84] John Wm. Padberg, "The Modernist Crisis Half a Century Later," *Proceedings of the Twentieth Annual Convention of the Catholic Theological Society of America* (1965), pp. 51–66.

emphasis on reason and its powers. Vatican Council I defined that God as the Creator can certainly be known from the things of creation through the natural light of human reason.[85] However, the conciliar section on divine revelation recalled the need for divine revelation so that man in the present condition of the human race can know God with firm certitude and without error.[86] Nevertheless, the Oath against Modernism states that God the Creator can be known and demonstrated from the things of creation. Although the Oath does not deny the need for revelation as stated in Vatican I, it tends to extol the power of reason by talking in terms of a demonstration and not mentioning any need for revelation.[87] Manuals of theology citing Leo XIII and Pius X maintain that it is theologically certain that the existence of God can be scientifically and intellectually demonstrated.[88] Leo XIII even claimed that the State could come to a knowledge of the one true religion since it was so evident.[89] Pius XII in the encyclical *Humani Generis* takes a slightly different tack. He says that although human reason can come to the knowledge of the existence of God, nevertheless there are many obstacles which prevent such a reasoning process.[90] The contemporary emphasis on the dialogue with atheism seems to go one step further. Reason, for the majority of men, does not bring them to a knowledge of God. Catholic theology today stresses the importance and need of faith and is even coming to grips with the problem of crises in faith. Excessive rationalism has also colored most of Catholic apologetics until recently. Reason was thought to prove the existence of God, the fact that Christ was the Son of God, and that the Church is the one true Church of Jesus Christ. Contemporary apologetics is different. In general, Catholic theology today is recognizing the excessive rationalism that has been a part of the theology of the manuals.

Moral theology has reflected the general rationalistic tendencies

---

[85] Denzinger and Schönmetzer, *op. cit.*, n. 3001.
[86] *Ibid.*, n. 3005.   [87] *Ibid.*, n. 3538.
[88] Iosephus M. Dalmau, S.L., *Sacrae Theologiae Summa II: De Deo Uno et Trino* (Madrid: Biblioteca de Autores Cristianos, 1955), Thesis 2: *Existentia Deo potest scientifice et intellectualiter demonstrari*, pp. 27 ff.
[89] "And if it be asked which of the many conflicting religions it is necessary to admit, reason and the natural law unhesitatingly tell us to practice that one which God enjoins, and which men can easily recognize by certain exterior notes, whereby Divine Providence has willed that it should be distinguished because, in a matter of such moment, the most terrible loss would be the consequence of error" (*Libertas Praestantissimum, Acta Leonis XIII*, Vol. 8 [1888], p. 230; Gilson, p. 72, n. 20).
[90] Denzinger and Schönmetzer, *op. cit.*, 3875.

in Catholic theology. Moral theology assumes that reason can solve all the complicated moral problems with clear and definite answers. A typical example of excessive rationalism is the proliferation of books and articles on medical moral problems in the present century. Reason has been invoked to give authoritative and clear-cut answers to such delicate moral problems as contraception, sterilization, euthanasia, artificial insemination, seminal analysis, etc. Many theologians are asking questions today precisely about these problems.[91] In the future, I think, Roman Catholic theology cannot expect reason to make the apodictic and absolute claims that have been made in the past.

Catholic moral theology is in the process of change and renewal. Moral theology is beginning a dialogue with Scripture, dogmatics, and above all with contemporary philosophy. Catholic theology is also aware of an overrationalistic spirit which characterized the theology manuals before Vatican II. Theological methodology is becoming more historically conscious and departing from a classicist world-view. Such changes, especially in methodology, will influence the insistence on absolute norms in moral theology. I do not categorically conclude that a more historically conscious methodology will deny absolute, universal norms; but such a methodology will not be as favorably disposed to such norms as the older, classicist methodology.

In conclusion, the scope and limits of the present chapter should be underscored. I have not tried to prove that there are no absolute, universally valid norms of conduct in moral theology. For three reasons, such an assertion is beyond the evidence submitted in the essay. First, there is a problem with the precise meaning of the term, "absolute norms of conduct." Many ethicists would agree on certain general and vague absolutes. Likewise, some confirmed situationalists will admit particular, absolute norms of moral conduct with regard to blasphemy, rape, and sexual promiscuity. Second, I have examined only the two factors frequently mentioned as contributing to the Catholic emphasis on absolutes. Third, every particular, absolute norm would have to be considered in itself before one could certainly prove that there are no specific, absolute norms in moral theology. Therefore, I have not undertaken to demonstrate that universal negative proposition. I have merely tried to prove that neither the natural law nor the teaching authority of the Church, the two reasons frequently proposed, explain the generic insistence on absolute norms in moral theology. In addition, two other factors, the ecclesiological

---

[91] Hurley, *The Furrow*, Vol. 17 (1966), pp. 619–623; Curran, *op. cit.*, pp. 128–129.

and sociological understanding of life in the Church as well as theological methodology, which in the past have contributed to the insistence on absolute norms, are now beginning to change. Since the reasons proposed do not explain the generic insistence on absolute norms in moral theology, I conclude that in the future the thrust in moral theology should be away from a generic insistence on such absolute norms. In the light of that thrust, moral theology must reevaluate its teachings on such delicate moral problems as divorce, direct abortion, masturbation, sterilization, and euthanasia, to mention just some of the problems that moral theology must face.

# 6

# *Calvin and the Prospects for a Christian Theory of Natural Law*

## DAVID LITTLE

It is more or less endemic to the character of the Christian gospel that natural law theory would have at once frustrated and intrigued the Church throughout most of its history. As is well known, primitive Christians understood their world to be profoundly corrupted and to be passing away in favor of a new heaven and a new earth. Not too much time needed to be spent in adjusting the radical claims of the kerygma to the everyday world, since Christians no longer lived an everyday life. The "natural" concerns of man—physical survival, procreation, social stability, and security—received little attention from the New Testament community. "The form of this world" gave very few clues as to the meaning of Christian existence or the style of life that until the last day was incumbent upon the Christian. Any attempt to move smoothly back and forth between the natural order and the order of the gospel was bound to encounter serious difficulty. The fact that the word "natural" itself has often meant "fallen" or "corrupt" in the Christian tradition bears testimony to this difficulty.

On the other hand, for the primitive Church, Christ was the "end" of things not simply in the sense that He *transformed* the natural world root and branch, but also in the sense that He *completed* in Himself and in the lives of His followers what the world was designed to be. The coming Kingdom represented both a decisive break with life as men knew it, and also a fulfillment of that for which the "whole creation has been waiting with eager longing." Any attempt, therefore, to divorce altogether the order of the gospel from the natural or created order was likewise destined to be resisted by the Church.

This central, though by no means unambiguous, notion of continuity between the established world and the in-breaking Kingdom helps to explain how it was that after the waning of eschatological fervor, the Church rather readily assimilated the Stoic doctrine of natural law to help cope with the complications of an everyday world. Even in the New Testament, of course, one finds an occasional reference to things men do "by nature" (Rom. 1:26–27; 2:14–15) as well as to the reasons for natural institutions like government, family, and so on (e.g., Rom. 13:1 ff.). As it became apparent that the established world was not doing much about passing away, these muted concerns required the kind of elaboration and systematization that could be supplied by the Stoic and Roman legal traditions. As a combination, then, between certain internal inclinations in the kerygma and the sobering demands of worldly life, the Church moved uncertainly and uneasily into the business of natural law thinking. Ever since, the Church has found it hard to live with as well as without such thinking.

Because of the peculiar ambiguity toward the natural order within their traditions, Christians have been pressed not only to satisfy the fundamental requirements of any natural law theory, but also to solve several additional self-imposed problems. Anyone, including a Christian, who sets out to develop a natural law theory would have to show two things, at the very least, about the everyday world: (1) that it is possible to establish a set of empirical generalizations about human nature that is constant, both spatially (cross-culturally) and temporally (historically); (2) that it is possible to move from this set of descriptive generalizations regarding how men do act, to a set of prescriptions regarding how they ought to act. As though these were not difficult enough, the Christian, as the result of his special stance toward the world, must add at least two more problems to his list: (3) he must be able to show on what grounds and in what sense human nature, though corrupted by sin, is still a reliable moral guide independent of Christian obligation; and (4) he must be able to relate his generalizations about natural moral obligation to Christian belief and obligation.

# I

In order to get some sense of how a Christian natural law theory has actually faced up to these problems, we shall examine one example in some depth. A figure who made a particularly valiant attempt to reconcile the conflicting tendencies within the Christian tradition, and to satisfy the four requirements we have lined out, was John Calvin. If any contemporary "rehabilitating" of Christian natural law theory is to be accomplished,[1] it is safe to say that the *way* Calvin tried to solve some of the abiding problems demands careful consideration. For Calvin's whole theological and moral enterprise was an endeavor to develop as best he could the specific connections between the natural world and the order of the gospel. Whether he succeeded or not, we may perhaps learn a few lessons from him for present-day cogitation on the subject of natural law.

Calvin's reflection on these matters begins with the theological assumption that all experience is ordered according to a divine design. Second, Calvin holds that right human action is not fully possible unless man acknowledges from his heart the Author of the design, namely God, and acts in conscious conformity with the purpose of the design, namely mutual love among men and with God. What Calvin calls the "moral law" or the "true and eternal rule of righteousness, prescribed for men of all nations and times" is simply that God "be worshipped by us all, and that we love one another."[2] In worshiping God genuinely, one perceives "the source and spirit [of righteousness] because from it men learn to live with one another in moderation without doing injury."[3]

Calvin makes clear that all legal as well as moral regulations and obligations derive from and point toward the "perpetual rule of love," which is the same as "God's eternal law" or what Calvin also calls the "scheme of equity."[4] That is, the rule of love is the law of creation, or the law according to which the entire natural-social order was designed.

> It is a fact that the law of God which we call the moral law is nothing else than a testimony of natural law and of that conscience which God has engraved upon the minds of men. Consequently, the entire scheme of this equity [rule of love] . . . is prescribed in it. Hence, this equity alone must be the goal and rule and limit of all laws.[5]

More specifically, the heart of God's created order is a social design entailing *cooperation* and *benevolent mutuality* among men. R. S. Wallace correctly describes Calvin's view: "The order of nature is that God has united all men together and has set them in this world so

---

[1] See Ian T. Ramsey's essay, "Towards a Rehabilitation of Natural Law," in *Christian Ethics and Contemporary Philosophy,* ed. Ian T. Ramsey (New York: Macmillan Co., 1966), pp. 382–396. Ramsey moves in a different direction from our own chapter.

[2] *Calvin: Institutes of the Christian Religion,* 2 vols., ed. John T. McNeill, trans. F. L. Battles (Philadelphia: Westminster Press, 1959), IV, 20, 15.

[3] *Institutes,* II, 8, 11.    [4] *Ibid.,* IV, 20, 15, 16.    [5] *Ibid.,* IV, 20, 16.

that each can help the other; unless we live in peace and concord one with another we prevent the order of nature." [6] Or, as Calvin himself puts it, "All men living . . . are linked together by a common nature. . . . The image of God ought to be particularly regarded as a bond of union." [7] Wherever the order of creation is fulfilled, there sharing of goods and services and unimpeded communication among men will take place.[8]

Against this background, Calvin's explicit exposition of the moral law is most interesting. As we noted, the moral law amounts to a declaration and specification of the natural law of God's created order. This specification takes place in the form of the Ten Commandments which, in turn, are the elaboration of the summary admonition to love God and man. Accordingly, Calvin's treatment of the Decalogue follows the traditional two-table division (commandments one through four pertaining to the duties owed God, and commandments five through ten the duties owed man).

Calvin begins his discussion by claiming that in the first commandment God "legitimates" His authority or His right to command: "If, then, 'from him are all things and in him all things abide,' it is right that all things should be referred to him. . . . Because it would be monstrous for us to want to withdraw from his rule when we cannot exist apart from him." [9] If there is a universal design and God is the designer, then, says Calvin, the goodness as well as the rightness of all things must be judged with reference to the purpose of the designer. "For God's will is so much the highest rule of righteousness that whatever he wills, by the very fact that he wills it, must be considered righteous. . . . But the will of God is not only free of all fault but is the highest rule of perfection, and even the law of all laws." [10] Calvin's argument, throughout his treatment of the first table, seems to proceed more or less as follows: the final purpose for which things are destined defines what is finally "good," "right," or "just." [11] God, being Himself final or ultimate, wills (or purposes) what is final; therefore, what God wills is good, right, and just.

The second table of the Decalogue is understood as the elaboration of the order or design of God. It is "the rule of [God's] righteousness," the set of fundamental imperatives that are "engraved upon the hearts

---

[6] Ronald S. Wallace, *Calvin's Doctrine of the Christian Life* (Grand Rapids: Wm. B. Eerdmans Co., 1961), p. 150.

[7] Calvin, *Commentary on Galatians*, 5:14.

[8] See André Biéler, *Social Humanism of Calvin* (Richmond, Va.: John Knox Press, 1964), pp. 17–18.

[9] *Institutes*, II, 8, 13; cf. I, 17, 1.   [10] *Ibid.*, III, 23, 2.

[11] These terms are not clearly distinguished by Calvin.

of all men." [12] What is particularly interesting about Calvin's treatment of the second table is the way he relates the commandments to what he conceives as God's final purpose. At several points, he imputes to the commandments "something more than what these phrases commonly signify. For by the virtue contrary to the vice, men usually mean abstinence from that vice. We say that the virtue goes beyond this to contrary duties and deeds." [13] That is, he understands some of the commandments not simply as prohibitory, but as recommending certain positive obligations, obligations that would appear to derive from the "perpetual rule of love."

Of the sixth commandment, "You shall not kill," Calvin says: "The purpose of this commandment is: the Lord has bound mankind together by a certain unity; hence each man ought to concern himself with the safety of all." [14] He continues: "Scripture notes that this commandment rests upon a twofold basis: man is both the image of God, and our flesh. Now, if we do not wish to violate the image of God, we ought to hold our neighbor sacred. And if we do not wish to renounce all humanity, we ought to cherish his as our own flesh." [15] This commandment means that man is not responsible simply to resist murder, but also that he must go out of his way to enhance the physical *and* spiritual well-being of his neighbor. Active attention to cooperation and mutuality is, Calvin argues, entailed in the structure of humanity itself.

The eighth commandment, "You shall not steal," Calvin broadens considerably to apply "not only in matters of money or in merchandise or land, but in the right of each [individual]; for we defraud our neighbors of their property if we repudiate the duties by which we are obligated to them." [16] In unmistakable terms Calvin interprets this commandment to have *benevolence* and *cooperation* as its end: "let us share the necessity of these whom we see pressed by the difficulty of affairs, assisting them in their need with our abundance." [17] "Let each man consider what, in his rank and station, he owes to his neighbors, and say what he owes. Moreover, . . . this rule was established for our hearts as well as for our hands, in order that men may strive to protect and promote the well-being and interests of others." [18]

Calvin exposits the ninth commandment, "You shall not bear

---

[12] *Ibid.*, II, 8, 1.
[13] *Ibid.*, II, 8, 9.
[14] *Ibid.*, II, 8, 39; cf. II, 8, 9.
[15] *Ibid.*, II, 8, 40.
[16] *Ibid.*, II, 8, 45. For an interesting discussion of "natural rights" in Calvin, see Arthur C. Cochrane, "Natural Law in Calvin," *Church-State Relations in Ecumenical Perspective*, ed. Elwyn A. Smith (Pittsburgh: Duquesne University Press, 1966), pp. 176–217.
[17] *Institutes*, II, 8, 46.
[18] *Ibid.*, II, 8, 46.

false witness against your neighbor," in a similar way. "This commandment is lawfully observed when our tongue, in declaring the truth, serves both the good repute and the advantage of our neighbors." "For he who does not allow a brother's name to be sullied by falsehood also wishes it to be kept unblemished as far as truth permits. Indeed, although he may guard it against lying only, he yet implies by this that it is entrusted to his care. That God is concerned about it should be enough to prompt us to keep safe our neighbor's good name." [19]

Finally, Calvin's interpretation of the Decalogue in the light of the "law of love" reaches a climax in his treatment of the tenth commandment, "You shall not covet your neighbor's house," etc. "The purpose of this commandment is: since God wills that our whole soul be possessed with a disposition to love, we must banish from our hearts all desire contrary to love." [20] We ought not, says Calvin, tolerate any desire that "tends to our neighbor's loss." "To this corresponds the opposite precept: Whatever we conceive, deliberate, will, or attempt is to be linked to our neighbor's good and advantage." [21] Calvin argues in this section that the prohibitions are really but the reverse side of the "law of love," that is, of a "deliberate consent of the will" in seeking the advantage of the neighbor.

Calvin also uses this opportunity to universalize the meaning of "neighbor" in no uncertain terms. "The term 'neighbor' includes even the most remote person; we are not expected to limit the precept of love to those in close relationships." "We ought to embrace the whole human race without exception in a single feeling of love; here there is no distinction between barbarian and Greek, worthy and unworthy, friend and enemy, since all should be contemplated in God, not in themselves." [22] Furthermore, Calvin takes strong exception to the Scholastic position on "counsels of perfection" by which the more radical precepts of Christian love were reserved for monks. "The reason they assign for not receiving them as laws is that they seem too burdensome and heavy, especially for Christians who are under the law of grace. Do they dare thus to abolish God's eternal law that we are to love our neighbor?" [23] The demands of the law of love are incumbent upon all men, for these demands make up the law of humanity, the law of human nature. Men were created precisely to practice the obligations of cooperation and mutuality; in fact, *by these standards Calvin defines the term "human nature."*

However, this discussion of the moral-natural law is not, of course,

[19] *Ibid.*, II, 8, 47, 8.   [20] *Ibid.*, II, 8, 49.   [21] *Ibid.*, II, 8, 49.
[22] *Ibid.*, II, 8, 55; cf. IV, 12, 7.   [23] *Ibid.*, II, 8, 56.

# Natural Law

the end of the matter. Calvin is well aware that he has disobedience and sin to contend with. He must handle the conflict inherent in Christian theology between the intended or "ideal" nature of man and his actual or "fallen" nature. Calvin needs, like any Christian thinker, to reconcile the present shape of things with the ultimate design that he has sketched out.

For Calvin the essence of love—of cooperativeness or benevolence—is a *voluntary* disposition to service. God instructed Adam regarding the tree of knowledge to "test his obedience and prove that he was willingly under God's command." [24] Adam's denial of God, his lack of voluntary submission, or love, "has perverted the whole order of nature in heaven and earth." [25] By all rights, Adam's disobedience should have been followed by "the destruction of our whole nature," [26] except that man, even in his sin, does not possess the power completely to undo God's design. Although the nature of man has been "despoiled of its true good" (voluntary cooperativeness),[27] certain "crumbs of righteousness," certain vestiges, remain to direct human action toward the good, and to enable man at least faintly to distinguish that good from its opposite. In other words, man continues to possess—minimally, to be sure—some conscious awareness of the demands of the law of love.

These crumbs or vestiges of righteousness make up Calvin's explicit doctrine of natural law. Despite all the corruption, God has left His law implanted in man's nature for two reasons: first, to prod man in the direction of his true end, and, second, to convict and condemn him because he must be prodded, and is not voluntarily disposed to act in accord with love of God and man. Let us comment on these two functions of natural law in order.

1. Though man since the fall has no access to true community with God and man short of an extra effort on God's part (i.e., special grace), God sees to it that the essential *social character* of human nature is maintained in man's "natural instinct to foster and preserve society." [28] "The fact remains that some seed of political order has been implanted in all men. And this is ample proof that in the arrangement of this life no man is without the light of reason." [29] Men also retain some useful knowledge of various arts that enhance man's social life: a capacity for government, economic management, mechanical skills, and liberal sciences.

There is some ambiguity in Calvin's thought about the precise status of these natural remnants. At times he appears to accord to

[24] *Ibid.*, II, 1, 4.
[25] *Ibid.*, II, 1, 5.
[26] *Ibid.*, II, 2, 17.
[27] *Ibid.*, II, 2, 15.
[28] *Ibid.*, II, 2, 13.
[29] *Ibid.*

man's rational and natural capabilities some sort of independence, so far as determining truth and moral rectitude goes. Not only does human nature—by its shortcomings—encourage men to look elsewhere for true goodness; it also seems to possess some distinctive moral legitimacy in itself. For example, Calvin suggests that people who reject or pervert commonly accepted laws and rules of justice (which are "implanted in all men") *"fight against manifest reason."* [30] In such cases one need not necessarily invoke God's law; apparently reason itself teaches general rectitude, at least in certain contexts.

That natural reason does have some independent moral status is the upshot of Calvin's distinction between "heavenly" and "earthly" understanding, or between "spiritual" and "political" life.[31] With respect to heavenly or spiritual matters, reason is "utterly blind and stupid." [32] But in matters earthly or political ("external conduct"), natural reason would appear to stand partly on its own. In the

---

[30] *Ibid.* (italics added).

[31] *Ibid.*, II, 2, 13; cf. III, 19, 15. At times Calvin comes very close to severing completely the spiritual and political realms. At these points he seems to imply that "manifest reason" is a sufficient guide to "outward behavior," while the "inner mind" alone is governed by God's Word. "Now these two, as we have divided them, must always be examined separately; and while one is being considered, we must call away and turn aside the mind from thinking about the other. There are in man, so to speak, two worlds, over which different kings and different laws have authority" (III, 19, 15; cf. IV, 20, 1). Here, of course, Calvin is trying to handle one dimension of the Christian tradition to which we alluded in the beginning of the chapter—namely, the asocial, "otherworldly" dimension, which is irrelevant to everyday structures. Other evidences of this side of Calvin's thought occur particularly in his treatment of the Christian life (III, 6 ff.).

Were this the only, or even the predominant, emphasis in Calvin's thought, we might have found a stronger inclination to develop a thoroughly independent natural law theory so as to handle the external world apart from the inner world of Christian freedom. This is, of course, exactly what happened in a figure like Richard Hooker. But Calvin found it hard to maintain the sharp distinction we quoted above. He also argues that the two kingdoms "are not at variance" (IV, 20, 2). On the contrary, political government ought to assure two related things: a public manifestation of true religion and the maintenance of humanity among men. That is, government should enforce both tables of the Decalogue (IV, 20, 3; cf. IV, 20, 9).

Actually, the two realms for Calvin join and interpenetrate one another in regard to the common end they both share: love. Love is the end of the law, as well as the end of grace. Consequently, while it is impossible to reduce the inner and outer worlds to each other, it is impossible completely to separate them either. The mutuality and cooperativeness demanded by the law of "outward behavior" is certainly not alien to the love granted in Christ, which affects the "inner mind." (See II, 8, 57–8.)

[32] *Institutes*, II, 2, 19.

# Natural Law

political, earthly realm, "man is educated for the *duties of humanity and citizenship* that must be maintained among men." [33] Apparently, Calvin believed that men naturally affirm the duties of humanity, which were but the second table of the Decalogue. Though there is diversity among the laws and customs of mankind, yet "together with one voice, they pronounce punishment against those crimes which God's eternal law has condemned, namely, murder, theft, adultery, and false witness." [34] Moreover, at certain points Calvin feels it adequate simply to invoke the duties of humanity against laws and customs that do not seem to conform to these duties. "For I do not think that these barbarous and savage laws such as gave honor to thieves, permitted promiscuous intercourse, and others both more filthy and more absurd, are to be regarded as laws. For they are abhorrent not only to all justice, but also *to all humanity.* ...." [35]

Finally, Calvin accords earthly reason at least provisional independence in the matter of determining the character and obligations of social office and station. "Natural reason itself shows and dictates that reverence ... is due to all lawful commands.[36] "The subjection of the inferior to the superior in the relationship of ruler to people, master to servant, husband to wife, child to parent is part of an inviolable order established by God the Father." [37]

However, while there are for Calvin these unmistakable "fixed points" [38] in natural moral experience, and while these do have something self-evident about them, Calvin is very far from divorcing natural morality altogether from the fundamental theological premises from which he starts. Not only have the "supernatural gifts" been lost in the fall, "but these natural ones remaining were corrupted" [39] as well. The very fact that men could simultaneously approve the second table of the Decalogue, and then in specific instances reject portions of it "on account of their lust," proves for Calvin "the frailty of the human mind" [40]—its inherent instability and unreliability. Natural capabilities then, prod man "to aspire to a good of which he is empty, to a freedom of which he has been deprived" [41] both by suggesting something of man's final destiny and by revealing his inadequacy and incompleteness apart from a full apprehension of that destiny.

---

[33] *Ibid.*, III, 19, 15 (italics added).     [34] *Ibid.*, IV, 20, 16.     [35] *Ibid.*, IV, 20, 15.

[36] *Commentary on Deuteronomy*, 17:12, quoted in Cochrane, *op. cit.*, p. 8.

[37] Wallace, *op. cit.*, p. 158; cf. *Sermon on Galatians*, 3:26–9, *Corpus Reformatorum* 50:567–568.

[38] This is a phrase used by Peter Winch in an interesting essay, "Nature and Convention," *Proceedings of the Aristotelian Society* (1960), p. 238.

[39] *Institutes*, II, 2, 16.     [40] *Ibid.*, II, 2, 13.

[41] *Ibid.*, II, 2, 1; cf. II, 8, 11, also, IV, 20, 15.

2. Because man must be driven or compelled to seek his real end, he must be condemned by the very thing that drives him, namely the natural law. "The purpose of the natural law, therefore, is to render man inexcusable." [42] Calvin elucidates as follows: "The sinner tries to evade his innate power to judge between good and evil. Still, he is continually drawn back to it, and is not so much as permitted to wink at it without being forced, whether he will or not, at times to open his eyes. It is falsely said, therefore, that man sins out of ignorance alone." [43] That man must be driven to do what he ought to do willingly is his severest condemnation.

The fact of coercion in the everyday affairs of politics and law is thus an expression and further elaboration of this two-sided character of the natural law. As the result of man's penchant for self-destruction and anarchy, political and legal institutions—as the manifestation of "natural inclinations"—remind man both of the final design and of his inability to act according to it save by a voluntary or loving disposition. These institutions are, therefore, necessary, and possess their own "functional demands," [44] which Calvin wishes to take very seriously. Nevertheless, the structures of politics and law, undergirding as they do the structures of the world, point beyond themselves to the "perpetual rule of love." The inclinations and institutions of the natural world have their "end," in both senses of that word, in the true and eternal rule of righteousness.

For Calvin it is, of course, Christ who, as the embodiment of God's love, is the fulfillment and the revelation of the ultimate design. "Now we know that apart from Christ there is nothing but confusion in this world. Although Christ has already begun to set up the Kingdom of God, his death was the real beginning of a right order and the full restoration of the world." [45] Christ alone *voluntarily* loves God and man, and thus becomes the mediator and exemplar through which men can at last be liberated from the "yoke of the law" (its coercive-condemning character) and "willingly obey God's Will." [46] Consequently, in His Body, the Church, the cooperativeness and mutuality that is the end of God's design becomes the pattern of life: "It is as if . . . the saints were gathered into the society of Christ on the principle that whatever benefits God confers upon them, they should in

---

[42] *Ibid.,* II, 2, 22.   [43] *Ibid.,* II, 2, 22; cf. II, 8, 1.

[44] *Calvin* devotes IV, 20 to a discussion of the functional demands of political institutions.

[45] *Calvin: Commentaries,* ed. and trans. Joseph Haroutunian (Philadelphia: Westminster Press, 1958), p. 339.

[46] *Institutes,* III, 19, 4; cf. II, 8, 57.

# Natural Law 185

turn share with one another." [47] As the matrix of love, as the representative of the order of the gospel, the Church becomes an independent community that at once fulfills, and yet remains qualitatively different from, the natural world in which it finds itself.

In one way or another, Calvin addressed himself to each of the four requirements of a Christian natural law theory that we listed earlier. (1) He developed a set of cross-cultural generalizations about human nature and reason in relation to social and political inclinations as well as to the six commandments of the second table of the Decalogue. (2) He moved from these descriptive generalizations to prescriptive or normative judgments about "good and evil" by viewing these generalizations as indicators or tokens of the purpose or design for which man was created. Man ought to act on these principles because they give evidence of what he was intended or designed to be. (3) Calvin accounted for the split in the concept of nature, which confronts every Christian theologian, and argued that within the limits of general social and political reflection, human nature and reason dictate a few unexceptionable moral principles and some capacity for successful moral reflection. (4) Most of Calvin's treatment of natural law was couched in terms of the distinction and complementarity between the natural law, as it functioned in a corrupted world, and the law of love as the "end" of law (again, in both senses of the word).

Calvin looks at natural law from the top, so to speak—from the perspective not first of all of nature, but of grace.[48] He has a theory of natural law, let there be no mistake about that. But he is not interested in developing a self-contained, independent doctrine. He has what

---

[47] *Ibid.*, IV, 1, s. See Biéler, *Social Humanism,* pp. 19 f.

[48] I believe myself to be in general agreement with Cochrane's conclusions in "Natural Law in Calvin." He remarks: ". . . In view of . . . the fallibility of conscience and natural law and the need for God's special, preserving grace, it is evident that Calvin did not mean that we could dispense with God's law and substitute a natural law. His point is that God's law is in harmony with the true order of man's creatureliness *which is itself from God's law"* (pp. 206 f.). Cochrane rightly emphasizes that even the natural gifts which men have are, after all, the products of God's grace.

One difficulty I have with Cochrane's very informative essay is whether Calvin ever makes the tidy distinction between the order of nature and the natural law that Cochrane makes (see p. 204). Cochrane seems to say that while the order of nature remains constant, man's apprehension of it varies. I do not fully understand what the term "constant" means, but, in any case, I should have thought that when Calvin says Adam "perverted the whole order of nature in heaven and earth" (II, 1, 5), he means a serious change has taken place in that order. Cochrane himself recognizes that Calvin is not always consistent in discussing the relation between natural law and natural order (see p. 204).

we may call a derivative theory of natural law, one that has always to be seen in relation to a more inclusive theological and moral design. The theory starts from the notion of love (or, variously, mutuality, cooperativeness, benevolence) as the central ethical principle embodied in Christian revelation, and then "works back" to make room for those generalizations of human nature that Calvin considered the conditions or prerequisites for making the realization of love possible.

How are we to evaluate Calvin's attempt at constructing a Christian theory of natural law? Is there anything here upon which present-day Christian ethics can build, anything which can meet the standards of contemporary social science and moral reflection, as well as make some contribution to a "theory of human nature which bears on ethical questions"?[49] Our response will be in two parts: (1) We shall examine some current anthropological observations relevant to the question of human nature to discover possible points of contact with Calvin's conclusion; (2) We shall examine the more strictly ethical problems involved in justifying and applying a Christian theory of natural law.

## II

1. The impossibility of discovering any essential definition of human nature has recently been asserted by Professor Kai Nielsen in his challenging essay, "The Myth of Natural Law."[50] Though Nielsen is aware of the growing "conditional absolutes,"[51] he is unwilling to make much of these constant features of human life:

---

[49] William Frankena, *Ethics* (Englewood Cliffs, N.J.: Prentice-Hall, 1963), p. 4.

[50] In *Law and Philosophy*, ed. Sidney Hook (New York: New York University Press, 1964), pp. 122–143.

[51] There is a growing literature on the subject of "ethical universals" and a unified theory of human nature. E.g., Philip Selznick, "Natural Law and Sociology," in *Natural Law and Modern Society*, John Cogley, et al. (Cleveland: World Publishing Co., 1963); Ralph Linton, "Universal Ethical Principles: an Anthropological View," in *Moral Principles in Action*, ed. R. N. Anshen (New York: Harper & Row, 1952); Linton, "The Problem of Universal Values," in *Method and Perspective in Anthropology*, ed. R. F. Spencer (Minneapolis: University of Minnesota Press, 1954); Clyde Kluckhohn, "Universal Categories of Culture," in *Anthropology Today*, ed. A. L. Kroeber (Chicago: University of Chicago Press, 1953); Kluckhohn, "Common Humanity and Diverse Cultures," in *Human Meaning of the Social Sciences*, ed. Daniel Lerner (Cleveland: World Publishing Co., 1962); Kluckhohn, "Values and Value-Orientations in the Theory of Action," in *Toward a General Theory of Action*, eds. Talcott Parsons and Edward A. Shils (New York: Harper & Row, 1962); Kluckhohn, "Ethical Relativity: *Sic et Non*," in *Culture and Behavior*, ed. Richard Kluckhohn (Glencoe: Free Press, 1964); Margaret Mead, *Continuities in*

> It may well be that men have a certain nature . . . that there is a property or some set of properties that all men and only men . . . in fact possess. A language and a culture may be just such properties. But this does not entail that man, like an artifact, has some essential nature, some function that he was cut out or made to achieve.[52]

Nielsen argues that if there were beings who resembled men physically and lived together doing many of the things men do but had no language or culture, "we still would not be justified in refusing to call them men." [53]

However, Nielsen's argument is not completely persuasive. Even he appears to squirm a little in a footnote on this subject: this issue is not, he says, "as simple as it may seem." "As a matter of brute fact, many of the characteristic things human beings do involve speech; take this away and there would be little distinctively human behavior left." [54] Yet he assures the reader—somewhat arbitrarily, it seems to me—that even without language a group of beings could still manifest enough manlike behavior to warrant the title "human." If this is true, we must have it on more convincing authority than Nielsen's assertion of it.

Some recent anthropological studies appear, in fact, to call into question Nielsen's conclusions. If the findings of Marshall Sahlins, Elman Service, and Walter Goldschmidt, for example, are correct,[55] we may be approaching a rudimentary, but very significant, empirical definition of what the term "human being," as distinct from other primate beings, means. And the bearing of this definition on ethical reflection is striking.

According to Sahlins' extensive investigations, human nature is characterized by two distinguishing features that are very much interrelated: culture or symbol-using, and sharing or cooperation.[56]

---

*Cultural Evolution* (New Haven: Yale University Press, 1966); Mead, "Some Anthropological Considerations Concerning Natural Law," *Natural Law Forum*, VI (1961), pp. 51–64. See also Richard B. Brandt, *Ethical Theory* (Englewood Cliffs, N.J.: Prentice-Hall, 1959), chap. 11.

[52] Nielsen, *op. cit.*, p. 132.   [53] *Ibid.*, p. 132.   [54] *Ibid.*, p. 12 n., 141.

[55] Marshall D. Sahlins, "The Social Life of Monkeys, Apes and Primitive Men," in *Readings in Anthropology*, Vol. II, ed. Morton H. Fried (New York: Thomas Y. Crowell Co., 1959); Elman R. Service, *Primitive Social Organization: An Evolutionary Perspective* (New York: Random House, 1965); Service, "Kinship Terminology and Evolution," *American Anthropologist*, Vol. 62 (1960), pp. 747–763; Walter Goldschmidt, *Comparative Functionalism* (Berkeley: University of California Press, 1966).

[56] See also Goldschmidt's account of the distinctive traits of "humanity," *op. cit.*, pp. 40 ff.

> A comparison of subhuman primates and primitive society must recognize a qualitative difference between the two. Human society is cultural society. . . . The social life of subhuman primates is governed by anatomy and physiology. Variations in human society are independent of, and are not expressions of biological variations of the organism. Variations in primate society are direct expressions and concomitants of biological variations.[57]

The fact that "man lives his life in a symbolic universe" involves, of course, language usage and other forms of cultural communication,[58] but it also involves "teamwork" or cooperation. "Economic teamwork and mutual aid are nearly zero among the primates, including anthropoids. Spontaneous cooperation has not been observed among them." [59] Sahlins adds, furthermore, that "spontaneous teamwork supposes symbolling: 'Teamwork makes intellectual demands of the same order as those made by language. Psychologically, it may, in fact, be difficult to distinguish between the two.' " [60]

Along the same lines, Service claims that the critical combination of symboling and sharing becomes, as it were, "written into" the physical as well as the psychological and social character of man's nature. "The acquisition of culture depended upon a development of the primate brain to the point which made possible the use of symbols in communication and thought. With symbols human [beings] *can plan ways to cooperate and create means to enhance and perpetuate cooperative relationships.*" [61] In other words, the fact that "nonhuman primates do not share," [62] means at the same time that they have no culture; for culture is predicated on the fact of communication and cooperation.

We are, then, coming close to an empirical definition of "humanity" as distinct from the primates (to whom man is obviously similar in many respects): *to be human is to order life cooperatively.*[63] Such a definition, if empirically valid, raises a number of questions about the fashionable ideas regarding the nature of man. For example, H. L. A. Hart, who has so influenced Nielsen and other contemporary philosophers,[64] gives what appears to be a mistaken impression in

---

[57] Sahlins, *op. cit.*, pp. 187–188.
[58] See Kluckhohn, "The Concept of Culture," *Culture and Behavior*, p. 73.
[59] Sahlins, *op. cit.*, p. 195.   [60] *Ibid.*   [61] Service, *op. cit.*, p. 41.   [62] *Ibid.*, p. 39.
[63] We stress that "cooperatively" implies cultural as well as other kinds of sharing. This fact is, of coure, what distinguishes man from lower orders of insects (e.g., ants) that cooperate nonculturally.
[64] The influence of Hart's *Concept of Law* (Oxford: Clarendon Press, 1965) is remarkable. In chap. 9, "Law and Morals," he develops his famous "minimum content of natural law."

developing his (basically Humean) theory of natural law. Hart understands man to be primarily concerned with continuing his physical existence. Therefore, he feels, man cultivates cooperative associations that have their own functional requisites or "natural laws." *If* man wants to survive physically, *then* he must choose to obey these minimal laws of association.[65] This way of viewing things implies, with Nielsen, that the term "man" or "human being" has some residual meaning apart from a cultural-cooperative pattern of behavior. It implies, very misleadingly, that man "opts for" human association and culture, which he can somehow take or leave and still remain man. However, if our anthropologists are right, *for man to remain man* (and not become some other kind of survival-seeking animal), *his cultural-cooperative characteristics must survive along with his biological existence.* Beings become human insofar as they are capable of symboling and sharing.[66] There is, as it were, a certain fixed design to the concept "human" which designates what man must do and be, if he will survive *as man*.

The bearing of all this on moral experience is important. It explains why in all known societies cooperation or mutuality, along with physical survival, is a morally crucial consideration. Indeed, it explains the fact that the dictates of cooperativeness often morally *outweigh* the concern for physical life and limb. It is a common religious-moral assumption (for example, in primitive Christianity) that a man should give up his life (physical survival) in order to find "true" survival—namely, life that is lived in genuine mutuality and cooperation, such as is found in the Kingdom of God. If physical survival is the basic concern of man, from which all other imperatives flow, it is not clear why so often moral priority is given to the *quality* rather than to the quantity of survival.

But beyond these considerations, our anthropological definition of human nature helps us to understand a little better the character and function of the cross-cultural "ethical universals" that are now widely recognized to exist in all societies. When one takes a close look at these universals, they can be seen as simply *a specification and elaboration of the conditions for social cooperation.* Kluckhohn col-

[65] Hume's general treatment in *A Treatise of Human Nature* (especially Book III) in many ways anticipates Hart.

[66] This fact helps us to understand why, for example, when a dog appears to communicate with his master, or to "know" what is going on, or to take his master's interests into account, we normally say the dog is "almost human." Conversely, we can understand why, when a man cannot communicate or share in any way, we normally say, "he just vegetates." These are not arbitrary uses of language. They express what the term "human" means.

lected a list of six such universals:[67] (a) prohibition against murder (wanton killing within the in-group), as distinguished from other forms of justifiable homicide; (b) prohibition against stealing within the in-group; (c) prohibition against incest, and other regulations on sexual behavior; (d) prohibition under defined circumstances against lying; (e) regulations and stipulations regarding the restitution and reciprocity of property; (f) stimulation of mutual obligations between parents and children. As Kluckhohn states without qualification: "Ethical universals are the product of universal human nature, which is based, in turn, upon a common biology, psychology, and generalized situation."[68]

For our purposes, what is of course so striking about the results of these findings is their congeniality with the natural law thinking of Calvin.[69] Surely, it is more than accidental that the six universals which Kluckhohn singled out correspond almost exactly to the six commandments of the second table of the Decalogue, something on which Calvin spent so much time. Furthermore, the apparent relation of the universals to cooperativeness or sharing, so essential to the realization and maintenance of human nature, seems to confirm in a rather uncanny way Calvin's argument that the end of the natural-moral law is more than prohibitory, "it contains . . . the requirement that we give our neighbor's life all the help we can." In short, Calvin would appear to have been on reasonably sound empirical ground in implying that man's social inclinations, his disposition for cooperativeness, together with the ethical universals of the second table that are imprinted on man's nature, all constitute fixed points in understanding what the term "human" or "humanity" means.

2. Despite these considerations, however, the problems for natural law theory are hardly all solved. First, though the six universals may be relatively fixed cross-culturally, they can be and have been institutionalized in widely divergent and sometimes contradictory ways.[70] Can one judge "naturally" which is best of all the possible ways there are to build a society around patterns of cooperation and prohibitions against murder, stealing, lying, etc.? Moreover, can these universals, unassisted, carry us very far in serious ethical reflection? Second, have

---

[67] "Ethical Relativity: *Sic et Non*"; although Kluckhohn does not mention the prohibition against stealing (b) in this essay, he does include it in "Values and Value-Orientations," p. 418.

[68] "Ethical Relativity: *Sic et Non*," p. 285.

[69] Not only with Calvin, of course. The whole tradition of natural law, on which Calvin drew, is relevant here.

[70] See Kluckhohn, "Ethical Relativity: *Sic et Non*," p. 279.

we yet established that even these universals, or the "natural" human inclinations to sharing and symboling are "good" and that it is "right" to obey them?

In laying the foundations for a Christian theory of natural law, the general ways in which Calvin tried to answer these questions are, at least, a useful start. As we have seen, the whole matter of natural law is looked at by Calvin from the perspective of the final end or purpose for which God designed man, namely *voluntary cooperativeness* (love) among men and with God. It is quite clear that for Calvin human nature could not finally be properly understood, let alone properly ordered, without reference to Christian revelation, that is, without reference to the partial realization of God's design here and now in Christ. This is true for him both because what is revealed in Christ *is* the final design, and also because man has so corrupted his nature as to need assistance in perceiving what human nature is really for.

Accordingly, the Christian apprehension of voluntary cooperativeness as the final purpose for which man was created becomes the ultimate norm for evaluating human nature and for appraising institutional ways of organizing it. While the relation of love to human nature is by no means a simple or unambiguous matter in Calvin, the central normative place of love is unmistakable. As the treatment of the Decalogue makes clear, love directs and shapes the character of the natural-moral law. Three substantive ethical principles would appear to be suggested in Calvin's notion of love: *universalism, active benevolence,* and *voluntarism.*

First, the ethical constants of the Decalogue are radically universalized at Calvin's hands. The prescriptions against murder, stealing, etc., no longer apply simply to the "in-group," but to every man, "even the most remote person." In God's design, neighbor "includes the whole of mankind."[71] Second, love informs the law in such a way as to add concern for the neighbor's welfare, or for the common good, to the negative prescriptions of the law. The natural law is not properly grasped, save in relation to active benevolence.

Third, love, as an essentially voluntary, self-giving activity, implies two things about human nature: in order for the human self to have the possibility for fulfilling its potentialities, its "base of operations" (the physical individual) must be regarded both as inviolable and as in need of opportunities for expressing cooperativeness. In other words, human nature possesses certain fundamental rights of existence and development. Indeed, several of the ethical constants

---

[71] *Calvin: Commentaries, op. cit.,* pp. 330–331.

of the Decalogue would seem to be an outline for just such a "bill of rights." Obviously, murder, stealing, bearing false witness are, by definition, arbitrary, unilateral acts that rule out the voluntary capacity of the victim. An individual who has either been murdered or robbed or misrepresented has quite precisely lost his rights to make choices regarding his life. He has no chance voluntarily to "give himself" (his life) or to "give of himself" (his possessions) or to "give account of himself" (speak for himself), for these matters have all been arbitrarily determined by someone else. In short, the possibility of manifesting a cooperative spirit has in each of these cases been seriously threatened, if not eliminated altogether.[72]

However, not only must the self be protected in these ways. It must also be given institutional opportunities for developing a willing cooperative spirit. As we suggested, Calvin's doctrine of the Church as an independent community, clearly differentiated (in theory) from political coercion, is premised on the assumption that Christian love is above all a spirit of voluntary mutuality, a "diversity of grace," and that, therefore, it must be given the opportunity of expressing itself in a voluntary, rather than in a politically controlled, social context. In my judgment, it is no accident that Calvinism in its English Puritan form, for example, moved so far in applying consensual and voluntaristic norms not only to the Church, but also to the wider institutional framework of government and family. Christian love understood as voluntary cooperativeness appears to have certain decided institutional implications.

Calvin does, then, supply us with a way of relating love to the ethical universals of human nature, as well as a way of shaping and arranging these universals according to the substantive principles of love: universalism, active benevolence, and voluntarism. Not only must the ethical constants be provided for, on this view; they must be provided for in keeping with the "law of love." Presumably, therefore, Christian ethics can begin to evaluate institutional patterns of behavior in relation to these substantive principles. That is, it can be asked whether legal, political, economic, and familial patterns, as they are established in a given society, are sufficiently universalistic (or nonpreferential), whether they encourage and allow for enough voluntaristic expression (or significant choice-making in family, politics, etc.), and whether they cultivate cooperativeness (or concern for

[72] In developing a "bill of rights" that is rooted in the notion of "man" as a sharing being, we do not, of course, suggest that there may never be any exceptions to the application of these rights. We simply suggest that the "burden of proof" will always rest upon recommendations that infringe these rights in any way.

the common welfare). There is, of course, no fixed answer to the application of these principles, nor may Calvin's own particular application be taken as final. Some of his views on social and ecclesiastical institutions may, I believe, be held wanting precisely with reference to these principles.[73] Nevertheless, we are beginning to generate here a set of principles which would appear to be entailed in the idea of Christian love, and which may be used to make social ethical judgments among and within different institutional systems.

But in the light of this interpretation, what becomes of natural law as such? If natural law, on Calvin's view, is not self-authenticating or self-sufficient, neither is it completely swallowed up in Christian revelation. In general terms, Calvin's understanding of natural law serves very much as do contemporary anthropological findings, namely to remind us of the fixed points of human nature which define as well as ensure the "humanity" of man. These fixed points, including the capacity to share goods as well as symbols, and the six ethical conditions of cooperativeness, enable us to come much closer to a "theory of human nature which bears on ethical questions" than Nielsen and others have grasped.

With the help of anthropology, it is becoming possible to discover certain fundamental rights that delineate what Calvin called the "duties of humanity." If there is to be man at all (i.e., a culturally and economically cooperative being), then the rights to life, property, and self-expression[74] must be ensured and enforced in some institutional fashion. It may even be that we have here a basis for understanding what the term "natural justice" means; it may be the "natural" human inclination to establish reasonably secure patterns of expectation around the six ethical universals and against their arbitrary, unilateral infringement. Without such guarantees, of course, cooperativeness and, therefore, humanity is in jeopardy.

As Calvin saw, there would appear to be a "lower boundary" of

---

[73] As well as institutional assurances regarding the regulation of property, marriage, and family. There may well be more than simply these six. See D. F. Aoerle, A. K. Cohen, A. K. Davis, M. J. Levy, and F. X. Sutton, "Functional Prerequisites of a Society," *Ethics*, Vol. LX (1950), pp. 100–111. When I mention "right to property" I do not necessarily mean what Locke meant by the term. I do have in mind individual control over some "wherewithal" to make meaningful choices about what a person shall do and be.

[74] As we saw above, Calvin affirmed a hierarchical social order grounded in nature. This assumption very much colored Calvin's views of state and church and impeded the full development of the consensualist equalitarian themes that are also present in his thought. Therefore, some aspects of his thought may be used to criticize other aspects.

human nature, below which the "image" or "design" of humanity is lost altogether. Social institutions—most obviously political and legal ones—maintain order and justice to the degree they prevent men from crossing that boundary, to the degree, that is, that they maintain the conditions and expectations of humanity against arbitrariness (or non-cooperativeness). To be sure, the character of this boundary tells us only a minimal amount about the "upper boundary" or "true end" of the design of human nature. At this point, revelation becomes important, as we have seen. Still, on Calvin's view, serious and resolute attention to the maintenance of the lower boundary is one of the crucial duties of humanity just so the true end of voluntary cooperativeness may be reached at all. What natural reason can perceive about the conditions of human nature has a great deal of significance in Calvin's moral thinking.

Finally, we come to the matter of legitimating or justifying a Christian natural law theory as a serious ethical position. Nielsen, in his aforementioned essay, takes issue with all religious natural law theories for two reasons. First, they make unverifiable statements about the "ultimate purposes" of man and, therefore, can hardly qualify as natural or empirical theories. In fact, Nielsen is skeptical that there are any constant purposes that human beings "by nature" pursue.[75] Second, whether or not theological assertions about the destiny of man become persuasive, there is no logical way to move from these descriptive assertions to prescriptive judgments. "Even if there

---

[75] Nielsen, *op. cit.*, p. 133. We have indicated above why we think Nielsen's unwillingness to speak of a structure of human nature is unfortunate. Though I am in no better position than Nielsen to be authoritative about these matters, I would like to suggest, on the basis of the evidence I have cited, that it does make sense to speak of men "by nature" seeking (intending or purposing) to live life cooperatively. Man does this by nature because, as we have seen, *this is what it means to be man*. On this point I find myself very much in agreement with Lon Fuller in *Morality of Law* (New Haven: Yale University Press, 1965). He states: "I believe that if we were forced to select the principle that supports and infuses all human aspiration we would find it *in the objective of maintaining communication with our fellows. Communication is something more than a means of staying alive. It is a way of being alive*" (pp. 185–186; italics added). This is not to say that it is the only purpose, but it is most certainly to say that this is a natural and very central purpose.

As to Nielsen's objection that religious natural law theories assert unverifiable purposes regarding man's nature, this is, I believe, only partly true in the case of Calvin. We have argued throughout that while the ultimate purpose for which man was created is known only in revelation and never naturally, this purpose is, for Calvin, related to natural purposes, that is, purposes of a verifiable character. Therefore, there is an aspect of Calvin's theory of the end of man that is always open to rational, empirical observation.

is such a God and man was made for such a purpose, no moral conclusions could be derived or grounded on such 'metaphysical facts.'"[76]

Now, both these objections center around the problem of purposive language. To begin with, it seems quite clear that evaluative language is closely related to the notion of purpose.[77] If one knows, for example, what a particular artifact—say, a refrigerator or a screwdriver—was designed to do, it is perfectly proper to apply the words "good" and "right" to the artifact. The sentence, "This is a good refrigerator," or, "It works right," can simply mean that the refrigerator does what is expected of it. No logical sins have been committed in speaking this way, since the prescriptions (what the artifact is "good for") were already determined when the object was designed. Indeed, "to design" appears to *mean* prescribing. To ascertain purpose or design, then, is to describe prescriptions. If a refrigerator is designed to keep food cold, then there is nothing wrong with saying that the refrigerator *ought* to keep food cold, and in evaluating it accordingly.

This is the way Calvin understood the relation between man and God. To know God is to know One who designs man's final purpose. In good biblical imagery, Calvin described man as "an artifact" who is "made by" God to function in particular ways (according to the "ways of God"). It is not a question, at least in Calvin's scheme, of moving from a set of metaphysical facts to moral conclusions. In apprehending God, man apprehends the purpose for which he was created, and he is judged (or evaluated) by this standard or "law." In short, man ought to act as he was intended or created to act. This does not seem to be an illicit way of talking. Whether or not Calvin's claims about God are true, his God can be known, if at all, *only as designer*. As such, prescriptive as well as descriptive language is certainly appropriate to the relation between man and God. Thus, the second of Nielsen's objections misses several important points.

However, even if the language of purpose helps us over, or around, some of the problems Nielsen raises, we still do not know on what grounds it is "good" to obey the purposes of God, assuming for the moment that to be a Christian is to apprehend the purpose for which man was designed. Even in everyday speech, a functional or instrumental use of the terms "good" and "right" does not appear to exhaust the possible uses of the terms. Merely to be made aware of the purpose for which a gun was designed, and therefore to be able to

---

[76] Nielsen, *op. cit.*, p. 136.
[77] See R. M. Hare's very helpful discussion of this matter in *Language of Morals* (New York: Oxford University Press, 1952), chaps. 6 ff.

judge whether the gun is a good one (functions well), does not tell us under what circumstances the gun ought to be used, or whether it is good to use guns at all. In the case of guns, we would probably say that we must consider the "higher" purposes for which the gun is being used (self-protection, hunting, etc.) before we can settle the moral problem of the use of guns.

However, when Calvin uses the term "purpose of God," he is speaking by definition of the highest or most ultimate purpose. When one speaks of God, there is no higher consideration, standard, or purpose by which to judge a function or an act. Very much as we normally ascribe to an author the authority over or rights to an invention or manuscript as to its use, so Calvin ascribes the final authority or right as to the proper use of man to the author or designer of man. The ethical basis of Calvin's thought (and one which needs a great deal more exploration) seems to rest on the interesting and important connection between the terms "author" and "authority."

## III

It is worthwhile examining a figure like Calvin, if only to begin to sort out some of the central questions in thinking about a Christian theory of natural law. But more than this, Calvin provides an attractive starting point for natural law thinking, because he employs natural law categories without doing what, in my estimation, a Christian ethicist must never do: make too much of, or make too all-encompassing, a theory of natural law. In Christian ethics natural law must remain at best a companion theory, one that is seen in relation to, and complementary with, the norms of Christian revelation. It will, in some sense, always remain minimal, or, to use Calvin's word, "vestigial." For the Christian who takes the fallenness of nature seriously, natural law will always be but suggestive or indicative of ethical norms beyond itself, norms which will have to be legitimated on grounds other than that they are "natural" or "empirical." Without the revealed knowledge of the purpose for which man was designed, the Christian will not be able finally to justify the "goodness" or "rightness" of even the ethical universals. (Without appealing to some prescriptive assumptions, it is difficult to understand how anyone, Christian or no, will be able to justify natural inclinations.)

Calvin's thought is a good place to start also because he does not make what is, especially these days, as grave a mistake as overdoing natural law. He does not reject it or neglect it altogether. Calvin's notion of humanity was never, as we have shown, simply derived from theological assertions. It had a very strong empirical ingredient, and it made room for moral reflection on the basis of reason and nature. Some of Calvin's insights correspond remarkably with recent anthropological findings. Others, such as his views about natural social hierarchies, do not. But to develop a theory of natural law, as he did, is to encourage the use of rational, scientific investigation in ethical discourse. In other words, to construct a theory of natural law, in the limited sense we have been describing, permits the use of science in ethics, without, of course, reducing the latter to the former.

Calvin's general approach suggests a pattern of religious-ethical reflection that meets our tests of a natural law theory without doing injustice to the Christian tradition or to the canons of rational and scientific procedure.

# 7

# Dynamism and Continuity in a Personalistic Approach to Natural Law

BERNARD HÄRING

If we are to speak of natural law we must know the historical context in which the subject arose and developed. In the very conceptualization of natural law there is unavoidably contained a "contextual," historical element. The classic Roman jurists and before them the philosophers of the natural law had as their starting point the experience of common elements of morality and law among the nations to which Rome had brought its "peace." The Roman lawgiver wished to be as broadminded as possible in view of the variety of customs and concepts of justice; but he always kept in mind his unifying role. The *ius gentium,* the common law in the different parts of the Roman empire, meant a tremendous growth, a widening of the horizons in comparison with the tribal narrowness of the older little Rome that had not yet come into contact with other cultures. And yet, the Romans could have no idea how small this whole world around the Mediterranean "lake" would appear to later epochs. Nor could they realize to what extent their intention of stabilizing the Roman "peace" was to influence their natural law thinking.

Another historical source or stream of our natural law thinking is "cosmopolitanism"—the idea of the "worldwide city" common among the Stoics and throughout the whole Hellenistic epoch. Some admirable theories of natural law were elaborated just at the time when the Greeks were growing out of the narrowness of the old culture of the single town into an "all-embracing" culture with a common language and a common ethical understanding. However, they could not even imagine that this encounter of cultures in the Hellenistic melting-pot was but a modest beginning in comparison with later eras. Neither could they realize to what extent the old culture and its transition depended on the philosophical thought of Plato and Aristotle.

The Greek and Roman epoch in which natural law theories were formulated was a heroic age, an age of growth, expansion, and planning. The Greek culture had subdued the Roman conquerors, and these had subdued not only the many nations around the Mediterranean but also "nature," for instance, by their admirable highways stretching from one end of the empire to the other. And yet they could not even dream of the extent to which man would later on be able to harness "nature" to his planning. They could not yet explore the very meaning of man's relationship to "nature."

The writings on natural law are "situated" in or influenced by the historical context of the thinker to such an extent that the content of what was considered as *the* nature of man allows us to reconstruct the cultural, sociological, and religious context or environment in which this or that was considered to belong to an eternal "natural law." What is even more important, we can reconstruct the context in which this way of thinking and arguing was meaningful and vitally related to reality.

Most of the natural law theories of the last century are influenced by the rationalism of that era which in turn seems to reflect the political situation of restoration and conservatism. The sometimes all too static concept of natural law reflected the rather static character of the society of that era. Our natural law thinking today unavoidably reflects the tremendous dynamism of modern society. We are, and we have to be, fully conscious of this fact. A failure to realize this existential context could diminish the value of our approach.

In view of the contextual element of natural law theories we have to ask: In what sense can be speak of "continuity" in such a doctrine? What do we as Christians and modern men mean by natural law? Can we speak of an unchangeable, abiding element?

## I. *The Meaning of Natural Law*

In ethics we understand natural law to mean the nature or meaning of man insofar as man has the capacity of understanding his nature, meaning, and vocation; and consequently of realizing what preserves to the greatest extent the full meaning of his person, what corresponds to his relationship with God, his fellow men, and the created universe.

We distinguish natural law from the positive revelation of God's will in the course of the history of salvation. But we should not think of it as a mere "natural order" beside the order of salvation. The distinction touches only the way in which we come to the knowledge of God's will, namely the capacity of our reason, our mind, our heart, our innermost being to grasp what is good, right, and just.

This distinction as to the ways in which man can reach self-understanding and moral knowledge by no means implies the thesis that there is no influence of the grace of God when man reaches a moral judgment on the level merely of reason, or "natural law."

In view of our definition of natural law it is easy to see immediately some aspects of continuity and also a great variety.

It belongs to the very idea of humanity and the unity of mankind that man has some capacity—in community with other people —to ask himself what he is meant to be and to do. *Homo sapiens* begins to "exist" as a really human being only when he goes beyond the stage of merely caring for his food and nourishment, protecting himself against the elements and learning how to use tools. He begins to "exist" in a human way only when he has developed some capacity to feel a moral problem, that is, to reflect upon what he ought to do or should have done—especially in relation to his fellow men.

The history of salvation or the unity of mankind in a religious perspective begins only when man, in one way or another, realizes that God has disclosed Himself "to the eye of his reason," and that therefore he can and must honor God and render Him thanks. When God discloses Himself to the eye of man's reason "in the things He has made" (Rom. 1:20) then man is faced with the basic religious event which I would consider the most fundamental part of natural law. However imperfect the element of "knowledge" may be, it marks the beginning of a real continuity of wisdom and religion. But I do not think that this experience must have been accompanied by a capacity to conceptualize it. To "realize" and to "conceptualize" are two different things. Natural law begins before natural law philosophy. However, it does not begin at all until man has, to some extent, reflected on himself and on himself as bound by or to some moral values.

Though I am convinced that natural law has its ultimate foundation in the existence of God who is love, I would not dare to assert that the reality of "natural law" entered into the history only with explicit faith in God. Neither history nor philosophy can enlighten us on whether man's first experience was one of religious awe or, rather, a sense of moral obligation toward his fellow men. A vague moral experience may have preceded the sense of religious dependence.

The fundamental beginning of "natural law" may have been a spontaneous understanding of the relationship to one's fellow men—without knowing the radical implication that all men could really be "fellow men"—an understanding which could be conceptualized in the "golden rule": "Do to no one what you would not wish done to you" (Tobit 4:16). But once more it must be said that there is a great difference between a human experience which practically or implicitly includes such a principle and an actual capacity to conceptualize such an experience.

The rationalistic understanding of natural law started with abstract principles; and, finding that these principles remain always the same "truths," this understanding admitted variety only in different "applications" according to the varying "circumstances." Our approach starts with the real man, as a historical being, with his real capacity for understanding himself in his essential relationship to his fellow men, to the world around himself, and to God. From this follows continuity, insofar as we are always concerned with "man" and the natural power of man to know something of his destiny. But there is a twofold source of a profound dynamism: (1) Though it is always a question of the nature of man, there is a great difference between the man of the stone era and the man of the modern scientific era; the differences affect his whole biological, psychological, social, and cultural life and his most urgent needs. (2) The basic capacity of self-understanding undergoes deep changes. Though truth from the viewpoint of God remains always the same, the human way of thinking, of approaching existential problems shows a wide variety on many points. It is not only a matter of different "application" of "eternal" principles; it is to a great extent also a matter of the fundamental way of experience and thinking. Thus we are faced with a changing man gifted with a somewhat changing faculty of self-understanding.

## II. *The Historicity of Man*

In our explanation of the differences in the moral thinking of man we have already touched on some aspects of man's historicity and of "natural law." It was impossible not only for primitive man but also for the Greek thinkers even to imagine the dimensions of the historicity of man. And perhaps we ourselves are only beginning to realize the tremendous perspectives and possibilities—and consequently the responsibilities involved on many of the great moral questions. We are more conscious than the man of earlier centuries that we have to content ourselves with our historical heritage, with the limited nature of our possibilities; we have to build on what we have received. But on the other hand we have to face new and undreamed of possibilities of changing our own heritage, of interfering in biological and psychological processes.

Historicity belongs to the constitutive structure of man, to his human vocation as well as his power of thinking, his freedom, his sexual determination, his faculties of joy and laughter—even to the extent that the manner of reasoning, the measure, depth, extent, and objects of freedom, the degrees and kinds of humor all have their history.

The entrance of the Jewish and Christian faith into human history with its typical understanding of history—especially of the oneness of human history in view of the one Creator and Father in heaven—has greatly affected not only the understanding of history but also history itself. It has greatly contributed to the fact that today, believers and "unbelievers" take it for granted that all men belong to the human race, to a human family with a common responsibility. For the believing man, the human race is one before God and therefore is called to live according to this oneness in unity and diversity. Perhaps the tremendous concern for solidarity and oneness among many "unbelievers" will be the most efficacious way to faith in one God, Father and Creator of all.

## III. *The Law of Growth*

The child of four years has a human nature. However, the expression of "natural law" in his life is quite different from that of a wise man of seventy years. And the fullness of moral insight and sensitivity will be different both for the child and the mature old man according to the richness or poverty of the moral values embodied in their environment. Human life means growth; the growth, however, is not automatic. Human life is a demand for growth. The higher values and the finer distinctions can be reached only gradually in a progressive effort. Where no effort toward growth is made, everything is endangered. But this human effort does not allow us to take the third step before the first and the second.

We find this most clearly in the divine pedagogy in the Old and New Testaments. "There is still much that I could say to you, but the burden would be too great for you now" (John 16:12). A long religious history and human experience was needed until in the Old Testament polygamy disappeared. Christians similarly took a long time to realize that Christian brotherhood under the Father in heaven has to eliminate all traces of slavery and racial discrimination. When an evolution has taken place men may fall back into underdeveloped attitudes, but they will not so easily be able to do so in good conscience, at least at the beginning of a period of regression.

## IV. *Natural Law and Revelation*

Though by natural law we mean that which is accessible to man's intellect, of course, his intellect is deeply rooted in and connected with the whole human existence. A man who has spent a life in the service of the poor has a different intellectual grasp of the dignity of the poor and of the honor of serving them than has the man who had no such experience. By revelation we understand an undeserved, gracious, divine intervention bringing men to an awareness or understanding of realities that are simply beyond the horizon of man's intelligence or at least transcend the level which he could reach at that moment without such an intervention.

Revelation and the response to it in a lively faith is an event which shapes history, which inscribes itself in man's life. Therefore, after revelation, the individuals and the communities of the people of God and also those who do not yet explicitly belong to it, even by reason alone have a greater accessibility to many moral values. Once a full-developed religious and moral life is lived convincingly by persons and by communities, it transforms man in a certain direction and enriches his capacity for self-understanding. Therefore the natural law thinking of Christians cannot be unrelated to the history of salvation. It is situated within it.

We can make a further step which seems to be typical of the *Pastoral Constitution on the Church in the Modern World* issued by Vatican Council II. We have there an effort of natural law thinking with a view to a dialogue with all men of good will, a dialogue in which, however, the Church does not wish to betray her own identity. On one side, she wishes to use arguments which could be understood even by non-Christians; on the other side, a very conscious effort was made not only to seek some accessible arguments in the Bible, but also to judge all arguments and this way of thinking in the light of the Bible, and see how they conform to the spirit of Christ's message to his people.

## V. *The Biblical Ethics of Vigilance toward the "Kairos"*

Immature individuals and communities need a good number of detailed "rules" of conduct. These tend to become absolute laws in proportion to the immaturity of the leaders and the greater number of the members of the community, in proportion also to the ability or inability to distinguish the moral value from the approximative "rule" which protects it. The people of Israel needed a good deal of protective and restrictive rules in order to guarantee internal unity and external protection against the alien religious attitudes of the nations around them. So we find an antagonism between, on the one hand, an all too "natural" tendency of the greater number, priests, rulers, and subjects, to cling to the bare external form of the rules, and on the other, the prophetic spirit which stresses their deeper meaning and leads to a synthesis in true love of God and mercy to one's neighbor.

In the New Testament the prophetic approach reaches its high point. The disciple of Christ is no longer faced with impersonal rules, but with his master who showed the full extent of his love, and with his brother whom he can love with Christ and in the manner of Christ. The morality of the disciple of Christ is marked by spontaneity and generosity. But spontaneity has nothing in common with arbitrariness. This comes through in the biblical concept of *kairos* (the moment of favor, the moment of decision, the present opportunity). It is God who prepares the present opportunities within the framework of the external events and even on "days" which appear to be bad. God gives the internal light and the capacity to understand the present hour and to use it to the full (cf. Eph. 5:16). The attitude which conforms the disciple of Christ to the real opportunities within history is one of vigilance, watchfulness, and attention.

The virtue of vigilance leads to an ever fuller understanding of the present moment—the "situation" or the "context" accordingly as man becomes more docile toward God in humble prayer and meditation and open-minded toward his neighbor. Since the real meaning of the "present opportunity" tends toward the growth and manifestation of fraternal love to the glory of God, only true love can guarantee and foster vigilance and the understanding of the hour of grace.

The full understanding of the meaning of history, of the "hour of favor," and of vigilance for the coming of Christ in these events belongs to the realm of faith. However, after the discovery of such a fundamental attitude as vigilance for the present opportunities, good human reasoning appreciates how important it is for a fully developed moral life, for maturity in ethics.

## VI. *Personalism in Natural Law Ethics*

The soul of vigilance and watchfulness is love between person and person, between person and community, between community and community. The Christian takes all created things seriously. But "man is the only creature on earth which God willed for itself." All the created things receive their full meaning in view of the manifestation of God's love for man and in view of the use man makes of them for the building up of a community in justice and love to the honor of the Creator. On a certain moral and religious level we can understand and ever more deeply realize that "man cannot fully find himself except through a sincere gift of himself." [1]

The all-embracing law which expresses human nature, the "nature of a person" is love. By love I do not mean mere sentimentality. Love is the way in which a person reveres the same dignity in his fellow men, opens himself to the goodness of others, contributes to the dignity and happiness of his neighbor and to the welfare of the human community. Love does indeed include affectivity, but it is above all an attitude of the free will and mind.

Everything in human life derives its measure and value from its fitness in expressing and strengthening the adoring love of man for his Creator, and in honoring the Creator through the building up of a worthy relationship among human persons. This applies also to man's own biological and psychological reality. We understand more and more that man cannot dominate only the "nature" that is outside himself. Man has to become more and more a wise administrator of his own biological and psychological "nature," without arbitrariness, without yielding to a self-destructive selfishness. Man must not be dominated by mere processes of a biological or psychological kind if he can modify these processes in the direction of greater moral freedom and a better interpersonal relationship.

A personalistic "natural law ethics" does not accept any taboo, since it does not adore created things. It is always a matter of understanding their final goal in view of the dignity of the persons and their relationship. Monotheism gives man a tremendous freedom toward the nonpersonal world, a responsible freedom which could never have become a common attitude under animism or pantheism. Man is called to shape the events, to transform the natural processes, and even to administrate his own biological and psychological heritage. The only moral limit is the dignity of every person and the building up of a brotherhood which as such gives honor to the Creator.

[1] *Pastoral Constitution on the Church in the Modern World* (*The Documents of Vatican II*, ed. Walter M. Abbott. New York: Guild, America and Association Presses, 1966), Art. 24.

## VII. *The True Countenance of Love*

In a personalistic ethics love is not a mere commandment or law. It is not a superstructure, but the very expression and fullness of person in community. Love is the heart of all things. It is man's destiny. Before he receives love as a commandment or moral law he receives the experience—at least an initial experience—of the reality of love and thus of an ever greater possibility of loving.

In a certain sense it can be said that love is the only absolute value, and that nothing apart from it is an absolute value or law. But then everything depends on the meaning we give to the words "apart from" or "besides." Sincerity, gentleness, temperance, justice, humility, respect are not something apart from love or besides love. They belong to the fullness of love. In them and through them love shows its true countenance. Love is the fullness of morality, not in the sense of excluding the other virtues but, rather, in the sense of including them and giving them their full meaning and value.

The thesis of the extreme situation ethics asserts that everything except love is relative, changeable, and open to any interpretation. This means in the final analysis that love is a "sphinx," a thing or behavior without a clear countenance. At one time it may look like a human being, at another like a lion, finally like a wolf. It could even be at the same time *"agapeic* and unselfish" and also "utilitarian and pragmatic." Or can it fall from the sky in the form of the atom bombs on Hiroshima and Nagasaki?

For a theistic and personalistic ethics it is evident that no law can be absolute or valid if (or insofar as) it contradicts the exigencies of true love. Every moral principle has to justify itself in its capacity to express the basic reality of love and promote it.

However, a truly personalistic ethics does not start with love as one law among others. It sees love as a "revelation" of the love of God Himself, who wished to have concelebrants of His own love. Love is the constitution of man, his destiny, but it points in a definite direction. The resulting development in ethics is not material laws, but the features of love, the exigencies of personal dignity and life in a community of free persons.

All agree that the biblical moral message is not centered on laws "apart from" love. The Sermon on the Mount as well as the farewell discourses of Christ proclaim the blissful and compelling power of God's love and man's happy capacity to respond. Nothing is merely added as something apart from love. The chief help given to the mature Christian is the ability to discern between true love and its counterfeits, between the harvest of the Spirit—unselfish love awakened by the Holy Spirit who is Self-giving Love—and the fruits of the selfish way of life (*sarx*). "The harvest of the Spirit is love, joy, peace, patience, kindness, goodness, fidelity, gentleness, and self-control. There is no law dealing with such things as these" (Gal. 5:22–23). On the other side are the features of the selfish "nature" which can never be expressions or features of true love. "Anyone can see the kind of behavior that belongs to the self-centered nature: fornication, impurity, and indecency, idolatry and sorcery, quarrels, a contentious temper, envy, fits of rage, selfish ambitions, dissensions, party intrigues, and jealousies, drinking bouts, orgies, and the like. I warn you, as I warned before, that those who behave in such ways will never inherit the kingdom of God" (Gal. 5:19–21). Love has a definite physiognomy. "Love is never boastful, nor conceited, nor rude, never selfish, not quick to take offense; love keeps no score of wrongs; does not gloat over other men's sins, but delights in the truth" (1 Cor. 13:4–7).

A personalistic "natural law ethics" comes to similar results; the developed human personality and community can recognize in this the true countenance of love, since this image of man has become and is a reality in human history; once it has shown itself in reality and in convincing words, it becomes self-evident as something which really expresses the full meaning of person and interpersonal relationships.

## VIII. *The Ethics of Values*

In the present discussions of an unprincipled situation ethics there is too much emphasis on the tension between love and law. The ethics of the signs of discernment is not sufficiently developed; consequently the more fundamental relationship between love and its true countenance, on the one hand, and those elements which can never fit into the true physiognomy of love, on the other, does not appear. Situation ethics not infrequently becomes degenerate by reason of pragmatism and utilitarian tendencies. A more fully developed ethics of values could be a most precious contribution. There should be no treatment of the problems of law before the study of an ethics of values. If we are to deal adequately with the question of what abides and what changes in the ethics of natural law, we cannot overlook the important contribution made by the modern philosophy of values (R. H. Lotze, W. Windelband, H. Rickert, W. Dilthey, F. Brentano) and by the ethics of values which is based on it. The ethics of values showed clearly the incompatibility of ethical value and "nonvalue" (*Un-Wert*). In his moral problems man is not simply faced with imperatives. The mature person responds to the appeal of values, and resists the seduction of moral "nonvalues" which appeal to his selfish desires. The human person feels guilty when he has chosen the nonvalue instead of an absolute value or a lower instead of a higher value. The ethics of values recognizes the legitimate interest of the person in his own integrity and fulfillment. But it does not describe morality in terms of virtue when and to the extent that this latter approach puts in the foreground the question of self-perfection. For this could be misinterpreted as a pragmatic concern for oneself. The ethical values of justice, temperance, purity, humility are more than means in order to reach "my fulfillment." They must be acknowledged in themselves in the relationship between persons. The person must be outgoing, must revere values; thus the right response to value brings fulfillment, dignity, and happiness to the individual person. Morality is not a business of perfecting oneself, but an openness to what is "good in itself."

The final justification of the concept "good in itself" is not always to be found in the ethics of values. Sometimes there is a heritage of a Kantian Rationalism, of a Categorical Imperative in relation to the concept of the whole of "mankind"; sometimes it looks like a Platonic "heaven of ideas" or "heaven of values" which has no clear connection with the history of mankind, with man on pilgrimage. However, successful efforts have been made toward a synthesis between the ethics of "objective values" and the psychology of development (E. Spranger). In the school of phenomenology the relating of the "person in community" brings the values nearer to man (A. Pfänder, M. Scheler, N. Hartmann, D. von Hildebrand). The ethics of values offers precious elements for an ethical personalism which concentrates on the "true countenance of love" and does not try to simplify ethics to a "conflict of values" in difficult situations. Not only does it develop the idea of "the hierarchy of values" (order of values), from which it draws the basic ethical norm: "preference of the higher values to the lower ones" and "sacrifice for the absolute values," but it indicates also the rule for the itinerary situation: how to cultivate the more urgent values of the here and now without denying the order of values. Obviously, in a realistic ethics there remain always the hard questions of "conflict of values" where it is not absolutely clear how some urgent values are to be cultivated in the direction of the fully manifest countenance of love in the harmony of all values. But the order of values indicates definite norms to which man has to conform more and more if he wishes to realize his own value and not become guilty in regard to his neighbor.

No human being can put all the values into practice. In relation to the fullness of values, man is always imperfect. But there are attitudes which are definitely in contradiction with absolute values, attitudes which make man guilty insofar as they are a free "no" to absolute values or to the order of values.

## IX. Epikeia *in Natural Law?*

It belongs to the common tradition of Western culture that no man-made law ("positive law") can oblige under all circumstances. The lawgiver must have the virtue of *epikeia*—that means he cannot include under his judgment a literal obedience to the law which would be meaningless, or harmful for the common good, or a burden out of proportion with the goal of the law. In those subject to the law, "*epikeia* must impose moderation on the literal following of a law." [2] To cling to the letter of the law, when this is not fitting, is wicked. Therefore the Book of Laws says, "Doubtless, one sins against the law when one clings to the words and thereby acts contrary to the intention of the legislator." [3] Since human laws have their justification in view of the common welfare, everything in the situation that is really required by legal justice and for the common welfare is good, even if it does not follow the letter of the law made by men.

In European history natural law ethics provided a bulwark against tyranny and authoritarian regimes, allowing man to invoke a higher justice against them. In normal times natural law ethics, especially in its emphasis on *epikeia*, promoted a mature attitude toward civil and church law and customs, thus ensuring a constant drive toward growth in insight and responsibility.

But as soon as natural law ethics proposed a detailed catalogue of principles it tended to become a cause of immobilism. And so again and again the question arose: Are all the principles of natural law absolute? Do they change in the course of history? Do norms of the natural law admit the use of *epikeia* in extraordinary situations? Everyone can see that these questions are similar to those of today's situation ethics. The answers given were not always the same.

Usually a distinction was made between the basic principles (*prima principia*) of natural law—which are the same for all men and

---

[2] Thomas Aquinas, *Summa Theologica*, I–II, q. 120, a. 2, ad. 3.
[3] *Ibid.*, a. 1, ad. 1.

can be known by all people—and the secondary principles. The first principles were called the primary natural law. The more numerous conclusions made from these basic principles were considered as valid for all times and all people with, however, two restrictions: (1) because of very particular circumstances and obstacles, these conclusions do not always express (fully) the real good; (2) sometimes the conclusions —insofar as their actual knowledge is concerned—do not belong to the natural law. A typical and oft-quoted example of this was the case of certain German tribes who did not consider robbery wicked, especially if it was done out of allegiance to their princes, though among cultivated peoples, robbery is clearly against natural law. In this connection we could mention the striking blindness of many people today in the matter of racial discrimination.

Thomas Aquinas follows the earlier tradition when he says that the precepts of the Decalogue are universally valid and indispensable "insofar as the precepts of the first table contain the very ordination toward God, and the precepts of the second table contain the order of justice among men; namely that nobody should be wronged and everyone should receive what is his right." [4] By this thesis many questions remained open. "Thus the precepts of the Decalogue are immutable as to the very justice which they contain; but as to the determination in view of the application to individual acts (for instance whether this or that is murder, theft, adultery, or not) there is place for change; sometimes only through God's authority, namely in those things which are instituted by God alone, as matrimony and other things like this; sometimes through human authority, namely in those things which are entrusted to men's authority." [5]

A widespread opinion held that only God could grant a dispensation from natural law. But this solution had its own difficulties. How can something be considered by right human reason as absolutely good and "obligatory of its very nature" when God can declare that it is not so in this case? The answer seems to be: It is not absolutely an exigency of natural law; but since man would not be able to judge in these exceptional cases only God can grant "dispensation." Such a solution brings other difficulties. However, the word "dispensation" should not be forced or explained in the sense of a dispensation from a man-made law given by the competent human authority. The opinion mentioned above assumed that the cases in which God grants a dispensation belonged to the sphere of the natural law. Observation of the law, however, was impossible because of some obstacle and,

[4] *Ibid.*, q. 100, a. 8.    [5] *Ibid.*, ad. 3.

as a result of God's intervention (as in the law of Moses on divorce), no longer binding. Some thinkers added: In evident cases man is free from obligation even without dispensation. In cases of bare doubt, conscience is bound by the general principles of natural law. The thinkers of the Middle Ages treated these questions chiefly in view of problems arising from the Old Testament.

In epochs of greater sociological and cultural change the inadequacy of some formulations of natural law ethics was felt. While the general validity of these principles was commonly accepted, the moralists were seeking for a more humane solution of difficult cases. For many, the use of *epikeia* seemed to be the most viable solution. Even such a cautious moralist as Alphonsus de Liguori did not hesitate to admit it. "*Epikeia* means the exception of a case because of the circumstances (the situation) from which can be judged, with certainty or at least with probability, that the legislator did not intend to include it under the law. This *epikeia* has its place not only in human laws but also in natural laws where, because of the circumstances, the action could be freed from malice." [6]

There can be no doubt that this assertion means a kind of situation ethics. However, it is by no means the same as the modern situation ethics of Griesebach, Ernst Michel, or Joseph Fletcher, since the older moralists applied the use of *epikeia* only to the secondary principles of natural law. In regard to the first principles of natural law and such conclusions as the Decalogue they did not allow the use of *epikeia*. In the Decalogue they distinguished the two positive laws (the law of the Sabbath and the prohibition to make an image of God) from the other parts which express the unchangeable exigencies of human nature. No one, except a few radical nominalists, would have argued (as do Robinson and Fletcher): Since the Sabbath was made for the sake of man and not man for the Sabbath (Mark 2:27), therefore law (in the sense which includes all the rules of morality except love) is made for the sake of man, and not man for the sake of law. What can be asserted of positive laws (even divine positive laws) and to some extent of imperfect, detailed formulations of natural law cannot be applied to natural law as such; for natural law, in its essence, is not a law given externally to man, but a "law" which expresses the innermost being and vocation of man. Natural law, in its substance, is not a restrictive law, not even merely a protective law; it is not in any way a law imposed from without; it is not only given for man; it is, rather, "given" (a given reality) with man's origin and being.

[6] *Theologica Moralis,* Liber I, n. 201.

Man's fidelity to his own origin, existence, and goal, man's dignity and integrity urge him to a constant effort to understand it ever better and to put it into practice so that he may be existentially what he is in God's intention (which finds its expression in the innermost being of man's nature).

The opinion that there is place for the use of *epikeia* in matters of the natural law gave only an imperfect solution. It was an opinion inspired by a sense of equity; but it is based on an understanding of natural law which should be rejected. These moralists looked on the traditional formulations of natural law as the natural law itself. They did not see clearly enough the historical nature of man; therefore they did not give sufficient attention to the task of "distinguishing eternal realities from their changing expressions." [7] Theology and natural law thinking were not always fully aware of the most basic necessity which John XXIII expressed at the opening of Vatican Council II: "The deposit of faith itself or the truth which is contained in our time-honored teaching is one thing; the manner in which it is set forth, in its full integrity and meaning, is another. Indeed, much consideration must be devoted to this manner of presentation, and if needs be painstaking effort must be made to elaborate it."

By admitting the possibility of *epikeia*, the older moralists found their own way of reducing the all too great number of absolutes; practically, they admitted the use of *epikeia* only with regard to those "natural law" principles which contained a historical element that was no longer fully in tune with new insights and new realities.

An example of some importance for discussions in the present day may illustrate the problem: Alphonsus de Liguori held, like all the other moralists, that interrupted intercourse as a method of birth limitation was against natural law. But this did not hinder him from urging a mild pastoral attitude toward those spouses who in good faith used interrupted intercourse because they were poor and already overburdened with numerous children. And not only that: he held that the wife not only may but should cooperate if the husband wishes to interrupt the intercourse, whenever she cannot change his mind.[8] Nor does he consider the natural law "not to interrupt intercourse" in its materiality as something absolute. "It is lawful to interrupt intercourse, provided there is a just cause for interrupting, e.g. if danger of illness, or death from an enemy should result from the continuation of the act. . . ." [9] Under these or similar circumstances the act,

---

[7] *Pastoral Constitution on the Church in the Modern World*, Art. 52.
[8] *Op. cit.*, Liber VI, N. 947.     [9] *Ibid.*, n. 954.

which generally would be "against natural law," would be "free from malice." So it is evident that he does not consider—at least in his final moral judgment—the mere external aspect of the act in its materiality but, rather, its moral significance.

Our way of thinking is somewhat different. We consider very consciously the whole historical context in which a particular principle was understood as an expression of natural law. Then we distinguish the abiding values (which the principle set out to protect) from the historical context; we distinguish them from the whole outlook of a period upon certain problems, or from an understanding of problems within a prescientific approach to natural, social, and sociopsychological data. We look for concrete possibilities of introducing distinctions, and so on. In so doing we do not yield to "historism" because we believe that besides the many historical varieties and processes there are some absolute values which, however, must be set forth according to the new context, according to the new objective reality, and according to our more developed knowledge.

From the best Scholastic tradition we preserve the awareness which was already expressed clearly by Thomas Aquinas: We must be most careful in the explanation of general principles where there is a question of making an application to a concrete case "whether this or that really is murder, theft or adultery or not." [10] The definition of a natural law principle must always put in first place the values and nonvalues which are at stake.

For instance, we keep the general principle that suicide is immoral (in other words against the basic vocation of man). But I do not think that it is all that easy to give an ethical definition of suicide. The Japanese nobleman who, when he is condemned to death, performs hara-kiri, does not intend to commit suicide; Socrates who drank the hemlock in compliance with the unjust judgment against him had no such intention as suicide. The pilot who goes down with his plane on an important military target sacrifices his life. Though he knows with certainty that his action will deprive him of his life he would not call his action suicide.

Can a spy who "does away with his life" in order to protect a very important secret and so preserve peace be said to commit suicide? Would you call his action suicide even if he does so by order of his government which has entrusted to him this service for the common good? Only after taking a closer look at the variety of these phenomena can we try to give a definition of what we mean by suicide, and of

---

[10] *Summa Theologica*, I–II, q. 100, a. 8.

what we mean when we say that suicide is against natural law. This belongs to the very heart of the matter. Only then can we avoid the oversimplification of the legalistic trend in natural law ethics and the carelessness of some of the representatives of situation ethics.

There may be fewer absolutes than we thought in earlier times, but there certainly are absolutes in ethics. For instance, blasphemy is always and absolutely immoral. But even here we must make a thorough effort to express well what blasphemy as a moral or immoral phenomenon really is. It is a way of acting or speaking by which a human person freely intends to insult his Creator or to deny God directly the honor which is His due. It is a conscious use, with full awareness of their significance, of actions or words which clearly imply an insult against God. Similarly, to disown God is always immoral. The "loving" intention of doing so only in order to go into the underground church[11] cannot justify it, if it is really an act of disowning God. St. Peter did not try to justify his action of disowning his Lord, though he may have had the good intention of preserving himself for an underground church. However, in the definition of the phenomenon of "disowning God" much care must be given to the full and concrete meaning. Hiding oneself or the refusal to give any serious answer (as, for instance, the babbling of a mixture of sense and nonsense in order to resist the assaults of brain-washing) may not fall under the definition of disowning God. An expression which, in normal circumstances, would imply disowning the faith may receive another meaning in a totally different situation. But then we would not say that the situation justified the disowning of faith. We would rather say that it justified an action or an expression which in those circumstances did not, or at least not necessarily, signify a disowning of the faith.

## X. *Dangerous Emphasis on Marginal Problems*

In the moral message of the New Testament the chief emphasis is on those moral guidelines which indicate the direction to the height of spiritual growth. "Love one another as I have loved you" (John 15:12) or "Be all goodness just as your heavenly Father is all good" (Matt. 5:48). This commandment and the entire Sermon on the Mount concentrate on the goal toward which the disciple of Christ has to strive if he wishes to be what he is called to be. There are then the numerous criteria for the discernment of spirits. They have to be taken all together. And the chief question of conscience is whether one is

---

[11] Joseph Fletcher: *Situation Ethics* (Philadelphia: Westminster Press, 1966), p. 72.

sincerely striving in this direction according to the measure of the gifts God has bestowed upon him, according to the *kairos* (the present opportunities). Here indeed is the place for a Christian situation ethics, the ethics of the *kairos*. But the *kairos* is within the order of love, of justice, of temperance, and so on. Besides these norms which indicate the direction, there are some definite restrictive norms in the Bible which indicate an absolute opposition and contradiction to the way of salvation.

For mature men, the emphasis in a Christian ethics and even in natural law ethics must not be put on those exceptional situations in which what is generally considered robbery, theft, suicide, or murder may be considered as falling outside the more accurate definition of these sins. These problems can and must also be studied. But unless they are integrated into a fuller perspective they will give occasion for a dangerous minimalism which would go even beyond the limits of the licit and illicit.

## XI. *Similar Results within Different Vocabularies*

Quite often different traditions will express almost the same concern for truth in very different vocabularies. Thus many get the impression of insurmountable oppositions when in reality there may be only a difference of approach. Brotherhood in a pluralistic society and especially ecumenism impose upon us the task of finding the basic unity in the variety of systems and vocabularies. In the matter under discussion we are faced with a typical example of a Catholic way of thinking and speaking, which can disturb thinkers of the Reformed or Oriental churches. But the differences are not so great as they appear at first sight.

In a Western (Latin) Catholic tradition there is a very strong distinction between the "objective moral norms" and practical pastoral counseling. The moral norm tries to express (1) the borderline or minimum below which there is definite contradiction or opposition to absolute laws or values (objectively), though not necessarily "subjectively," i.e., in the conscience of the individual person, (2) those itinerary norms which express the Christian vocation to holiness. On the other side pastoral prudence deals (1) with those steps which may be considered as a real break for a man who has come a long way and had not yet light and force enough to conform to the necessary minimum of restrictive laws, (2) with the signs of the time and the concrete opportunities within the limits of the universal laws of morality; in other words, the common typical human effort to help one another to find the next possible step in the direction of an ever fuller realization of the Christian ideal.

There are some absolute norms which forbid attitudes that are in clear opposition to human dignity and love; there is also a definite obligation to follow the Christian vocation to holiness according to the gifts God has bestowed upon man in great variety. But pastoral counseling does not simply put these norms before men; it remembers always the concern of the Lord: "There is still much that I could say to you, but the burden would be too great for you now" (John 16:15). There are the numerous cases of "invincible ignorance" where pastoral gentleness and prudence realize that a "material" transgression of moral laws is a lesser evil—no personal sin—than an outburst of rebellion or desperation that might be provoked by an inopportune admonition.

Other philosophical and theological traditions manifest the same or a similar concern for the plight of the weak ones and those hampered by the low moral standards of their environment; but their concern finds expression in attitudes which give less importance to the distinctions we have made between the objective norms, on the one hand, and respect for the real possibilities of the man who follows an upright conscience, on the other.

An example may make our meaning clearer: The objective moral judgment on marriage after divorce is, in our tradition, clearly negative. The words of the apostle are looked on as an always valid norm: "A wife must not separate herself from her husband; if she does she must either remain unmarried or be reconciled to her husband" (1 Cor. 7:10–11). Those who act against this norm will never be given doctrinal approval; in other words, a second marriage during the lifetime of the first spouse (after a valid marriage) will be considered as incompatible with an objective norm. But pastoral counseling may in some difficult situations look on the second marriage as "the lesser evil." Pastoral prudence will act differently in cases where the people live in a second marriage with a peaceful conscience and in cases where they are fully aware that their marriage is against the evangelical norm (as understood in the Western Catholic tradition). Pastoral prudence, generally, will not speak out on the concrete obligation to separate unless this can really be hoped and looked for as now a step forward for the persons concerned and the community. In view of the psychological and moral balance of the two spouses (living in a second marriage after divorce) and especially in view of the children who need the warmth of a home, pastoral wisdom and charity are content with the advice: "Do what you can and pray for what you cannot yet do." The parties may have taken some concrete steps which give evidence of a sincere good will, a growth in humility, penance, and self-control. These steps can be acknowledged as a real, concrete way in which these people are beginning "already," "initially," and gradually to fulfill the will of God.

This distinction between the "objective" moral norms (which include already the general consideration of "historicity") and pastoral prudence is based on another important distinction which is found very clearly in other schools and traditions too, namely, the distinction between a valid system or theory of ethics and the existential decisions of the individual person or the community taken in view of the concrete possibilities of the present insight and conscience. The individual person manifests a fundamental agreement with the "natural law" (and with the evangelical "law") as far as he is earnestly seeking truth and an ever better understanding of the moral exigencies, and follows the appeal of an upright conscience. Whoever acts in conformity with the judgment of an upright conscience, though it be an erroneous one, "gains always light" (Cardinal Newman).

A clear distinction among the objective moral norms, the ever imperfect but earnest endeavor of an upright conscience in the concrete decision, and the pastoral prudence of the counselor has several advantages over an oversimplified situation ethics. The latter does not clearly distinguish the existential effort of the conscience within its limits and its possible errors from the valid objective standards of an ethics based either on the moral experience and insight of the best thinkers and people or on Christian faith. It is a good thing to pay full respect to the first sincere steps of a person emerging from darkness and striving toward fuller light. But it is another thing to equate such an imperfect decision-making with the standards or norms of an ethics meant for mature and responsible persons.

The great dangers of a situation ethics which asserts that apart from love nothing is absolute are, first, arbitrariness and, more important, the growth of a most sophisticated self-righteousness. Instead of humility, penance, and constant striving, an easier way is encouraged—a way that takes as its slogan: What I did I did out of true love, out of *agapeic*, pragmatic, and utilitarian love, or "we tailor our ethical cloth to fit the back of each occasion. We are deliberately closing the gap between our overt professions and our covert practices." [12]

[12] *Ibid.*, p. 147.

# Toward an Epistemology of Ethics*

JOHN G. MILHAVEN

The following pages aim merely at articulating some questions, directing them at those more competent than the present writer to answer them. Catholic ethicists and moral theologians generally rely on certain axioms when they deal with questions of the day. At least one of the axioms often fails to be understood outside the ranks of the ethical specialists and, surprisingly enough, is rarely brought to light and discussed in its general bearing by them. The neglect in explaining this principle, coupled with the frequency in invoking it, may well be cause of much present-day bewilderment among nonspecialists concerning what is presented as natural law—for example, in sexual matters. The present chapter, composed by one who is not a professional moralist, seeks to win light on this principle by focusing questions on it and finally suggesting an answer. The ethical principle under question is the axiom that the essential purpose of a particular act suffices to determine its moral and immoral use. The context of the questions is that of natural law morality and not of values or imperatives imparted only by Christian revelation.

As it stands, the principle is unexceptionable. Clearly, everything created should be used for the purpose God has marked for it. And God's purpose is its purpose. But when the principle is applied, e.g., to marriage, to the physical life of deformed babies, to sexual activity,

---

* Reprinted, with permission of the Editor, from *Theological Studies,* Vol. 27, No. 2 (June, 1966), pp. 228–241.

to man's speech, its meaning loses clarity, even becomes ambiguous, at least in the eyes of the nonspecialist.[1]

Seemingly, the source of the confusion lies in two different ethico-intellectual syndromes. Many ordinary educated American Catholics of 1966, perhaps unlike their fathers, and apparently unlike the professional ethicists, do not in forming their moral judgments instinctively look first to God's *particular* purpose for the thing to be used. They would not at all contest in principle such a point of reference, but their minds implicitly move another way. They look first to God's *general* purpose for man and they measure the questioned action against it.

One might articulate their understanding of God's general purpose as *gloria Dei vivens homo*. The glory God would have of a man is simply that he live—that he live fully. One day the life will be the vision and intimate love of God; today it is an imperfect anticipation of that goal through the understanding and love a man ekes out in the world for God and for his fellow men and for himself. When the question arises how to act in a certain situation, the ordinary man today does not normally inspect the total complexity of the object to be used in order to deduce what God must have envisioned in all these details. Rather, he finds out what he can do. From what he can do he chooses as morally right those actions by which human life, i.e., life of understanding and love, his own and his neighbor's, can be further realized. For example, speech which misrepresents one's views is wrong, and wrong before God, because it thwarts a life of understanding and love among men. Ordinarily, a man feels no need

---

[1] Thus, the application of this principle in papal texts to reject all contraception as intrinsically immoral bewilders many today. Fathers Ford and Kelly have assembled pertinent texts from the teachings of Pius XI and Pius XII and bring out in their analysis that "the principle stressed in all the papal texts is the principle of 'divine institution,' 'divinely established order,' 'divinely established design.' In other words: God has written a certain definite plan into the nature of the generative process, and human beings are not free to change it" (John C. Ford, S.J., and Gerald Kelly, S.J., *Contemporary Moral Theology*, Vol. 2: *Marriage Questions* [Westminster, Md.: Newman Press, 1963] p. 286; this point is repeated throughout the analysis, pp. 286–91. Cf. Kelly's "Contraception and the Natural Law," *Proceedings of the Eighteenth Annual Convention* [1963] *of the Catholic Theological Society of America*, pp. 28–33). The point of the present writer is obviously not that such an application of principle is invalid. His point at the moment is sociological: it leaves uncomprehending many educated Catholics today, many a husband and wife facing their large family and their love and need for each other, many a priest trying to counsel them. The subsequent point of the writer will be epistemological: How, in general, does one come to know principles that can be applied in this way?

to inspect the complex details of tongue, larynx, lungs, etc., and discern God's specific purpose for the faculty in order to make his moral decision.

There are, then, apparently two approaches to moral evaluation. Both base their moral judgment on the "purpose" of the prospective action,[2] but they do not envisage the same thing as the morally decisive purpose. One traces out first the specific purpose of the action and does not doubt that the ultimate purpose and good of the whole man will be attained thereby.[3] The other measures the action directly in the light of man's general purpose, a full life of understanding and love, and does not doubt that the relation to the general purpose coincides with the specific end. It may be that the dichotomy appears only on the surface. Nevertheless, it is the dichotomy many men today do find: the way the moralists think and the way he thinks.[4] From this dichotomy, real or imagined, arise conflict and confusion of conscience.

The confusion permeates discussion of significant issues and raises questions in the popular mind. The prolonged existence of a baby extensively deformed in body and soul may be demanded by the specific purpose of man's physical existence in this world, but does it constitute the *vivens homo* who alone is God's glory? Should not conjugal morality for given families in a given society be governed by the fact that the general good of this society and this family can be most practically furthered by generous childbearing to a certain

[2] Or, if one prefer, the purpose of the object to be used. In this context one can speak indifferently of the purpose of speaking or of the purpose of the faculty of speech, the purpose of living a married life or the purpose of the institution of marriage.

[3] Arthur Vermeersch, S.J., discussing his proof of the grave immorality of contraception, expressed well the first approach: "This argument is free from any consideration of the moment which that rightness [*honestas*, i.e., the essential order which man should observe in his use of the conjugal act] has for the private or the common good. True, the provident God himself, while He lays down the order to be kept, is the guardian and protector of the common good. But we should not weigh what advantage or harm each act may bring in order to determine from this that there is a serious or light fault. Mortal sin . . . is *formally* an act substantially *against order* laid down by divine law, but not *formally* an act against the common good" (A. Vermeersch, S.J., *De Castitate et de Vitiis Contrariis* [Rome, 1921] p. 256, n. 258; italics are V.'s, translation mine).

[4] At very least it must be granted that ethicists in recent years have intensified their efforts to complement the argumentation from specific purposes with other approaches more congenial to contemporary thinking, e.g., from the symbolism or "sense" of a given act. However, since many ethicists still offer the first-mentioned argumentation as by itself decisive and since the new, complementary approaches are far from having attained universal acceptance, the dichotomy is, if only as a distorting epiphenomenon, widespread today.

extent and then by continuing expression of conjugal love with the use of contraceptives? Are the mental gymnastics of a *reservatio mentalis* necessary or even worthy of a grown man in circumstances where mutual love and understanding indisputably demand that a certain other person entertain a false opinion?

Questions of this type, met at every turn today, may betray subjective confusion of the popular mind rather than obscurities in the presentation of the ethicist. Nor does the present writer espouse all the presuppositions that the questions would seem to imply. But he does feel that the vague, implicit attitude behind the questions is not without insight and should be articulated by more precise questions in the hope that the reply of the ethicists may bring needed light.

The first attempt at a more precise question is offered by way of foundation for further questions. When a process (e.g., the total physiological process that brings about ocular vision) regularly terminates in the same result, in what sense is the result necessarily the "purpose" of the process? The regular result is, of course, purpose of the process in the sense that anything that happens can be called the purpose of the action immediately producing it and therefore of the divine concurrence. Furthermore, one need not contest the principle (concerning whose meaning and basis, however, *disputatur inter scholasticos*) that whatever acts regularly in the same way is necessarily ordered to its term by an intelligent director; for so watered a sense of purpose neither requires nor invites the kind of moral response at stake. The mere fact that my hair regularly tends to grow long has, as such, no decisive influence on any moral judgment. Clearly, the constant term of a process is not *eo ipso* the kind of purpose under present discussion, one intended, in a stricter sense of the word, by nature and God, i.e., one absolutely incorporating intrinsic value, orienting means, demanding unconditionally moral respect, prohibiting any violation or frustration.

Similarly, even when the process only through a complex convergence of numerous factors produces its regular result, does it follow necessarily that the result is the kind of absolute purpose under present discussion? One could take once more the example of the process that makes vision possible. Does the degree of complexity argue the degree of importance the term has? Even the most anthropomorphically conceived divine watchmaker must labor effortlessly; He has no need of proportioning the complexity of His created processes to the value of their term. Yet there are moralists for whom the relatively small proportion of a total bodily system that participates in a given activity proves the relatively small importance intended by God for that activity within the system.⁵ One wonders how they would discern the primary importance God envisioned for man in the universe.

The point of these two tendentious questions is not that the purposes which the tradition found in human processes are irrelevant to moral decision. On the contrary! But how does one know the proportionate value of each? The point is that neither mere regularity nor mere degree of complex convergence reveals the proportionate value of the term or "purpose" of a process. To prolong a *simpliste* image often invoked: if a man's father gives him a watch, the son recognizes its purpose in the regular term of its complex processes, namely, that it tells time for him. But would this suffice to situate the proportionate value of the term or purpose, i.e., the importance the father gave to it in his mind? Might there not be other purposes indeterminately envisaged by the father? How would the obvious proximate purpose be measured with a given remote one? Would the father be excluding the sale of the watch if this were the only way of paying for an operation for the son's wife, or the use of the watch as a hammer (and thus its destruction) if this alone on a given occasion could save the son's life?

How, then, can a man know the absolute and inviolable purpose of anything? How can one know . . . ? This epistemological question is the central one the present writer would like to pose. It seems to him that urged in its universality it could profitably receive more consideration from the ethicists.

To reword the question: How can one know inviolable values in this world? Certain values, it would seem, are recognized immediately on discerning what they are. If one discerns what can be the authentic love between a man and a woman, one recognizes its absolute worth. One sees that no man may seek to frustrate or destroy it. The discerning required is clearly no indirect, superficial conceptualization; to reveal the worth of human love, genuine understanding and therefore some experience of it are needed. One could use here the overused word "insight." But once human love is understood, once the insight is had, man sees immediately its absolute worth. Obviously, it is a

⁵ "Further if we consider the totality and complexity of the generative system—a complexity that is neural, glandular, vascular, muscular, with internal and external organs—what a small part of that whole system actually participates in the mere bodily union of intercourse, and what a small part of that whole system is the site of pleasure and bodily satisfaction. Surely, if God had envisioned the personal satisfaction of His individual spouses as the equal or primary purpose of the generative function in marriage, He would have fashioned man and woman in a different mold" (Joseph S. Duhamel, S.J., *The Catholic Church and Birth Control* [New York: Paulist Press, 1962] p. 16).

question here of an immediacy of evidence, not necessarily of time. No further evidence is required. One need not consult the further consequences of the act. To know what it is, i.e., to know its direct, specifying object, is to stand before an intrinsic, absolute value. It is, therefore, one way of coming to an absolute, inviolable purpose of God.

Can the same immediate evidence be found for all acts where moral decision is called for? Evidently not. A man may well understand what marriage is and what dissolubility would be, but does that immediately reveal to him that marriage should always be contracted as indissoluble? It would seem not. The ethicists themselves adduce ulterior evidence for the point. A man may well understand what is *locutio contra mentem* and not yet have enough evidence to discern its immorality. On this point, too, ethicists feel constrained to adduce further evidence.[6]

This is the final focus of the epistemological question: What is the nature of the "further evidence"? For, although the ethicists themselves at times invoke it, the universal nature of the further evidence seems to be neglected when principles of morality are brought to bear on other questions of the day. Thus, in the recent controversy concerning abortion, some Catholic moralists confronted humanitarian outcries *simply* with the assertion of the inviolability of human life.[7] But the inviolability of human life is not a first principle. It is not

---

[6] References to some ethicists will be given presently, when the nature of this evidence is discussed. See notes 12, 16, and 18.

[7] For example, Richard McCormick, S.J., in an article on "Abortion" (*America*, June 19, 1965, pp. 877–881), explains carefully what is the absolute inviolability of any innocent man's physical life. But he never indicates the reasons that prove there is an absolute inviolability, holding under all circumstances. He invokes the dignity and inviolability of the human *person,* but does not show that there follows from this an equally absolute inviolability of human *physical existence.* He does adduce pertinently the harmful consequences a merely relative inviolability of human life could entail. But he never makes clear whether it is these consequences that ground the absoluteness. If he would actually ground it on this basis, his solution could fit well with the general epistemological orientation that the present chapter is about to suggest. But such a grounding needs to be drawn into the clear and justified directly and fully. An analogous criticism could be made of the several comments published in *America* concerning the killing of babies deformed by thalidomide (Aug. 18, 1962, p. 605; Sept. 22, 1962, p. 763; Nov. 10, 1962, pp. 1118 and 1128). The present writer is not criticizing the stand taken on abortion and mercy killing or the relevance of many points made. But he submits that the above articles and comments neglected a question uppermost in the minds of many readers: What proves that innocent human life is inviolable under all circumstances? How do we know this?

evident simply on understanding what human life is (i.e., physical existence in this world) and what its physical suppression would be.[8] It is a conclusion of further premises. The main contention of the present article is that thematizing epistemologically the nature of such further premises or evidence, not merely for the particular case of abortion, but insofar as they are relevant throughout the science of morals, would bring invaluable light to the nonspecialist and perhaps to the moralist as well.

One final example of what would seem to be neglect of this epistemological question: recently several moralists have pointed out that the argument condemning all contraception cannot be based on the invalid principle that *no* faculty or act may be used against its purpose. On the contrary, they say, the force of the traditional argument proceeds from a principle which considers the specific nature of the *procreative* faculty or act: "Just as innocent human life itself is inviolable, so those things which immediately pertain to the beginning of human life are also inviolable." [9] This represents a valuable clarification of the traditional viewpoint, but the moralists have characteristically left unanswered one question many of their contemporaries would ask them: What is the evidence for this principle? How do we know it is absolutely and universally true? In other words, granted the inviolability of human life, why does it follow from that inviolability that the life-giving processes are equally inviolable? Recall that the principle, as used by the moralists, does not mean simply that one may not violate the processes in such a way as to harm life. It means that one may not violate the processes even when life would suffer no harm as a result, e.g., in the cases where the only reasonable alternative to contraception would be continence. Taken in this sense, the principle is not self-evident. What is the evidence for it? Once more

---

[8] It should be clear that the "human life" meant here is not the *vita hominis* mentioned above, the life of human understanding and love which alone constitutes formally the glory of God. The "human life" in question here is merely the physical existence of a human being on earth, which might be without any understanding or love and which is opposed to the afterlife.

[9] Gerald Kelly, S.J., "Contraception and the Natural Law," *Proceedings of the Eighteenth Annual Convention* [1963] *of the Catholic Theological Society of America*, p. 30. J. J. Lynch, S.J., in "Notes on Moral Theology," *Theological Studies*, Vol. 25 (1964), p. 234, refers to this argument of Father Kelly as one which "would appear to throw some new light on the teleology of the generative act." He also notes that J. L. Thomas, S.J., expressed the same thought a few years ago in *The Family Clinic* (Westminster, Md.: Newman Press, 1958), p. 186. Cf. also Ford and Kelly, *op. cit.*, pp. 286–291.

one finds unanswered the question concerning the nature of the further evidence which would ground an absolutely universal prohibition of certain actions.[10]

In conclusion, let a possible answer be suggested for this question. It may serve at least to concretize further discussion. What is the nature of the further moral evidence for those acts where a simple understanding of what they are is not decisive? This epistemologist would suggest that such further evidence in the last analysis is always empirical. It is the evidence of the probable or certain consequences, of what is going to result from the act in question. Will its eventual result be to contribute to, or to oppose, the concrete realization of those absolute values already recognized through the immediate evidence discussed above (e.g., the absolute value of human love)? And the evidence of what is going to result can only be, as David Hume showed more lucidly than anyone else, the evidence of the past sequence of individual events: they indicate "what generally happens." One suggests, therefore, that it is empirical evidence, not direct insight into what something is, but the observation, correlation, and weighing out of numerous facts, which reveals the value of most human acts; for they show what effect these acts will have in the concrete, existing world on those absolute values a man discerns by immediate insight.[11]

Traditional moralists do not ignore such empirical evidence. They do not condemn divorce simply by describing what marriage is and what dissolubility means. They do describe these, but then appeal to what is going to result, namely, what is going to result in marriage if its dissolution be licit: the hindrance to the fitting education of the

[10] Recently an important study has treated this question extensively: Germain G. Grisez, *Contraception and the Natural Law* (Milwaukee, Wis.: Bruce Publishing Co., 1964). The present article and Dr. Grisez's book are mutually independent, and though they follow a similar course in the first steps of the problem, are far from coming to the same solution. Cf. the present writer's "Contraception and the Natural Law: A Recent Study," *Theological Studies*, Vol. 26 (1965), pp. 421–427.

[11] Germain Grisez, *op. cit.*, describes well the epistemology of ethics that the present writer is suggesting. He points out that this sort of epistemology characterizes most of the contemporary attitudes that are hostile to traditional natural law and, in particular, refuse to condemn any particular external behavior unconditionally, i.e., under all circumstances. Without denying this, the present writer submits, and tries to develop in the following pages, that the same kind of epistemology can be found also in the natural law tradition and that it *can* ground the unconditional prohibition of certain external actions, although the great refinement and extension that empirical knowledge enjoys today may well diminish the number of actions that, considered abstractly, can be condemned without any qualification.

child, the damage to married love, etc.[12] And to show what is going to result, they are appealing implicitly to empirical evidence (at least to what a man has through analogy or vicariously through observation), e.g., of what generally happens to a child whose parents are separated, of what generally happens when one has committed oneself totally to another and knows one can be abandoned, etc. That the *condigna prolis educatio* and the *amicitia* between husband and wife are absolute values and purposes is clear to anyone who understands what they are. But it is only empirical evidence that reveals that the liceity of divorce opposes these absolute values and therefore that divorce itself is absolutely wrong. Only in the empirical context does it make sense to say, by way of conclusion, that divorce is wrong because it violates the nature or purpose of marriage. Could not this simple case provide a paradigm for more complex moral evidence?

Nor do the ethicists condemn lying by simply describing what it is. Here, however, they disagree on the nature of the decisive evidence.[13] Some hold that the very nature and purpose of speech, the manifestation of one's thoughts, suffices to prove the intrinsic evil of lying, since the lie by definition violates this nature and purpose.[14] Of these, some advance also an empirical argument, based on the consequences for social life, but they proffer it as a parallel proof, not as the foundation for the argument from nature or purpose.[15] They find no need to offer any evidence that this nature or purpose is of such a kind as to be respected absolutely. They neglect completely the general epistemological problem which the present article is attempting to pose in sharp focus and which it claims lies behind much contemporary confusion.

[12] E.g., V. Cathrein, *Philosophia moralis* (2nd ed.; Freiburg, 1895), pp. 309–311, nn. 448–449; E. Elter, *Compendium philosophiae moralis* (3rd ed.; Rome, 1950), pp. 182–183; I. Gonzalez, *Ethica (Philosophiae scholasticae summa* 3 [2nd ed.; Madrid, 1957]), pp. 754–760, nn. 931–942; V. Bartocetti, "Divorce," *Dictionary of Moral Theology* (Westminster, Md.: Newman Press, 1962), pp. 427–428.

[13] Cf. E. Elter, *op. cit.*, pp. 149–151.

[14] St. Thomas Aquinas, *Summa Theologiae* 2-2, q. 110, a. 3, c, and 4 ad 4m; H. Davis, *Moral and Pastoral Theology* (New York: Sheed and Ward, 1952), p. 114; E. Elter, *op. cit.*, pp. 151–154; E. Genicot and J. Salsmans, *Institutiones Theologiae Moralis* 1 (14th ed.; Buenos Aires, n.d.), p. 340, n. 415; H. Noldin and A. Schmitt, *Summa Theologiae Moralis* 2 (27th ed.; Barcelona, 1951), p. 578, n. 638; A. Sabetti and T. Barrett, *Compendium Theologiae Moralis* (34th ed.; New York: Pustet, 1939), p. 300, n. 312.

[15] Thus Elter (although he does not believe that the empirical argument suffices to demonstrate that lying is by its very nature immoral and absolutely illicit in every case), Noldin-Schmitt, and Sabetti-Barrett, *loc. cit.*

Other ethicists, however, after describing what lying is, appeal ultimately not to the nature and immediate purpose of speech, but to what is going to result, namely, what is going to result in society if lying be licit: the damaging of social life itself.[16] And to show what is going to result, they are appealing implicitly to man's empirical evidence of what generally happens when one cannot tell if his neighbor is speaking the truth. That man's social life is an absolute value and purpose is clear to anyone who understands what it is. But it is only empirical evidence that reveals that the liceity of lying opposes the absolute value of social life and therefore that lying itself is absolutely wrong. Only in the empirical context does it make sense to say, by way of conclusion, that lying is wrong because it violates the nature or purpose of speech. Could not the presentation of these moralists provide a paradigm for most moral evidence?

The discussion, it might seem, has come full turn. The problem set up at the beginning of the chapter, the dichotomy between the intellectual syndromes of the ethicists and the popular mind, appears to have been neither problem nor dichotomy. At least in the cases just seen, both ethicist and nonspecialist ultimately invoke empirical evidence: to evaluate certain actions, they compare what is going to result from the actions for certain absolute values, those intrinsic and formal values which constitute a "living man." The implicit attitude of the man on the street coincides with the last reasons of the traditional proofs of the ethicist.

Nevertheless, it is respectfully submitted that the examples cited of divorce and lying are not universally paradigmatic in the presentation of contemporary ethics, that the ethicist does not keep in mind as often as he could the empirical nature of his evidence, that he does not work out and apply systematically an epistemology of ethics. The

---

[16] L. Bender, "Lying," *Dictionary of Moral Theology*, pp. 720–721; V. Cathrein, *op. cit.*, pp. 212–213, n. 298; I. Gonzalez, *op. cit.*, pp. 598–599, n. 636; J. De Lugo, *De Virtute Fidei Divinae* (Venice, 1718), 4, 1, 11; 4, 1, 9; 4, 4, 57; 14, 5, 74; *De Justitia et Jure* (Venice, 1718), 16, 2, 29; F. Suarez, *De Fide Theologica* (Paris, 1872), 3, 5, 8. One is tempted to put St. Thomas in this group rather than in the one previously given (supra n. 14). True, in question 110, article 3, he reasons purely from "innaturale et indebitum," with no reference to the empirical. But in question 109, article 3, ad 1m, he explains that the virtue of veracity "aliquo modo attendit rationem debiti." For ". . . naturaliter unus homo debet alteri id sine quo societas humana servari non posset. Non autem possent homines ad invicem convivere nisi sibi invicem crederent, tanquam sibi invicem veritatem manifestantibus." This is clearly an empirical argument. However, the context of question 109 is different from that of 110, and it is perhaps pressing the word *debitum* too much to conclude that St. Thomas is thinking of the same thing in both places.

epistemology proposed here could be summed up once more from a negative point of view. An act is seen to be wrong in one of two ways. Either it (e.g., cowardice) betokens by definition the absence of a quality (courage) whose absolute value is seen intuitively on understanding what it is, or the empirical observation of a number of cases indicates that the act (e.g., divorce) will result in some absolute evil, itself recognized in the former way (e.g., damage to the fitting education of the child). It is suggested that any talk of frustration of purposes merely expresses in a derived fashion one or both of the evidences mentioned above.

Such an epistemology makes large place for the empirical. Few are the acts whose value simple direct insight suffices to establish. They would be restricted to acts such as "love and honor and pity and pride and compassion and sacrifice." Moreover, although moral qualities are needed to appreciate these and live them fully, they pose no intellectual problems for the educated Christian. On the other hand, for the numerous acts whose value direct insight does not suffice to establish, e.g., sexual actions, the question is frequently open or being reopened. If the epistemology suggested here is justified, such questions could be more fruitfully explored or at least their answers more convincingly communicated, if it were kept in mind that the decisive evidence is empirical.

Not that empirical evidence would make all conclusions contingent and revocable. An empirically established necessity can be a true necessity.[17] Just as arsenic, placed in the diet, would necessarily destroy the physical life of men, so the liceity of lying would necessarily damage their social life. Even when extreme exceptions be conceivable, no sane man decides his action in these cases on the basis of the remotely possible exception.

According to the suggested epistemology of ethics, moreover, it is precisely such empirically discovered necessity that founds, and alone founds, most moral judgments. To uncover these necessities, the exacting complexity of empirical techniques, evolved to fine perfection by the sciences in the last few centuries, must be brought to bear. Should Christian ethics neglect these techniques, or apply them merely as gratuitous reinforcement? Should it not, rather, see in them the main source of light for the involute obscurity of many moral problems? Can, for example, the evil of homosexuality be certain—even for the specialist—unless the methods of contemporary social sciences

---

[17] This has been traditionally recognized as the thesis of the knowability of miracles illustrates.

attest its disastrous consequences: e.g., that the homosexual relation generally results in an unstable, stunted caricature of love? And would not this scientific attestation merely render more clear and convincing the empirical insight behind the old formula that homosexuality violates the nature of the faculty?

On the other hand, many empirical conclusions are contingent and revisable. The necessity is in these cases relative. The ethicist readily admits this for the "nature" of money or of occasions of sin in the matter of chastity. For this reason he rightly disclaims any reversal of position when he declares to be licit what was formerly condemned. Empirical evidence has revealed to him that something different from that heretofore is going to result from the use of money or the wearing of a certain costume. Consequently and consistently the morality is different. The nonspecialist would ask only whether the ethicist should not recognize more thematically his empirical evidence and show himself more widely sensitive to contingency in conclusions and change in evidence. The nonspecialist often has the feeling that some arguments of the ethicist are based not on an absolute necessity that evil is going to result from a given action, but on a relative necessity, on a likelihood of the result within the area observed so far. The Church seems at times to come along and, going beyond the evidence, validly and wisely imposes an absolute obligation, which furthers the general good and moves the Christian people toward a higher ideal of life. As a matter of fact, ethicists, especially moral theologians, are often modest on the force of their purely rational arguments, but a more precise methodological modesty might be helpful all around.

A case in point might be that of euthanasia and suicide. The final and decisive argument against them is not the inviolability of physical life, although this is a valid, relevant link in the reasoning. Ultimately the ethicist faces the question why a man cannot in a given case, because of the enormous good at stake, presume God's permission to take a life. The ethicist answers with the empirical argument of what is going to result if men be permitted, even if only in exceptional cases, to end directly their own lives at their own good judgment.[18] The empirically evident likelihood of abusive extension of the privi-

---

[18] E.g., C. Boyer, *Cursus philosophiae*, Vol. 2 (Rome, 1939), p. 508; V. Cathrein, *op. cit.*, p. 203, n. 282. One would, of course, like to substantiate the thesis of this chapter and show that the other arguments used in this context by these and other authors could, or at least should, be reduced to an empirical methodology. But this would go beyond the limits of my present purpose, which merely seeks to raise and urge the question.

lege would come into play here. This empirical, *ex semel licito* argument is strong, but perhaps not strong enough to be absolutely necessary, applying indubitably in all cases. One would touch here not so much the natural limits of human intelligence, but the particular limits of the empirical evidence in question. Yet that evidence would be strong enough to ground a general principle of action and to explain and justify—if justification were needed—the more universal condemnation by Christ's Church.

A general advantage envisaged in recognizing more extensively the empirical evidence of moral judgments would be a gain in force and clarity, at least in the eyes of the contemporary Christian who is not a trained ethicist. Too many educated, committed Christians are turning from the ethicists with one word, "Casuistry!" One hears more and more often, "I simply follow my conscience." Tragic is this progressive alienation from an indispensable tradition. But what are the causes? According to the argument of the present chapter, one cause is the empirical tenor of contemporary thinking, at a loss before the rationalistic garb of much professional moralizing. In the last four hundred years Western thought has grown more and more consciously empirical. In Christian circles one is wont to condemn the creeping empiricism for its exaggerations. But has it not also been a progress? Has it not clarified and uncovered resources of man's knowledge? Is not the critical sense of the empirically oriented contemporary, which he brings to bear on the ethicist's solution, in part something good and sound, a gain over the contemporary of Thomas Aquinas? Might not the ethicist profit from it more methodologically and systematically than he has heretofore? Might he not thereby be more faithful to the best in his own tradition and more relevant to the problems of his contemporaries?

The present chapter is no more than a question—a leading question, but one honestly meant as a question. To appraise the worth of the question, and *a fortiori* to answer it, a full-scale review of ethical principles with a view to epistemological synthesis would be in order. If the review is ever carried out, whatever be its outcome and however naïve and misleading the original question turn out to be, the raising of it should have been worthwhile, at least for the nonspecialist.

# 9

# Human Significance and Christian Significance

RICHARD A. McCORMICK

It has been unaccountably true that anyone who seriously holds the validity of general principles in the Christian moral life stands convicted of some rather black methodological suppositions. Such a person will feel it necessary to set the record straight before he makes his entry into the target issue. This is particularly true, I think, of the Catholic moral theologian who must candidly admit that the splendid casuistic achievements of his precursors too often hid the specifically Christian rootage of their moral thought and provided no small degree of credibility to the accusation of unilateralism. The Catholic moral theologian, therefore, may be more readily forgiven if he insists on checking the doors before he settles in the room.

I am aware that some of these doors stand loosely ajar and resist the type of definitive closing and locking which would make things tidier and easier—opening as they do on areas which constitute the theological heart of the discussion of Christian ethics. One man's premises are another man's problems. Hence James Gustafson is surely correct when he says that the debate on "contextualism vs. principles" has tended to assume that the matter of how moral decisions are made could be separated from other considerations.[1] In stating these "other considerations" as premises or presuppositions I do not wish to be understood as sharing these assumptions in every respect. But getting down to business can never mean passing over

---

[1] "Context Versus Principles: A Misplaced Debate in Christian Ethics," *Harvard Theological Review*, Vol. 58 (1965), pp. 171–202.

basic business. I mean only to hurry to a point where those who do ethics (as they say) within the Catholic tradition have encountered, or may encounter, or should encounter a problem.

# I

The following remarks constitute the premises out of which, or the contexts within which, it seems safe to assume that most Catholic moral thought takes its beginning. If these suppositions remain arguable, there is all the more reason for detailing them. Let us consider five premises:

1. *The primacy of charity (agapé)*. The good news of Christ is not a group of propositional truths but, rather, a way of being, a life. Being heirs of God and co-heirs of Christ (Rom. 8:17), having received of Christ's fulness (John 1:16) and become branches of the vine which is Christ (John 15:1-8), being members of a body of which He is the head (Eph. 4:15 ff.); our moral lives consist in a maturing and unfolding, a growth process in the Christlife, in *agapé*. This teaching is written unmistakably and emphatically in God's revealed word.

The following of Christ (Luke 9:23) will mean loving God by keeping His commandments (John 14:21) and loving one's neighbor as Jesus loved us (John 13:33-35), even to death (John 15:12-13). There is no greater commandment than this (Matt. 22:37-38). This love of God and neighbor is the epitome of the entire law (Rom. 13:8-9; Gal. 5:14) and is a way more elevated than all charisms and is the beginning of eternal life (I Cor. 13:1-13). It is the root from which other virtues flow (Eph. 3:17) and is the bond of perfection (Gal. 3:12-14). This love is a new law (John 13:4) and is so characteristic of Christians that one is to recognize them by its observance (John 13:35), and see in them through this love a revelation of the unity of the divine Persons and the mission of Christ (John 17:20-23).[2]

The Christlife is well summarized by St. John when he writes: "In this is charity: not as though we had loved God, but because He has first loved us, and sent his Son to be a propitiation for our sins. Beloved, if God has so loved us, we also ought to love one another" (I John 4:10-12). Oscar Cullmann has noted of this passage that it is the "catechism of the ethics of the New Testament."[3] The well-known exegete L. Cerfaux states simply that "charity is the normal

[2] Cf. Gérard Gilleman, S.J., *The Primacy of Charity in Moral Theology* (Westminster, Md.: Newman Press, 1959).

[3] *Christ and Time* (Philadelphia, Penn.: The Westminster Press, 1952), p. 230.

occupation of Christians while they wait and prepare themselves for the judgment of the 'parousia.' "[4] The Fathers of Vatican Council II made it quite clear that they share this view:

> For charity, as the bond of perfection and the fulfillment of the law (cf. Col. 3:14; Rom. 13:10), rules over all the means of attaining holiness, gives life to them, and makes them work. Hence it is the love of God and of neighbor which points out the true disciple of Christ.[5]

Ethical reflection, if it is to be Christian, must begin then from the fact that the human personality has, so to speak, been seized by the divine grasp, quickened with a new life so that every virtue and every virtuous act is an expression, a mediation of this new life-tendency. John L. McKenzie, S.J., has remarked that "the New Testament reduces all morality to the commandment of love."[6] This is not to deny the function of reason in the discovery of moral doctrine, nor is it to erase the distinct nuances of moral value which reason discovers. It is merely to assert that reason's task within theological ethics is to discover the demands of Christian love. In short, our Christlikeness (if it is true Christlikeness) must burst forth in different forms of virtuous action. But these different forms of virtuous action are simply the interior drive of charity becoming the external gift of charity in the world. If this be the type of "love-monism" with which James Gustafson has taken issue,[7] then there are among us, I am afraid, many unrepentant monists.

2. *The essential interiority of law in the New Covenant.* One of the properties of law is said to be its external character. By this is meant not its merely positive character (given externally by a competent authority), nor its external proposition but, rather, its coercive character, whereby it is understood to move men to action *ab extra*. Taken in this way it is certainly opposed to a law which moves man by internal motivation. And this opposition highlights the analogous character of the word "law." May we not accept the fact that for the "new man in Christ," law (as the imperative of our indicative, our "being in Christ") is to be understood as the unfolding of the internal motion of the Holy Spirit? May we not accept the fact

---

[4] "La charitè fraternelle et le retour du Christ," *Ephemerides Theologicae Lovanienses*, Vol. 24 (1948), p. 326.

[5] Cf. *The Documents of Vatican II*, ed. Walter M. Abbott, S.J. (New York: Guild Press, America Press, Association Press, 1966), p. 71.

[6] "Reflections on the Church's Teaching Authority," *The Catholic World*, Vol. 203 (1966), pp. 86–90.

[7] "How Does Love Reign?" *The Christian Century*, Vol. 83 (1966), p. 655.

that the law of Christ does indeed oblige us, but that it obliges us not as an external-coercive agent but, rather, as an internal law? As Rudolph Schnackenburg notes:

> The apostle requires, therefore, that the law of God should be done; but with the Christian this fulfillment takes place in a different way from that of the old law. He does not receive a multitude of precepts coming to him from without, and with which he cannot adequately comply; he hears within him the voice of the Spirit, simultaneously impelling him towards what is good and enabling him to do it. Thus the "law of the Spirit" is not a new code of laws (condensed into the commandment to love, perhaps), but rather an impulse towards the good coming from the Holy Spirit.[8]

Thus those who are led by the Spirit and by grace are not under the (external coercive) law. Franz Böckle has completed this point as follows:

> However, this "Law of the Spirit" should not be pictured simply as an inner encouragement from the Holy Spirit. This is so because its fulfillment in love that looks back to the preaching of the great commandment by Jesus and Paul also makes special reference to the instructions of Jesus.[9]

It is this same point which W. D. Davies makes when he says that Christian life is freedom in the Spirit, "but it is freedom informed by a moral tradition stemming from the words of Jesus himself."[10] If we read the New Testament in any other way (e.g., in terms of a rigid understanding of the Pauline antithesis of grace and law), Davies contends, we ignore three things: the tumultuous, tortuous nature of Paul himself; the exaggerations engendered by the historical controversy out of which that antithesis arose; and, above all, much evidence pointing to a law which remains in the new covenant of grace, one rooted in the words of Jesus.

When one accepts this balanced sense of the interiority of the law, he also thereby endorses the following assertions, and need no more prove that he believes these things: (*a*) Observance of the law, *as such*, is in no sense justifying. (*b*) The law as externally proposed, and therefore as universal, cannot assert concretely all that the individual man here and now must do. God's call, made known in the

---

[8] *The Moral Teaching of the New Testament* (New York: Herder and Herder, 1965), pp. 201–202.

[9] *Law and Conscience* (New York: Sheed and Ward, 1966), p. 39.

[10] *The Setting of the Sermon on the Mount* (Cambridge, Eng.: Cambridge University Press, 1964), p. 440.

Spirit, is always to an individual person in a concrete situation. Hence knowledge of this call is personal and cannot be adequately formulated. Here Karl Rahner's remarks on an existential ethics are in place.[11] (c) Law is not the principal element governing the present moral order. The principal element is the motion of the Spirit and of grace. This principal element is only served by the law.

3. *The existence of the natural law.* In an important article, Bruno Schüller, S.J., after pointing out that moral knowledge is knowledge of values and that values are known only in immediate moral experience, asks: Is, then, faith in the Word of God the primary, original manner and the logically prior manner in which man grasps an equally original moral value—for example, humility or fidelity? Schüller answers this with a categorical negative. His explanation is extremely interesting:

> The Christian faith is knowledge founded on the witness of God. This encounter between the believer and the God who serves as his own witness comes about through the medium of word and language. But this is only possible if the language God uses in revealing himself is known in advance by the man who is called, if it is the language proper to man. And how broad is the ethical "vocabulary" of this human language? It is just as broad as man's natural ethical experience, his natural ethical consciousness. Divine revelation cannot be considered as the foundation which determines the breadth of expression of human language, since precisely the whole question is to find out what possibilities of expression God finds in language when He wants to reveal Himself to man. If, therefore, it is the natural ethical consciousness of man which grounds the expressive possibilities of human language, then it seems to follow that God through this revelation can only communicate to man that aspect of moral insight which man already knows by means of his natural ethical experience, or at least which he can know.[12]

Schüller refuses to draw this conclusion quite that simply. For if left unnuanced it would seem to deny the possibility of a substantially supernatural revelation. Rather, he points out that in his natural existence man is already a likeness of God. Therefore the language which man uses to express understanding of his natural existence must be apt to become a parable or sign which reflects a higher reality, a reality no longer human but divine. Obviously by revealing Himself,

---

[11] *Theological Investigations,* Vol. II, *Man in the Church* (Baltimore: Helicon, 1963), pp. 217–234.

[12] "Wieweit kann die Moraltheologie das Naturrecht entbehren?" *Lebendiges Zeugnis,* März (1965), pp. 41–65 at pp. 47–48.

God can communicate immeasurably more than we already understand simply by reason of our human existence. Indeed, He has done so in Christ Jesus. Therefore, Schüller continues:

> In no way does the moral message of the New Testament have as its primary objective the announcing of a natural moral law already accessible to us. It calls man insofar as he is or should be a "new creature" in Christ. Therefore it reveals to us the *lex gratiae*. Now in comparison with the *lex naturae*, the *lex gratiae* represents something that is radically new, a supernatural reality. The *lex gratiae* is in fact the *gratia Christi* itself insofar as this is entrusted to man not only as a gift, but also confided to him as a task. How is it possible that this totally new element which radically transcends nature is communicated in human language? . . . Because grace finds in nature, and the *lex gratiae* in the *lex naturae*, an analogical image, therefore the ethical concepts of our language (concepts which correspond to the *lex naturae*) can symbolically point to the supernatural reality of the *lex gratiae*.[13]

On the basis of this analysis Schüller concludes that man is capable of hearing and giving intelligent belief to the ethical message of the New Testament only because (logically) prior to the revelation of God's Word he already grasps and expresses himself as an ethical being. From the divine point of view, so to speak, this means that it is only by the very fact of having established man in his natural existence (and thus providing the ontological basis for the *lex naturae*) that God endows him with the capacity to hear the Word which He means to address to man as Savior and Redeemer. Or as Schüller says: *"The fact that the natural moral law concerns him is for man his 'obediential potency' for the fact that the* lex Christi *can concern him."*

Schüller concludes this remarkable analysis as follows:

> And so we have the answer to the question whether the Christian, in searching for the will of God, can simply refer either to the moral message of Christ or to the *lex naturae*. There is no genuine alternative here. The man who turns seriously to Christ in order to learn from him what he must do, proves therewith that, before any response of Christ, he understands himself as an ethical being, and one who knows that he is called to orient his whole life according to the divine will. . . . For otherwise he would be in no condition to understand this *lex Christi*, which is really only intelligible for man to the extent that it is reflected analogically in the natural moral law.[14]

"Man's grasp of himself as an ethical being" states quite well another premise on which theological ethics must build; for it states the

[13] *Ibid.*, p. 48.　　[14] *Ibid.*, pp. 48–49.

ontological basis of the natural law (concrete, existing man) and the general epistemological implications of this basis (man's limited grasp of his own being). Unfortunately the strength of this premise is often undermined by the caricatures of the natural law so often encountered in literature on the subject. John Courtney Murray, S.J., has better than anyone identified these caricatures and convincingly disowned them.[15] For example, he refers to abstractionism (which undertakes "to pull all its moral precepts like so many magician's rabbits out of the metaphysical hat of an abstract human 'essence' "); intuitionism (which regards *all* natural imperatives as self-evident); legalism (which reduces the natural law to a detailed code "nicely drawn up with the aid of deductive logic alone, absolutely normative in all possible circumstances, ready for automatic application"); immobilism (which denies the historicity of the human person); biologism (which confuses brute facticity with the normatively natural); rationalism (an "alleged deafness to the resonances of intersubjectivity"). Murray rightly contends that by and large those who dislike the natural law are forever burying the wrong corpse. And if the natural law is any one of the above caricatures, one would be happy to join a tearless Murray at its wake.

Louis Monden, S.J., is much closer to the truth when he contends that the natural law is "an ordering of man towards his self-perfection and his self-realization."[16] Rather than an abstract blueprint, it is, he says, a *"dynamically inviting possibility,* a concrete project to be carried out in the midst of a concrete situation in which man's 'self' presents its demands to an 'ego' consciously realizing itself." In other words, it is man's being charting his becoming.

This can be better understood (or, perhaps, more readily accepted) when we see the same structure at work in the Pauline presentation of the Christian life. In Paul's thought the Christian life is the execution of the imperative implied in an indicative. It is the fully free and responsible acceptance of the gift of newness of life. The reality which has been worked in us sacramentally is still something to be developed and lived out. It is given as a pledge (Eph. 1:14), an as yet hidden gift (Col. 3:3) which can still be lost (1 Cor. 10:12). Thus Paul constantly asserts that our death and resurrection is both achieved and to be achieved; that we have been conformed to Christ and therefore must conform our lives to His. The gift of God is, even as gift, a call and a challenge. Thus: "They that are Christ's have crucified their flesh, with the vices and concupiscences" (Gal. 5:24). Yet the Colossians are urged to "mortify therefore your members which are upon the

---

[15] *We Hold These Truths* (New York: Sheed and Ward, 1960), pp. 295-296.
[16] *Sin, Liberty and Law* (New York: Sheed and Ward, 1965), p. 89.

earth" (Col. 3:5). Similarly, "as many of you as have been baptized in Christ have put on Christ" (Gal. 3:27). Yet the Romans are exhorted to "put ye on the Lord Jesus Christ" (Rom. 13:14). We live in the Spirit, now we must walk in the Spirit (Gal. 5:25); the old man has been crucified with Christ (Rom. 6:6) but we must put off the old man and take on the new (Eph. 4:22-24).

Something very similar can be said of the natural law. It is the imperative implied in our very being. We have received (and continue to receive) the gift of being from God, and this very gift is a challenge which reads: "Become what thou art." Because the natural law is fundamentally man's being as implying his becoming, it is above all an inner reality or imperative, and therefore, as "law," as analogous as is the "Law of the Spirit."

When adequately understood, therefore, the notion of a natural law in no sense attacks the idea of a personal relationship with God, a personal call from God at each moment of life inviting to a personal decision. With contemporary Christian thought, the authentic natural law tradition sees the situation (and the synthesis of relationships constituting it) as a religious reality in which God and the individual confront each other in an I-Thou relationship, a continuous dialogue of gift and acceptance, a continual word of love from God awaiting our response, which takes the form of abandon. The situation is necessarily religious and the individual response is necessarily religious. But this tradition also insists that the call of God is constituted by the ensemble of real elements which constitute the situation and that an ineradicable, basic datum is the fact of being a man, a human person. If this escapes us we muffle the call of God by depriving the situation of some of its reality and make a complete religious abandon impossible. For the I-Thou relationship based on God's call to me is clearly present not only in His saving intervention in human history and in the immediate inspirations of grace, but also in the call of God issued through creation.

How we know these claims, what they are, how they are to be formulated are, for the moment, other and secondary concerns. But the claim of others on my love is inseparable from my being and their being. And because man is reasonable, he can discover, if only with difficulty, the larger outlines of these demands. All that the authentic natural law tradition asserts is that a person's loving and lovability may not be defined short of his full humanity. Being a work of God, man *as man* is a word of God.

4. *The relationship of natural law to gospel morality.* The contents of the previous and the present supposition represent areas of

some disagreement between the Catholic ethical tradition and Protestant ethical traditions. I am aware of this and of the importance of pursuing the matter single-mindedly and in depth. However, for present purposes, it must suffice to make a single point for those inclined to accept the validity of a natural law: to speak of the natural law and the gospel morality as two different moralities involves a false notion of the place of the natural law in the *Heilsordnung*. There is no such thing as a natural law existentially separable from the law of Christ, and there never was. There is only Christian morality, not a natural and a Christian morality.

This last sentence implies many things. It asserts, for example, that what we sometimes call "natural" institutions (such as marriage, the family, the State) have, in fact and by the Creator's intent, a function and meaning beyond themselves as natural, i.e., to serve the Kingdom of Christ. Therefore parents and politicians who are good parents and good politicians even though they are ignorant of Christ, achieve materially that whereby and wherein the Kingdom of Christ can better develop and expand.[17] Second, it asserts that the observance of the natural law, since it is part of the law of Christ, is a means to salvation—not of itself as natural, but by reason of grace with which it takes place. Third, it suggests that the (materially) good acts of nonbelievers are often or at least potentially performed out of a believing, a Christian love. This love does not exist, it is true, at the level of explicit or reflective awareness, but only at a depth of the soul beyond the grasp of reflective consciousness where a fundamental option occurs. Not only the Christian, but also the atheist and the agnostic make a deep personal disposition of themselves in the depths of their beings before the God of life. This basic option is made in confrontation with the grace of Christ. Hence the correct moral behavior of non-Christians at least can be an expression or mediation of the new life and love which Christ works in them even though they do not recognize it as such.

But from the sentence "there is only Christian morality" I should like to draw out and emphasize above all the fact that to admit a natural law and yet to conceive it independently from or as in competition with the law of Christ is to conceive it as a mere abstraction. As Murray notes, "what the follower of Christ chooses to perfect is, and can only be, a humanity." [18] In still other words, far from denying what theologians refer to as natural law obligations, it is precisely

---

[17] Cf. Joseph Fuchs, S.J., *Theologia Moralis Generalis* (Roma: Editrice Universita Gregoriana, 1960), pp. 86–87.

[18] Murray, *op. cit.*, p. 298.

because Christ charged us with love of the neighbor that He must be thought to have asserted them. One who would claim to love his neighbor (or live out *koinonia,* or call it what we will), while at the same time refusing to acknowledge the basic claims that the human person makes on this love, would not accept and communicate with the total reality of that person. In failing to do so, he would be victimized by an otherworldly supernaturalism, and would, incidentally, be underestimating the affirmation of the dignity and worth of men implied in Christ's very incarnation (His God-*manhood*).

Obviously there is something of the mysterious in the continuing significance and validity of human claims in the newly "divinized" being. But this is to be expected. It is a mystery that God became man. It is a mystery that the divine and the human were conjoined to the point of oneness of person, yet without confusion or absorption. Refractions of this conjoining will also be mysterious. It is a reality, but has always been a mystery, that a drink of water to a thirsty indigent can be an incarnate act of Christ's love for another. It is even perhaps more mysterious (but nonetheless true) that Christ's life, hence Christ's love for another in our persons, can only survive and grow through such concrete, *human* actions. It is the greatest risk to our new empowerments in Christ, to our charity, to think that it does or can ride above the human scene. Ever since the incarnation it has been clear (but only mysteriously so) that our loves cannot be divine unless they struggle to be perfectly human.

5. *The rejection of moralism.* Needless to say, the Christian is committed to the discernment of right conduct and to the avoidance of sin. This commitment, if it is to be any more than nominal, carries right to the heart of the complexities of modern life: to expense account conduct, to racial attitudes and reactions, to tax responsibility, to the use of force, to premarital mores, etc. But inseparable from the fact that moral conduct is concrete is the temptation to view the moral life as a series of disengaged acts, a series of (merely external) omissions and commissions without sense or direction.

Such an attitude is moralism, that is, an exclusive concern with an individual external act insofar as it is thought of as sinful or not. At its worst this is a form of codalism which quickly becomes minimalism, a framework within which the strict minimum requirements for avoidance of sin tend to become the measure of one's following of Christ. The thought-structure is "permissible-not permissible." Within this framework spiritual brinkmanship (how far can I go?) is too easily the moral ideal, and conformism the pernicious implication of this ideal.

If the moral life is conceived in these terms, it ends in being nothing more than a tedious attempt to avoid infraction of a legally conceived code. The adventuresome pursuit of Christ is gone, and in its place we find a stoic correctness unfamiliar with the notions of growth, dedication, heroism. In a sense Christ might as well never have come. Not even Christian sin is committed, but in its stead there is but a pale gray violation of a static code. This is simple spiritual sterility.

It must be accepted from the start that whether one defends universally valid moral principles or not his position need not be and therefore should not be stamped as moralistic or legalistic. In this sense one can only agree completely with the emphasis in the writings, for example, of Joseph Fletcher, Canon Douglas A. Rhymes, and Bishop John A. T. Robinson. If it seems repetitious, and even ungracious, to insist that this is an emphasis, one can only counter that it is sometimes accepted as more than that, i.e., as a methodology established by satisfactory answers to the questions which validate a methodology. Yet even after these recent writings, Paul Ramsey has been able to note (and correctly, I believe):

> The real issue is whether there are any *agapé-* or *koinonia-*embodying rules; and, if there are, what these rules may be. Theologians today are simply deceiving themselves and playing tricks with their readers when they pit the freedom and ultimacy of *agapé* (or covenant-obedience, or *koinonia,* or community, or any other primary theological or ethical concept) against rules, without asking whether *agapé* can and may or must work through rules and embody itself in certain principles which are regulative, or the guides of practice.[19]

These, then, are some of the premises accepted by the Catholic moral theologian.

## II

These have—happily and not without a certain malice of organizational forethought—brought us to Ramsey's statement of the issue of rules. There may be some merit in recasting Ramsey's statement if such a reworking can hope to lay bare the problem or problems underlying this issue. Let us put it this way. Schnackenburg has remarked that the law of the Spirit is not a new code of laws but, rather, "an impulse towards the good coming from the Holy Spirit." [20] The prob-

---

[19] *Deeds and Rules in Christian Ethics* (New York: Charles Scribner's Sons, 1967), pp. 4–5.
[20] Schnackenburg, *op. cit.,* p. 202.

lem of norms is, it would seem, to know whether, to what extent, and by what criteria this good can be captured through reflective processes and be meaningfully, validly formulated.

It should be noted at the outset that the good cannot be formulated with complete adequacy; for it is known in the immediacy of experience. This fact suggests several reasons for the limitations we must put on reflective formulations.

First, the good we know directly and seek to formulate is known also through the aid and inspiration of the Holy Spirit. But such divine activity is, of course, ineffable and beyond formulation. On the other hand, the Spirit visits and sanctifies a human being, and is moving him to love as only a human being can, humanly. The basic outlines or demands of this love are founded in the being of man. For man, being as man a creature of and thereby an image of God, it must be supposed that the Spirit will not be in contradiction with the Creator whose Spirit He is. Therefore the question of norms involves the more modest quest of the determination of the good at this objective-material level.

Second, some (e.g., Maritain) have suggested that our primary moral knowing pertains to the level of preformulated, nonobjectifying intellection, and is a kind of knowledge by inclination or congeniality. If this is the case, conceptual formulation of this intellection will obviously be not only of secondary importance, but to some extent inadequate to the experience.

Third, everyone is disposed to admit the inherent deficiencies of human formulation. Men swim in the historico-cultural stream. This means that their formulations are historically conditioned, that is, enunciated through a form peculiar to a historical moment. These will share both the qualities and the limitations characteristic of the historical moment in which they are uttered.

But these limitations on norms should not lead us to conclude that they represent a dispensable academic luxury. The human intellect, by its own dynamism, moves toward formulation and achieves in the clarity and distinctness of formulation a kind of perfection, relative though it may be. Hence, if we accept the ontological identity of the good and the true, and the wisdom of the maxim that "the truth will make us free," it is obvious that formulated knowledge of the good will help to make us free. For by bringing greater clarity to the range of moral choices, it will enlighten the deliberative processes and thus expand freedom.

All epistemologies accept the fact that man as man is perfected by the pursuit of good or value. Hence every epistemology of moral knowing has attempted to show that and how man knows goods or values. They differ only in the goods they identify as controlling and the manner of identification of these goods. Somewhat similarly, every ethic has attempted to show how and what sort of human conduct does or does not incarnate value. The result of this attempt has led in the past to the existence of both formal and material norms. Formal norms are understood as those which enshrine a value without stating concretely or materially what acts embody this value or attack it. Thus, nearly everyone would accept the universal and absolute validity of formal norms such as the following: "one must always act justly," "one must always act temperately," "one should always act humbly, authentically," etc. Material norms are contractions of these formal norms to concrete pieces of human conduct. If a concrete act embodies a value, it is prescribable. If it generally embodies an attack on value, it is generally proscribed. If it always embodies an attack on value, it is always proscribed.

Norms, therefore, are statements about value or disvalue. And if they are material norms (the only ones truly in question in contemporary Christian ethical discussion), they are statements of the value or disvalue of concrete acts, of the significance of the act. Therefore, it seems that the problem of material norms is above all the problem of identifying accurately the significance of concrete human actions.

This point comes through clean by a consideration of the inconsistencies in the writings of Bishop John A. T. Robinson. After stating in *Honest to God* that love alone makes a thing right or wrong, he hastens to conclude that nothing in itself is wrong and instances premarital relations as a case in point. "For nothing can of itself always be labeled as 'wrong.' One cannot, for instance, start from the position 'sex relations before marriage' or 'divorce' are wrong or sinful in themselves. They may be in 99 cases or even 100 cases out of 100, but they are not intrinsically so, for the only intrinsic evil is lack of love." [21]

Later, in *Christian Morals Today,* Robinson writes that "there are some things of which one may say that it is so inconceivable that they could ever be an expression of love—like cruelty to children or rape —that one might say without much fear of contradiction that they are for Christians always wrong." [22] Then when treating of premarital relations, Robinson states that "outside marriage sex is bound to be

---

[21] *Honest to God* (Philadephia: Westminster Press, 1963), p. 118.
[22] Robinson, *Christian Morals Today* (Philadephia: Westminster Press, 1964), p. 16.

the expression of less than an unreserved sharing and commitment of one person to another." [23]

Here we see a man trying to establish in the name of love an ethic of the exceptional instance (and therefore the invalidity of any absolute norms) and yet being unable in the name of love to do so when he faces certain exceptional instances. And the reason? Robinson has, I submit, run smack into the meaning of human actions and is too honest-to-God a man to think he can change this significance.

Ramsey's splendid analysis has caught this point.[24] Admitting that stealing, lying, killing, committing adultery are so fundamentally destructive of human relationships that no differences of century or society can change their character, Robinson had nevertheless insisted: "But this does not, of course, mean that stealing and lying can in certain circumstances never be right. All Christians would admit that they would be." [25]

Ramsey is right on target when he replies:

> Never have Christians—at least not those Christians whose vocation it is to reflect as ethicists upon the nature of the Christian life—admitted any such thing. Instead they have asked: *what is the meaning of the forbidden theft, what is the meaning of truth-telling, what is the forbidden murder? They have explored or deepened or restricted the moral meaning of these categories or rules of conduct.*[26]

The problem of norms or rules of conduct, therefore, is fundamentally the problem of the significance or meaning of human actions. One may suspect that Karl Rahner, S.J. had this in mind when he labeled extreme situationism a "massive nominalism." [27] More narrowly, the problem could be put as follows: How do we determine significance? What criteria do we use to determine whether an individual act (coitus with another's wife, for instance) embodies a value or an attack on it? One thing is clear: we do not *prove* that an individual act (and all like it—a category, therefore) contains an attack on value, if by proof we mean a type of logical argumentation which all but traps the mind into assent. Hence, too, we do not *prove* the validity of norms based on this recognition of value or disvalue. Since the meaning or significance of a piece of conduct involves its relation to value, and since value is something utterly original, we can only describe, point to, and assert significance. We cannot prove it. We can

---

[23] *Ibid.*, p. 42.
[25] *Christian Morals Today*, p. 16.
[27] See note 11, above.

[24] Ramsey, *op. cit.*, pp. 37–38.
[26] Ramsey, *op. cit.*, p. 37 (italics added).

make logical statements about it, but we cannot logically demonstrate it.

## III

This being the case, I should like to list a number of factors to be weighed, attended to, or discounted as we pursue the altogether Christian effort to state the meaning or significance of certain pieces of human conduct. If these reflections do not immediately resolve the issue of norms as earlier stated by Ramsey (and they do not propose to), it can be hoped that they will, insofar as they are valid, at least point us more resolutely toward the only basis (i.e., significance) upon which a resolution can avoid being arbitrary. In the examples chosen for purposes of illustration I shall limit myself to the area of sexuality, and that for two reasons. First, it is a constantly recurring example in contextualist writing. Second, it makes for simplification and consistency.

1. *The dynamic character of natural law.* A static notion of natural law which indiscriminately identifies primary moral perceptions with detailed conclusions can blind us to value as easily as the summary refusal to allow man's created being to function normatively at all. Man's being is the basis for the norms of his becoming. In still other words, man's being is the basis of the significance of his actions. It is an accepted fact that a man changes, matures, develops, transforms himself. This individual process is but an instance of the often imperceptible but nonetheless real growth of the human race itself, as Chardin has so pointedly reminded us.

On the other hand, man always remains man. Hence, as Schüller points out, it is necessary to distinguish between norms founded on man's being as changeable and man's being as providing continuity in change, as stable and suprahistorical. Or more proximately, it is necessary to distinguish between acts embodying meaning in a stable fashion and actions involving meaning in a more or less variable way. This is important if one is to avoid the misleading insinuation that because a conclusion is of natural law, it is fixed and unchanging.

Ramsey has made this point extremely well while treating Robinson's ethic of the exceptional case. He uses as his example the traditional treatment of justified theft.

> This was an "exception" only when externally or statistically viewed. The moral reasoning on which this piece of casuistry was based was a love-informed determination of the created destination of property right to the common good or common use. This was "love's casuistry," and

then with the principles governing property in mind love proceeded to the ordering of human reality generally and to particular cases of application. *It was the bourgeois period with its notions of absolute property right that made the prohibition of theft not only a fixed rule, but a fixed rule with a certain and a non-Christian moral meaning so that thereafter theft could only be a (forbidden) exception.*[28]

We are all, of course, capable of a bourgeois parochialism of outlook, perhaps all the more so the more we think we are immunized against it. But it would be unfair to shift the burden of this weakness to the wrong shoulder. For example, even traditional Scholastic epistemology has provided the basis for the distinction mentioned above (between stable meaning and variable meaning, and therefore between changeable and unchangeable norms). In his intriguing essay on natural law, Columba Ryan, O.P., sees the basic and primary moral knowledge of man (based on urges to and primary recognitions of quite general goods in the concrete) as involving statements such as "some arrangements must be made for the preservation of life," "some for the organization of society," etc.[29] What these arrangements should be is, in each case, open to experience and inquiry. From these quite general principles one arrives at others by way of conclusions (not, be it noted, by deduction but, rather, by subsumption). Ryan puts it as follows:

> The natural law has different levels; basically it consists of those highest principles which are simply given and indemonstrable—whether as the rules of moral conduct or as the primary axioms of an entirely general moral awareness; but it comprises also anything which may be derived by way of conclusion, from such axioms, and which may serve in turn as principles in reaching individual decisions as to conduct. In this way, the natural law is indefinitely extendable, as we come into fuller and fuller possession of what we see to be derivable from the original premises. *But, and it is important to notice this, such development is not to be had without constant reference to a wider and more sensitive assessment of experience; nor is it to be had without danger of making mistakes, and without exacting enquiry.*[30]

It is clear, therefore, that if we are to determine the significance of concrete actions (and therefore the norms generated by this significance)

---

[28] Ramsey, *op. cit.*, pp. 37–38 (italics added).

[29] "The Traditional Concept of Natural Law: An Interpretation," in *Light on the Natural Law*, ed. Illtud Evans, O.P. (Baltimore: Helicon, 1965), p. 29.

[30] *Ibid.*, pp. 29–30 (italics added).

we must often rely heavily on the data of other (than theological) disciplines.

2. *The pertinence of other disciplines to the recognition of significance.* Not only does man himself change and develop, but his grasp of this change is a continually deepening thing. This growth is worked especially by attention to the findings of, e.g., the sciences and incorporation of them into one's reflective processes. An excellent example of this would be the discoveries of the depth sciences and their pertinence to our notions of human sexuality.

For centuries it was common coin to speak of the "generative faculty" and its finality and to base this on an observable anatomical structure. On the basis of this finality so determined, a basic significance was attributed to the biological intactness of acts of sexual communion. Somewhat analogously, moralists spoke of acts of adultery and fornication as being somehow *secundum naturam* because in their external manner of execution they mirrored this intactness. It has been noted by any number of authors[31] that these analyses derive significance from the brute facticity of biological organs, thereby revealing the level at which significance was supposedly located.

The depth sciences have made it clear that we can no longer talk about the meaning of human sexuality as if this were to be derived especially from a finality based on the observation of external organs. These sciences have shown that sexual acts are an engagement of the whole person, involving the whole range and depth of the instinctive-emotional register. They have shown us that no act of sexual expression can be viewed as the simple manipulation or coupling of organs and that one who views human sexuality in this way is speaking out of another century. The depth sciences have thus provided the empirical evidence to corroborate an analysis of coitus which understands it as the expression of a total personal sharing and donation. Far from undermining traditional moral norms, this evidence has provided a more realistic and adequate basis in which to anchor them. Thus, the rejection of adultery and fornication must be based on an analysis of sexuality which does justice to its true depth. Similarly, if one is to condemn contraception, his rejection can hope to be credible only if it grows out of awareness of the awesome depths of human sexuality.

Ironically, those who reject an analysis of sexuality which founds significance on brute facticity sometimes unwittingly reveal that they

---

[31] E.g., Robert O. Johann, S.J., "Responsible Parenthood: A Philosophical View," *Proceedings of the Twentieth Annual Convention* (Catholic Theological Society of America), pp. 115–128.

have been victimized by this analysis. Take, for example, the instance cited by Joseph Fletcher. Fletcher presented the case of a mother who gained her release from a Soviet prison-farm and reunion with her family by means of an adulterous pregnancy. This was her only way back to her family, which, it can be supposed, needed her badly. This action, Fletcher says, "would have the situationist's solemn but ready approval." [32] Now let us grant immediately that those who balk at this "ready approval" have nothing against reassembling separated families; indeed, let us grant that they would do all they humanly could to achieve this worthy purpose. "Humanly" is the issue. Is not Fletcher constrained to say that in this instance coitus was not the incarnation of a total sharing, of a total personal relationship, of a lived two-in-oneness? If it was not this, then what was it but a bit of high-minded expediency, a "use of the generative organs"? What was it but the sundering of the personal from the sexual?

Actually, if the significance of coitus is derived exclusively from the intent or exclusively from the good results it might produce, do we not have to view this piece of human conduct as *of itself* insignificant, a kind of empty container ready for any meaning that a good intent or good effects might give it? This is not to deny that these circumstantial factors influence, even greatly, the meaning of an act. It is only to suggest that the meaning-giving capabilities of human intent are not unlimited. All in all, it is easy to see in Fletcher's conclusion the implications of a dualism which must derive significance from other than human and bodily activity. This can only mean that coitus (and therewith human sexuality) has been returned to the level of brute facticity to await the arrival of meaning from without. That was the accusation brought against "biologized" natural law.

Schüller has provided another example where traditional moral thought needs nuancing because of the insights of a cognate discipline. It is the matter of deception. For centuries Catholic moral tradition has regarded the lie as *per se* slight moral matter. This conclusion is based on an analysis of the meaning of speech and language which sees it structurally as a medium for the communication of ideas or information. This it surely is. But cannot language mean more than this? The legitimate insights of philosophical personalism have taught us to view speech as often more than a communication of information and, rather, as a medium for the encounter of persons. In their words, the speakers share not only their ideas but they share themselves. Deception, in this light, is not merely false information; it is the falsification

---

[32] "Love is the Only Measure," *Commonweal*, Vol. 83 (1966), p. 428.

of a basic human relationship. Philosophical personalism has sharpened our perception of the possible meaning of human speech.

3. *Consequence-empiricism and the significance of acts.* The "empiricism of consequences" is so important in modern thought about the meaning of human activity that it should be singled out for specialized treatment. We have seen Fletcher's use of it. Harvey Cox also shows to what extent it functions as decisive in his thought. While dealing with premarital relations he says: "Premarital sexual conduct should therefore serve to strengthen the chances of sexual success and fidelity in marriage, and we must face the real question of whether avoidance of intercourse beforehand is always the best preparation." [33] Here Cox tips his hand as to what is his criterion for judging the significance of this particular type of conduct. This is somewhat surprising in the light of his clear hold on the significance of coitus and of the genuine wisdom of much of what he says about contemporary attitudes toward sex. There are many ways in which the matter of consequence-empiricism might be approached. One must suffice here.

In Chapter 8 of the present volume, John G. Milhaven, S.J., asks the question: "How can one know inviolable values in this world?" One must know the answer to this question before the absoluteness of a moral position is clear. Milhaven proceeds as follows.

First, there are certain values which we recognize immediately and intuitively as absolute without need of further evidence of any kind. Thus he says: "If one discerns what can be the authentic love between a man and a woman, one recognizes its absolute worth. One sees that no man may seek to frustrate it or destroy it. . . . once human love is understood, once the insight is had, man sees immediately its absolute worth" (see p. 223).

What Milhaven is saying, it seems, is that man knows moral values "intuitively" or directly, somewhat as we know colors. He feels that rather few values fit this category of absolute worth. He mentions love, honor, pity, pride, compassion, sacrifice, the proper upbringing of a child.

Second, one recognizes acts as immoral when the empirical observation of a number of cases indicates that the act (e.g., divorce) will result in some absolute evil. By empirical evidence Milhaven means "the evidence of the probable or certain consequences of what is going to result from the act in question." It is only empirical evidence in this sense that shows that divorce will oppose the absolute values embedded in marriage. He summarizes as follows:

[33] *The Secular City* (New York: Macmillan Co., 1965), p. 215.

> An act is seen to be wrong in one of two ways. Either it (e.g., cowardice) betokens by definition the absence of a quality (courage) whose absolute value is seen intuitively on understanding what it is, or the empirical observation of a number of cases indicates that the act (e.g., divorce) will result in some absolute evil, itself recognized in the former way (e.g., damage to the fitting education of the child). [See p. 229.]

It is easy to agree with Milhaven that we depend on empirical evidence (in his limited sense) more often than we think. It is also true that this type of evidence can become so impressive that it would provide the basis for a general rule of conduct binding on all who want to remain good empiricists. But how large is the area in which such evidence is needed before the basic significance of an action is clear? Are there not some areas of human activity where consequence-empiricism only confirms (or perhaps does not) what we already genuinely know without it? Milhaven gave cowardice as an example of that which betokens by definition the absence of a quality (courage). Are there really so few others?

A single example may serve to illustrate the point. Milhaven asserts that the decisive evidence for the morality of sexual acts must be empirical—and recall that he means by this only a calculation of consequences. The presupposition of such a statement must be that other sources (above all, the accumulated wisdom of revelation and Church teaching) cannot lead us or have not led us, if only gradually, to a perception of the meaning of coitus which relates it to the love of man and woman. Is there not a meaning to human coitus which we perceive even without the aid of consequence-empiricism, indeed, a sense which this empiricism could conceivably never establish?

Concretely, why is it wrong to assert that anyone who knows what the true love of man and woman is will know that adulterous coitus is immoral? Or in Milhaven's words: "it [e.g., adultery] betokens *by definition* the absence of a quality [love and/or fidelity] whose absolute value is seen intuitively on understanding what it is" (*italics added*). I am suggesting that human sexual intercourse has a sense and meaning prior to the individual purposes of those who engage in it, a significance which is a part of their situation whether or not the partners turn their minds to it. It is an act of love, and therefore has a definition which relates it immediately to the love of man and woman —with all the demands of this love. Furthermore, I am suggesting that we can come to know this meaning even if the scientific empiricism of our time has not proved it and cannot prove it.[34]

[34] Cf. *Theological Studies,* Vol. 27 (1966) under title of "Notes on Moral Theology" where I have treated this matter at greater length.

Is this not what is implied in Robinson's statement that "outside marriage sex is bound to be the expression of less than an unreserved sharing and commitment of one person to another"? [35] Is not this what Vatican II meant when it said that "this love is uniquely expressed and perfected through the marital act"?—a love it had earlier described as "total fidelity . . . unbreakable oneness between them . . . undivided affection . . . mutual gift of themselves . . . total love." [36]

These statements are statements concerning *significance* and they reach beyond consequence-empiricism. Furthermore, they have roots in a wisdom which even a good empiricist would hardly question: the Bible. If the Bible tells us anything about sexual intimacy, it tells us that it is a communication between persons, a sign and language so unique that *of itself* it expresses a two-in-oneship exclusive and irrevocable.[37]

That is why one must insist against Harvey Cox that whether or not premarital relations aid marital adjustment (a harrowing determination even at the general, statistical level) can become a primary and dominant moral determinant only if one assumes the primacy of consequence-empiricism as that which establishes the meaning of human conduct. More specifically, one must insist that sexual intimacy, because it expresses the person (or *is* the person become his act), must correspond to the existing personal relationship. To the extent that it does not correspond to the existing relationship, it does not express the person, but something else, infrahuman and divisive. To perform or to ask another to perform an act that prescinds from the personal is to ask him or her to act in a nonhuman way, hence to do something harmful to oneself. Regardless of the emotional concomitants, the high purpose, the repeated protestations of love, this cannot be an act of love toward that person, but must remain objectively, even if not consciously, an act of manipulation. And in the Christian ethic it is always immoral to manipulate another person.

In this perspective the cardinal rule of sexual conduct was and always will remain: physical expressions of intimacy express the person and therefore must correspond to the existing relationship of the persons. The unmarried are only preparing for the total relationship of marriage. They are learning, not chiefly but among other things, to fill their expressions of love with respect and protection, with more of the person. They are not given to each other. Since their love is protective, not possessive, they will give themselves to each other only

---

[35] *Christian Morals Today*, p. 42.
[36] *The Documents of Vatican II*, pp. 250–256.
[37] Cf. *America*, Vol. 115 (1966), p. 116.

to the extent that the person can be given at this moment—in a limited way. Consequently, they will avoid those acts that of themselves signify total personal oblation (if they signify anything), not out of blind servility to a negative "thou shalt not," but because, being in love, they will wish to speak a personal, and therefore genuinely human, language to each other. Since sexual intercourse and its proximate antecedents represent *total personal* exchange, they can be separated from total personal relationship (marriage) only by undermining their truly human, their expressive character—in short their significance.

4. *The subjective aspects of the perception of significance.* It has been accepted for centuries that the basic process of moral knowing (which reflective ethics must presume and upon which it builds) is not simply a matter of cerebralization. Contrarily, it is colored, qualified, conditioned by a host of personal factors.

For instance, man's very constitution is an indication of this. His knowledge of the good is first of all in his direct experience, his concrete affirmations and choices. Reflective analysis comes afterward. But such direct experience is the terminus of man's radical affective-cognoscitive "bent" to the good, a kind of spontaneous bearing of the person toward good and away from evil, which, as implicit in every moral judgment, is the kernel or nucleus of moral perception. From the very beginning of the process of moral perception it is clear that knowledge of the good is intertwined with the love of the good.

Such an affective orientation of the individual colors his perception and affirmation of value all down the line. His very fundamental option, being a basic self-disposition in the face of the Absolute, is thereby a kind of opening or a closing to all derivative values and goods. Thus if a person's basic personal posture before God is one of rejection and self-exaltation, it is bound to induce a creeping blindness to moral value itself.

Similarly, the strength or weakness, presence or absence, of a particular virtue will affect moral judgment. For it is virtue that orders the appetite and it is the well-ordered appetite which orders the person to *objective* goals.[38] And finally it is such an ordering of the person which helps guarantee truth in his prudential (or value) judgments in the concrete. We are familiar with the everyday wisdom that only the truly chaste man can make genuinely secure judgments about the morality of individual acts in the area of sexual expression. Only the charitable man possesses the security that his fraternal correction is an act of charity. Contrarily, it is often the alcoholic who is con-

---

[38] In this connection cf. John R. Connery, S.J., "Prudence and Morality," *Theological Studies*, Vol. 13 (1952), pp. 564–582.

vinced that only one drink "just this once" is possible. The difference between antecedent and consequent conscience judgments measures the extent to which appetite can control judgment. A sinful habit not only makes virtuous conduct more difficult; it makes it more difficult to recognize.

Furthermore we bring to our moral knowing all the sensitivities and defects of our early life and training. More often than we would care to admit, our perception and affirmation of value is the working out of imperfectly abandoned infantile images and structures. The zealot is sometimes far less devoted to a good cause than he is tied to the need to project and live out his aggressiveness.

Similarly, if one's personality structure will directly affect his recognition and affirmation of value, it will also do so indirectly—by molding his relationship to his environment and culture. For instance, a strong relationship of dependency can easily mean that one does not reflect in his conduct and judgments an independent and genuinely interiorized grasp of value but, rather, mirrors those values which are dominant in his culture and milieu.

One's perception and retention of significance is, then, a fairly fragile, even capricious thing. Awareness of this will issue in a salutary hesitation to make oneself (on the basis of one's own assessments) the exceptional case. This fragility also suggests the wisdom of continual humility and self-criticism in the area of reflective ethics. For, as noted above, reflective ethics will always depend upon and to a large extent reflect the quality of our personal and communal direct experience.

5. *The communal aspects of the perception of significance.* Contemporary philosophy sees man as a person only in relation to other persons. In this sense his personality is established by his relation to others. (Is it, incidentally, really surprising that man, created in the image of God, is in his radical constitution a refraction of the inner life of God where personality is described in terms of relation to another? Do not the sometimes dramatic discoveries of the depth sciences only point more conclusively to the fact that all about man conspires to relational life?) If man is a person only in relation to others, he is also to some extent a knower only in relation to other knowers. For *agere* still follows ineluctably upon *esse*.

This is clearer than ever from the specifically Christian point of view. Man's new being in Christ is, above all, being in a community. Assumption into Christ means assumption into the whole Christ—which is His Body, His People. Hence, "Saul, Saul, why do you persecute *me?*" (Acts 9:4) was the apostle's first lesson in Christian ontology. Similarly, "if any man says I love God and hate his brother, he is a liar" (1 John 4:20) must be seen as John's way of making the same ontological point. Being of Christ we are necessarily in a community. We cannot exist as Christians except in community and we cannot define ourselves except as "of a Body." Hence it is theologically axiomatic that the community of believers (the Church) is the extension of the incarnation. It is similarly axiomatic that those actions wherein we initiate into, fortify, restore, intensify the Christlife are at once Christ's actions and the actions of the community which is His Church.

If we cannot exist as Christians in isolation, neither can we know as Christians in isolation, and it would be unchristian to think we do or hope that we could. Our shared knowing is concerned, of course, with the *Magnalia Dei,* God's wonderful saving events. However, since it is *men* who are being conformed to Christ by being swept into these events, and since the Christ to whom we are being conformed is the God-*man,* and since we extend and intensify this conformity by *human* actions, it must be clear that the Christian experience under the guidance of the Spirit will lead even to a growing sensitivity to human (natural) values and significances. This has always been the Church's understanding of the depth of the riches she possesses. This fine sensitivity to human values will itself be a communal possession, and a communal enterprise in its growth and extension.

If the Christian experience involves a growing sensitivity to human value and if Christian thinking is necessarily community thinking, it is clear that the Christian will draw instinctively (this instinct being partially identifiable with the guidance of the Holy Spirit) upon his ethos for the meaning of human actions. This is the very meaning of a distinctive "value system." Theologians are only beginning to probe the significance of *consensus fidelium* as a theological source where even human values are concerned.

Since norms are based on significance, if there have been certain cherished norms in the Christian community (regardless of how clumsily they have been formulated, or how much they have been legalized in their execution), this can only mean that Christians have seen a significance in a piece of human conduct and have refused to slip their grasp on this significance. Is it any wonder, for example, that those who have read and cherished Ephesians 5 should view the marriage relationship somewhat more profoundly than those who, by force of historical circumstances, have never been exposed to it? Is it any wonder, therefore, that their attitude toward coitus (and hence adulterous coitus) should be distinctive? To reject this significance, even in an instance (perhaps, *especially* in an instance), could easily amount to thinking in isolation, to a failure in *Christian* empiricism. Such cloistered thinking is, *pace* Harvey Cox, a genuine risk for those who must make their way in the faceless impersonalism of contemporary Western culture.

These pages have been concerned with *significance* as the problem underlying the problem of norms—first, with the premises some use to approach significance, then with some methodological criteria for its determination. That the more basic problem does not directly concern the moral norms in control of conduct but, rather, the meaning of conduct can also be made negatively, i.e., by showing the growing disappearance of significance in a single area (sexuality) of human conduct. Specifically, I submit that our culture has gone far along the road toward emptying sexuality of genuine significance. This is, of course, quite a feat. The insignificant is always morally problematic simply because morality concerns good and evil and the insignificant is neither. Where significance disappears, so do good and evil.[39]

To say that we are unwittingly succeeding in rendering sexuality insignificant calls for clarification. Recent thinkers suggest that instead of a joyous but challenging expression of total personal commitment, total personal encounter in fidelity—variously mysterious, humiliating, frivolous, refreshing, playful, hallowing, dutiful, boring, etc.—sex has too often become a mechanized, manipulatable, tabulated, microscoped thing always on call. We know all about it: its incidences, its glands, its controls, its nerves, its deviations, its selling powers. There are hundreds of books telling us what button to push and how. As Leslie Farber noted in *Commentary*:[40] "Our residence in the laboratory is recent; really only since the turn of the century has the act of sex been interviewed, witnessed, probed, measured, timed, taped, photographed, judged." The process going on here, he suggests, is that of objectification, a wrenching from the human context.

This objectification appears even in our language, as Farber trenchantly observes:

> Qualities such as modesty, privacy, reticence, abstinence, chastity, fidelity, shame—could now be questioned as rather arbitrary matters which interfered with the health of the sexual parts. And in their place came an increasing assortment of objective terms like *ejaculatio praecox*, foreplay, forepleasure, frigidity—all intended to describe not human experience, but rather the behaviour of the sexual parts. The quite

[39] I have borrowed the following paragraphs from my article "Toward a New Sexual Morality?" *The Catholic World*, Vol. 202 (1965), pp. 10–16, with the permission of the publisher.

[40] "I'm Sorry, Dear," *Commentary*, Vol. 38 (1964), pp. 47–54 at p. 52.

preposterous situation arose in which the patient sought treatment of *ejaculatio praecox* or impotence and the healer sought to find out whether he liked his partner.[41]

First, then, there was objectification, a situation where "knowing about" was too easily substituted for biblical knowing. It was then inevitable that such knowledge should lead to greater dominance by the human will, and that this dominance should gradually assume its easiest form, mechanization. Thus we not only have contraceptives, but we have pills and the IUD (intrauterine contraceptive device) which operate with minimum tax upon human intelligence. We seek the perfect rhythm calendar or regulator. The controls are increasingly external and automatic. We have become the masters of techniques, the clinicians of quality precisely in an area where quality escapes the mere clinician. The euphemisms "affair," "sleeping with," "her favors," "going to bed with" reflect the ultimate cultural achievement of mechanization, casualness.

This dominance-by-will and ultimate mechanization means the growing autonomy of sexuality. Thus Farber, in discussing the laboratory experiments of Dr. William H. Masters on female orgasm, sees them as symbolic of our real cultural dilemma. For those involved, "sexuality would have to be autonomous, separate from and unaffected by her ordinary world. 'World' here would have to include not only affection but all those exigencies of human existence which tend to shape our erotic possibilities." [42]

Once there is autonomy, there is depersonalization and decontextualization of human sexuality. Depersonalized sex is simply inhuman. It is mere coupling, and eventually arrives at the point where even coupling becomes an inconvenience in comparison with the swift assurances of autosexuality. Farber concludes that "over the last fifty years sex has for the most part lost its viability as a human experience." Such a reduction of sexuality to facility led Paul Ricoeur to remark that "it may be that tomorrow's greatest problem will be to preserve the expressive and meaningful value of sexuality." [43] And if it will be tomorrow's problem it is already today's.

Certainly these sweeping strokes represent a caricature. But the broad lines of the process of objectification-autonomy-depersonalization are sufficiently discernible to suggest that our characteristic threat is an increasingly dim perception of the meaning of sexuality. If hu-

[41] *Ibid.*, p. 53.  [42] *Ibid.*, p. 50.
[43] In *Cross Currents*, Vol. 14 (1964), p. 247.

man sexuality is gradually losing its significance for men, then of course a new significance must be discovered in another world. Is this not precisely what is happening? The symbol par excellence of this search for meaning is *Playboy* magazine. It presents an unreal, hence basically antisexual sexuality, as Harvey Cox has so brilliantly shown.[44]

Cox shows that *Playboy*'s ultimate formula for significance is: Sex equals fun. It is extremely interesting to note how woman (and through her, sexuality in general) has been developed into a packageable item for the consumer market. As the eminent moralist from Bonn, Werner Schöllgen, has indicated,[45] everyone experiences a craving to be taken out of the ordinary, everyday world into a state of exaltation. This is particularly true of the adolescent whose basic insecurity makes the never-never world even more appealing. Escape into the imaginative provides a release from the pressures of day-to-day worries.

Schöllgen points out that this release can be achieved in either of two ways: by seeing the everyday in a context which transcends and sanctifies or by flight into the subspiritual. It is in this latter that one finds all forms of intoxication leading to the world of fantasy. The ego exercises omnipotence in this world. "His majesty, the ego" as Freud is reputed to have said. The barriers of time and place disappear; one reaches goals arbitrarily. Whereas in reality there are fellow men, practical repercussions, legions of obstacles, rebuffs, failures, and in general the limitation of the earthly, in the world of fantasy there is only interior stupefaction. There is fulfillment without effort, achievement without work; there is no striving, no encounter with painful situations, no conflict, no development of coping mechanisms. There is only the swift build-up of desire and immediate, exaggerated satisfaction. Quite expectedly there is also the increasing tendency to resort to this world of ego-kingship in the face of challenge. And just as expectedly there is in the real world one notable effect: lack of growth. There is, in brief, unreality.

Benjamin De Mott has pointed out that *Playboy* and its blunter sycophants achieve their effect precisely by a process of abstraction which ends in the world of fantasy.[46] That is, they present experience, especially sexual experience, in a purely imaginative way. The only substantial emerging realities are sexual need and sexual deprivation. By thus simplifying sexual experience, one produces sexual absorp-

[44] *The Secular City*, pp. 197 ff.
[45] *Moral Problems Today* (New York: Herder and Herder, 1963), pp. 170-197.
[46] "The Anatomy of 'Playboy,'" *Commentary*, Vol. 36 (1962), pp. 111-119.

tion. Every means is used to block out memories of reality and any knowledge which ties one to reality. The chief means in the campaign to simplify sexual experience and produce absorption is a continuing attack on the notion that with women reluctance is the norm, eagerness the exception. The magazine's subtle attempt, De Mott insists, is to create the illusion that women burn insistently and insatiably, and that this is sexual reality. Thus the "sex-bomb" is identified with the girl next door. They include the writings of recognized authors to reinforce the illusion that they deal with reality. Once this illusion is created, one is completely in the imaginative world. The "essential woman" of the communications media is the woman of the male imagination; she it is who is then established as the *real* woman.

Thus into the growing vacuum created by the objectification-autonomy-depersonalization process, a new significance is being injected. Its basic characteristic is unreality. Because it is a product of the imagination it can only be discovered there. Hence it can only hasten the flight into the fanciful and imaginative—and back to the age so thoroughly vulnerable to this flight, adolescence.

It is hardly surprising, therefore, that a culture which is losing its grip on the meaning of sexuality and rediscovering it in a dream world is simultaneously obsessed with sex. For the dream world is the adolescent world and the adolescent world is the world of sex-obsession. Malcolm Muggeridge remarked that "never, it is safe to say, in the history of the world has a country been as sex-ridden as America is today." [47] With due allowance made for Muggeridge's Cassandraism, was he not saying that never has a country so thoroughly derived the meaning of sexuality from the imagination? Was he not saying: Never has a country been as obsessed with, hence as adolescent about, sex as America is today? Was he not saying, then, in effect: Never has a country so thoroughly lost its grip on the meaning and significance of genuine sexuality as America has? Good methodology cannot afford to deny such a possibility out of hand.

The problem of norms, then, seems to be the problem of the significance of concrete pieces of human conduct. If the problem is seen as one of *absolute* norms (particularly absolute prohibitions), it must be candidly admitted that it is not much of a problem; for even traditional theological categories—when properly understood—admitted very few absolute prohibitions. The preoccupation of the "new morality" with these absolutes may actually represent nothing

---

[47] "Down with Sex!" *Esquire,* Vol. 63 (1965), pp. 72–74.

more than an uneasy struggle to recover significance. It may also represent the birth-pangs—entirely transitional in character, as they proved to be in Europe in the early fifties—of a wholesome effort to move toward a more genuinely interiorized moral life, toward a concept of morality in which interiorized value is central and essential.

*PART THREE*

Reformation Themes:
The Uses of the Law

# 10

# Soteriological Implications of Norm and Context

EDWARD LEROY LONG, JR.

There are times in the development of theological thinking when a contemporary discussion can be illuminated by categories devised for a previous analysis. Ideas do not necessarily repeat themselves, but issues formulated one way in the past often turn up in new forms in subsequent ages. If contemporary discussions ignore—through default or by intention—such past formulations, theological analysis is often robbed of insights it might otherwise enjoy or falls into errors it could otherwise avoid.

The considerable concern about the place of norms and contexts in contemporary debates between ethics of rules (or principles) and situational ethics should prompt us to return to older discussions of these same problems. Many insights that seem to their contemporary exponents to be "new" in either appearance or emphasis have been centrally significant in previous discussions. Despite some of the implied claims ours is not the first generation to sense the difficulties in legalistic morality or to propose a way for dealing with moral choices without binding men to fixed rules.

I shall examine in this chapter the categories that were articulated in the period of the Reformation for dealing with the role and function of law in Christian experience, seeking thereby to shed light upon both the strengths and the inadequacies in contemporary treatments of norms and contexts in Christian moral decision. Such an examination must be selective; in one chapter, I cannot consider all previous discussions. I shall take up but one or two categories from the past and look at their relevance for the present discussion of the significance of law in Christian ethics.

## I. *The Law as a Goad to Repentance*

The Reformers discussed the place of norms in Christian ethics under the rubric of the uses of the law. Luther set forth a contrast between the law and the gospel by developing his moral analysis in terms of two uses of the law. According to Luther, the first use of the law is to serve as an instrument of civil order (*usus civilis*), restraining sinful men from transgression. The restraint of the law holds in check the consequences of evil from both the Christian and the unchristian segments of the social order. In a second use of the law (*usus theologicus*) man comes to see and understand his sinful rebellion against God. Luther felt that this second use of the law was of primary importance, and described it as follows:

> . . . the true function and the chief and proper use of the Law is to reveal to man his sin, blindness, misery, wickedness, ignorance, hate and contempt of God, death, hell, judgment, and the well-deserved wrath of God. Yet this use of the Law is completely unknown to the hypocrites, the sophists in the universities, and to all men who go along in the presumption of the righteousness of the Law or of their own righteousness.[1]

Melanchthon eventually added a third function to Luther's two categories, that of teaching the redeemed man which works are pleasing to God (*usus didacticum*). Melanchthon also put Luther's second use of the law, in which the law serves as the pedagogue for repentance, into first place and gave it the fullest and most complete exposition. Among other observations about the use of the law as a goad to repentance, Melanchthon remarked, "One needs the preaching of the law, as St. Paul says, for 'Through the law comes knowledge of sin' [Romans 3:20]. Yes, the law is not only a witness to what sin is, but to what God is; one must learn what sin is if one is to know what God is and what is repugnant to his divine wisdom and order." [2]

---

[1] Martin Luther, "Lectures on Galatians" in Jaroslav Pelikan (ed.), *Luther's Works, American Edition*, Vol. 26 (St. Louis: Concordia, 1963), p. 309.

[2] Philip Melanchthon, "On Divine Law" in Clyde L. Manschreck, *Melanchthon on Christian Doctrine: Loci Communes* 1955 (New York: Oxford University Press, 1965), p. 125. Melanchthon's exposition of the three uses of the law became explicit only in editions of the *Loci Communes* after 1525, but his emphasis upon the primary importance of law as a goad to repentance was present from the edition of 1521.

John Calvin followed Melanchthon, both in the order in which he discussed the functions of the law and in the number of functions which he delineated. His description of the role of law in fostering repentance before God reads in part:

> ... while [the law] shows God's righteousness, that is, the righteousness alone acceptable to God, it warns, informs, convicts, and lastly condemns, every man of his own unrighteousness. For man, blinded and drunk with self-love, must be compelled to know and to confess his own feebleness and impurity. If man is not clearly convinced of his own vanity, he is puffed up with insane confidence in his own mental powers, and can never be induced to recognize their slenderness as long as he measures them by a measure of his own choice. But as soon as he begins to compare his powers with the difficulty of the law, he has something to diminish his bravado.[3]

In contrast with Melanchthon, with whom he otherwise agreed, Calvin made the third use of the law primary. In the third use Calvin found the comforting assurance that the saints could learn each day the will of God which they were committed to serve. Calvin sharply criticized those ignorant persons who sought to cast away the guidance that comes from this use of the law.

In writing about the uses of the law the Reformers generally had in mind the Ten Commandments. In both Melanchthon and Calvin the discussion of the three uses of the law is found along with the presentation of the laws of Moses and their appropriate application to the life of the faithful Christian. The Reformers wrote in heavy dependence upon biblical categories and it is only natural that their conception of the law should reflect such concerns. But the three uses they found for biblical injunctions (*triplex usus legis*) can also be applied to norms in general, which play a role in contemporary discussion analogous to the role played by the biblical conception of law in the work of the Reformers.

One of the functions of the law (*usus civilis*, the first function for Luther, the second for Calvin and Melanchthon) is basically societal. The law prescribes those restraints that keep the body politic preserved from the wrongdoing of sinful men. It is useful in checking sin in both believer and nonbeliever and thus in sustaining justice and order. A sweeping look at the dominant themes in Christian ethics in the literature of the past twenty or twenty-five years will, I believe, reveal a

---

[3] John Calvin, *Institutes of the Christian Religion,* ed. John T. McNeill, and trans. Ford Lewis Battles (Philadelphia: Westminster Press, 1960), pp. 354 f. (Book II, chap. VII, par. 6).

strong tendency to overlook these civil functions of the law as more and more attention has been focused on the relationship of norms to decisions made by individuals. Emil Brunner gave much attention to the interest of the classical Reformers in the societal functions of law as he wrote about the state and its laws as dikes against sin. Karl Barth spoke of the same matters in a somewhat different form, as did Dietrich Bonhoeffer. But since their time there has been a subtle change in the focus of attention. More and more consideration has been given to questions about the use of norms, or the rejection of their use, in the making of individual decisions. The consequent discussion of differences between ethics of norms and ethics of situations has tended to become preoccupied with the internal methodology of choice rather than with the external questions of social policy, until in some literature of the new morality the discussion of social policy is practically ignored.[4]

There is both the opportunity and the obligation in this area for an extended rethinking of Christian imperatives. Even if we become convinced that norms should not play decisive roles when persons are thinking about individual responses to situations it is by no means clear that this insight can be applied to social policy and corporate procedures. Shall a bank, or the legal supervisor of financial institutions, proceed on the basis that embezzlement of funds should be condoned when greater human needs are served than they are by strict accounting rigor? Should speed laws be written with allowance for them to be ignored when love is better served by their abrogation? Can educational institutions dispense with rules of group guidance on the grounds that all moral questions are matters of unique individual responses to special circumstances? It may be possible to devise social policies that permit the free response of individuals to the uniqueness of their own situational experiences, but it certainly will be less easy to do this than it has been to treat individual decisions in a situational manner. It is one thing to argue that an individual should, in certain circumstances, break a law in order to serve a greater good and quite another to devise social controls which function without the use of normative prescription.

While the societal function of law as restraint against sin deserves extensive new thinking, that is not the concern of this chapter. The following discussion explores the interrelationship between law seen as the source of guidance (Calvin and Melanchthon's third use of the

---

[4] See, for example, the chapter on "The New Morality" in John A. T. Robinson, *Honest to God* (London: SCM Press; Philadelphia: Westminster Press, 1963).

law) and the law seen as a source of judgment leading to repentance (their first use). It is concerned with the bearing of soteriology on the ethical life. While there are significant differences between the normative approach and the contextualist approach to ethics there may be even more significant differences between the manner in which either type of choice-making is understood to relate to man's relationship to God and his personal salvation.

The guidance function of the law has not always been discussed in relation to the soteriological function. Luther, for example, omitted the normative function of the law from his formal categories, though he had things to say about it in his own exhortations to his followers. Those contemporary situationalists who cite Luther rather than Calvin as the exemplar of the Reformation,[5] or who read the New Testament with Lutherlike eyes,[6] not only ignore the third function of the law and its possible bearing upon the first function, but specifically deny the value of the guidance function. But this, in a curious sense, focuses the discussion about the third (guidance) function to the exclusion of the first (accusative) one, for it concentrates inordinate attention on whether or not there should be a third function to the law. The consequent polarization leaves an apparent choice between two antithetical and mutually exclusive alternatives. In one it is supposed that the Christian assents to some inviolable conception of the morally right and applies the norm to the decisions he makes. He follows rules or remains faithful to ideals. Even if he develops a casuistry for coping with the unique and mitigating factors of particular cases, his concern is to remain faithful to the extrinsic requirements of a predefined measure of the good or the right. In the other approach it is supposed that the Christian responds in fidelity to the love of God as made known in Christ by becoming a neighbor to the person to whom he finds himself related by circumstance and situation. He expresses this neighborliness, not by seeking conformity (either in his own actions or in what is expected from the other person) to a specified prescription of the right, but by dealing with the unique variable in such a way as to meet the other man with maturely demonstrated concern.

It may be significant that the most pure form of each of these positions has been expressed polemically by the opposing point of view, but theologians are not the only group that tears down caricatures of

---

[5] See, for example, the relative importance given to Luther and the little attention afforded Calvin in Joseph Fletcher, *Situation Ethics: The New Morality* (Philadelphia: Westminster Press, 1966).

[6] See Joseph Sittler, *The Structure of Christian Ethics* (Baton Rouge: Louisiana State University Press, 1958).

the opposition in order to make a case for its own side. From the contextualist side, for example, we are told:

> Situation ethics always suspects prescriptive law of falsifying life and dwarfing moral stature, whether it be the Scripture legalism of Biblicist Protestants and Mohammedans or the nature legalism (natural law) of the Catholics and disciples of Confucius. One American theologian has complained that situation ethics fails to realize people are unwilling to grapple with what he calls "paradoxical ambiguities"—that they want something more definite and exact than ethical relativism offers. Of course; they want the Grand Inquisitor. T. S. Eliot was right to say that people cannot bear too much reality. But there is no escape for them. To learn love's sensitive tactics, such people are going to have to put away their childish rules.[7]

From the other side, in equally assertive judgments, we are told that those who would dispense with principles and norms destroy the ethical enterprise.

> The sentimentalist buries morals in a mud-bath of maudlin compassion. The analytic philosopher assists by proving that it is all emotive anyway. The psychotherapist and the sociologist carefully skirt the use of ethical categories. The theologian puts morals out of sight by burying them underground, by elevating them to the skies, or by dissipating them into the self or into society. The sophisticate views the whole affair with contempt. And the respectable chap, even when he conforms, is at heart a cultural relativist. All conspire to a common end—that ethics should become obsolete.[8]

The sharp antithesis evidenced by these quotations develops from the tendency to make the acceptance or rejection of the guidance function of the law the sole factor to be considered in accounting for the worth of an ethical stance. It comes from an oversimplistic measure of what makes an ethic viable. It does not ask whether there are conditions under which prescriptive definitions of obligations can be maturely and profoundly embraced, while there are other conditions under which this would lead to unfortunate rigidity. It does not explore whether there are conditions in which reliance upon contexts is a wise and fruitful way of dealing with problems and other conditions in which such a reliance aborts the ethical process itself.

There is a significant difference within the literature of the new morality between those who take an exclusionist line that rules out all

---

[7] Joseph Fletcher, *op. cit.*, p. 140.
[8] Robert E. Fitch, "The Obsolescence of Ethics," in *Christianity and Crisis*, Vol. XIX, No. 19 (November 16, 1959), p. 165.

other options as faulty and those who think of concern about situations as a corrective which is supplementary and complementary to the older ways of formulating ethical decisions. The quotations given above illustrate exclusivism in the debate, but the following statement from Bishop Robinson evidences a more melioristic attitude.

> I believe that the "old" and the "new morality" (in any sense in which I am interested in defending the latter) correspond with two starting-points, two approaches to certain perennial polarities in Christian ethics, which are not antithetical but complementary. Each begins from one point without denying the other, but each tends to suspect the other of abandoning what it holds most vital because it reaches it from the other end. Inevitably, in any genuine dialectic, one will come as a corrective to the other, and at a particular time or for particular persons one may seem the way to the exclusion of the other. But one cannot be true simply at the expense of the other. In seeking to interpret what I believe "the new morality" is trying to say, I hope I shall not guy or deny the old—and all I would merely ask for in return is a similar sympathy and understanding.[9]

Moreover, many observers of the current scene have questioned the wisdom of dividing all ethical approaches into the normative and the contextual categories and all thinkers into advocates of only one point of view. James Gustafson has termed the discussion as carried out in polarized debate as "misplaced" and warned that due attention must be given to the unique features of each individual statement of either position.[10] George Woods has declared that the basic problem in discussing the value of "situation ethics" is a lack of clarity in the use of terms. Woods believes the debate over situation ethics can be solved if more adequate understandings of the nature of a situation can be obtained.[11]

It will not do simply to take the difference between ethics of rules or principles and ethics of contexts as the decisive measure of the contrast between the good and the bad in Christian morality. But neither is it sufficient to hope these two approaches can be kept in some sort of harmony by mutual forbearance alone. It may not even be possible

---

[9] John A. T. Robinson, *Christian Morals Today* (London: SCM Press; Philadelphia: Westminster Press, 1964), pp. 10 f.

[10] James M. Gustafson, "Context Versus Principles: A Misplaced Debate in Christian Ethics," in *Harvard Theological Review*, Vol. 58, No. 2 (April, 1965), pp. 171–202. Also in Martin E. Marty and Dean G. Peerman, *New Theology, No. 3* (New York: Macmillan Co., 1966), pp. 69–102.

[11] George Woods, "Situation Ethics" *Christian Ethics and Contemporary Philosophy*, ed. Ian T. Ramsey (London: SCM Press, 1966), pp. 329–339.

to hope that a proper appreciation of the mutual relationships between these two approaches can come from clarifying their use of terms. We need a more adequate set of judgments for determining when ethics of rules are detrimental to human experience and when they aid it, for noting when contextual approaches are helpful and when they are dangerous or abortive.

There are several criteria which can help to make such judgments, but one of the most important ones seems to involve the way in which the performance of an ethical action is related to the salvation of the person who construes his moral action to be a function of religious duty. This factor has played an important role in the history of Christian ethics, as discussions of the uses of the law as a pedagogue for repentance point out. To ignore the first function of the law in relationship to the way in which the third function is carried out is to overlook one of the most significant theological variables. In the analysis that follows we will look at the possible combinations of two kinds of ethics and two views of soteriology. Much of the available literature can be understood in new perspectives if studied in light of such categories.

## II. *An Ethic of Rules under a Soteriology of Works: The Anatomy of Legalism*

There is no single factor which taken by itself is sufficiently decisive to produce a legalistic syndrome, perhaps least of all the mere employment of norms in the determination of Christian choices. Ethical legalism can have several different causes. It can arise in situations in which the norm has become a symbol for authority. If, for example, the specific provisions of biblical codes are viewed as the direct content of revelation, then the prescriptive character of such codes acquires rigidity. Even though conservative evangelicalism formally eschews a doctrine of works it can develop a moral legalism on the basis of its authoritarian view of biblical law as a propositional revelation of God's eternal will. Thus John Murray, speaking from this perspective, says:

> It is easy to see the difficulties that would embarrass love if it were left to devise the ways and means of self-realization. We think very naively indeed if we suppose that love can spontaneously decide the mode of its expression. It is only because we have become habilitated to the biblical revelation of law and commandment, because our thinking has been informed to such an extent by the revelation of God's will as deposited in the Scripture, that we could ever have entertained

the thought that love dictates the law of its activity or the modes of its behaviour.[12]

If a doctrine of plenary or propositional revelation thrusts conservative Protestant thinking toward legalism, a corresponding emphasis upon authority functions in a similar way in traditional Roman Catholic moral theology. In the extensive work of Henry Davis, a work in which the legalistic tenor is obvious, we are told at the beginning: "The science of correct moral conduct is based on the teaching of legitimate authority and the principles of right reason." [13] In another book Joseph P. Fitzpatrick puts it this way: "This, then, I would say is the specific character of the Catholic's approach to moral decision, that he recognizes one source of final moral authority in this world that speaks with the authority of God Himself." [14]

One of the difficulties in describing the anatomy of legalism is the fact that no Christian theologian wants to call himself a legalist. The term is a slur word, used by most theologians to describe an ethical stance they wish to avoid. Murray, Davis, and Fitzpatrick would not describe themselves as legalists, so that the charges against their approach reflect the evaluation of others. Indeed, Fitzpatrick goes to great lengths to show that Roman Catholic thinking can take account of individual response, and declares: "Catholic life is not a series of formulas, not a rigid blueprint, nor a succession of these prohibitions, although in the heat of controversy a defense of the Church's position may make it appear that way." [15] The Pharisees are probably the only group that *all* Christians view as legalistic. Of them it may also be said that the element of authority contributed to the way in which they used the law.

The authoritarian element can create a legalism from either codes of right conduct or rational ideals of good behavior. The possibility of a rigid legalism in the case of prescriptive codes is obviously greater than the possibility of legalism within a morality of principles, but forms of legalism have sprung up in both kinds of normative ethic. To the extent that the reason prompts a desire for consistency or is viewed as a divinely sanctioned set of conclusions it may contribute to a legalistic tendency. The very concept of a natural law based upon

---

[12] *Principles of Conduct: Aspects of Biblical Ethics* (London: Tyndale, 1957), pp. 24 f.

[13] *Moral and Pastoral Theology*, Vol. I (London: Sheed and Ward, 1935), p. 6.

[14] "Ethics of Roman Catholicism," in *Patterns of Ethics in America Today*, ed. F. E. Johnson (New York: Institute for Religious and Social Studies. Distributed by Harper, 1960; Collier, 1962), p. 45 in Collier edition.

[15] *Ibid.*, p. 63 (Collier edition).

reason is presumed to point to a set of standards or norms that are binding upon all men in the same way precisely because of their universal foundation in reason. Moreover, rational principles are often assumed to be permanent, to endure despite changes in cultural mores. In the face of changing attitudes and practices the defense of rational principles as fixed standards can become legalistic, especially when supported by authoritarian impulses.

But the foregoing factor seems to pale alongside of a soteriology of works as an explanation for legalism in religious morality. Indeed, it is common for us to identify ethics of codes with a soteriology of works. But this combination—it is a combination of two factors—occurs when particular accidents conspire to couple the use of rules to the hunger for a salvation that can be grasped by human achievement. The "terror of the law" occurs when the fulfillment of a code is used as a means to ensure salvation; it is not an inevitable product of a normative ethic *per se*.

The use of the law as a goad to repentance takes on particular characteristics under a legalistic system. Legalistic repentance catalogues many degrees and types of transgression and prescribes specific forms of satisfaction for wrongdoing. This form of the first use of the law is petty in its conceptualizations of moral responsibility and oppressive in its demands for obedience to the letter of both the law itself and the devices that are created to remedy transgressions of the law so as to aid the salvation of the individual. The oppressive anxiety and sense of bondage that attend legalism are products of the soteriology of works even more than they are products of a normative element in ethics.

Kenneth E. Kirk pointed this out by using different categories. He argued that the early Church gradually eroded the gospel of grace into a formalistic system of law—not merely by adopting standards but by allowing such standards to become measures of goodness. Speaking of this process he declared:

> We have glanced at two simultaneous developments: the one, that steady elaboration of the Christian code by which more and more offences were disentangled from one another and placarded as grave sin; the other, that by which the disciplinary weapon of penance and excommunication was brought into effective and tyrannical use—a use entirely different from that to which it was normally put in the New Testament. What resulted from the convergence of these two movements? First of all, as was suggested above, a wholly wrong attitude toward ethical principles or maxims. *Less-and-less are they thought of as means to secure the purity of life which achieves, and the energy of*

> *service which retains and attests, the vision of God. More and more they become mere conditions of membership in a society where external conformity will be rewarded with assured salvation.*[16]

Kirk's distinction between two ways of embracing the law permits a rejection of legalism without requiring a simultaneous distrust of normative ethics. This kind of thinking can produce different consequences from those which emerge when works/righteousness is treated as a single monolith.

Calvin perceived the way in which a soteriology of works turns the law into an instrument of negation. Calvin rejected "law righteousness" rather than "law" by itself. He had much to say about Christian freedom, which begins with release from "law righteousness" and entails the capacity to become joyously obedient. Calvin regarded many matters with indifference and showed how a thrust for security through obedience to rules about minor matters can destroy all possibility of creative living.

> . . . when consciences once ensnare themselves, they enter a long and inextricable maze, not easy to get out of. If a man begins to doubt whether he may use linen for sheets, shirts, handkerchiefs, and napkins, he will afterwards be uncertain also about hemp; finally, doubt will even arise over tow. For he will turn over in his mind whether he can sup without napkins, or go without a handkerchief. If any man should consider daintier food unlawful, in the end he will not be at peace before God, when he eats either black bread or common victuals, while it occurs to him that he could sustain his body on even coarser foods. If he boggles at sweet wine, he will not dare to touch water if sweeter and cleaner than other water. To sum up, he will come to the point of considering it wrong to step upon a straw across his path, as the saying goes.[17]

This description of the process of negation which springs from the reliance upon codes to produce morally safe actions shows how keenly Calvin was aware of the potential dangers in the use of the law to attain security before God. It puts a finger on the fundamental impulse that breeds legalism, the impulse for ethical achievement. If one presupposes that his salvation is dependent upon his fulfillment of the law then he is obliged to become anxious whether or not he does enough

---

[16] Kenneth E. Kirk, *The Vision of God: The Christian Doctrine of the Summun Bonum* (London: Longman's Green, 1931); reissued as a Harper Torchbook (1966), p. 172.

[17] John Calvin, *Institutes of the Christian Religion*, p. 839 (Book III, chap. XIX, par. 7).

to merit a heavenly reward. Since the heavenly reward is ultimately important, anxiety concerning one's fulfillment of the law becomes acute. When this anxiety reaches an intolerable level, as it did in Luther's personal experience, a legalistic interpretation of Christian faith focused in a works/righteousness is overthrown in favor of another understanding of the gospel. Often such an understanding takes the form of an ethic of response within a soteriology of grace.

## III. *An Ethic of Contexts with a Soteriology of Grace: Protests against Legalism*

In legalism the law becomes a terror because it must be fulfilled with inordinate completeness in order to attain status before God. It often becomes foolish as devout seekers for salvation define with increasing precision just which rules apply and how they apply to every contingent circumstance of life. The believer cannot slip. He cannot be uncertain of the law's requirements. He must therefore spend anxious attention to how rules are to be followed in cases of conflict or doubt and to creating the conditions which make obedience to the rules most likely and most complete.[18]

When legalistic morality has developed in the history and life of the Church, significant protests have arisen against it. Because legalistic morality is a combination in which normative ethics are combined with a soteriology of works, these protests have often taken the form of an ethic that abrogates the role of law as well as declares salvation to come by grace through faith. Such a reaction occurred in Paul's rejection of Jewish legalism and the outlook of the Jerusalem Christians which taught the New Covenant as law. (In this respect Paul was faithful to the stance of Jesus, who also rejected the works/righteousness of the Pharisees.) Luther responded negatively to the moral rigor of the monastic effort to grasp salvation through a life of earnest obedience to the law. In more recent years men like Brunner, Bonhoeffer, Sittler, Lehmann, and Ebeling have articulated an evangelical ethic based upon the radical primacy of justification by faith. While these three responses vary in details they are similar in basic form and motivation.

Paul's rejection of salvation through works was flat and unequivocal. There is no salvation through the law. The law has not worked

---

[18] For an illuminating discussion of the functions of code morality in relationship to religion see Paul Ramsey, *Basic Christian Ethics* (New York: Charles Scribner's Sons, 1950), pp. 46–54.

even for the descendants of Abraham, to whom the promise actually came by faith despite its subsequent transmission as a covenant of works (Rom. 2-4). In place of standing under obedience to the law the Christian finds himself in a new relationship to Christ. He is free from the tyranny of works—free to be helpful to his neighbor as love requires—but nevertheless obligated to obey the will of God as he perceives it. Paul seemed to describe a wholly new orientation of the believer toward moral obligation. The believer is a new creature, set free of the need to earn his salvation by works that he cannot adequately perform. This freedom abrogates the terror of the law. The Christian is a new man in Christ because he is justified by faith. He has peace with God, making possible a new and living response to His will.

While Paul usually avoided the use of the term "law" for defining the life of devotion expected from the man of faith, he did not categorically reject the use of norms in describing the new life (cf. Rom. 12-13). Subsequent interpreters have debated what Paul meant by the phrases "the law of Christ" and "the will of the Father." Some contend that Paul rejected all prescriptive aspects entirely; others argue that his use of these categories involved the normative aspects of the law freed from the tyranny of a soteriology of works. This debate sometimes says more about the understandings of those who carry it on than it settles about Paul's thinking.

Luther's experience with the penance system of Roman Catholicism prompted a breakthrough to a new conception of the gospel as a free gift of grace. In Luther's experience a modestly rigorous system of works/righteousness (it was less oppressive in practice to most Catholics than it was to Luther, who took it with inordinate seriousness) was replaced with a theology of grace and accompanied by a serious distrust of the law as a source of ethical guidance. For Luther the chief function of the law is the condemnation of sin, leading to the repentance prerequisite for grace. Luther set law and gospel into sharp contrast:

> According to the apostle in Romans 1 [vv. 3-6], the gospel is a preaching of the incarnate Son of God, given to us without any merit on our part for salvation and peace. It is a word of salvation, a word of grace, a word of comfort, a word of joy, a voice of the bridegroom and the bride, a good word, a word of peace.... But the law is a word of destruction, a word of wrath, a word of sadness, a word of grief, a voice of the judge and the defendant, a word of restlessness, a word of curse. For according to the apostle, "The law is the power of sin" [cf. 1 Cor.

15:56], and "the law brings wrath" [Rom. 4:15]; it is a law of death [Rom. 7:5, 13].[19]

Luther emphasized the first function of the law as a source of judgment and condemnation because such a function is entirely compatible with his view that law is the antithesis of gospel. He interpreted the second, or societal, function of the law in repressive terms and made no separate place for a third, or guidance, function of the law. Gerhard Ebeling has suggested that the term "law" for Luther described a condition or a state rather than a set of moral norms. "The law is primarily event and only secondarily teaching." [20] The Christian is, therefore, no longer under the law once he has experienced the grace in Christ. He is a new being whose criteria for ethical action and motivations for moral endeavor come from a new and different source. Luther described the impulse of the new man in Christ as follows:

> ... a Christian who lives in this confidence toward God, knows all things, can do all things, undertakes all things that are to be done, and does everything cheerfully and freely; not that he may gather many merits and good works, but because it is a pleasure for him to please God thereby, and he serves God purely for nothing, content that his service pleases God. On the other hand, he who is not at one with God, or doubts, hunts and worries in what way he may do enough and with many works move God.[21]

Luther was shocked whenever men used his attacks upon the law as an excuse for unwanton liberty or as a justification for behavior that would violate the requirements of the law without thereby serving love more completely. He foresaw the possibility of actions which served love while violating a particular provision of the law seen as a code, but he wrote a sharply critical comment about those who turned the liberty of faith into an occasion of license. The Christian man is free, but he is also in bondage to the needs of the neighbor. Moreover, Luther's close associate, Melanchthon, soon made a place for the law's didactic function ". . . that the saints may know and have a testimony of the works which please God." [22]

The neo-Reformation ethics developed in both Europe and Amer-

---

[19] Martin Luther, "Explanations of the Ninety-five Theses," in Harold J. Grimm (ed.), *Luther's Works*, American Edition, Vol. 31 (Philadelphia: Muhlenberg Press, 1957), p. 231.

[20] Gerhard Ebeling, "Reflexions on the Doctrine of the Law," in *Word and Faith* (Philadelphia: Fortress Press, 1963), p. 278.

[21] Martin Luther, "Treatise on Good Works" in *Works of Martin Luther*, Vol. I (Philadelphia: A. J. Holman Company, 1915), p. 191.

[22] "Of Divine Law" in Clyde L. Manschreck, *op. cit.*, p. 127.

ica since the nineteen-thirties bear many similarities to the Lutheran outlook, which they have frequently cited with approval. However, the situation from which they arose has been quite different. While code moralities and legalistic penance systems had not entirely disappeared from the Christian tradition by the time of these writings, an expanded and broadened type of confidence in moral achievement had grown up as a result of Kantian influence upon Protestant thinking. Belief in the independent value of a rational procedure for determining ethical choices had become coupled to a confidence in human powers to achieve a good life by acting in accordance with universally accepted principles or ideals that specify the goals all men ought to pursue. Consequently, in the literature of the neo-Reformation the attack upon extrinsic norms in ethics and a soteriology of achievement has been more complex, concerned to refute both the code moralism of legalistic religion and the autonomous ethic of trust in man's capacity to achieve a satisfactory solution to the moral problems of life without submissive dependence upon divine grace.

Emil Brunner is frequently credited with making the initial and possibly most thorough development in modern times of a Christian ethic squarely based upon the doctrine of justification by faith—an ethic successfully overcoming both religious code moralism and autonomous rational ethics. In reacting against both traditional and recent ethics of norms and soteriologies of works Brunner declared the primacy of the divine command. This command has no relation to an "intrinsic good" and cannot be defined in theory by any prior categories. Instead,

> The Good is simply what *God* wills that we should do, not that which we would do on the basis of a principle of love. God wills to do something quite definite and particular through us, here and now, something which no other person could do at any other time. Just as the commandment of love is absolutely universal, so also it is absolutely individual. But just as it is absolutely individual so also it is absolutely devoid of all caprice. "I will guide thee with Mine eye." No one can experience this "moment" save I myself. The Divine Command is made known to us "in the secret place." Therefore it is impossible for us to know it beforehand; to wish to know it beforehand—legalism—is an infringement of the divine honour. The fact that the holiness of God must be remembered when we dwell on His love means that we cannot have His love at our disposal, that it cannot ever be perceived as a universal principle, but only in the act in which He speaks to us Himself.[23]

[23] Emil Brunner, *The Divine Imperative* (Philadelphia: Westminster Press, 1947), pp. 117 f.

The influence of Brunner's work has been enormous on subsequent discussions. But some commentators have felt that he remained dependent upon a conception of the divine command too colored by law and compulsion. Brunner allowed the idea of law to re-enter his thinking as a penultimate category despite the way in which he excluded it as the primary means of forming ethical directives. Other writers have attempted to state the case for a radical ethic of grace which flatly negates any use of prescription.[24] Thus has arisen the contextualist position in Christian ethics, in which context has been defined in radical contrast to norm.

A comparison of the three developments outlined reveals a curious process at work. In each succeeding case the moral pattern being protested seems to be less legalistic. The code morality of the Pharisees was probably more stringent than the penance system of medieval Catholicism; the legalism of the penance system more prevalent than the presence of code morality in twentieth-century Christianity. Indeed, in the latter, the use of rational principles represented a serious effort to introduce flexibility and concern for contingency into the making of ethical decisions. But while the legalism being protested has been increasingly less evident in each succeeding case the rejection of the extrinsically normative element has been more complete. Paul's rejection of the law was sufficiently ambiguous to make the interpretation of his intentions a matter for serious subsequent debate by the scholars, many of whom are convinced that he held to some place for extrinsic norms. Luther could not bring himself to defend that function of the law providing guidance to the believer, but he was ill-at-ease when his teaching was taken as justifying contempt for normal and decent standards of behavior. The contextualism that has sprung up in recent neo-Reformation theology was at first willing to speak of the penultimate value of norms but has more recently become thoroughly consistent and absolutistic in its rejection of their legitimacy on any level. Some of the resulting statements about the relation of norms to grace might look to any previous defenders of the context/grace alternative as flagrantly oblivious to obligations that have been assumed aspects of obedience to God, even under the gospel.

In the legalistic repentance associated with schemes of works/righteousness, specific sins are confessed and specific penance is prescribed according to quantitative measures of guilt. But in the contextualism related to a theology of grace the whole conception of repent-

[24] See H. Richard Niebuhr, *The Responsible Self* (New York: Harper & Row, 1963), and Joseph Sittler, *The Structure of Christian Ethics* (Baton Rouge: University of Louisiana Press, 1961).

ance is modified. Dietrich Bonhoeffer described the type of confession appropriate to an ethic of response as follows:

> The only way to turn back is through recognition of the guilt incurred towards Christ. What must be recognized as guilt is not the occasional lapse of error, or transgressions against an abstract law, but the defection from Christ, from the form which was ready to take form in us and lead us to our own true form. True acknowledgement of guilt does not arise from the experience of disruption and decay, but for us, who have encountered the form of Christ, solely from this form.[25]

This statement is significant for two reasons. First it reveals the primary importance assigned by Bonhoeffer to confession of guilt. He also declared, "If anyone stifles or corrupts the Church's confession of guilt, his guilt towards Christ is beyond hope." [26] But the statement is also significant because it transforms the act of repentance into consistency with the idea of a contextual morality. It changes legalized repentance into a generalized repentance. In the latter the Christian confesses his apostasy from Christ rather than his transgression of the law. While Bonhoeffer seems, at times, to have confessed the very same sort of things the legalist might feel guilty about,[27] he did not use such repentance as a device for gaining salvation. He criticized any tendency to compare the self with others in "a weighing up and calculation of guilt" leading to self-justification. "In a way which is totally incomprehensible to the moralist there is no seeking for the actual guilty party; there is no demand for a condign expiation of the guilt, punishment of the wicked and reward of the good." [28] While this understanding of repentance rejects salvation by works it still relies upon the need of grace. With Bonhoeffer, as with many of his fellow neo-Reformation theologians, Christian ethics has a profound soteriology.

## IV. *An Ethic of Contexts without Soteriology: Tendencies in the "New Morality"*

A third way of dealing with these matters is often identified with the second way because it rejects the use of norms in favor of contexts as the source of ethical guidance. It has attracted a great deal of interest because it has been set forth in a series of popular essays, mostly in the English language, that have appeared in the mid-1960's, and goes under the general title of the "new morality." The phrase the "new morality" is not very precise because there are diverse expressions of

---

[25] Dietrich Bonhoeffer, *Ethics* (New York: Macmillan Co., 1962), p. 46.
[26] *Ibid.*, p. 51.   [27] *Ibid.*, see pp. 48–50.   [28] *Ibid.*, pp. 47 f.

this approach, few of which have been developed into full and mature form. It is too early to tell whether this will become a sufficiently well-developed movement to go down in the annals of Christian theology as a major trend or whether it is merely an ephemeral enthusiasm. It has, as in the case of the present volume, precipitated an extended discussion of the relative importance of norm and context in Christian ethics. Among the spokesmen for this approach are John A. T. Robinson, Douglas A. Rhymes, Joseph Fletcher, and (with slightly different concerns) Harvey Cox.

The new morality is unequivocably negative with respect to the function of law as a guide for the behavior of believers. Norms have no place in Christian ethics, at least insofar as they are extrinsic specifications of the right or the good. Rhymes speaks for this position when he writes:

> I would claim that this new approach to ethics in which the emphasis is laid upon love rather than law, on freedom rather than fixity, on relativism within the situation which calls for the maximum wellbeing of all involved rather than on adherence to fixed principles, is more in accord with what we learn from the Bible of the approach of Christ than the traditional attitudes of many parts of the church. I would also claim that an ethic which lays emphasis on the full maturity of man as a responsible, deciding, acting human being within a given situation is also in accord with the whole teaching of Christ on the wholeness of man.[29]

But while the new morality is similar to neo-Reformation contextualism in its rejection of the law as a compelling guide to behavior, it is quite different in its attitude toward repentance. Indeed, the spokesmen for this point of view seem to have very little, if anything, to say about the soteriological question. This silence about the first use of the law and the whole range of theological considerations that are related to repentance and to justification may not be deliberately intended. It may result simply from the preoccupation of these writers with the need to question the place that extrinsic norms play in traditional morality, a preoccupation that has tended to make them forget other kinds of considerations. But even if this is the case, the omission can be significant, for it shows that the soteriological question has ceased to have a primary place in their thinking and that they believe Christian morals can be discussed without reference to this factor.

The likelihood, however, is that this silence is not merely default,

---

[29] Douglas A. Rhymes, "The New Morality: What, Why—and Why Not?" in *Religion in Life*, Vol. XXXV, No. 2 (Spring, 1966), p. 175.

but a natural by-product of a completely different orientation toward many of the problems and issues related to man and the question of his salvation. The sharp antithesis between an autonomous ethic of human reason and a relational ethic of response to the mighty redeeming activity of God—an antithesis of central significance in the thinking of men like Brunner, Bonhoeffer, and Sittler—has all but slipped out of sight in representative writings by the new moralists. This contrast is mentioned by Robinson,[30] but he seems more concerned to distrust the heteronomous use of religious authority than to question the value of human independence symbolized by autonomy. Rhymes argues that the Christian can make no claims for moral truths based upon a special relationship to God, since modern man will recognize only such authority as can be justified by empirical experiences common to all. Indeed, he points out, "One of the difficulties today of an authoritarian ethic rooted in the authority of God is that the very authority in which it is rooted is questioned." [31] Rather than seeking to reinstate the authority of God by proclaiming His mighty acts and preaching the good news of the gospel, Rhymes prefers to find ways in which Christian ethics can be commended to men on the basis of commonly accepted experience. Joseph Fletcher, for his part, seems quite unconcerned about the element of response that was set by neo-Reformation contextualists in such sharp contrast with the autonomous ethics of humanism, and declares, ". . . situation ethics is not particularly Catholic or Protestant or Orthodox or humanist. It extricates us from the *odium theologicum*." [32]

Each of these ways of describing the moral situation of the Christian tends to ignore the unique role played by the engendering activity of God. Each of them finds it less difficult than did the contextualism of a neo-Reformation tradition to make a *rapprochement* with humanist ethics, provided only that such humanist ethics understands the relativistic character of moral choices and shares in the movement to reject extrinsic measures of good and bad conduct. The tension between the gospel and the world has been relaxed in terms congenial to the world. The new moralists, therefore, can accept with considerable equanimity changes and shifts in moral practices and social mores that are disturbing to those of a more traditional outlook.

The new moralists frequently employ the term "maturity" to describe a whole complex of wisdom, adulthood, love-directed-coping-with-life, and openness to novelty and change that avoids aimlessness,

---

[30] *Honest to God*, pp. 113 f.     [31] Rhymes, *op. cit.*, p. 172.
[32] Joseph Fletcher, *Situation Ethics*, p. 13.

on the one hand, and rigidity, on the other. The term "therapeutic" might also be used for the same ideas, for the new morality is much less judgmental than traditional ethics and seeks to cultivate authentic individuals who meet situations with a wellspring of resources based upon an ability to cope with all the variables in each crisis.

> ... the new morality means the imaginative reappropriation of our moral traditions to enable us to cope productively with new and unprecedented situations. ...
>
> Secularization has resulted not only in a society of differentiated pluralism, a radical variety of values and points of view, but in a secular mentality which no longer assumes that the values handed down by parents, church, or the past of the tribe are valid for today. How do we celebrate this new freedom? How do we embrace it joyously and thankfully and accept the discipline of maturity and accountability to which it calls us? [33]

This maturity is, moreover, generally assumed to be an achievement. It comes to the Christian much as it would come to any man, through the artful cultivation of one's selfhood. It is not a radical renewal coming from divine grace. We get it by seeking it, by casting aside those false notions and attitudes of the old morality that inhibit human freedom and that distort the ethical enterprise into legalism and rigidity. It is not a unique possibility for the believer alone, but can be shared alike by believer and nonbeliever. The "new man" and the "new man in Christ" are pretty much the same, both mature citizens of a dynamic, secular, world of many-sided values and commitments. Christians can boast, "Yes, we too are human (or humane)."

If the phrase "works/righteousness" can be applied to the legalism that couples obedience to the law with a soteriology of works, is it too strong to call this new outlook an example of "context/righteousness"? The absence of soteriological considerations is really a subtle embrace of a covert doctrine of salvation by works in humanistic categories. This makes for a curious similarity with one aspect of legalism. While it consistently rejects every function of the law, explicitly casting out the third use, ignoring the second, and implicitly rejecting the first one, like legalism it places the initiative, responsibility, and locus of fulfillment upon man and his achievements. It is not a theology of grace, at least in any usual theological sense of this term.

In Joseph Fletcher's writings these implicit implications come to quite explicit form. He severely criticizes theological efforts to attach

---

[33] Harvey Cox, "Maturity and Secularity" in *Religion and Life,* Vol. XXXV, No. 2 (Spring, 1966), p. 215.

implications of guilt to actions done under situational compulsion. He complains that the idea of the "lesser evil"—an idea basic to neo-casuistry—only breeds confusion. To suppose that men should repent for their violation of an extrinsic idea of the good when circumstances have required them, for love's sake, to resort to some other kind of action is only to confuse the issue.

> If a lie is told unlovingly it is wrong, evil; if it is told in love it is good, right. Kant's legalism produced a "universal"—that a lie is always wrong. But what if you have to tell a lie to keep a promised secret? Maybe you lie, and if so, good for you if you follow love's lead. Paul's "speaking the truth in love" (Eph. 4:15) illuminates the point: we are to tell the truth for love's sake, not for its own sake. If love vetoes the truth, so be it. Right and wrong, good and bad, are things that *happen* to what we say and do, whether they are "veracious" or not, depending upon how much love is served in the situation.
> . . . *The situationist holds that whatever is the most loving thing in the situation is the right and good thing*. It is not excusably evil, it is positively good.[34]

This understanding of ethics abrogates every vestige of the first use of the law. It sweeps aside a range of theological analysis that has had a powerful effect upon the thinking of many men, particularly those who have wrestled with questions of Christian responsibility in situations of conflict. The need for repentance, whether the legalistic repentance of specific acts or the generalized repentance which admits the inherent human dilemma, is denied any necessary place in Christian experience. This is Pelagian. Indeed it is more than Pelagian, for it has even less to say about grace than did Pelagius. While silent about the necessity and the forms of grace it comforts those who think of the Christian life as an achievement. We may not yet have become fully aware of the extent to which the new morality transforms the presuppositions of the gospel message. This transformation is present as omission rather than as polemic and consequently fails to announce its break with the classical contextualism from which it has sprung in a way that demands immediate attention. There is more at work here than a declaration of freedom from the law. There is a covert transformation of the entire conception of man's relationship to God, perhaps even the repudiation of the significance and importance of such a relationship.

---

[34] Joseph Fletcher, *Situation Ethics*, p. 65.

## V. *An Ethic of Norms with a Soteriology of Grace: Calvinism, Puritanism, and Neo-Casuistry*

In setting forth the third function of the law as guidance for the saints Calvin was to father a series of Protestant moralities in which a soteriology of justification by faith was coupled to an appreciative use of the law as guidance and direction for sound Christian living. This tradition has come down through the Puritan heritage as represented in men like Richard Baxter and Jeremy Taylor.

The Puritans believed that a justified man will show forth the fruits of his freedom by living a life of joyful and disciplined response to God. Moral obedience becomes a means of celebrating the experience of salvation and of glorifying the majesty and sovereignty of God. Such obedience may be guided by "directions" for respecting and honoring God and for cultivating both a right attitude of devotion and a life that is in harmony with the will of God. As Richard Baxter put it: ". . . you would hence have this further advantage, that you would have less backwardness to any duty, and less weariness in duty; you would find more delight in prayer, meditation, and speech of God, when once God himself were more lovely and delightful in your eyes." [35]

The Puritan conception of obedience to law as a mode of response to God's grace has not always been appreciatively understood. Many have cited the Puritans as proof that if law is granted any place within the Christian life it will take command of the entire relationship of God to man and destroy the freedom expressed in the gospel. The Puritans have often been presented as narrow and fearful in their understanding of the relationship of God to man despite all they said about the joy of response to a gracious and loving God. Apparently such charges were made against the Puritans during their own times, for Baxter took note of them as follows:

> And if any reader should be discouraged at the number of duties and directions set before him, I entreat him to consider, 1. that it is God, and not I, that imposeth all these duties on you: and who will question his wisdom, goodness, or power to make laws for us and all the world? 2. That every duty and direction is a mercy to you; and therefore should not be a matter of grief, but of thanks. They are but like the commands of parents to their children, when they bid them "eat

[35] "The Right Method for a Settled Peace of Conscience and Spiritual Comfort," in *The Practical Works of Richard Baxter*, ed. William Orme; Vol. IX (London: James Duncan, 1830), p. 29.

their meat, and wear their clothes, and go to bed, and eat no poison, and tumble not in the dirt; and cut not your fingers, and take heed of fire and water, &c." To leave out any such law and duty, were but to deprive you of an excellent mercy; you will not cut off or cast away any member of your body; any vein, or sinew, or artery, upon pretence that the number maketh them troublesome, when the diminishing of that number would kill or maim you. A student is not offended that he hath many books in his library; nor a tradesman that he hath store of tools; nor the rich at the number of his farms or flocks. Believe it, reader, if thou bring not a malignant quarrelsome mind, thou wilt find that God hath not burdened, but blessed thee with his holy precepts, and that he hath not appointed thee one unnecessary or unprofitable duty; but only such as tend to thy consent, and joy, and happiness.[36]

Baxter felt release from the terror and burden of the law without feeling that it is necessary to reject the guidance of the law. Justification by faith changes the relationship of man to God by encouraging the acceptance of the law in a new frame of mind and under different conditions of assent. Justification by faith overcomes the antinomy between law and gospel rather than perpetuating it. This is no less a miracle of grace than the freedom from the law proposed by the contextualist. It may be more difficult to remain free from the terror of the law if one rejects only its soteriological value than if one rejects it completely, but the Puritan solution to the problem of Christian ethics has an integrity that should be acknowledged even by those who judge it inadequate. The Puritan might be regarded as saying, "All things are lawful to the Christian, even obedience to the law."

The Puritans belong in that group of Christian moralists that have found values in a system of casuistry for relating law to circumstances. Classical forms of casuistry do not have a uniformly good reputation and modified forms of neo-casuistry are difficult to evaluate. There can be no doubt that casuistry has often been a handmaiden of a theology of works and closely associated with legalistic ethics. It has functioned both to tighten the grip of the law by specifying every minutial requirement to be fulfilled as the condition of righteousness and also to abrogate the moral claim by defining as allowable questionable fulfillments of moral obligation. It is therefore not clear whether, on balance, it intensifies or subverts the moral life, but in either case it has these consequences when used in conjunction with a soteriology of works.

Casuistry can be quite different if defined and embraced in relation to a soteriology of grace. Such a casuistry can provide a flexible

---

[36] "A Christian Directory," in William Orme, ed. *op. cit.*, Vol. II, p. 4.

and helpful guidance without creating a form of legalism. It can work both as a guide to action in particular circumstances (because it permits the demands to be tailored to occasions) and as a goad to repentance (because it always preserves a sense of the moral requirement above the action). It can provide a reasonable, yet never totally definitive, guide for action while also increasing man's sense of need for divine grace. It can free men from the terror of the law without leaving them in a sea of uncertainty. A casuistry that presupposes salvation by faith, unlike situational ethics that adapts to the circumstance with an easy conscience, can look upon every action as a compromise between the obedience appropriate to the faithful man and what can actually be accomplished in a particular action. Compromise makes sense if engaged in with continued reliance upon the mercy of God. Under such conditions extrinsic norms can be acknowledged as meaningful even when they cannot be completely followed. Man need not settle for the sense of spurious satisfaction that rests content with doing the best he can under the circumstances.

Karl Barth has attempted to redefine the relationship between law and gospel in such a way as to preserve the priority of justification by faith while keeping the possibility of a normative element in the divine command. His efforts have been heralded by his friends as faithful to the balance between grace and obligation and criticized by his detractors for failing to break with normative morality.

Barth places the hearing of the gospel prior to knowing the law. This reverses the common assumption that men who first come under judgment are then in a position to hear the gospel because they have failed at obedience to the law. God's Word comes as both gospel and law; for ". . . if we speak of Gospel *and* if we speak of Law, we mean God's Word. God's Word can indeed say many things to us. It can not only comfort us, heal us, vivify us, it not only can instruct and enlighten us, it can also judge us, punish us, kill us, and it actually does all of these." [37] For Barth, "In the true Christian concept of the covenant of God with man the doctrine of the divine election of grace is the first element, and the doctrine of the divine command is the second." [38]

Much that Barth says about the priority of grace over command repeats what Brunner and other neo-Reformation contextualists say about it. God is the essence of the good and cannot be subordinated to any autonomous value or authoritative law extrinsic to Himself. Yet

---

[37] Karl Barth, "Gospel and Law," in *Community, State and Church*, ed. Will Herberg (Garden City: Doubleday & Co., 1960), p. 72.

[38] *Church Dogmatics*, Vol. II, Part 2 (Edinburgh: T. and T. Clark, 1957), p. 509.

neither does Barth look upon the Command as a function of context alone.

> The Law of God cannot be compared with any human law. For it is not merely a general rule but also a specific prescription and norm for each individual case. . . . For as God is not only the God of the general but also of the particular, of the most particular, and the glory of the latter is Him, so is it with His command. His command is not at all an empty form to which we have to give specific content (approximate to this or that moment of our lives) by our action and the accompanying judgment of our ethical reflection. It is not a generalized thing to which particularized expression must accrue from elsewhere. The command of God is an integral whole. For in it form and content, general prescription and concrete application are not two things but one.[39]

By allowing law to be a source of guidance as part of the Word of God, by permitting it to have a normative function for guidance without giving it significance for salvation, Barth uncovers possibilities that cannot be explored in terms of only a single function of the law. As opposed to those who overstress the function of the law as a guide to moral decision, Barth insists that the guidance of law is always subordinate to the Word. As opposed to those who reject the possible role of law in favor of guidance from context, Barth suggests that the guidance of the law is preferable to the whim of circumstance. He criticizes and accepts aspects of both sides of a polarized debate. Moreover, he shares a great deal in common with the thinking of a man like Baxter while at the same time improving upon it.

Paul Althaus, a Lutheran scholar, has likewise attempted to deal creatively with the relationship between law and gospel, between the freedom stressed by the contextualist and the kind of guidance deemed important by the casuist. Althaus formally rejects the third use of the law as Calvin described it, but provides for a similar function under the rubric of "command." According to Althaus we must distinguish between the command of God, which is the original life-giving call which puts man under a claim, and law, which refers to the negative prohibitionary teaching symbolized by the Decalogue. Through the fall, command turns into law, life-creating guidance into life-restricting negation:

> The divine command speaks only of the love of God, and of the fact that we are made for this love. The law, unfortunately, must also speak continually of our iniquities. The command presupposes, as the indicative on which it rests, only the love of God as expressed in his

[39] *Ibid.*, p. 663.

creation of mankind. The law presupposes also the indicative of the fall, of sin. Thus the command is, in its form, determined purely theocentrically; but the form the law takes is determined also anthropocentrically.[40]

The experience of release granted by God to man through the gospel is central. It cancels the law as an experience of terror, as a legalistic way of regulating the Christian life for purposes of meriting salvation. But it does not lead to a relativistic contextualism in which the guidance function of law is flatly rejected. Instead, as Christians, ". . . we are well advised to pay attention to the moral teachings of the New Testament, to the apostolic imperatives. We need these as the norm and corrective for our own apprehension of the will of God for us today. The same is true of the Ten Commandments. God's spirit teaches me through my attending to the moral imperatives of the Bible." [41] While this language is different (Althaus uses "law" as we have used "legalism," and "command" as we have used "norm") the basic understanding of Christian morality presented in his argument comes closer to being an ethic of norms under a soteriology of grace than it comes to being a situationalism that rejects all normative elements in the life of faith.

The formulations of Barth and Althaus deal with a delicate balance of two contrasting aspects of the Christian's relationship to God. They are not easily balanced. H. Richard Niebuhr criticized Barth for using the categories of law and commandment to interpret the biblical ethic, declaring, ". . . the use of this pattern of interpretation does violence to what we find there." [42] But if Barth has had critics who complain that he makes a mistake using the categories of law and commandment, he has also had critics who regard him as not making enough positive use of these concepts. N. H. G. Robinson feels that Barth has rejected morality in rejecting moralism:

> . . . Dr. Barth seems to have failed to distinguish between hostility to the unique magnification of a thing and hostility to the thing itself. And yet such a distinction is clearly demanded by the facts. The alternative to tyranny and dictatorship is not anarchy. Likewise the alternative to moralism in theology is anti-moralism with a hyphen and not antimoralism without it.[43]

---

[40] Paul Althaus, *The Divine Command: A New Perspective on Law and Gospel*, trans., Franklin Sherman; introduction by William H. Lazareth (Philadelphia: Fortress Press, 1966), p. 14.

[41] *Ibid.*, pp. 44 f.   [42] *The Responsible Self*, p. 66.

[43] N. H. G. Robinson, *Christ and Conscience* (London: Nisbet, 1956), p. 139.

Carl F. H. Henry, for whom the "significance of the Law is that it inscripturates God's command in propositional form as a fixed rule of life," [44] also finds Barth's treatment of the law unsatisfactory. He feels it is contrary to the biblical conception of ethics for precisely the opposite reason that H. Richard Niebuhr feels it is unbiblical. The fact that Barth displeases two contrasting points of view does not prove he is right but it may well show that he balances two emphases within his thinking.

Repentance within an ethic of guidance under a soteriology of grace will be so formed as to reflect a sense of man's total dependence upon God's forgiving love, but it will also understand the causes of man's needs in terms of wrongs committed and obligations left unfulfilled. It will acknowledge both the estrangement of man from the divine ground of being and the transgression of man against the divine will. N. H. G. Robinson has suggested the double focus of repentance as follows:

> "Come unto me" and "Follow me," said Jesus; and they mean the same thing: But, while the one emphasizes the practical directive, the moral claim, the other stresses the gift which it includes. But if it is a gift of mercy and forgiveness, then it is also a judgment, representing another side to the moral reasoning of our meeting with God in Christ. This claim judges us in the whole length and breadth of our being, not only in respect of our individual deeds and misdeeds, but also in respect to the standards we have acknowledged and the aspirations we have cherished, not only with regard to ourselves as individual men and women, but also as members of human society in the broadest possible sense. If we at our best are not what we aim to be, then even our dreams are brought to judgment.[45]

An ethic of norms under a soteriology of grace has much in common with a neo-Reformation contextualism—so much in fact that the differences between them pale in comparison with their common difference from both legalistic and autonomous ethics. Calvin and Luther stood closer to each other than either stood to the Catholic or the sectarian legalists of their time. Barth and Brunner are more often considered as protagonists of a common theological movement than as antagonists in a side debate about the nature of Christian ethics. Althaus and Bonhoeffer can both be considered neo-Lutherans who happen to put accent marks upon different parts of similar formula-

---

[44] *Christian Personal Ethics* (Grand Rapids, Mich.: Wm. B. Eerdmans, 1957), p. 350.

[45] *Christ and Conscience, op. cit.*, p. 19.

tions. Neo-casuists share many of the impulses expressed in contextualist ethics even though they use different ways of expressing those impulses. Nevertheless, despite these similarities and the close relationship between both kinds of Christian ethic based upon justification by faith, there is a significant difference between those who can include a modified place for the normative element in Christian ethics and those who feel obliged to expurgate it.

## VI. *Conclusion*

The conclusions to be drawn from the foregoing analysis are largely implicit in much that has been set forth. There is a place, however, for both summarizing the implicit themes and a fuller explication of their consequences.

It is by no means clear that a mature ethic will emerge from just one way of understanding these factors. While much contemporary ethical writing takes great pains to permit and encourage a freedom and diversity of judgment concerning the possible content of conduct, it is often rigid in its demands as to how the moral life is to be understood by Christians. Such a rigidity may bind men's thinking as much as moral legalism has bound their actions. A "para-legalism" that insists upon a particular way of describing the moral stance of the Christian can become more ideological than empirical in character. If this happens freedom is threatened just as much as it is threatened by a morality of rigid laws.

There is clearly a large consensus in the contemporary discussions calling for a rejection of legalism, a consensus that increasingly includes Roman Catholic as well as Protestant spokesmen. But it is not necessary to reject the third function of the law in order to break with a scheme of works/righteousness. Since legalism is a combination of an ethic of norms with a soteriology of works, its grip upon the conscience of the religious man can be broken by rejecting obedience to the law as a means of achieving salvation without necessarily rejecting the role of law as guidance. While it is understandable that the rejection of legalism frequently involves the rejection of both the normative and the soteriological functions of the law, it is neither logically nor religiously necessary for this to take place.

When the rejection of legalism becomes an overriding preoccupation to do away with norms, works/righteousness is replaced by a context/righteousness in which the soteriological significance of the gospel as an experience of grace is poorly understood. The most blatant forms of this possibility are too recent for us to be sure just how they will fare under scrutiny. Perhaps they will quietly modify themselves back into a neo-Reformation contextualism in which justification by faith plays a significant soteriological role as soon as the extent of their deviation from classical contextualism is widely recognized. Perhaps they will continue to argue an increasingly popular case, oblivious to soteriological questions, until their heyday of enthusiastic acceptance has passed and they suffer the fate of many other theological enthusiasms. Perhaps they will give increasing attention to the multitude of variables that must be taken into account in considering what constitutes mature Christian behavior and quietly embrace a wider band of possible aspects of the Christian life, including law as a source of flexible guidance. The quiet modification would probably produce more lasting wisdom than a continued preoccupation with purity of method that would engender a compensating reaction.

The discussion of these matters should never be divorced from their relationship to the conditions of human life and society at a given period. The contextualists in the neo-Reformation tradition usually wrote out of experiences in which they understood the exigencies of the situation to require violations of an extrinsic view of normative love. These experiences were usually encountered in wartime resistance activities, and the contextualism of men like Bonhoeffer spoke very powerfully to the crisis of the time. Many postwar contextualists have portrayed the crisis character of human life with illustrative situations drawn from literary sources or life experiences. Both approaches have tended to think of the most appropriate ethical response to situations of unusual complexity and difficulty rather than to the more routine daily nature of decision. Can the crisis situation be made paradigmatically normative without distorting the ethical situation?

If the only possible threat to healthy social and personal living is moral legalism then the contextualists are right in calling for a free and spontaneous encounter with circumstances. But is contemporary society threatened only by a strait-jacketing by law? In the medieval world and in the personal experience of Luther the law obviously had strong, oppressive impact. In those situations the protest against the law made a significant contribution toward recovering the message of freedom under the gospel. But to apply that experience to the conditions of today may be to have a very different effect. Do men in our age, even Christians, feel oppressed by law in their everyday experience? Or, is Paul Holmer right in suggesting that

> A modern man seldom feels obliged by a law; he is seldom motivated by a legal command; he is only frequently fearful of a law. Furthermore, our norms of conduct are not any longer engendered by legal sanctions. Once the expression "law" bespoke all kinds of norm and conduct inducing behavior. The combination of actual law and belief in a higher law, moral and awful, was extremely powerful. Whether we agree or not with the trend, the idea of natural law (or the corresponding notion of the higher moral law) has become only a polite mode of speech; and positive legislation is now thought to be governed only by proximate needs, and laws are accorded only the respect due temporary and pragmatic devices.[46]

A terror of the law born of the attempt to fulfill it is fundamentally different from the resentment of restrictions that comes with the effort to escape them. To suppose that the mood of rebellion in contemporary society is similar to Luther's despair with the law is to confuse the issue. Luther and Paul both protested vigorously when their attacks upon the terror of the law were taken as invitations to license. Had Luther and Paul been dealing with religious situations in which the absence rather than the oppression of law was prevalent their response would probably have been different.

In this chapter we have examined four options or types of approach to the norm/context problem from the point of view of soteriology. These are: (1) an ethics of rules under a soteriology of works (legalism); (2) an ethics of contexts under a soteriology of grace; (3) an ethics of contexts without a soteriology of grace—or with a soteriology of context/righteousness; and (4) an ethics of norms under a soteriology of grace. In (1) and (3), extremes meet. The choice seems to lie between (2) and (4) in giving an account of the Christian life.

In deciding, therefore, whether the second option of a neo-Reformation contextualism or the fourth option of a neo-casuistry is the most viable in contemporary Christian ethics we may well need to take the context into account. In some situations the second option proclaims the necessary word of freedom; in others, the fourth proclaims a necessary aspect of obligation. The relevance of these strategies depends in part upon the situations to which we must speak and within which Christians must act. There is a potential dialectic between these two options, a dialectic in which one functions to keep the other from becoming an exclusive polar emphasis. If classical contextualism can keep a neo-casuistry from overplaying the role of

---

[46] "Law and Gospel," in *The Lutheran Quarterly*, Vol. XI, No. 2 (May, 1959), pp. 129 f.

norms and turning them into oppressive rules, the neo-casuistical emphasis can warn against trying to deal with life without any guidance. A dialectic of this sort presupposes a stance in which both the internal thrust toward ideological consistency and the moral thrust toward purity are superseded by the experience of justifying grace.

# 11

# The Three "Uses" of the Law

## N. H. SØE

In his famous explanation of the first article of the Apostles' Creed, Luther immediately concentrates on God's creative work and providential care for me, the individual, my body and corporeal endowments, my soul and all that is of importance for my human existence. Luther has been praised for calling our attention not to the very beginnings of the created world but rather to the need for trust and thanksgiving for everything which is actually and immediately meaningful to me (*pro me*). Of course he could not imagine how close he, in doing so, would come to modern existentialist theology, e.g., that of Bultmann and Gogarten, which forbids us to speak of God's action or actions in the past and calls our attention to our actual encounter here and now with the Christian kerygma. Karl Barth may not be entirely wrong when he asks whether Bultmann is not finally to be understood only from the Lutheran tradition.[1]

But is Luther entitled to speak in this way of God's providential care for me? Who am I? What has shaped the present conditions of my existence? Certainly not only God my creator and preserver, but also many different human beings in their good will, wisdom, and folly, their sinfulness and selfishness. And I myself have contributed, making wrong decisions and seeking my own in a sinful way. The

---

[1] Karl Barth, "*Rudolf Bultmann: Ein Versuch ihn zu verstehen,*" *Theologische Studien*, Vol. 34 (Zollikon-Zürich: Evangelischer Verlag, 1952). English translation by Reginald H. Fuller in Hans-Werner Bartsch, ed., *Kerygma and Myth*, Vol. II (London: S.P.C.K., 1962), pp. 83–132.

structure of my life's web, as I received it this morning, is a strange mixture of divine providence and forces more or less antagonistic to God's will. Am I then entitled or even obliged to offer thanksgiving to the Almighty Creator for this my present life?

We are here touching very difficult and, as far as I can judge, extremely important questions. I must, however, be very brief. As is well known, Luther in his highly praised and severely criticized book, *De Servo Arbitrio,* has spoken of God, not only as omnipotent in His redeeming work, but also as the all-working Power whose will dominates all of the created universe.[2] This theology is, however, not that of the Bible but, rather, a philosophy which was subsequently fully elaborated by Spinoza with the consequence that what human beings call evil (*malum*) has this name only because of our limited human viewpoints, our inadequate knowledge.[3] And we must, when reading Luther, be grateful that Spinoza has worked out this way of thinking of God's almighty power in a fashion that certainly would have horrified Luther. This might have caused Luther to reconsider his position.

To our generation this problem is extremely important. Today from several quarters, Christians are criticized for having a too narrow, a too limited conception of God. Hindus tell us that their deities are richer, comprehending in their unfathomable nature all the forces and possibilities of the universe, both the powers creative of and the powers destructive of life in its fullness. And, to mention only one other example, psychoanalysts of the school of C. G. Jung often make the same critical point. The Christian concept of God is, they aver, that of a God of ethical perfection. We are, however, called upon to understand God as a God of totality, as completeness, as not simply holy, but whole, comprehending also that which in its isolation is not only dangerous, but pernicious, or worldly. It is well known how Jung himself called for an acknowledgment of the divine quaternity in which the "earthly" element was included, instead of the "orthodox" doctrine of the Trinity which is, as it were, a curtailed form of the true archetypical concept of the divine fullness. Still more explicitly this "completion" has been claimed by one of Jung's most skillful disciples, the Jewish-born Erich Neumann.[4]

---

[2] "Omnipotentiam vero Dei voco, non illam potentiam, qua multa non facit quae protest sed actualem illam, qua potenter omnia facit in omnibus, quo modo scriptura vocat eum omnipotentem" (*Weimar Ausgabe,* 18, 718).

[3] "Cognitio mali cognito est inadaequata," Spinoza states directly (*Ethica* IV, 64).

[4] See, e.g., his *Tiefenpsychologie und neue Ethik* (Zürich: Rascher Verlag, 1952), p. 124.

Here Christians must be in very clear and definite opposition, without being perplexed by the fact that the demand for such a revision of the concept of God is very often, especially in the psychology of the Jungian school, combined with a most legitimate fight against what is usually called an ethic of perfectionism. The teaching of the New Testament is at this point transparently clear. Of course we do not know for certain whether the author of 1 John had certain heretical Gnostic teachings in mind. But it is at any rate noteworthy that immediately after having introduced himself as an eyewitness of Jesus Christ he proceeds to say: "This is the message that we heard from him and announce to you: God is light; there is no darkness at all in him" (1:5).

Two consequences must be derived from all this: we cannot take our present existence, our life and being today, directly from God's creative or governing hand. Second, it is already impossible from a theological point of view—not to speak of possible philosophical objections—to derive knowledge of God from the world as we know it.

Consider the first point. Assuming we cannot say that God has given us our being as it is *de facto*, because other "powers" have contributed so largely, how then do we come to that confidence in the Creator which should be characteristic of a Christian life and be convinced that we are safe in God's hand? The only possible answer is, as far as I can judge, that Christ has vanquished the evil and disastrous or dubious powers, powers tainted by or dominated by sin or nihilism. This does not mean that these powers can do no real harm any more, as Barth seems to think, but that they cannot hurt those who are set free to be members of Christ's Kingdom. The whole "background" of our present existence, life as it was given us anew this morning, we take from God's hand, not because he has made it—that is an inextricable mixture of creation and sin (*Schöpfung und Sünde*, to make use of the title of a book by Emanuel Hirsch); rather, we take it as God's gift to us because of the redeeming victory of Jesus Christ. Paul does not say that all things work together for good. He does not even say that this is so because of Christ's victory over the powers of darkness. He says, rather, that all things work together for good to them that love God, to them who are called according to his purpose (Rom. 8:28). And from this, because of this, we try to comprehend those extremely difficult words in the Epistle to the Ephesians (5:20) where it is affirmed that we have to give thanks always for all things unto God and to the Father in the name of our Lord Jesus Christ. Most of us have not yet learned the lesson here given. But if we are following the way of thinking indicated here, we understand that the last words, pointing to the name of Christ, are not just a pious commonplace befitting an apostle, but that which also renders the exhortation altogether intelligible.

Only in this way does it seem possible to acquire a Christian understanding of what Barth calls the "horizontal" line of Christian ethics, which simply is there and must be accepted. And if I understand Bultmann rightly, this at any rate comes very close to what he intends to say when he, borrowing the phraseology of the earlier Heidegger, says that the Christian kerygma allows us to move from an inauthentic to an authentic existence.[5] We are liberated from the powers that entangled us, liberated to God's service. Or we might even concentrate the result of our inquiry up to this point in the two short sentences which to Herbert Braun, a New Testament professor in Mainz and disciple of Bultmann, are the whole content of the Christian message: "I am set free to" and "I am under the obligation to" (*Ich darf und ich soll*).[6]

Now we come to the second of the points mentioned above: we certainly cannot know either God or His will from the created world, since it presents itself to us as a strange mixture of creation and sinfulness. It certainly should not be necessary to enter deeply into the discussions of the so-called proofs of God's existence. Pascal knew the dubious character of an appeal to the teleological argument when one is actually trying to convince atheists or skeptics. The same conclusion was seen by Kierkegaard (in his *Philosophical Fragments*). David Hume's and Immanuel Kant's criticism is certainly well known, although it is sometimes overlooked that Kant in his third critique (*Kritik der Urteilskraft*) is well aware of the fact that the seemingly great power of the teleological argument for proving God's existence depends partly on our unconscious smuggling of moral concepts into that idea of God which we claim to derive simply from the "purposes" we discover in nature.

The main reason for negating any possible "natural" knowledge of God is, however, a strictly theological one. Since the beginnings of the so-called I-Thou philosophy and theology it has been made

---

[5] This is, as far as I know, the usual translation of Heidegger's terms *eigentliche und uneigentliche Existenz*. Mrs. Magda King has proposed the terminology "owned and disowned existence" (*Heidegger's Philosophy* [New York: Macmillan Co., 1964], p. 56). It is clear that Heidegger does not consider the kerygma as the necessary condition of reaching an "owned" or "authentic" existence.

[6] H. Braun, "Gottes Existenz und meine Geschichtlichkeit im Neuen Testament," *Zeit und Geschichte,* Festschrift an R. Bultmann (Tübingen: J.C.B. Mohr, 1964), p. 410.

clearer than ever before that if God is really personal, we cannot treat Him as an object which we can find and examine and to a certain extent control. God is only known where and when He in His free grace enters into contact with us, reveals Himself in His Word as a person meets a person. Roger Mehl correctly observes: "Let us recognize that if reasoning could give us God, this would be precisely because God then had ceased to be a person." [7]

The question of most direct importance in a brief survey of ethical problems is of course the following: how far, before and outside of God's revelation in Jesus Christ, can we know, partly or wholly, God's will regarding our duties as human beings? We enter hereby into the endlessly debated question of "natural law."

Notwithstanding all discussions on this problem it seems evident to me that there is no legitimate way of passing from an examination of given facts to a moral obligation. Professor R. B. Braithwaite (Cambridge) rightly speaks of "the gravest of all category mistakes— that of supposing that an *ought* can follow from an *is*." And he adds: "How can one commit oneself to an empirical fact? How can a fact have a claim upon one?" [8] We all here think of what G. E. Moore has taught us to call "the naturalistic fallacy." And we think of the passage in which Henri Poincaré in his way pointed to the same fallacy. Usually David Hume is supposed to be the first philosopher who (in his *Treatise on Human Nature*) called attention to the logical error of passing from an is or is not to an ought or ought not. However, it is noteworthy that men like Karl Barth and Søren Kierkegaard without any knowledge of Hume and his successors, also very clearly saw the error committed here.

Karl Barth accuses Roman Catholic moral theology of founding obligation on existence and says that "the order of ought erected on the order of being can as such be *no* order of ought, at any rate no divinely commanding ought, as it has revealed itself in Jesus Christ." Instead of the Lord of the Bible revealing Himself in his Lordship we have in Roman Catholic theology "the idol of being, the concept of God taken over from ancient philosophy." In an extremely sharp

---

[7] *La Condition du Philosophe Chrétien* (Neuchatel et Paris: Délachaux et Niestlé, 1947), p. 82. In an amusing way H. J. Iwand (1899–1960, professor of systematic theology in Bonn) says: "The change which today is exacted from theology is to hand over the revelation to the present aeon and the natural theology to the coming." *Nach-gelassene Werke*, Vol. I (München: Chr. Kaiser Verlag, 1962), p. 291.

[8] *Christian Ethics and Contemporary Philosophy*, ed. Ian T. Ramsey (London: SCM Press, 1966), p. 93.

attack Barth concludes: "This idol may, as befits such demonic figures, do many things. It can however not really command." "What has this metaphysics of being to do with God who is the foundation and lord of the church?" [9] And Kierkegaard says: "To convey decision through knowledge or knowledge through decision is turning things upside down, but in our days it has come to be . . . the truly deep, the true penetrating insight of deep thinking." [10] But of course, modern English philosophy has the honor of emphasizing that it certainly is "a logical howler to suppose that prescriptive assertions are derivable from descriptions" (to use a phrase coined but not accepted by Ian T. Ramsey).[11]

If this is true, it means that we can come to know what is God's will in our life only when He reveals Himself in Jesus Christ and thus creates a personal encounter which we cannot establish. True morality, as Christians must understand this phrase, is founded in "true religion." But, of course, this does not involve that foolish position that people who have no knowledge of God should not be able to create a morality or very many different forms of morality that make life decent and human. Human beings know how to behave in order to preserve a stable and even in the best sense of the word a prosperous society. They have their moral ideals and "know-how" to promote them. And they even very often share many common ideals and thus they can work together. The concept of "natural law" is ultimately false, but practically a quite reasonable expression of this fact. It is in my opinion an overstatement when H. L. A. Hart characterizes the Thomist tradition by stating: "There are certain principles of true morality or justice, discoverable by human reason without the aid of revelation even though they have a divine origin." [12] But certainly it is divine providence that human beings "by nature" are endowed with so much reason and moral sense that they ever and again have proved themselves able to find a *modus vivendi*. Perhaps Henri Bergson in his once so famous and now almost forgotten book, *Les deux sources de la morale et de la religion* (1932), comes near the

---

[9] *Kirchliche Dogmatik*, II/2 (Zollikon-Zürich: Evangelischer Verlag A.G., 1942), pp. 586 ff. Barth finds a kinship between Roman moral theology and the spirit of neo-Protestantism. The Romans are, however, masters and the neo-Protestants "obvious dilettantes."

[10] Søren Kierkegaard, *Kjerlighedens Gjerninger* (*Works of Love*), second Danish edition (København: Gyldendal, 1927), Vol. IX, p. 263 (translation by Søe).

[11] *Op. cit.*, p. 384.

[12] Quoted by Ian T. Ramsey, *op. cit.*, p. 383.

## Reformation Themes

truth. It would, however, in this context be superfluous to dwell further on all the problems involved here.

But if we appeal to divine revelation in Jesus Christ as the foundation of true morality, many thinkers claim that here again a logical fallacy is committed. We are deriving an ethical obligation, they maintain, from theologically given facts or something that is rightly or wrongly accepted as factual. On the contrary, they claim it is a prior ethical conviction which makes us accept just this or that, perhaps even the Christian faith. So R. B. Braithwaite can write: "To say that it is the belief in the dogmas of religion which is the cause of the believer's intending to behave as he does is to put the cart before the horse: it is the intention to behave which constitutes what is known as religious conviction." [13] And Kai Nielsen (New York University), to mention only one other author, makes exactly the same point: "We, as moral agents, form moral convictions and decide that such a Being must be good and his commandments must be followed. But this is so *not* because he utters them but because God, being God, is good. But we have here used our own moral awareness and sensitivity to decide that God is *good* and that God *ought* to be obeyed.[14]

This objection against founding Christian morality on a special revelation or on special given dogmas reminds one in a most striking way of the position held in the beginning of this century by Ritschlian theologians. Rather often they proposed the thesis that a thoroughgoing investigation of what it means to be a human being establishes that there is in man an almost Kantian knowledge of what ethical obligation means and involves. This then provides the clue that leads a man to choose just that religion bestowing the deepest satisfaction on his truly human nature. Already Albrecht Ritschl himself thought on these lines, and Emil Brunner retorted sharply that according to this view Christ was simply the representative (*der Träger*) of a religious-moral idea which had its validity in itself.[15] Revelation then would not be true revelation, but only a "divine" recognition of that which already was known and accepted.

The answer is, of course, that a philosopher like Braithwaite completely misunderstands what divine revelation means to a Christian. It is certainly not a set of dogmas to which one assents, but the experience of that liberating action of God in Christ mentioned at

---

[13] In Ian T. Ramsey (ed.), *op. cit.*, p. 62.
[14] In Ian T. Ramsey (ed.), *op. cit.*, p. 141.
[15] *Der Mittler* (Tübingen: J. C. B. Mohr, 1927), p. 73. English translation by Olive Wyon: *The Mediator* (Philadelphia: Westminster Press, 1947).

the beginning of the present chapter. Christ saves us from our forlorn and finally empty, nihilistic existence and gives us new life as God's liberated children. That of course means that Christ is the Lord of this new life He has imparted to us. We have not chosen Him out of some considerations as to what suits our innermost nature or satisfies our deepest desires. If this had been the case, we might perhaps later come to the conclusion that we ought to revise our first choice. Instead, Christ had delivered us from the power of darkness and into His Kingdom, where we have redemption through His blood (Col. 1:13-14).

## I. *The "Second" Use of the Law*

Precisely in this context St. Paul speaks of "redemption" as forgiveness of sins. And is not that the central point in all Christian teaching? Does not such centrality signify that before we can experience this redemptive act we must know of our deepest misery, our sins and our fundamental need, i.e., even our need of forgiveness? And does not this in turn mean that a knowledge of sin is a necessary predisposition for experiencing the liberating power of forgiveness? And is such knowledge possible without some, perhaps very imperfect, natural perception of divine law? Is not Paul alluding to this when in Romans 1:20 he claims that the non-Jewish, non-Christian world is "without excuse"?

This traditional Christian doctrine is worked out in rather different ways. Often Paul's very peripheral remark on the "conscience bearing witness," the work of the law written in the heart of "natural" man (Rom. 2:14), has been emphasized very strongly, thus building a bridge to the Stoic doctrine of an inborn knowledge of fundamental ethical principles, e.g., in the Thomist doctrine of the "synteresis." As in Lutheran tradition, especially in the interpretation given by outstanding modern scholars (e.g., Gustaf Wingren in Lund), we are told that here we have a most important part of God's action in the "secular realm." (The latter is sometimes, strangely enough, identified with the biblical term "the present aeon" by, e.g., Anders Nygren, Ragner Bring, and Gustaf Wingren.) If man sincerely enters into the "created" conditions of human life, his "vocation" in the broad Lutheran understanding of this term, he will experience his shortcomings, his helplessness, and so be open or opened to the glad tidings of forgiveness of sins.

Or the emphasis is put on the republication of natural law as given in the Decalogue (perhaps adding an allusion to the interpretation given in the Sermon on the Mount). As a rule Luther's *Small Catechism* has been understood in this way. The thunder from Sinai must be heard and people convicted of sin before the ground is ready to receive "the good seed." And we are often told that the reason people do not listen to the gospel is that the traditional respect for God's holy law has gone. What we need, it is claimed, is a new John the Baptist who can crush the hardened hearts and help the hearers to realize their forlorn condition.

The way in which Søren Kierkegaard deals with this problem is very interesting, especially in the *Concluding Unscientific Postscript*. He does not point to the Decalogue, but to the fact that people, prior to any knowledge of Christ, may come to an acknowledgment of God's Lordship. Men may acknowledge a supreme claim, being absolutely bound by the absolute and only relatively by the relative entities of this world. It is the ethical idealism of his day which Kierkegaard here expounds, but in a way entirely different from, say, a man like Fichte. To Fichte the ideals testify to our true nature, to our being one with the holy, divine world, the innermost core of being. The ideals call forth our free obedience, lift us upward above the sensible world which has no reality of its own and make us understand that life is divine (calling us not to the quietism of an Indian mysticism, but to the most wholehearted obedience to the divine voice of our conscience). Kierkegaard, on the contrary, loves the ideals that hurt or wound. Therefore he emphasizes idealistic religiosity, in his terminology, "Religiousness A." This "stage," when taken seriously, leads to a complete breakdown under the burden of guilt. Kierkegaard is misunderstood if we suppose that his so-called "stages on life's way" are to follow one after another in everybody's life. But he eagerly points out that it would lead to the assumption that divine grace is a matter of course if we tried to realize "Religiousness B," the specific Christian stage, without having experienced the deep feeling of complete guilt that is the final result of taking "Religiousness A" seriously.

In other writings, however, especially in *The Sickness unto Death*, Kierkegaard tries to reveal not the all-pervading guilt but the fundamental despair lurking everywhere in human existence. His intention is to make people understand that if one takes life seriously, there is only one possibility for being saved from the emptiness and forlornness of being a man, and that is faith in God. Here Kierkegaard has perhaps most directly influenced the German theologian Karl Heim (1874–1958), who tries to make people understand that finally there are only two possibilities: nihilism or faith. Like Kierkegaard, Heim also insists on the necessity of choosing, and this is in accord with a broad stream in the existentialist movement.

Now, certainly, it must not only be admitted but emphasized that to modern man the fundamental problem as a rule is not that of sin and forgiveness but the question whether life has a real meaning or whether, as Shakespeare said, everything finally is vanity, "full of sound and fury, signifying nothing." The glad tidings of justification by faith mean little to modern man (a state of affairs to which the General Assembly of the Lutheran World Federation in Helsinki in 1963 was also sensitive).

But even here when we try to approach modern man not in his need for justification but in his need for rescue from the engulfing emptiness and meaninglessness of human existence, radical thinkers arise and question us in a most searching way. In his famous *Letters and Papers from Prison* Dietrich Bonhoeffer speaks of modern man as one who has reached maturity, who is able to handle and solve the problems of his own life without seeking divine assistance. He severely criticizes and ridicules those successors of Christian theologians: the modern existentialists and psychotherapists who are eager to detect the vulnerable points in human existence, to prove how the most healthy of men are suffering from veiled frustration, weakness, and insecurity. This way of approaching people is, first, without meaning; second, ignoble; and third, unchristian. We must try to learn to preach Christ to the man of full maturity who feels secure in his achievements and abilities, the healthy man at the summit of his strength. This is the way Paul was approached by Christ on the road to Damascus, not in a state of misery under the burden of an accusing conscience, but just when he thought himself performing his duty in full integrity and to the utmost of his ability.

Here a tremendous series of questions are raised. But from a traditional theological point of view the central one certainly is: what then about the so-called "second use" of the law, the law as "our schoolmaster to bring us to Christ," "our attendant on our way to Christ" (two translations of Gal. 3:24)? And is not this "use" central in the Christian teaching that the law precedes the gospel and thus performs its *usus paedagogicus sive elenchticus?*

We are here confronted with the vehemently debated question whether we rightly say "law and gospel" or turn this sequence around and say "gospel and law." It has often been affirmed that the theological tradition here was unbroken in favor of the sequence "law and gospel" until Karl Barth in 1934 published his famous booklet *Evangelium und Gesetz*. The tradition has often included a more or less clear theory of the Old Testament as mainly law and the New Testament as gospel.

Modern Old Testament scholars, e.g., Walther Eichrodt, Gerhard von Rad and Martin Noth, to mention only some of the best-known German names, have shown, however, what in my opinion should be evident, that in the Old Testament the law (*torah*) is God's gracious gift to his children. Yahweh does not first and foremost come to Israel as the Lord who demands strict obedience and is ready to punish transgressions, but as the savior who rescues His freely chosen people who have been doing nothing to make themselves worthy of His grace, out of their state of slavery in Egyptian bondage. He acts to establish and to uphold His covenant, irrespective of their rebellion. And to these adopted children of His He makes known His holy and gracious will, so that the pious Israelite could praise God for this gift (as we hear, e.g., in Ps. 119). Or, as Karl Barth has put it in his famous statement: the tables of the law were kept in the ark of the covenant of grace. The central teaching of the Pentateuch is not God's strict or even merciless punishments, but His trustworthiness, His faithfulness to His covenant, notwithstanding all the grumbling and transgression of His people.

And it is just the same in the New Testament. Everything is here directly centered around the name of Jesus Christ. And Luther was correct, quite apart from some commentaries to which we shall later return, when he emphasized that Christ certainly is no legislator but the Savior and Redeemer. We can allude only to the most famous instance: the Sermon on the Mount. This is not a new and stricter proclamation of divine law, promulgated in order to crush the hard consciences of men and so prepare them to listen to the gospel. The very first comment on this "sermon" of which we know, is that given by the author of what is called "the Gospel according to Matthew." It is given as an introductory note in Matthew 4:23 where we hear that Jesus went about all Galilee, "preaching the gospel of the Kingdom." It is evident that the author in "the Sermon on the Mount" tells us in concentrated form what this gospel was. The man who received the name of Jesus because (according to Matt. 1:21) He should "save his people from their sins," here proclaims the glad tidings of the Kingdom which is incarnated in Him.

From a historical point of view it seems natural that the first part of Luther's *Small Catechism* is the Decalogue, although from Christian prepossessions Calvin in *Le Catéchisme de l'Église de Genève* (1542) legitimately started with the "articles of faith." But Luther's greatest mistake in this connection is that he left out the opening words of the proclamation of the Ten Commandments: "I am the Lord, your God who brought you out of the land of Egypt, out of the state of slavery." These few words are a most important reminder of that which had been broadly described in the preceding nineteen chapters of the book of Exodus: God's faithfulness to His promises to the fathers.

What ought to have been said here by Luther is, however, in fact affirmed by him in his famous explanation of the second article of the Apostles' Creed. Here Luther speaks of the fact that Christ with His precious blood and sinless and holy life and death has redeemed us from all the powers of evil, sin, death, and the devil, in order that we should be His own, and in His Kingdom live under Him and serve Him in everlasting righteousness, innocence, and blessedness. At this juncture he echoes Paul who in Romans 6:16 speaks of gospel and law, gospel and new obedience or obedience unto righteousness.

But what then about the "knowledge of sin" which seems to be the predisposition necessary for hearing the glad tidings of Him who came and comes to save us from our sins? Perhaps we must be careful not to proffer too many definite solutions. Here also God's ways finally are unsearchable. And yet I venture to say this much: all that we as Christians have to proclaim is centered in the name of Jesus Christ. We should not deny that modern man can come to know of the burden of his guilt or, more often, of the emptiness and absurdity of human existence without knowing Christ. And this may, as it were, be an introduction into the right listening to the Christian message of salvation. But not until man is confronted with divine *agapé* as revealed in Christ will he come to real knowledge of sin and of the utter vanity of life left to its own resources.

We have an old Danish adage which runs: "He weeps not for gold who never possessed any gold." When this adage is applied to interpret the Christian context, as a rule it is said to point to the so-called fact that when human beings are longing for God, it is because they were created for Him and they have retained some obscure remembrance of this fact. This means that the adage is applied along the lines known from Plato or perhaps along those of the famous passage from Augustine: "Thou madest us for Thyself, and our heart is restless, until it repose in Thee" (G. B. Pusey's translation), a passage which even Bultmann, who ought to know better, can quote with approval.[16] The right application of the Danish adage would be, as far as I can judge, to say that only on seeing some glimpse of the light that in Christ shines out of darkness can we really and truly come to know our forlorn state, perhaps first the emptiness of our life and then finally our deepest misery, our sin. Again I call attention to Bonhoeffer's warnings.

A well-known Danish pastor who did not represent any "special" theology, at any rate not the "Barthian" one, once gave some indications of how he tried to make boys and girls at the age of fourteen (confirmation age) understand a little of what the word "sin" means. To my surprise this pastor, who was considered rather traditional, did not mention any appeal to the Decalogue or similar passages. I point, he would say, to the story in Luke 5:1–11 of how Simon Peter, having toiled all night without catching anything, at Jesus' word and command let down the net again and, in utmost astonishment at the great draught of fishes which then were taken, fell down at Jesus' knees and cried out, "Depart from me, for I am a sinful man, O Lord." Or this pastor would call the children's attention to the divine love revealed at its fullest in the story of the crucifixion. So much, he said, was needed to rescue us.

From this background it is possible to tell something of how far we have gone astray, how removed our life and doings are from God's holy will and commandments. We should not say that the "second" use of the law is hereby restored. It is not. It is, according to John 16:8–9, the Holy Spirit who brings conviction to the world about sin because men do not believe in Christ. Or, as Paul has it in Romans 3:27, it is not by the law of works but by the law of faith that our "boasting" is excluded. And yet, the law is hereby not overthrown, it is confirmed (cf. Rom. 3:31). But first and foremost it is shown what God's gracious will really is and to what purpose it was revealed.

## II. *The "Third" Use of the Law*

We have come to what is traditionally called "the third use of the law" (*usus tertius legis*), i.e., the law as our adviser, our guide to keep us on the right path, to teach us the righteousness that exceeds that of the scribes and Pharisees, to quote Matthew's version of the Sermon on the Mount.

---

[16] *Jesus Christ and Mythology* (New York: Charles Scribner's Sons, 1958). Here quoted from *Glaube und Verstehen,* Vol. IV (Tübingen: J. C. B. Mohr, 1965), p. 167.

We are here confronted with numerous questions, of which we shall be able to consider only a few of the more important.

First, there is the central question whether or not it is permissible in a truly evangelistic ethics to speak of this "third" use of the law. Does this mean that we leave Luther and join Tridentinism in making of Christ a legislator?[17] Do we not run the risk of perverting Christianity into "a new law"? Is not the doctrine of "the third use of the law" an innovation by Melanchthon and Calvin, coming near to Roman Catholicism, and foreign to Luther? It must, as far as I can judge, be admitted that Luther did not use the term.[18] But Helmut Thielicke is certainly right when after a careful examination of the whole problem he states that Calvin certainly not only used the term but accentuated that to which the term points much more strongly than Luther did. But actually there was no essential difference between these two Reformers on this question.[19]

The essential problem, however, is of course not what Luther, Melanchthon, and Calvin taught, but what we find in the New Testament. We limit ourselves to taking up two passages from the Gospels: (1) the way in which our Lord, according to Matthew's fifth chapter, proclaims a new righteousness and gives a thoroughgoing revision of traditional Old Testament and Jewish teaching; and (2) the meaning of John 13:34, when Jesus, according to the evangelist, says: "A new commandment I give unto you: Love one another. Just as I have loved you, you must love one another." What does the word "new" here involve?

We take up the Johannine passage first. And we refrain from entering into the complicated question regarding how far the commandment of mutual love is different from the seemingly identical commandment or commandments of the Old Testament.[20] We confine

---

[17] The Council of Trent explicitly states that Christ not only was redemptor but also legislator (see Denzinger-Brannwart, *Euchiridion Symbolorum*, 831).

[18] Modern scholars (see, e.g., W. Elert, *Das christliche Ethos*, [Hamburg: Furche-Verlag, 2 Supl. 1961], pp. 388 ff.) have shown that the only passage where Luther seems to make use of this term (*W.A.* 39.1.485) is a falsification.

[19] See H. Thielicke, *Theologische Ethik*, Vol. I (Tübingen: J. C. B. Mohr, 1951), pp. 214 ff. Of great interest in studying the Lutheran tradition is a small book by the famous Swedish scholar Ragnar Bring, *Gesetz und Evangelium und der dritte Gebrauch des Gesetzes in der lutherischen Theologie* (Helsinki, 1943). Bring here tries to show that the teaching on this point in *Formula Concordiae*, notwithstanding its non-Lutheran wording, is in accordance with Luther. Elert likewise argues along these lines, *loc. cit.*

[20] Of course it has often been said that the "new" in Jesus' commandments is to be found in the way in which He appeals to His own example.

## Reformation Themes

ourselves to that question which has been so eagerly debated in modern Lutheranism, especially on the European continent. The question is often formulated in a curious way: is there a "special" Christian ethic? Or is not morality a human affair where Christians and non-Christians are discussing on equal terms and able to reach the same answers? This question is posed as if Christianity were a specialty for certain people, as if Christ had not died for every human being, as if it were not God's will that everything in heaven and on earth should be unified in Christ (cf. Eph. 1:10).

We are here thrown back on the question of natural law alluded to previously. Here it is sufficient to point to the fact which John Locke has already underlined, that there is no general consensus on moral questions. What we of the European-American tradition are inclined to call "natural law," is actually the product of a historical development in which the heritage from Palestine and from Greece and Rome are interwoven with one another and combined with several other elements. When it is asserted that Christian ethics is materially identical with the ethics of every decent person it should therefore be sufficient only to point to Eastern Europe or to African and Asiatic traditions.

But if we are right so far, what then is the "new" in Christ's "new" commandment of love? What is the "special" in a "special" Christian ethics? In his much-debated book *Situation Ethics*, Joseph Fletcher writes: "Pinned down to its precise meaning, Christian love is benevolence, literally goodwill." A little later he states that this love is radical "because of its non-reciprocal, non-congenial outreach. It is for the deserving and the undeserving alike." [21] This affirmation has of course often been made. It is primarily an interpretation of the well-known demand on the children of the coming Kingdom, that they are to love even their enemies.

This certainly is essential in Christian ethical teaching. But is this demand specifically Christian? And even if this be so, does it indicate the most central characteristic of Christian ethical teaching? It is a fact that "realistic" psychoanalysts like Freud have protested against this call to love even our enemies, maintaining that it entails a very dangerous or even pernicious repression of our aggressive instincts. Yet some theologians have claimed that even a non-Christian must admit that "non-reciprocal" love is what we, if we grope deeply enough into our own hearts, must admit to be the ethical demand upon us, at any rate if we agree that our life is a gift and not some-

---

[21] Philadelphia: Westminster Press, 1966, p. 105.

thing to which we are entitled. This is perhaps the most essential point in the Danish Professor K. E. Løgstrup's very widely read *Den etiske Fordring (The Ethical Demand)*.[22] That is to say, Løgstrup derives the challenge of "non-reciprocal" love not from the revelation in Christ or from the doctrine of creation interpreted in the light of Christ, but from an isolated first article of the Creed. It is, however, very doubtful whether he has succeeded in proving his point.[23] And if he has not, we may agree that Fletcher has pointed to something of utmost importance if we wish to delineate the specific characteristic of Christian ethics.

But perhaps there is more to be said. In the same context Joseph Fletcher[24] quotes Bishop Stephen Neill, who has called Christian love "the steady directing of the human will towards the eternal well-being of another." If this is correct, we certainly have a still more characteristic feature of Christian ethics. Bishop Neill's definition reminds us of a better-known Danish thinker, Søren Kierkegaard. When he in his *Works of Love* tries to elaborate that which in his opinion makes Christian love radically different from merely human love, he points especially to the fact that Christian love always has to do with God, with eternity. God is always the "middle term" in Christian relations —between husband and wife, friend and friend, neighbor and neighbor. We are called upon to help our neighbor to understand what human life really is and means in the light of Christian revelation, to help man to know God, to love and obey Him.

This of course does not mean that Kierkegaard leaves out of consideration the fact that we are also called upon to relieve the purely "secular," "natural" needs of our neighbor. Scholars have often thus misunderstood Kierkegaard. But this certainly is a gross misinterpretation. In this work he is, however, especially interested in emphasizing precisely what non-Christians do not see or acknowledge. Our obvious duty to assist a man in "ordinary" need is casually mentioned as a matter of course, but is not emphasized.

Perhaps we now are very near a true interpretation of John 13:34. Bultmann's commentary on the Gospel of John is here noteworthy. As a rule Bultmann is extremely keen in telling us that we certainly need no advice when we are called upon to love the man who confronts us. Love, he tells us, immediately; without any special theories,

---

[22] German translation: *Die ethische Forderung* (Tübingen: H. Laupp'sche Buchhandlung, 1959).

[23] Is it really "natural to all normal human beings to consider life as a gracious gift"?

[24] *Op. cit.*, p. 104.

love sees what has to be done. But when he has to comment on John 13:34–35 he says that Christian love takes a form that is alien to this present world. Christian love must have *den Charakter der Entweltlichung,* the character of aloofness from what is worldly. And Bultmann directly quotes from Kierkegaard's *Works of Love,* that God is the "middle term" in Christian love (*die Zwischen Bestimmung*).

Now, let us take up the other question, concerning the new righteousness proclaimed in the Sermon on the Mount. It has previously been said that this is no "new law" and Christ is here no new "legislator," but the Sermon is given to us by Matthew as an example of the preaching of the glad tidings of the coming Kingdom of God.

But is this a true interpretation of the text, especially Matthew 5:17–48? Already Matthew 23:8 speaks of Jesus as "master" or "teacher," and Justin Martyr directly calls Jesus a "new legislator." Not only has the Roman Church retained this term, but it is also used in a Reformed confession of faith, the famous *Confessio Scotia* of 1560, where Christ is called "our just law giver" (*justus noster legislator,* cap. 11). And a man like Reinhold Niebuhr defends in this connection the decision of the Council of Trent.[25] If we consult modern exegesis, we may confine ourselves to the outstanding but unfinished commentary *The Gospel According to Matthew* by Ernst Lohmeyer, edited posthumously, where at one point he observes that Christ is both Lord and servant of the law, "exegete of the old Torah and herein founder of the new one, as 5:21–48 clearly enough teaches." [26]

Yet Matthew is right when in 4:23 he places the whole "sermon" under the "headline": "proclamation of the good news of the kingdom." This means that we are confronted with no "law" (*nomos* or *torah*) in the sense in which this term was understood in late Judaism. It is not something like an "eternal law" (*lex aeterna*) which man has strictly to obey in order to deserve eternal reward. Everything has to be understood in the light of Him who "preached" the "sermon," He who was on His way to Golgotha, He who was bringing that Kingdom in which He and He alone performed complete obedience to God's will which is here made known. The "new law"—if we venture to make use of that term which is easily distorted—is a kind guide, friendly advice to those who by divine grace have come to be children of the new Kingdom. Rightly understood, there is no "Thou

---

[25] *Nature and Destiny of Man,* Vol. II (London: Nisbet and Co., 1943), p. 147, n. 1. Niebuhr claims that the Council here was right in opposing a "tendency toward moral defeatism and antinomianism in the Reformation."

[26] Ernst Lohmeyer, *Das Evangelium des Matthäus* (Göttingen: Vandenhoeck und Ruprecht, 1956), p. 110.

shalt"; but all is changed into a "Thou art set free to, thou art permitted to." [27]

If we, to use Pauline phraseology, "speak after the manner of men because of the infirmity of your flesh" (Rom. 6:19), we may talk of a divine commandment, an imperative, or even of a servitude, of being "slaves of God." But we have to remember that this divine imperative is founded in, and as it were permeated by, the divine indicative, the divine liberation from the powers of darkness, the divine love. "This is why," to quote Paul Lehmann, "the definitive question with which Christian ethics has to do has been formulated, not as 'What *ought* I . . .' but rather as 'What *am* I, as a believer in Jesus Christ and as a member of his church, to do?" [28]

Of course different theologians, also of the tradition of the Reformation, have somewhat varying emphases. Calvin could teach that the "law" is a "whip" for the lazy,[29] whereas modern opponents of Calvinism like H. F. Kohlbrügge and Alfred de Quervain are eager to make it clear that fundamentally "law" to a Christian is not a "Thou shalt" but "Thou art permitted to." The whole truth cannot be stated in one sentence. But the latter emphasis certainly comes closer to the central intention of the gospel than does Calvin. And yet he is not entirely wrong. Life is larger than all our limiting definitions.

Strangely enough, some modern Lutheran theologians think that when we accept a doctrine of the "third" use of the law such as we espouse, this must mean that interest is diverted from our "neighbor," from the "Thou" here and now, and concentrated instead on the subject himself, his individual "sanctification," his achievements and shortcomings. This, of course, is a gross misunderstanding. That God has revealed His holy will to His children and admonished them to live in that love which Christ realized, quite directly turns us to our neighbor and shows us what it means that our life should be a sacrifice

---

[27] A most helpful study of the shift in the understanding of "law" in older Israel and later Judaism is given in Martin Noth's essay, "The Laws in the Pentateuch" ("Die Gesetze im Pentateuch") in *Gesammelte Studien zum Alten Testament* (München: Chr. Kaiser Verlag, 1957), pp. 9–141.

[28] Paul Lehmann, *Ethics in a Christian Context* (London: SCM Press, 1963), p. 159. See also the whole paragraph. Very helpful also are the observations made by Anders Nygren in his well-known *Commentary of the Epistle to the Romans* (Swedish edition, 1944), especially concerning the connection between the indicatives of Romans 6:1–11 and the imperatives of 6:12–14. We completely misunderstand Paul if we think that the indicatives make the imperatives superfluous. On the contrary, the former alone gives the latter meaning.

[29] *Institutio Christianae Religionis,* 1559, II, 7, 12.

to the glory of God and thanksgiving to Him. "The works that God demands from man are his care for our neighbour." [30]

## III. *The "First" Use of the Law*

If we so far are on the right path, we are, however, confronted with a problem that often has been considered as extremely difficult, and which certainly is of the utmost importance. If Christian ethics has a theological foundation, a foundation in the revelation in Christ, are we then not contradicting or ignoring the insight of non-Christian ethics? Is there not a "common ethical predicament," in which believers and unbelievers alike are involved? Do we not find exceedingly noteworthy alternatives to Christian ethics?[31]

Or we might state the problem in a slightly different way: is not our Creator's law for His creation accessible, at any rate in principle, to all human beings? Is it not a fact that Christian ethics has had very much to learn from non-Christian ethical insight, from Plato, Aristotle, the Stoics, and onward to Voltaire, Marx, Nietzsche, and Freud? Must we not here appeal to "the sphere of general revelation"? It is said not to be difficult to see that we have here (God be thanked!) "the basis upon which Christians may co-operate in all kinds of useful social and political enterprises with men of good will who do not call themselves Christians." [32]

Again we are confronted with the problem of "natural law," *jus naturale*. Or we might say that we have to take up the question, which in "orthodox" Lutheran and Reformed theology was called "the first or civil or political use of the law" (*usus primus, civilis seu politicus*). Do we know of such a "natural" or "civil" law? And can it be the duty of the church to help people to see this law and as far as possible to keep it? Have we any right thus to separate "the law" from "the gospel" and to expect that people who will not believe "the gospel" may be willing to accept "the law"? Is the proclamation of such a

---

[30] H. J. Iwand, *loc. cit.*
[31] This passage is almost a quotation from Paul Lehmann, *op. cit.*, p. 165.
[32] See Alan Richardson, *Christian Apologetics* (London: SCM Press, 1947), p. 126. Richardson has some ironical comments on the fact that the Western allies during Hitler's war always were fighting for "Christian principles." What then were the Muslim subjects of King George or the Russians fighting for? "Of course, Mohammedans, Russians, and British (insofar as they were fighting for principles at all) were fighting, not for distinctively Christian principles, but for those fundamental human values of which mankind has knowledge through the grace of God in general revelation." And Richardson adds: "Distinctively Christian truth cannot be either defended or propagated by the sword" (*ibid.*, note 3).

"civil" law acceptable because it is only a clarification of that "natural" law which is common to all human beings?

In his unfinished *Ethik*, edited in 1949, Bonhoeffer takes up some of the most fundamental questions of the right understanding and the proper place of the *usus primus* of the law. He goes so far as to say that this "use" has its origin and terminus (goal) in the gospel. "The law cannot be preached without the gospel." We have no right to separate law and gospel. Christian preaching has no exclusive or particular interest in establishing definite human orders of society. It calls to order because it calls to faith. Because God in Christ has loved all men and the world, therefore orderly life in the world and in society is to be upheld.[33]

We emphasize the point that the "first" use of the law has its foundation in the gospel and not in a very dubious "natural law." From God's revelation in Christ the "civil" or "political" use of the law is to be understood. And we shall try to draw closer to the central problem of the relation between non-Christian ethics and Christian proclamation of God's will by taking up the much-debated problem of how justice and love are related to one another.

It is a fact that many feel a remarkable tension or almost an opposition between these two concepts, while admitting that they cannot do without both. The Danish physicist Niels Bohr, who was the first to use the term "complementary" to describe that special relationship between physical experiences which modern atomic physics has revealed, has ventilated the idea that justice and love are so related to one another that here we have "one of the most striking analogies to the complementary relationship between physical phenomena described by different elementary concepts which were combined in the mechanical conception of nature, but whose strict applications in wide fields of physical experience exclude each other." [34]

In the theological world Emil Brunner stands out as a vigorous proponent of the idea that justice and love are ethical concepts, each needing the other, but derived from different sources of knowledge. To him justice is essentially a philosophical concept. Here we can learn very much from Aristotle and the Stoics. And yet Brunner claims that only the Christian understanding of what it is to be a human

---

[33] D. Bonhoeffer, *Ethik*, ed. Eberhard Bethge (München: Chr. Kaiser Verlag, 1949). In the German text the whole problem is treated on pp. 237–249. It is, however, evident that this passage is only a first outline. It proved impossible for Bonhoeffer to give final elaboration to his thought.

[34] See Bohr's article "Physical Science and the Study of Religions" in *Studia Orientalia* dedicated to Professor Johannes Pedersen, (1953), p. 389.

being can help us to understand both the fundamental equality of all men and that inequality which is given in God's creative activity. Brunner praises Calvin as the one among the Reformers who here saw most clearly both sides of this difficult question of equality and inequality. But this does not mean that now we have passed on to a doctrine that is fundamentally Christian. Every human being, Christian or non-Christian, can understand and accept this teaching. It has only to do with God's will as Creator, not with His redemptive work. It remains a philosophical doctrine to such an extent that it can be explained and defended by sheer rational arguments. And we are here in a sphere not only where it is possible to reach agreement, but where we are confronted with claims that human beings can fulfill.

Love, or New Testament *agapé*, is, on the contrary, something that transcends all justice. It never violates or sets aside what justice exacts, but is of another nature. It calls for selflessness, self-renunciation, and its claims can never be fulfilled. Here we are always falling short, always in debt (cf. Rom. 13:8–10).[35]

It is of the utmost importance to ascertain whether Brunner here is essentially right. It therefore should not be too startling that at the very beginning of his book *Basic Christian Ethics*, Paul Ramsey makes clear his fundamental disagreement with Brunner on this question: "This book deliberately adopts a procedure the reverse of Brunner's. The meaning and measure of full human obligation are to be found only in the biblical conception of righteousness, and not elsewhere in some moral norms derived from reason operating apart from the Hebrew-Christian religious heritage." [36]

It certainly has proved to be of great importance to inquire about the true content of the Hebrew words that are traditionally translated by "justice," and to show how misleading this translation is if we think of justice in the sense of Roman *justitia*. Here Albrecht Ritschl has done a great service in clarifying theological insight. And especially in this century much care has been devoted to showing the shift in content when translations take us from Hebrew to Greek and then to Latin. Much harm has been done, perhaps especially in dogmatics, principally in the doctrine of atonement, by not seeing this clearly enough. But it certainly also is of the utmost importance to Christian ethics here to be *en garde*.

---

[35] See especially Emil Brunner, *Gerechtigkeit* (Zürich: Zwingli Verlag, 1943). English translation: *Justice and the Social Order*, trans. Mary Hottinger (New York: Harper & Row, 1945).

[36] Paul Ramsey, *Basic Christian Ethics* (New York: Charles Scribner's Sons, 1950), p. 3.

Still more important, however, is a confrontation of modern Christian and philosophical thinking about ethics like that which is attempted by Paul Lehmann.[37] Of course I cannot here enter into details. It must be sufficient to state that in my opinion Lehmann is perfectly right when (p. 283, n. 1) he speaks of "the fundamental incompatibility between Christian and philosophical ethics." But I fail to see that he is right when (p. 275) he adduces the following fundamental result of his examinations: "The methodological fact is that Christian ethics need not, cannot, and does not reject philosophical ethics; it is philosophical ethics which must and does reject Christian ethics." And when Lehmann in this context appeals to Karl Barth, I think that he is slightly "mellowing" the great Swiss theologian. He quotes Barth as saying: "The grace of God protects against every human established ethic as such. The protest, however, is positive: grace not only negates man but still more affirms man by pursuing the solution of the ethical problem which grace provides in active refutation, resolution and suspension of all human answers to that problem."[38] The crucial word "resolution" and "suspension" are here translations of the German *Überwindung* and *Aufhebung*. It seems to me the German phrases are more polemical than the English ones.

Perhaps I deviate from Barth. I certainly do from Lehmann in saying that Christian ethics for several reasons cannot accept philosophical ethics.

When here we listen to Barth, we must, however, be prepared for a surprise. In the most recent volume of his *Kirchliche Dogmatik* (IV/3), precisely in a paragraph which has as its motto the most central clause in the strictly Christocentric Barmen Confession of Faith of 1934, we find that Barth dwells upon the "fact" that God also can grant to people "outside the walls of the church" (*extra muros ecclesiae*), even pronounced antagonists of Christianity, the capacity to speak "true words" (*wahre Worte*). They may be able to see certain aspects of true Christian ethics just as clearly and precisely and often perhaps better and earlier and more clearly than do the Christians (pp. 140 f.). Barth gives no examples. But I wonder whether we ought not to think of what the Christian "West" has to learn from Marxism or the Communist world of today. Previously I mentioned that we also have had lessons to learn from men like Voltaire, Nietzsche, and Freud, notwithstanding their pronounced anti-Christian philosophy of life.

[37] *Op. cit.*, pp. 167–284.
[38] See Lehmann, *op. cit.*, pp. 275–276. The quotation is from *Kirchliche Dogmatik*, II/2, p. 573.

Can we accept this? Are there "true words" spoken by God to us through the medium of such thinkers? Here, I think, we have to be extremely careful, and perhaps more careful than Barth is. We take Voltaire as an example. He certainly has contributed largely to promoting tolerance on religious and similar questions. The Christian Church is actually indebted to him. Was it then given him from above to say "true words"? It should be evident that Christians could not take over either his arguments for tolerance or the conclusions he proposed. According to Voltaire, tolerance was founded in skepticism, as already Bayle's argumentation had been. And therefore the result was a pale, seemingly all-embracing mildness, with no real room for definite and unyielding convictions. He did not really accept religious liberty, i.e., the liberty of certain groups of people to stick vigorously to their confession and to do the utmost to propagate them by using only spiritual means and no direct or indirect unspiritual force.

Therefore, Voltaire's contribution to the cause of tolerance had to be transformed, translated into Christian thinking, grounded in the Christian understanding of religious faith as a free, personal decision and leaving room for people of completely different views and for a real and true spiritual fight between those differing views. This "translation" has in our time proved to be of the greatest importance. In some societies the real danger is not intolerance in the old sense of the word, but a strong antipathy and even antagonism toward those who are convinced that they know so much of the one and only truth that it is their duty to try to "proselytize" for their religion. Therefore, to take only one example, a very "tolerant" philosopher like Karl Jaspers immediately becomes intolerant when confronted with the Christian conviction that in Christ and here alone *the* truth is revealed. Then he is reminded of the bonfire where Calvin had Serveto burned! This is a hopeless misunderstanding of what true religious liberty implies. What religious liberty really means and what is the true and unshakeable basis of that demand only biblical revelation as such can teach.[39]

An example like this may also serve to indicate how far cooperation between Christians and non-Christians in social and political questions is possible. We are in the fortunate position that such cooperation is not only widely possible but easy and almost a matter of course. Different religious or nonreligious groups may join in fighting poverty, social injustice, racial discrimination, the threat of war, etc.

---

[39] For a further treatment of this question see my article "The Theological Basis of Religious Liberty," *Ecumenical Review* (October, 1958), pp. 36 ff.

Often there are no problems whatsoever. We may, e.g., think of the situation in a secularized state like modern India where Hindus, Muslims, Christians, etc., work together for the benefit of the whole nation, and where disagreements do not always follow the divisions between religious traditions. A Christian must consider this as a divine gift. The non-Christian world is not left alone or simply handed over to malicious spirits. There is so much left of ethical insight and of sheer reason that nations outside of any Christian influence have been able to establish a somewhat decent and durable society. And yet, behind all these agreements and cooperations there is a fundamental difference between those who know of divine *agapé* and those who do not. Sometimes this difference comes to the surface, although it often is found only in the basic convictions from which action is motivated.

If this exposition is correct, it means that the old doctrine of the "first" or "civil" or "political" use of the law is absorbed into the "third" use. Jesus Christ is the Lord of all creation. His will must guide us everywhere. There is no "secular" realm that should be dominated either by a "law" prior to the gospel, by for example the Decalogue, or by a so-called natural law. In principle Dr. W. A. Visser 't Hooft was right when in his well-known book *La Royauté de Jésus-Christ,* he had a closing chapter on the Kingdom of Jesus Christ in the world.[40]

Of course this may appear extremely dangerous teaching. Perhaps we are immediately reminded of the traditional Roman Church and its tendencies toward a theocracy which really signified an ecclesiocracy. To modern Roman Catholicism this, however, is obsolete and may even be regarded as a heresy. And it certainly is no temptation to a Protestant thinker. Moreover Visser 't Hooft stands directly against this misinterpretation of what he wants to say. But the danger certainly exists that we try to "translate" the biblical commandments into paragraphs of a law for the State and society, and so we may be doing our utmost to establish, perhaps not "the Kingdom of God" on earth, but at any rate something that comes as close to this "Kingdom" as possible under the conditions of the present aeon.

Here it is helpful to be reminded of Luther's famous doctrine of the two realms, or two kingdoms. We cannot accept what Luther taught on these matters and we shall soon return to the problems in such teaching. But some truth inherent in this doctrine certainly remains. We must always remember that laws and legal conditions for state and society have to do with this our present, "earthly" life. We

---

[40] *La Royauté de Jésus-Christ* (Genève: Boulet, 1948).

cannot and should not treat a "mixed" society as if it were built up of sincere Christians only. Our Christian understanding of what it means to be a human being must be applied to the conditions under which we have to live until the end of the world. There is some truth in the assertion made by a number of modern Lutheran theologians (e.g., Gogarten and Løgstrup) that Christianity has brought about modern "secularized" society. This certainly is not the whole truth. On the contrary, Christianity will help people to see more clearly what this earthly, "secular" life, according to God's intention, should be, and what lawgiving should strive to achieve. To this extent Christianity is, rather, the born enemy of secularization.

Consider the following illustration. The Christian knows that matrimony is sacred and that married people should respect their union. But it is obvious that Jesus in emphasizing this did not intend to create a legislation that made divorce impossible. In a society like ours a law to that effect would do tremendous harm "because of the hardness of our hearts" (Matt. 19:8). And yet, the Christian knowledge of God's will as to the sacredness of matrimony will influence his decisions if he is responsible for lawgiving. He will try to prevent divorce from becoming a too easy solution to matrimonial troubles.

How far have we now deviated from Luther and the Lutheran tradition? We have emphasized the "third" use of the law more strongly and explicitly than did Luther. But here we are to a large degree in accordance with Lutheran orthodoxy. We have severely questioned the "second" use and appealed to John 16:9, where it is said that it is the Holy Spirit who reproves the world of sin, "because they believe not on me," as Jesus says. And the "first" use of the law has actually been absorbed into the rightly understood "third."

This last point calls for some special remarks on Luther's doctrine of the two kingdoms or "realms": God's "secular" rule whereby He upholds and governs the world, and His "spiritual" rule which He exercises in the preaching of the gospel and the administration of the sacraments.

The question concerning how this doctrine is rightly to be understood and how the division is made between the two "kingdoms" was extensively discussed a few decades ago among German and Swedish scholars. Perhaps the ripest fruit of these researches is a comparatively small book by the professor in church history in Leipzig, Franz Lau.[41]

[41] *"Luthers Lehre van der beiden Reichen"* (*Luther's Doctrine of the Two Kingdoms*), *Luthertum,* Heft 8 (Berlin: Lutherisches Verlaghaus, 1953).

The most important point that Lau makes for our purposes here is that Luther's doctrine is constructed in such a way that the worldly kingdom, the secular rule, actually does not need any Christians, neither among the governors nor the governed, in order to exist. He points to the fact that Luther directly identifies the commandment of love with the natural law and understands this commandment in a quite general and "worldly" fashion. Reason is, in Luther's opinion, in agreement with the commandment of love.

But then, toward the end of his study, Lau very briefly takes up some searching questions which might be put to Luther. He defends Luther as "realistic" and claims that all "Christocratic" theories are oriented around a concept of Christ which is foreign to the Bible. They speak, Lau says, of a Kingdom of Christ of which the Bible knows nothing. Nevertheless, Lau is convinced that we have to take the question seriously whether or not Luther is right in his interpretation of the Bible. He confines himself to saying that we are obliged in a careful study of the Bible to discover whether Christ has not given commandments which are new, not only in regard to their motivation, but also their content, and to examine whether these "new commandments" might be relevant for the activity of Christians and Christianity in this world, the "worldly" Kingdom.

One of the major objectives of this chapter has been to show that this certainly is so. I have tried to say what this involves, without succumbing to the danger of promoting a new "Kingdom of God Movement." This need not be the result in Christian theological ethics of absorbing the first use of the law into the third. Instead, this is a correction of the Reformation tradition which is needed in our understanding today of the Christian life. "The Lutheran church," as Lau says, "knows no infallible Luther."

# PART FOUR

# Situation Ethics: Defense and Critique

# 12

# What's in a Rule?: A Situationist's View

## JOSEPH FLETCHER

Does it make any sense to claim that (*a*) all rules (e.g., "keeping promises is a good thing") have validity as statistically preponderant generalizations, but (*b*) are not absolutely valid or universally obliging because it might be wrong to follow them in some or many situations? The latter claim obviously implies the existence of a fixed criterion or *summum bonum* (e.g., *agapeic* concern for others) with which rules could come into conflict in practice. This therefore denies them any transcendent or intrinsic force. At all times it treats them as behavioral maxims or principles subordinate to concern for others in every situation.

In this stance, therefore, rules are to be followed only when and because they happen to serve the *archē* or *prōton* or predominant principle of the good—e.g., *agapeic* concern as in both Christian and humanistic ethics, or the classless society in Marxian ethics, egoistic gratification in classical hedonism, escape from the wheel of life in Buddhist ethics (unless you are a *bodhisattva*), and so on.

What follows is an attempt to justify the answers given to the questions above, and especially to "make sense" of the position which acknowledges empirical (but not fiat) generalizations about good and evil and right and wrong while at the same time seriously qualifying and limiting their ethical or normative validity—actually to the point of rejecting any claim of absolute or universal validity for any rule.

## I. *The Context*

The two basic analytic questions are (*a*) how do we judge a past action or decide a future one, and (*b*) by what norms, if any, are we to do so? These questions are being examined in this volume in most of its chapters within a theological frame of reference; we see them as problems posed to both theological and philosophical ethics. (These are, incidentally, poor labels for these categories. The terms ought instead to be "theistic" and "nontheistic." As currently labeled there is a false suggestion that theistic ethics are undisciplined philosophically; and, equally falsely, that nontheistic ethics are theologically ignorant or indifferent.) And since many of us approach the whole question of rules and deeds from the theological perspective let me first try, as far as my own understanding goes, to set the discussion in the broader context of the New Reformation. Certainly *Christian situation ethics* has to be seen in this way to be fully appreciated.

By the "New Reformation" I mean what Cardinal Bea had in mind when he characterized Vatican Council II as the end of the Counter-Reformation.[1] A new spirit of *aggiornamento* is at work in the Protestant world too; we may indeed say that the Old Reformation has ended along with its counterpoise. Ours is a revolutionary era, one in which the change that is a continuous feature of civilization is abnormally rapid—due, I believe, fundamentally to the "new world" of thought and practice opened up by science and technology. Theologizing, or God-thought and God-talk, is never carried forward in a vacuum. Theology works in a socio-cultural context just as all human inquiry and reasoning do. And in sensitive response to the world revolution a New Reformation is taking shape. We can describe it, for our purposes here, as having three basic features: (*a*) the new theology, (*b*) the new evangelism, and (*c*) the new morality.

The new theology has many exponents running from the conservative question-asking of Bishop Pike through the central position on the spectrum occupied by Bishop Robinson to the "way out" thinking of the death-of-God theologians. There is a wide spectrum here from orthodoxy to heterodoxy to multidoxy to minidoxy to nondoxy. I suggest that we can characterize it all as a shift away from metaphysics and speculative or "perennial" philosophy toward a more historical, empirical and this-worldly focus, deriving its conceptual

---

[1] Cf. John A. T. Robinson, *The New Reformation?* (Philadelphia: Westminster Press, 1965), p. 9.

apparatus from science and the verification method, rather than from ancient myths or from "nature" or from revelations of truth by way of Sacred Scriptures, councils, and autonomous illuminations. There is much more that could be said about the new theology, such as its primarily christological rather than theological starting point, but this is enough for our present purposes.

The new evangelism appears to be a significant shift away from treating the Word of God or the Judeo-Christian biblically based faith as a "word" for *proclamation,* as Barth for so long insisted, toward treating it as a word or message for *demonstration.* This is, bluntly put, a shift from verbal to actual behavioral mission, from the *kerygmatic* strategy with its claims and demands and threats to a *digmatic* or *paradigmatic* strategy based on exemplifying the faith by "presence" and action and "doing the truth." This is the basic difference between a Billy Graham and a Harvey Cox. There is in this secular age a new intellectual humility in theology and evangelism—the same humility which is expressed morally in the openness and tolerance and relativism of situation ethics and the new morality.

The new morality—for which situation ethics claims to be the appropriate method—can be located at various points along a line which includes, for example, Paul Lehmann's *Ethics in a Christian Context.*[2] For reasons to be explained shortly we can join with Lehmann's ethics John A. T. Robinson's, and with his Canon Douglas Rhymes', whose book *No New Morality*[3] professes to be an elaboration of an ethics in which guidance or intuition is the controlling factor (it is hard to be sure which it is). I would put my own *Situation Ethics*[4] in a more conservative position; epistemologically, a position much closer to the unelaborated but pregnant essay by Joseph Sittler, *The Structure of Christian Ethics.*[5] This is a species of theological ethics in which there is a place for any system or kind of ethics which makes room for both decisional freedom and generally valid principles. This spectrum cannot, however, include an ethic which is by nature legalistic, e.g., the ethics of Orthodox Judaism and of Protestantism, segments of which are legalistic for reasons of revealed theology, or the ethics of Roman Catholicism which is legalistic for reasons of both revealed *and* natural theology.

In the same way this spectrum cannot include those ethics which

[2] New York: Harper & Row, 1963.
[3] Indianapolis: Bobbs-Merrill Company, 1964.
[4] Philadelphia: Westminster Press, 1966.
[5] Baton Rouge: Louisiana State University Press, 1958.

are by nature entirely unprincipled and spontaneous, e.g., the antinomian morality mentioned by Paul in 1 Corinthians 6:12–20, which laid claim to a clairvoyant "conscience" without need of any rules even in the sense of maxims and moral generalities. Nor can it include the kind of extemporism which rejects all rules on the ground that moral experience is radically discontinuous and therefore cannot provide any meaningful carry-over from one situation to another. In her recent work on ethics, Hazel Barnes, Sartre's translator and an eminent existentialist philosopher, says: "The New Theologians are in complete harmony with humanistic existentialism in declaring that there are no rules, codes, or commandments which may not be set aside." [6] But for consistent existentialists there simply are no rules possible. Sartre has held more steadily that ethics is irrelevant, escapist, and impossible—"bad faith." And Barnes herself compares reality to a giant Chinese-checkerboard with no pattern or regularity in the holes and no uniformity in the size of the marbles.[7] In short, a stoutly *atheistic* view of reality, and one which permits no generalizing or principle-finding.

But the spectrum of the new morality has a place for any ethic in which it is possible on any ground to justify a given deed without subordination to a given rule for a given situation.

In capsule fashion, it seems to me that we can characterize the new morality as a shift away from moral law and prescriptive rules and ontologically grounded values to situational particularities and to a commitment to persons rather than principles. My own way of formulating the essence of this is in two propositions: (*a*) We are commanded to love people, not principles, so that the needs of human beings come before adherence to any rule—although adherence to rules is often less opposed to human welfare than sentimental or unreflective persons may be willing to appreciate; and (*b*) We are to love people and use things, "things" including abstractions such as moral principles as well as material objects, so that the clue to immorality lies in loving things and using people—that is, subordinating persons to principles, thus reducing them from subjects to objects.

There is a sense in which we can regard situation ethics as a contribution to the literature and reflection sometimes called, in Daniel Bell's phrase, "the end of ideology"—i.e., the contemporary growing out of and away from traditional *a prioristic* and doctrinaire or ideologic thinking about both social policy and interpersonal rela-

---

[6] *An Existentialist Ethics* (New York: Alfred A. Knopf, 1967), p. 12.
[7] *Ibid.*, p. 106.

tions.[8] Situation ethics could be as well represented by political pragmatism and social pluralism as by personal relativism and adaptability, for social ethics is as subject to contextual variety as personal behavior is. In Geneva at the World Council of Churches meeting on Church and Society (1966), this posture was described *viva voce* and very succinctly by Margaret Mead: "A secular world means a world in which there is never only one answer to any problem, for a diffusion of vocation and responsibility creates openness and the possibility of change."

Noting that moralists and sociologists can help each other in enlarging their understanding of the situations in which judgments are to be made, the British philosopher Dorothy Emmet, formerly of Manchester University, puts it this way:

> Morality may thus call for distinct categories, but it does not exist in splendid isolation. A judgement as to what is right has to be made in a "situation," and a situation is comprised of facts seen as bounded and related to human interests, problems or attitudes. . . . The moral judgment has to take account of the "facts of the situation." A purely autonomous ethics, not in any way beholden to empirical facts or to our interest in them, would be, as Kant saw, an ethics of *a priori* principles, which would have to be both self-authenticating and incapable of conflicting. I have questioned whether morality can be like this; what place it has nevertheless for rules and principles needs further definition. They may be important, but [they are] not sufficient guides to moral judgment.[9]

## II. *The Debate*

What is needed at the outset is a plain statement of the perimeters within which the debate is being pursued. I should say that *the debate is about how to do ethics*. That is, it is about ethical method, not about "content"—which would be, presumably, what kind of ethical principles are to be adumbrated, how they are to be established, formulated and validated, their source (reason and revelation), how they are to be related coherently in logic and practice (doubt and perplexity in casuistry), and so on. *It is only the methodological issue which situation ethics, as such, raises and poses.* Of course, others have a right to ask situationists what their "content" or normative principles are; or, more carefully put, which ethical generalizations they tend to take fairly seriously and follow fairly regularly, and why. However, the

---

[8] *The End of Ideology* (New York: Collier Books, 1961 rev. ed.), pp. 393–407.
[9] *Rules, Roles and Relations* (New York: St. Martin's Press, 1966), p. 54.

why-question, which in some sense is really the first question, is the province of metaethics or one's pre-ethical foundations in a theological or philosophical world-view. It is impossible rationally to discuss either the method of ethics or its normative content without adverting to metaethical considerations, as this chapter and the entire book amply illustrate.

In the first place, the book *Situation Ethics* was, of course, an attempt to draw into the debate about "how to do ethics" a wider range of nonprofessional and nontheological people. It was aimed against a far too arcane monopoly of method-discussion by academicians. It appears to have had a measure of success in these terms, yet its critics in some cases have faulted it for putting its ultimate metaethical presupposition (which is a christological faith-commitment, e.g., my answer to the prime query, "Why care at all about the right and the good?") in a post-scriptum instead of an ante-scriptum. To this it is enough to say in reply, "There is no point in scaring off the game by making strange and unfamiliar noises." In any case, it was not written for the professionals—as this chapter is. In the second place, it was tailored as a methodological essay, aimed to do two things: (1) to make a radical reduction of ethical strategies or methods to three alternatives—legalism, extemporism, and situationism, and (2) to show how one *Christian* situationist would employ the situational method and what some of the reasons are for doing so. It has been enlightening to watch the philosophical, theological, semantic, and logical defenses (some quite angry) used to block the path of situation ethics. They are in effect appeals to bow down and worship in the forum of conscience before moral generalizations treated *als ob,* as if they were valid universally. They have usually borne two retorts: (*a*) Of course we are all situationists actually, but you don't need to say it so flatly, and (*b*) You can't really mean what you say; you are just trying to stir us up and make us think!

In a book written for a general debate it seemed unprofitable to employ some of the tools of sophisticated discourse among the professional ethicists. For example, there is the Rawls-Frankena typology of ethical strategies as between act-ethics, rules-ethics, and modified rules-ethics. As we all know from the history of modern American discussion, this is really Rawls's analysis, even though Frankena has applied it interestingly to Christian ethics and Paul Ramsey has added a considerable commentary and further reflection in his *Deeds and Rules in Christian Ethics.*[10] With Rawls it arose as part of his discussion of the

---

[10] New York: Charles Scribner's Sons, 1967, pp. 104–122, 123 ff., etc.

place of punishment ("telishment") in utilitarian theory, as something contributive to future benefits.

It was almost only incidental that in discussing rules he distinguished between those that are summary, i.e., general guidelines based on a wide sampling of experience, and those that are "practice" rules, i.e., specified *directives* or what I would call legalistic prefabricated solutions or decisions. Nonsituationists usually fail to note that in Rawls's saying that there are rules of *both* kinds, summary rules with a "full option to use the guides or to discard them as the situation warrants" and practice rules under which "one's actions . . . are settled by reference to the rules which define the practice," he also explained quite plainly, "It is my feeling that relatively few actions of the moral life are defined by practices and that the practice conception is more relevant to understanding legal and legal-like arguments than it is to the more complex sort of *moral* arguments." [11]

Nevertheless, there is no complete symmetry between us. Certainly not. His use of "relatively few" in the quotation above puts him, even though guardedly, in the legalist camp. He is being only somewhat more cautious than Pascal, who once said that moral principles should have the same universal application and validity as Euclid's propositions! In ethics as in physics we have left behind the Newtonian world for the Einsteinian world; not mechanics now but dynamics. To be in the situationist camp Rawls would have to follow the full force of his own logic, and of his distinction between legal and moral problems. He would have to join me in saying that there are *no* actions that should be predetermined in practice by *any* moral rule whatsoever; that all rules lose their apodictic claims.

The most that can be hoped for any normative rule, such as the one against lying, is that it will be a "summary" wisely adumbrated and based on a wide, long, and mature experience. No such rule can be universalized as to its obligation or absolutized as to its validity. There is only one rule or norm or principle which it is always ethical to practice, and that is the Primary Value-Commitment or Boss Principle or Single Norm or Formal (nonoperational) Imperative—which for Christians, surely, is *agapé* or neighbor-concern or "love" for others. The *sophia* (normative principles) may illuminate a given situation in which we are trying to bring *agapé* and *kairos* together; if and when it does so its rules are useful—but only in that sense "valid."

It is entirely possible to speak of situation ethics either as "modi-

[11] John Rawls, "Two Concepts of Rules," *The Philosophical Review*, Vol. 64 (1955), pp. 3–32.

fied-rules-ethics" (as Frankena did when speaking of Christian "agapism") or as "modified act-ethics." [12] Situationism holds, on the one hand, that rules are not absolutely or universally valid, thus modifying legalism. At the same time it modifies the unprincipledness of extemporism by holding that general principles in normative ethics may sometimes, even often, be relevant and obliging because they happen to be consistent in concrete situations with the transnormative criterion or formal imperative. For Christians this criterion is *agapé*, for others it may be ego interest or ego annihilation or class victory or ecclesiastical dominance or whatever is their boss principle. In short, it is probably inevitable that legalists who live by "the tradition of the elders" will suspect the situationist of being a "soft" antinomian, while spontaneists will regard him warily as being a kind of "soft" legalist. Both are right, because both—each in his own way—are victims of their own polarizations. This is the cross that mediating, nonextremist positions always have to bear.

Frankena has complained that theologians avoid the question whether there is any real difference between agapism and utilitarianism, even though he himself answers both Yes and No—there is a difference, yet there is not! [13] Perhaps, then, this is the time and place to confess that up to now I too have avoided the issue. I have avoided it, in effect, by saying that we ought to unite in a coalition the Christian norm of love or *agapé* with the utilitarian "procedural principle" of general utility. In this gambit I have taken the procedure to be one of seeking the greatest amount of the "good" possible for the greatest number of neighbors possible, and the standard of the "good" to be *agapé* or loving concern for the neighbor—as judged by one's understanding of situations and human needs. But we can now cut through this issue cleanly: I am ready to turn the coalition into an organic union. Let's say plainly that *agapé* is utility; love is well-being; the Christian who does not individualize or sentimentalize love *is* a utilitarian. In Frankena's language, "Roughly speaking, where theologians talk about love, philosophers talk about beneficence or general utility." [14] Then what remains as a difference between the Christian and most utilitarians is only the language used, and their different answers given to the question, "Why be concerned, why care?"—which is again the metaethical question.

---

[12] William K. Frankena, "Love and Principle in Christian Ethics," in *Faith and Philosophy*, ed. Alvin Plantinga (Grand Rapids, Mich.: Wm. B. Eerdmans, 1964), pp. 203-225.

[13] *Ibid.*, p. 209.   [14] *Ibid.*, p. 207.

## III. *Ontology? No!*

To those who in this discussion still have a taste for metaphysics, let it be declared very plainly that normative principles or "rules" are really only maxims or guidelines or statistical preponderances about what is good and right. They are not universal "laws"—either natural or revealed. They are without any ontological status. They have no ontic integrity. By faith we may, and I do, assert as Christians that God is love and that therefore when a man tries to be loving he is trying to *approximate* the truth about ultimate reality. But in its fullness and actuality love *is* only in God, not in the world nor in men nor in human acts. The goodness or the rightness of a human act is at the most only an approximation of "the will of God." This is what it means to speak seriously of human finitude and creatureliness and imperfection. It means that the "good," short of and other than God's own lovingness, is always a predicate, never a property—that as far as men are concerned whatever they do that is "good" is something that happens *to* it extrinsically, something we predicate or say *about* it by way of judgment and evaluation; it is never intrinsically *in* it, in principle or by general rule.

This is what it means ethically to say with Isaiah 55:8–9, "For my thoughts are not your thoughts, neither are your ways my ways, says the Lord. For as the heavens are higher than the earth, so are my ways higher than your ways and my thoughts than your thoughts." Here is a prime example of what I mentioned above, the conscious and deliberate intellectual humility of the new theology and new morality. In some measure it truly threatens both the legalism and the revelationism of classical theological ethics by doing its work with a new, serious, and deliberate *relativism*. It rejects all ontological realisms and requires not only de-Hellenization in the discarding of ontology itself (God-talk in terms of "substance," etc.) but also demedievalization in the discarding of all ontological ethics (good-talk in terms of "nature" or "law" or biblical fiat). In such ways we can discover the radical entailments of the methodological debate, as it impinges upon metaethics. It is nominalism, back again on the theological stage in a new and contemporary form. Goodness is extrinsic, not intrinsic in human acts. (And to the philosophers I need only point out that Moore's *fin de siécle* idea of goodness as a "non-natural property" is not sufficiently disposed of by such critics as Stevenson, Toulmin, and Hare, until they more plainly reject the very notion of property altogether in relation to goodness and moral value.)

From the point of view of those Christians who challenge all attempts to absolutize and universalize any imperative, except the Summary of the Law, there is really no significance in distinctions between the natural law tradition of classical Catholic theology and the scriptural law tradition of classical Protestant theology. There are differences between them, of course, and these differences may or may not have great practical importance. For example, in the ethics of reproduction the Catholic law-of-nature position catches them in an intolerable predicament morally speaking in an era of planned parenthood and population pressure, while the Protestants are in a happier posture because in this respect, as in so many others, the Bible never happened to "lay down the law" on the subject in the way that Catholic moral theology has. It is hard to unmake an absolute, whether scriptural or natural.

Catholic legalism is in more trouble than Protestant legalism simply because Catholicism is richer, more detailed, nearer to us in time and experience than the Protestants' Bible basis. Yet Catholic ethics is impaled on its double claim to being able to think God's thoughts after Him by *both* the interpretation of "nature" with human reason *and* the light of revelation in Holy Writ. Dogmas are an attempt to capture and fix the mind of God. But his thoughts are his own final truth, and any attempt to capture or grasp them fully or certainly is impious. Dogmatic claims are always on the edge of magic, of using God. In the same way, moral rules treated as laws or "God's mind" are an attempt to capture and fix the will of God, and when men try to formulate and codify the ultimate or "real" good and right they are being idolatrous, practicing ethical magic.

There is every reason to hail with hope such "hands across the seas" as Father Häring's, when he says that a distinction between absolutizing "natural" laws and relativizing "positive" laws may help to close the distance. He writes:

> It is true that the positive human laws, under certain circumstances, must give way to the call of the moment. There is full agreement on this point between Catholic theologians and the proponents of situation-ethics. The reason for this lies in the fact that the positive human laws are not made in view of the unusual situation and, consequently, do not exclude a different course of action in exceptional cases. But under no circumstances can the call of the moment be in explicit opposition to the natural moral law rooted in man's nature by God's own design, because God cannot contradict Himself.[15]

---

[15] Bernard Häring, C.SS.R., *Towards a Christian Moral Theology* (Notre Dame: University of Notre Dame Press, 1966), p. 206.

But this really only clarifies the conflict, since situationists will not and cannot absolutize *any* kinds of laws or rules—natural, scriptural, or positive (whether ecclesiastical or civil).

## IV. *The Decalogue: A Test Case*

In order that this debate may be sharply put and clearly understood, in the theological camp as well as in philosophical circles, let us look again at the question how we are to regard the Ten Commandments.[16] For the very pious legalists who lean on "at least a few things that we can hold to as fundamental," the Ten Commandments are not to be questioned. This is equally true of Catholics and Protestants. The Decalogue ("The Ten Words") is in big type in popular editions of the Bible; it provides the whole structure of Jesuit moral theology; it is recited liturgically in Anglican and Lutheran churches —it is, in a word, the basis of all classical Christian and Jewish ethics.

What is more to the point, the Decalogue is *an example par excellence of ethical legalism,* according to the situationist's viewpoint. And why so? Because, to put the position in stark and necessary terms, only Jesus' summary (meaning his radical reduction or distillation) of all of the law or *torah*—the Ten Commandments just as much as the Mosaic legislation and the various codes and scribal elaborations or *midrash* and *mishnah*—only the Summary is an absolute and universally valid imperative. We cannot milk any more universals from a universal. We cannot adduce or deduce or derive or extract from a universal any more universals. The one universal requirement is to love others, God and men, as ourselves. Anything else, including those ancient theophanic-nomadic rules called the Ten Commandments, are *relatively* valid—relative to any situation in which their meaning might happen to be fitting to love's requirements. Only love is absolute, and it is this anchorage which makes it possible for situationism's relativization of all rules to be genuinely relativistic, and not merely chaotic and random and sheerly unrelated.

The first commandment is an indicative anyway, not an imperative. Either you do or you do not worship God, and only Him. As to the second, you might for love's sake have to deny God—to protect innocent lives depending upon your denial, for example, just as you might break the commandment never to take God's name "in vain" or the one about keeping "holy" the Sabbath day. In the second tablet (they were on stone because that was supposed to be hard and perma-

---

[16] Cf. Exod. 20:1–17; Deut. 5:6–21.

nent), we could for love's sake break any of them—whether the one about filial piety or taking life or committing adultery (the ancient Jews applied this only to *women*) or theft or telling the truth or "coveting" another's possessions. It all depends upon the situation, in actual practice.

There may be a few genuine legalists who never tell lies or who always keep the Sabbath or never kill others or always honor their parents, or who when they break such rules always honestly condemn themselves as evildoers. But most of the people who affirm and recite the Ten Commandments are hypocrites—especially if loving concern is really the first-order commitment in their ethical approach. It might even be said from the point of view of "love monism" that while it is best to be an honest situationist it is at least better to be a hypocritical legalist than an honest one.

In any case, the question whether the Ten Commandments are to be treated as laws or as maxims will, among Christians and Jews (and Muslims) separate the sheep from the goats in the debate about how to do ethics. Hence Karl Barth sees that "The question of good and evil is never answered by man's pointing to the authoritative Word of God in terms of a set of rules," and that to offer a man a rule in any *kairos* or "situation of choice" would be "to hold out a stone instead of bread." [17]

Permit me an example of the classical Christian dilemma, taken from the treasury of Catholic moral theology, with all its careful articulation and meticulous analysis. Among other things it shows how a good shove, if we can learn how to exert our situationist strength, will be more apt to move Catholics than Protestants into a faith-grounded relativism of the sort we advocate. If this is true, it is because Catholic casuistry is closer at least in temper to the neo-casuistry of situation ethics. In the tradition there has for long been a sensitive and troubled awareness that *in some situations* even the Ten Commandments cannot be absolutized if love is the highest good. The arresting formula *"Lex positiva obligat semper, sed non pro semper"* (a rule binds always but not in every situation) has evolved, under which it is held that an "affirmative" law binds always but not in every case, whereas a "negative" law binds both always and without exception in all cases. Thus in spite of the first four commandments a Christian is not bound in conscience to profess his faith under all circumstances, as for example under persecution, yet he is never allowed to deny it.

[17] *The Humanity of God* (Richmond, Va.: John Knox Press, 1966), p. 85.

This distinction is based on another methodological doctrine, i.e., that we are bound always to obey prohibitions but not always to obey positive commands. Thus because we are forbidden to mutilate our bodies (so it is thought) it follows that even though we wish to donate (pre-cadaver) a kidney or ovary or cornea to a neighbor who is dying of renal failure or remains childless or has become blind, the law subordinates sacrifical love and we must refuse. And this is decreed even though it is generally acknowledged that there is one exception to the rule of *obligat semper, sed non pro semper,* and that exception is "the law of charity," which binds always and for all time. In the case of the law of love they acknowledge that it is a positive command which is always binding. Catholics ought then to see that, given this one exception, there is no other law which is always binding— none at all. And that positives and negatives in rules are only two sides of the same coin. As Christian situationists put it, we are to live by the law of love and not by the love of law; two propositions, one positive and the other negative, yet both the same thing. No Christian can deny that charity is more important than chastity— or nonviolence, or promise-keeping, or filial piety, or private property, and so on.

Classical ethics asked whether an action is right or wrong, but situation ethics asks *when* it is right and *when* it is wrong. For the situationist there is only one thing about which the when-question is never in order. That is "love" or "justice" or "concern." It is always in order. Or more complexly put, as Paul Tillich did, "For love is both absolute and relative by its nature. An unchanging principle, it nevertheless always changes its concrete application. It 'listens' to the particular situation." [18] This is why I say it is a "formal" principle, which rules us and yet does so without content. What a pity that so few ethicists, at least among Christians, understand the distinctions between "principles"—between formal, substantive, normative, and prescriptive principles.

A *formal* ethical principle is imperative (which makes it ethical) but it is neither substantive nor normative, and certainly not prescriptive. For example, "The truth must be sought," is imperative but it says nothing about *what* truth is or about *how* it is to be sought. Or take the propositions "The good should be sought or done" and "The right should be done." They are formal; they assert nothing as to what the good is or how it is to be sought or done. So with "Act as lovingly, i.e., with as much concern (*agapé*) as possible." This

---

[18] *Morality and Beyond* (New York: Harper & Row, 1963), p. 42.

formal principle is an imperative but it states nothing about what love (concern, *agapé*) is, nor about *how* we are to do it. A *substantive* ethical principle gives substance ("content") to a formal imperative; it is expressed in the indicative as well as the imperative mood. For example, "The good, which must be sought or done, is pleasure"—the hedonist principle—is substantive but still not normative. (Classical hedonism left it open whether pleasure is mental or physical; the Marquis de Sade specified physical gratification.) Other examples are: "The good which should be sought or done is utility" (Bentham and Mill); "The good which should be sought or done is self-interest" (Ayn Rand's objectivist egoism).

A *normative* ethical principle is one which provides a "norm" or average or model; it asserts what is typical of the substantive, normal to it, its usual effectualization, a sort of statistically preponderant instrumentation of the substantive. It gives an operational meaning or description to a substantive principle. Examples are: "True self-interest lies in buying real estate rather than utility bonds" and "General utility is best served by respecting private property rights, by not stealing" and "Loving concern for our neighbors calls for telling them the truth." Therefore, *normative principles spell out the general conduct-maxims of substantive definitions of formal imperatives.* Thus far, situation ethics goes right along with other methods.

In the most precise language we may say that situation ethics balks at *prescriptive* ethical principles—it rejects peremptory orders, preset directives, ordained rules, any designating how its substantive (*agapé*) in the Christian's case is to be *done*. Situation ethics is a "hang loose" ethics when it comes to *pre*scriptives such as the Ten Commandments, canon and civil laws, codes (as in the Pentateuch or the Essenes' *Discipline*), or precepts of any kind. Imperatives, substantives, normatives—yes; prescriptions—no.

## V. *Conscience*

One of the complaints about situation ethics is that it is "so cold blooded" about love. Many critics seem to be put off by the rationality of treating *agapé* as an attitude or disposition or *Gessinungsethik* rather than as a matter of feeling or emotion. This is a hoary problem. It may even have become a bit threadbare. What else is there to say after we have acknowledged that even though the total experience of love may and ordinarily will comprehend "liking" as well as "loving," nevertheless what is aimed at in all talk about *agapé* (or the Old Testament's *aheb*) is a conative and not an emotive neighbor-concern? Or, in still another effort to capture the point in the shifting flow of language-meaning, what else can we say after we have said that *agapé* is concern? This word "concern" may be the more exact one. Even if we invest it with a component of feeling it is a word meaning primarily a disposition of will toward the welfare of others—of the neighbors. Philosophers, at any rate, will have no trouble in seeing that if "love" is to have any viable general relevance to ethics it cannot connote the subjective and selective nature of either friendship or romance.

Still, the distrust of rationality is very widespread. The emphasis upon it in situation ethics therefore poses another important issue. I am convinced that *en fin* and *au fond* there are only three ways of looking at conscience, just as there are only three ethical methods. The first is the intuitional view, in which conscience is regarded as basically a built-in, radarlike, direct (trans- or ultra-rational) voice within, a kind of "insight" into the right and the good in every situation. The second is the inspirational, in which conscience is understood to be guidance by some outside illumination or power, a "still small voice" without instead of within, beyond and other than the moral agent himself. Such a guide might be pentecostal or theomanic, a familiar spirit, or even the Holy Spirit in a direct or a more generalized charismatic-moral influence.

The third view is an empirical, situational, data-centered, fact-minded one—the rational view, in which it is supposed that conscience is the whole person critically examining the context of decision rationally, by the rules of discourse and logical analysis, "making up his mind." On this view, conscience is a human function, not a faculty. Aquinas came close to this by saying that conscience is reason making moral judgments. (We leave aside, here, the further fact that Aquinas spoke of both *synteresis,* which was a kind of nisus or built-in "insight" intuitively in men, and the leading of the Holy Spirit as an additional reinforcement. He rode all three horses in his ethical method. The situationist, however, rides only the third one, reason at work as value judgment. His, the situationist's, attempt to be humble and tolerant, already noted, will not allow him to lay grand claims to either of the other two—the radar of intuition or the alter-ego of inspiration.)

Parenthetically, let me say that I do not mean to embrace "reason" in the sense of a bag full of *a priori*s, nor the machinery of deductive argument. On the contrary, situationists will be disciplinedly empirical and inductive. It is true that in moral theology the second premise of the classical syllogism has recognized the bearing of the situation, but it was always the *first* premise, where the universals and absolutes lay, which was given the decisional and conclusional priority. The traditional morality has had its model in such paradigms as Zeno's: "All Greeks are liars, this man is a Greek, therefore he is a liar." Science and modern philosophy have dropped that kind of logic, and we have to drop that kind of ethics too! This *détente* is what situation ethics is all about.

The situationist's idea of conscience is functional; he does not see conscience as a faculty or a "power" either innate or ambient. Conscience is something we do, not anything we have. And fundamentally the word for it is "reason." Its work is "judgment" when it is retrospective, as in penitential ethics, and "decision" when it is prospective, as in situational analysis and moral choice. And so, when we get right down to it, conscience is a rational activity—and the colder it is, in the sense of fact-comprehensive and emotionally untied, the better.[19]

It is for this reason that I feel compelled to put Paul Lehmann's treatment of our problem, with all its theological sensitivity and elaboration, on the intuition-guidance wing of the new morality.[20] I have pointed out that he confuses our developing thesis by ambiguously speaking of both the Church (*koinonia*) and its faith as the "context" of Christian ethics, along with still a *third* meaning of context, i.e., the objective situation in which Christian conscience must make its decisions.[21] This is a matter which calls for further critical examination and discrimination.

I can only reiterate my own suggestion that all ambiguity on this score can be removed if we will only agree to speak of "situation" rather than "context," and mean by it *the priority in decision-making of the objective circumstances,* rather than any general principles or abstract theological doctrines or discrete in-groups such as the *koinonia*. But the main reason for referring to Professor Lehmann's work is because he has, in spite of his own widely revered humility and openness, offered us what in other hands inevitably becomes a pretentious, pride-prone nonrational notion of conscience. This seems

---

[19] Bishop James A. Pike takes direct issue with this method-thesis, even though he is a situationist by declaration, saying: "Christian moral theologians, basing their view on New Testament texts, give *agapé* the highest marks. . . . But it is not the best love, either for the lover or the loved. It is not enough. . . . *Agapé* is not only not the full good; it partakes of evil. In its 'pure' form, without admixture of *eros* or *philia*, it is a 'putting down' of the person thus 'loved'" (*You and the New Morality: 74 Cases* [New York: Harper & Row, 1967], pp. 70–71). I prefer the view of the moral theologians to Pike's.

[20] *Ethics in a Christian Context* (New York: Harper & Row, 1963).

[21] Fletcher, *Situation Ethics*, p. 14.

to me to be the thrust of his discussion of conscience.[22] How else are we to take his treatment than as a guidance theory, attributing moral choices to God's guidance in some unspecified way?

Bishop Robinson seems to take the same perilous ground when he says, "Love . . . has a built-in moral compass" which enables it "to 'home' intuitively upon the deepest need of the other, [and] can allow itself to be directed completely [sic] by the situation." [23] This is certainly an extemporist's rather than a situationist's way of speaking, an assertion of "pure act-agapism" indeed.

Lehmann distinguishes first the autonomous (but not necessarily individualistic) conscience, which he assigns to the extemporists. Then, second, he describes the heteronomous conscience of the legalist, the one who relies upon rules and law-making authorities. His third kind of conscience is the "theonomous" one. But this conscience, which he claims is "immediately sensitive" (clairvoyant?) to the situation, has the overtones of Spirit-guidance.

This third conscience is, after all, one more version of antinomianism, but religious rather than existential. It does not, it is true, entirely repudiate general moral principles, but nevertheless it does deny the need to *think* about them, pretending that the Spirit-led conscience can trust it is being "immediately sensitive" to the right action in the decisive situation. We wish Lehmann would adopt as his ethical epistemology what we prefer to call a "logonomous" conception of conscience. *This* conscience would be free in having its human rationality and initiative, yet still armed with the guidelines of faith and moral maxims. Thus we could leave "autonomy" to the spontaneity or extemporizing of existentialism. Then his "contextualism" might be able to keep house with situation ethics.

(I am grateful that Walter G. Muelder has decided that as between the "contextual" ethics of Barth, Lehmann, and myself, mine "shows the greatest understanding of the place of the empirical in moral judgments." [24] It is this *empirical* situationality, if I may so express it, which is the core consideration. Conscience must be data-centered, not either a natural or a divinely inspired homing pigeon.)

Paul Tillich's discussion in *Morality and Beyond* of the antinomy between faith-determined ethics and reason-determined ethics can be put in a different way.[25] At least in *Christian* ethics of the situational

---

[22] *Op. cit.*, pp. 358 ff.
[23] *Honest to God* (Philadelphia: Westminster Press, 1963), p. 115.
[24] *Moral Law in Christian Social Ethics* (Richmond, Va.: John Knox Press, 1967), p. 19.
[25] Tillich, *op. cit.*, p. 70.

stripe, faith determines the *summum bonum,* i.e., *agapeic* concern, and reason (logic plus perception) determines everything else. That is to say, reason decides (*a*) what general maxims or "summary" rules best express the operational meaning of love generally or by and large, and (*b*) what the moral agent or "decider" is to do in any particular situation, aided by the wisdom of the general maxims but finally required to "make up his own mind."

## VI. *Response and Responsibility*

However all this gets worked out in the end, the main point is that the new morality is an ethic of living response to situations rather than of either laws applied or impromptu impulse. H. Richard Niebuhr satisfied situationists when he set out an "ethics of response" over against the usual alternatives of the teleological ethics of goal-seeking, as in utilitarianism, and the deontological ethics of rules-obeying, as in formal systems.[26] Concerning that old antinomy I can only repeat what I have said in *Situation Ethics:* ". . . situation ethics is closer to teleology, no doubt. Yet one's duty is to seek the goal of the most love possible in every situation, and one's goal is to do just that! . . . There is no difference in practice." [27] Niebuhr agreed with Martin Buber in whose language pure moral autonomy (antinomian extemporism) is only freedom-from, not freedom-for; while pure moral heteronomy is obligation without freedom. The ethics of response is autonomous in that it recognizes the claims of the self, or the moral agent, and it is heteronomous in that it responds to the claims or appeals of others.

It is only this latter form or meaning of heteronomy which situation ethics takes with complete seriousness. Response to persons and to their needs is its only predominant rule. We have to reject outright Kant's first formulation of the categorical imperative, i.e., "Act always on such a maxim as thou canst at the same time will to be a universal law." Our moral relativism excludes this. And as to the second formulation, "So act as to treat humanity, whether in thine own person or that of any other, in every case as an end withal, never as a means only," the calculus of *agapeic* concern with which Christian situationism confronts questions in *social* ethics, as distinguished from interpersonal ethics, might in some situations have to relativize even this formula—when it is seeking the greatest good possible for the

---

[26] *The Responsible Self* (New York: Harper & Row, 1963), pp. 47–68.
[27] P. 96.

greatest number of people possible. When faced with the ineluctable problem of the one and the many, which arises in ethics as in politics and every other area, it may sometimes be necessary to sacrifice or ignore the well-being of one or some for the sake of more.

Any version of "personalism" which, in putting human values first in the order of priorities, renders itself individualistic and romantic by absolutizing discrete persons one by one is ethically irresponsible. This is because it chooses *not* to respond to many human beings by responding without reservation to the nearest neighbor, on a basis of first come first served. However, there is not only "the situation" to be considered but the *network* of situations. It is true for both legalists and situationists that remote as well as immediate symbioses are to be considered.

Someone has pointed out that only a free man (which is the same as saying only a *man*) acts in response to concrete situations. The unfree man, the man of rules and principles, can see in any situation only what is similar to other situations, how they resemble each other. The free man uses principles but is never used by them. Being free, he can respond, whereas the unfree legalist can only react. For man-the-answerer the question is never *primarily* what is the goal or what is the law but what is the situation and what is the fitting response.

Let us meditate on Adolf Eichmann's self-defense when he was on trial in Jerusalem for genocide under Hitler's orders: "I did not *will* the murder of human beings. This mass slaughter is *solely* the responsibility of the political leaders. *My guilt lies in my obedience.* . . . Obedience is praised as a virtue, and I therefore request that my having obeyed be the sole fact that is taken into account." This is the petulant yet monstrous voice of legalism.

The man whose ethics is one of response sees persons, people, at the center of every situation, and his relation to them morally is the heart of the matter—the thing that counts. It is concern for people, and response to their needs as the first order value and norm, which characterizes the ethics of response or situation ethics Christianly practiced. Situation ethics calls for fitting action, not legal or impulsive action—in the same way that H. Richard Niebuhr did and before him A. C. Ewing.[28] Walter Muelder in his doughty attempt to meliorate the situationist vs. classical debate,[29] is right in citing Maurice Mandelbaum's phrasing in his *Phenomenology of Moral Experience:* ". . . the

---

[28] Cf. Ewing's *The Definition of the Good* (London: Macmillan & Co., 1947), pp. 150-158, 169-179.

[29] *Op. cit.*, p. 90.

concept of fittingness is the basis upon which we judge" and a right action is one "which is a fitting response to what we take to be the dominant element in the total situation" we are facing.[30] "The first element in the theory of responsibility," said Niebuhr, "is the idea of response." [31]

This way of understanding responsibility as response has had an interesting history in modern theological ethics, running through the Big B's—Buber, Brunner, Barth, Berdyaev, and Bonhoeffer. Apparently it was the Jew Buber who first effectively formulated this concept of responsibility in 1923 in his *I and Thou*,[32] and then the Protestants took it up. The core of the concept was relationship (J. H. Oldham expressed it as "real life is meeting" [33]), the thought that to be authentically personal we have to be in "dialogue" with others. To Brunner goes the credit for the first adequate theological construction of the idea, even though there were uses made of it by Gogarten, Heim, and the radical existentialist Eberhard Griesbach.

Harvey Cox suggests that "sin" can best be understood as apathy.[34] Sociologists (Max Weber, for example) have had a great deal to say about the social evil of *anomie*—just as the classical theologians condemned *acedia*. All are referring to the same thing—to indifference, neutrality, not caring, irresponsibility or *not responding*. (Let me repeat myself from earlier discussions: the opposite of love is not hate but indifference.) The essence of moral guilt, or "sin" theologically speaking, lies in the failure or refusal to respond to the needs and calls of others. *It does not lie in the failure to obey an abstract rule or principle.* Indeed it is impossible to be responsible, i.e., *responsive*, to any abstraction—be it principle or rule—just as we cannot respond to an object.

We can only respond to the calls and claims of people, of others who like ourselves are persons rather than things, subjects and not objects. If we follow or obey or submit to principles and rules it will only be because doing so in the situation coincides with person-concern. True responsibility is always a response to a call from others. As Dietrich Bonhoeffer put it:

> The responsible man is dependent on the man who is concretely his neighbor in his concrete possibility. His conduct is not established in

[30] Glencoe: Free Press, 1955; p. 61.   [31] *The Responsible Self*, p. 61.
[32] New York: Charles Scribner's Sons, 2nd ed., 1958 (trans. Ronald Gregor Smith).
[33] *Real Life Is Meeting* (New York: Seabury Press, 1953).
[34] *God's Revolution and Man's Responsibility* (Valley Forge: Judson Press, 1965), p. 37.

advance, once and for all, that is to say, as a matter of principle, but it arises with the given situation. He has no principle at his disposal which possesses absolute validity and which he has to put into effect fanatically, overcoming all the resistance which is offered to it by reality, but he sees in the given situation what is necessary and what is "right" for him to grasp and to do.[35]

Helmut Thieliecke's *Grenzsituation* in his *Theological Ethics,* i.e., his "borderline" idea, is a cautious and timid but substantial version of the same situation ethics.[36] In Niebuhr's language, the situationist is an answerer, not a seeker or an obeyer. This personalism is as basic to situation ethics as is its relativism.

## VII. *Complaints*

Those who still take their stand in the classical tradition, along with its conventional wisdom, complain that situation ethics downgrades or neglects such doctrinal categories as grace and sin, guilt and forgiveness; and such moral categories as duty and self-denial. In the teeth of the evidence one critic has actually accused *Situation Ethics* of dropping obligation—presumably because he understands obligation to be duty-bound obedience to principles rather than loving care for persons. In the *legalistic* sense there is, confessedly and professedly, no "obligation" in situation ethics: it is admittedly "guilty" of treating all rules freely, though not lightly. As for the meaning of duty, one's duty is to seek or serve the goal of love (which H. Richard Niebuhr in *The Purpose of the Church and Its Ministry* has said is the Church's mission[37]), and one's goal or purpose is to "obey" or serve love's requirements as fully as may be in every situation. Therefore, in a real sense, duty ethics becomes the same as goal ethics, to be realized or worked out in response ethics. The situational methodology transforms the concept of duty, freeing it from the straitjacket of rules, yet it does not erase or drop them. And nobody could seriously examine the notion of an *agapeic* calculus, especially the propositions "Self-love means to love oneself only for the neighbor's sake," and "We are to aim at the greatest amount of love for the greatest number of neighbors," and still assert that there is no place in situation ethics for self-denial or for social concern.

There is only one "sin" just as there is only one "virtue," once

---

[35] *Ethics* (New York: Macmillan Co., 1965), p. 227.
[36] Vol. I, *Foundations* (Philadelphia: Fortress Press, 1966), p. 482.
[37] New York: Harper & Row, 1956; pp. 27 ff.

we see with the situationist's eye that ethical value or import is predicated of human acts and not a property *in* them. We "sin" when we knowingly betray love, when we cheat on the principle of loving concern. To be egocentric is the "original" sin—the source or basic sin. The question may arise, "*How* does one sin?" In some situations the answer could be, "By telling a lie." In other situations, "By telling the truth." Telling a lie, as such and in itself, is not a sin; nor is telling the truth a virtue. The truth is to be told not for *truth's* sake but for love's sake—and the same for lies. No deed is *malum* or *bonum in se,* only *malum* or *bonum per accidens, ex casu.* Therefore as better words than "sin" and "virtue," we ought to use "malevolence" and "benevolence." And thus to understand "sin" in terms of will or intention or attitude, rather than legalistically as a certain kind of action or deed, radically reduces the *materia gravis* of contrition. It means that we may be accused (by self or others) only when what we have done was a witting denial of loving concern, no matter "what" we have done—lie, steal, fornicate, or anything else "defined" as sinful. This is assuredly a radical criticism of and departure from classical penitential theology, and a narrowing of the range and frequency of the forgiving-business, of *mea culpa* and *peccavi, peccavi.* On this basis there is less call for the *absolvo te.*

Concerning the doctrinal category of grace, is there really any need to say anything more than that a Christian decision-maker *believes* that by his faith in God's love, i.e., by his faith in *God,* his own rational powers of analysis are sharpened and motivated to their "logonomous" task? This surely is grace—understood in a fashion consistent with both freedom and power. And so with "sin"— for what is sin but irresponsibility, the betrayal of *agapé?* (If it is "original" sin in the sense of finite man's egocentricity which is in view, let it suffice to say that there is nothing perfectionist about the situationist's strategy—either as to his claims for competence or his expectations. Indeed it is the relativism of his method-theory, about both his actions and his moral rules, which accounts for his distrust of all theories of transrational conscience.)

*Guilt* seems obviously to be a term that figures in the discourse of situational ethics, although in a different and less doctrinaire way than in legalistic ethics, for it arises as a result of failing love's call and *not from failing or violating a rule.* This means that guilt becomes more extensive in our lives yet less a matter of legal specifics or bills of particulars as in juridical ethics. On this view—the view that guilt is for failing *agapeic* concern—we have less clear reason for remorse and much more for regret. No longer will we accuse ourselves for breaking rules when we do it for love's sake, knowingly and freely and responsively. And that much, at least, is a reduction of the false guilt engendered by legalism. We never need forgiveness for breaking a rule unless it was done as a betrayal of *agapé*.

How revealingly insistent is the demand that if we situationists are to make love our boss principle, then we have to spell it out in some kind of operational or "nuts and bolts" terms. What this really means is "in some kind of *rules.*" The demand is for specifying what love is and what it is not, to "delineate" it. Here is the language of a legalism that will not be downed. When H. Richard Niebuhr once attempted to reduce "love"—which I would safeguard by holding it to be precisely a formal principle without content—he ended up with only four generalized entailments, all of them as nonspecific and nonoperational as "love" itself. They were *rejoicing* in others; *gratitude* to them for being; *reverence* of them rather than the possessive feelings of *philia* and *eros;* and *loyalty.* To reject these would be like opposing mother love and championing sin. They simply provide no "delineation" at all of who does what and when and under what circumstances.

There is a kind of persistent morphology of response and reaction to most new developments. Situation ethics is certainly not new; it is just that it is managing at last to break through legalism's defenses. The "new morality" is as old as Jesus' and Paul's revolt against Pharisaism and law ethics on behalf of freedom and grace. Franz Böckle in his *Law and Conscience* is able to see that it goes back to Luther as "a type of relative situation-ethics," [38] but actually it is the very *ur*-Christian ethic! Nonetheless the reaction to it follows the classic pattern of protest, as William James once pointed out in the case of pragmatism. First the retort is, "Nonsense. Ridiculous. It's perfectly absurd." Then it becomes, "It's obvious. A platitude. Not important." And at last it takes the form, "Very true. Essential. That's what I've been saying all along." But the new morality and its situational method are as yet only somewhere between stages one and two, by all reports.

## VIII. *Issues: Old and New Morality*

Out of the continuing debate about situation ethics I find certain issues which persist in explicit or implicit form. The debate has at least had the merit of provoking a re-examination of basic questions

[38] New York: Sheed and Ward, 1966; p. 93.

in a fresh manner. Leaving aside all theological rhetoric, and going to the marrow of innumerable complaints, reservations, challenges, and denials, there seem to me to be at least six core-problems. I simply list them:

1. Whether freedom and responsibility, in their paradoxical relation, necessarily presuppose each other.
2. Whether human deeds are inherently or only contingently good or evil, right or wrong.
3. Whether human acts are related to moral ideals as duty-bound or as goal-oriented.
4. Whether response ethics is an alternative to duty ethics and goal ethics.
5. Whether the spirit of ethical norms, or their letter, is to be followed.
6. Whether the locus of control and authority in moral acts is internal or external to the agent.

## IX. *The Context Again*

In the fall of 1966 a world congress of "evangelical" Christians was held in Berlin. Needless to say they did not conceive evangelism in *a new* way. Nor, indeed, did they see theology or morality in a new way. On the contrary, they concluded that there are four movements of life and thought today which are to be condemned. I cite them here because I seriously believe they represent a "package" from out of the classical metaphysical, legalistic, and dogmatic past. They condemned liberal theology, biblical criticism, the ecumenical movement, and situation ethics (morality "based on love" rather than on the "law of Scripture"). Here we have the full theological content of our problem in one coherent declaration.

But there is another part of the whole context—the "secular" part. G. F. Woods has listed the challenges to us in *A Defense of Theological Ethics*—challenges coming from the side of secular humanism.[39] There are several of a metaphysical kind—notably, and most vitally, doubt about the very existence of God. But on the side of moral challenges to theological ethics he lists two chief ones. The first is an attempt to establish the autonomy of moral principles, freeing them of reliance upon theological metaethics. It is doubtful whether this will long remain a serious philosophical debate since on all sides (except for

---

[39] Cambridge, Eng.: Cambridge University Press, 1966; p. 5.

a small party of "natural theology" champions) faith is agreed to be beyond the reach of empirical reasoning and of anything but speculation. But the second moral challenge is an attempt to establish the autonomy of the moral agent himself. The humanist wants to free the agent of "spiritual" controls and crutches, such as righteousness understood to be known by "special revelation" and under "eternal rules," i.e., fiat legalism. What is important to note is that on this second score, as compared to the first, the distance is not so great or so wide between the secular humanist and the rational love-ethics of Christian situationists. Their ultimate commitments differ, but their immediate methods are the same.

As a "Scripture" for the open-endedness of situation ethics turn to Romans 14:14. When Paul said, "I know and am persuaded in the Lord Jesus that nothing is unclean of itself," what he meant by "unclean" (once we step out of the situation in and to which he spoke), and what he could well have said, is "immoral." Nothing is immoral in itself, intrinsically. What love is, what morality is, always depends on the situation.

# 13

# Ideals, Roles, and Rules

## BASIL MITCHELL

"Christianly speaking . . . the norm or measure by which any thought or action is to be judged a success or failure, i.e. right or wrong, is love," writes Joseph Fletcher.[1]

There is a party game called "Adverbs" in which those present divide into two teams. One team, which goes out of the room, has to think of an adverb. When they have done this they are admitted to the room one by one and asked to perform a specified action "in the manner of the adverb." The other team has then to guess what the adverb is. The unsophisticated choose a word that is easy to act and an action that is easy to perform in the manner indicated by the word, e.g., the word is "angrily" and the action is shutting the door. But with more experienced players the fun consists in the one team choosing a word which will test the ability of the actors and the other team thinking of actions in the performance of which it is hard to evince emotion at all or which are normally associated with one very specific emotion. For example the word is "lovingly" and the action is putting on the kettle or strangling your wife.

In the game one of two things happens. Either the actor is baffled by the task of performing *this* action in a loving manner and communicates nothing to the audience; or he brings off a *tour de force* by which he performs the detestable deed with an impressive show of "tender loving care." The moral that might be drawn from

[1] *Situation Ethics* (Philadelphia: Westminster Press, 1966), p. 43.

the first actor's failure is that there are some *sorts* of action that cannot be performed lovingly. The moral to be drawn from the second actor's success might be that there are no actions that cannot be performed lovingly. Neither lends support to those situationists who wish to insist that love is the sole guide to action and that there are no sorts of action which are intrinsically incompatible with love.

It will be objected, and rightly, that there are such important differences between this game and life that the game is useless for purposes of illustration. The actors, restricted to dumb-show, cannot tell us their motives or explain their policies; and, even if they could, no context is provided which could render them intelligible. In real life, however, we can learn that the wife is suffering from an incurable disease and that the husband's motive is indeed love, because he wants to save her from further suffering. Love, as a policy, may dictate actions which are not ordinarily expressive of love and which, even in their context, do not express love in that comparatively straightforward sense of "express" in which, for example, an embrace expresses it. Love as a policy is an "orientation of the will."

But if love is to serve as "norm or measure," certain acts must be ruled out by it, at least in the sense that *in a given situation* love must indicate what is or is not to be done. Clearly, unless it does so, it cannot provide a guide for action. Love cannot help me to decide between alternatives if any action I might think of doing can, as well as any other, be inspired by love. Professor Fletcher believes that love, and only love, can determine our moral choices. But he does not make it very clear how love does it. Sometimes he seems to be propounding a straightforward act-utilitarianism. "In Christian situation ethics nothing is worth anything in and of itself. It gains or acquires its value only because it happens to help persons (thus being good) or to hurt persons (thus being bad)." [2] Insofar as this is his view, two familiar questions arise: (*a*) How are we to tell what is to count as "help" or "hurt," this being one of the issues about which people of different moral, and even metaphysical, standpoints disagree, (*b*) Does possession of a particular motive, in this case love, guarantee a right answer to the question, "What in this situation will help most and hurt least those persons involved?"

The classical utilitarians answered the first question simply and clearly, if not convincingly, by identifying "help" and "hurt" with "pleasure" and "pain," but Fletcher explicitly repudiates this solution. "For although the 'love ethic' . . . takes over from Bentham and

---

[2] *Ibid.*, p. 59.

Mill the strategic principles of 'the greatest good of the greatest number' ... it reshapes the 'good' of the utilitarians, replacing their pleasure principle with agapé."[3] So we are to act always from the motive of love and this means to act in such a way as to produce not pleasure but love. Always to seek to bring about a situation in which people love one another is certainly an intelligible policy, but it can scarcely be anyone's *entire* policy, for the question will always arise, what ends love seeks to achieve. In the case of euthanasia, for example, two people, the genuineness of whose love is not in doubt, may differ as to what ought to be done, and a single individual may be deeply perplexed about it, his love intensifying rather than resolving his perplexity. Anyone knows who has experienced such a dilemma that love is not enough. Love ensures that the only question before the lover's mind is "What can I do to help?" It does not answer the question. To answer it requires moral insight and to say this is to reopen all the controversies that moral philosophers have engaged in.

There is, as Fletcher notices, a close analogy with Kant's ethic of duty. I remember at the beginning of World War II being involved, like many of my generation in England who had been attracted to pacifism, in the agonizing decision whether to fight or register as a conscientous objector. A friend of mine, a noted Kantian scholar, was extremely puzzled by my state of mind. "There is no difficulty in deciding what is one's duty," he said. "The difficulty is only in doing it." "How do I decide then?" I exclaimed, and he replied, "Act as a man would act in whom reason had full command over the passions." I complained that this advice was useless unless accompanied by some indication of what such a reasonable man would choose or upon what principles he would make his choice. Professor Fletcher does, indeed, use language which echoes Kant. "Love is not a substantive—nothing of the kind. It is a principle, a "formal" principle expressing what type of real actions Christians are to call good. . . . It is the *only* principle that always obliges us in conscience."[4] Kant attempted to discover a pattern of ethical reasoning which would provide an answer to the question, "What ought I to do?" without presuming any prior agreement about ends, and perhaps this is what Professor Fletcher also intends. He may, that is, be advocating in a much less precise form the sort of moral theory so brilliantly worked out in Professor R. M. Hare's *Freedom and Reason*.[5] Professor Hare's basic

[3] *Ibid.*, p. 95.      [4] *Ibid.*, p. 60.
[5] New York: Oxford University Press, 1965. See especially chap. 6.

contention is that moral questions can be decided by the use of golden-rule arguments in association with knowledge of the facts of the case and the inclinations of those involved. The Golden Rule, "Do unto others as you would have them do unto you," is a scriptural formulation of the law of love, so that Professor Hare's position could well be regarded as a form of agapism. Hare warns us against a too literal interpretation of the common forms of expression—which constantly recur in arguments of this type—"How would you like it . . . ?" and "Do as you would be done by." He says, "We shall make the nature of the argument clearer, if when we are asking B to imagine himself in the position of his victim, we phrase our question, never in the form 'What *would* you say, or feel, or think, or how *would* you like it, if you were he?' but always in the form 'What *do* you say (*in propria persona*) about a hypothetical case in which you are in your victim's position?' . . . To involve him in contradiction, we have to show that he *now* holds an opinion about the hypothetical case, which is inconsistent with his opinion about the actual case."[6] Thus a Nazi might be asked whether he is prepared to be gassed in the hypothetical case of his being a Jew. Since he does not want to be gassed he is committed, insofar as he accepts the golden-rule argument, to condemning the gassing of Jews.

Professor Hare regards arguments of this sort as being concerned with the *interests* of all parties, and it would, of course, be generally agreed that it is not as a rule in someone's interest to die. However, even this may sometimes be a controversial question. In the case of the wife suffering from an incurable disease, is it or is it not in her interest to die? Hare himself relates the concept of "interest" very closely to what the individual wants. "To have an interest is, crudely speaking, for there to be something which one wants, or is likely in the future to want, or which is (or is likely to be) a means necessary or sufficient for the attainment of something which one wants (or is likely to want)."[7] "Is it in the patient's interest to die?" becomes (with the above qualifications) "Does the patient want to die?" or, perhaps, "Do I, on the hypothesis that I am the patient, want to die?" Hare would not, of course, take an affirmative answer to this question as justifying euthanasia without further ado. For there are other considerations:

> For example, it may be very much in the interest of a doctor to be freed from a troublesome patient; or it may be very much in the interest of a wife that her husband be allowed to die, so that she can have his money

[6] *Ibid.*, p. 108.  [7] *Ibid.*, p. 122.

and marry her lover. There are so many temptations here that neither in law nor in morality is it safe to say to people, "Consider the individual case, and, after weighing the interests of the parties, decide what is for the best." For in a great many cases people will weight the scales in their own favour. Therefore we need to have very strict and comparatively simple general principles and to stick to them—because of man's sinfulness. . . . For example, it is a very good principle that everyone in general and doctors in particular ought to preserve life wherever possible. But, it may be asked, are there not classes of cases in which to preserve life is not for the best—in which a person charged with the care of a sick man, even if he loved the sick man as himself (or, more correctly, especially if he loved the sick man as himself), would think it wrong to prolong his suffering. . . . If it were possible to formulate exceptions to our principle which were sufficiently clear and comprehensible not to give rise to abuses, there would be no practical objection to admitting them, since the principle has a practical purpose and is not an ultimate unalterable moral law.[8]

It is along such lines as these that Professor Fletcher's situation ethics could best be developed. One has, however, an uneasy feeling that Professor Hare's "powerful engine for producing moral agreement" is so constructed as to yield only answers which are conformable to the moral standpoint of a mid-twentieth-century Anglo-American liberal intellectual.[9] Professor Fletcher, indeed, makes no bones about this. Among the presuppositions of situation ethics, he tells us, is Pragmatism whose "idiom expresses the genius and ethos or style of life of American culture and of the techno-scientific era."[10] It may be that Christian ethics really has for the first time achieved full development in our own intellectual climate, but we ought, perhaps, to be a little cautious in advancing the claim. What do Professor Hare and Professor Fletcher have to say of moral theories that do not conform to their chosen pattern? Professor Hare relegates them to the realm of "Ideals"[11] and Professor Fletcher to that of "Ideology."[12] Professor Hare, with characteristic restraint, resists the temptation to say that moral questions can arise only where other people's interests (in his sense of the word) are involved. For there are "two distinct grounds on which we can commend or condemn actions, one of

---

[8] *Decisions about Life and Death: A Problem in Modern Medicine*, pp. 22–23. A Report published for the Church Assembly Board for Social Responsibility, Church Information Office, Church House, Westminster S.W.1, England.

[9] It is only fair to add that Hare anticipates this objection and denies its force. See *Freedom and Reason*, p. 192.

[10] *Situation Ethics*, p. 42.

[11] *Freedom and Reason*, chap. 8.  [12] *Ibid.*, pp. 137 ff.

which is connected with the interests of other people, and the other with ideals of human excellence." [13] Questions about ideals, he holds, cannot be settled by golden-rule arguments; indeed they often cannot be settled at all. Ideals have their place in human life. The man who allows his ideals to override the interests of others is called by Hare "the fanatic." Thus the Nazi is a fanatic if, in reply to the question, "Do you, in the hypothetical case that you are a Jew, wish to be gassed?" he replied, "Yes," for this is to rate the purity of the Aryan race as an ideal transcending all interests, even his own. This attitude would generally be regarded and condemned as "fanatical" by most people. But we need to remember that the term "fanatical" is to be applied to anyone who allows ideals, however estimable, to override interests in Hare's sense of the word. To take Hare's own example:

> Consider the question . . . of whether it is wrong for a pretty girl to earn good money by undressing herself at a "strip-club" for the pleasure of an audience of middle-aged business men. If this is not a moral question in an accepted sense of the word, it is hard to say what would be. . . . Yet those who call such exhibitions immoral do not do so because of their effect on other people's interests; for, since everybody gets what he or she wants, nobody's interests are harmed. They are likely, rather, to use such words as "degrading.". . . Such conduct offends against an ideal of human excellence held by many people; that is why they condemn it.[14]

The question is, given that ideals must not be allowed to override the interests of others, What sort of authority attaches to this branch of morality? It looks as if people's wants, so long as they are universalizable, must always take precedence over ideals on pain of fanaticism. To hold this is to maintain that it is more important, morally speaking, that people should do as they want than that they should conform to a well-founded ideal of human excellence. Many morally reflective people would reverse the priority. They would think that the girl ought not to engage in strip-tease, even if she wants and even if the audience and the management want her to. If this is fanaticism, it is a much more widespread and more reputable phenomenon than Professor Hare appears to think. That this is so is perhaps obscured in Hare's discussion by the fact that he uses the word "interest" in a special sense. As we normally use the word "interest" it is, of course, true that we do not think we ought to follow our ideals at the expense of other people's interests and we might well agree to condemn as "fanatical" anyone who did. But,

---

[13] *Ibid.*, p. 147.          [14] *Ibid.*

as we ordinarily use the word, a person who adopted an ideal of chastity would not think it in the girl's interest to earn her living in this way. In other words, our conception of people's interests is normally related to our conception of human excellence where this includes but is not restricted to moral excellence. The question in dispute is not simply a terminological one; the difference about the use of the word "interest" reflects a moral difference about the weight to be given to wants as such. In maintaining that ideals must not be allowed to affect our conception of interests, which must be interpreted solely in terms of desires, Hare is, in spite of his protestations to the contrary, embodying a certain type of liberal morality in his supposedly neutral method of moral argument.

I embarked on this discussion of Hare's argument in *Freedom and Reason* because it seemed to offer the best prospects of developing Fletcher's contention that love is a formal principle and the only principle that obliges in conscience. What seems clear in the light of it is that it is a necessary condition of a loving attitude that one should adopt the Golden Rule, but it is not a sufficient condition of enlightened moral choice. For a difference may still arise between two people who adopt the rule as to what really does help or harm themselves and others.

Professor Fletcher insists, and surely he is right here, that love's concern is in the end with persons, and this leads him to distrust forms of legalism which subordinate the interests of persons to respect for the moral law. But it is not easy to discover what he thinks is the proper place of rules in Christian (or any other) ethics. The "legalist," who is his chief object of criticism, apparently holds the following beliefs, (1) that there are absolute moral rules, which may never be broken, (2) that even when the breaking of a moral rule is justifiable, there remains an element of evil in the situation. The evil may be excused but not eliminated, (3) that moral rules are, in some sense, "given" or "objective," (4) that there are some moral rules which are universal in the sense of being recognized by all men, (5) that moral decisions can be "prefabricated," (6) that it makes sense to ask such questions as "Is premarital intercourse wrong?" Fletcher himself presumably rejects all these beliefs. Yet he strenuously resists the charge that he is an antinomian.

What then does Fletcher believe about rules? His *official* view is that there are, as he puts it, no rules, only maxims,[15] and these are to be understood as rules of thumb, like "Punt on fourth down" or

[15] *Situation Ethics*, p. 55.

"Take a pitch when the count is three balls." Such rules are useful summaries of experience, which the sensible man will do well to defer to in the absence of good reason to the contrary. If he knows enough about the situation before him to decide on the basis of the facts, he will disregard the rule without compunction. (Since the value of these rules is that they incapsulate the accumulated experience of mankind, it is not clear why some of them, at least, should not be "objective" and universally recognized). I call this Fletcher's *official* doctrine because he sometimes departs from it. His most striking departure occurs in his discussion of abortion,[16] where, after criticizing the Catholic moral theologians for "absolutizing their prohibition of abortion *absolutely*," he sketches the situationist's attitude to the problem and bases it, apparently, on the ground that *"no unwanted and unintended baby should ever be born."* [17] The author's italics suggest that this is not a momentary lapse, but that here is a moral principle which he is prepared to "absolutize absolutely." He nowhere else goes as far as this, but he does make other admissions which take him well beyond his official theory. For example, "Agapeic love is not a one-to-one affair. . . . Faced as we always are in the social complex with a web of duties, i.e., giving what is 'due' to others, love is compelled to be calculating, careful, prudent, distributive." [18]

What is this "social complex with a web of duties"? At the very least it must consist of those obligations which we have in virtue of the many and diverse roles we occupy in society, e.g., husband, wife, parent, child, teacher, pupil, employer, employee, and those more general rules which are necessary to the existence of any society. These constitute a "web" because they criss-cross one another and limit our individual freedom of action in innumerable ways. Indeed it is chiefly in relation to such a "social complex" that there arises a "situation" calling for moral decision. If I am asked for advice about a problem of conscience my first step is to ask, "What is the situation?" and I should not regard the question as satisfactorily answered if nothing was said about the agent's relationship to the other people concerned, what he had promised them or led them to expect, how frank he had been with them, how they would be justified in interpreting his actions. If the situation is awkward, delicate, distressing, problematic, it will be so largely because of conflicts or misunder-

---

[16] *Ibid.*, pp. 38–39. Contrast p. 43: "The situationist avoids words like 'never.'"

[17] It is not entirely clear how this is intended to be taken, but it bears a strong resemblance to such a "legalistic" principle as "No innocent person should ever be judicially punished."

[18] *Situation Ethics*, p. 89.

standings, doubts or dilemmas arising out of the varying roles these people occupy in relation to one another. To be sensitive to the situation is to appreciate all this and what it means for the participants. If a playgoer cannot understand how the characters are related to one another and what obligations they have incurred, he simply does not know the situation in which the dramatist has placed them.[19] Thus we find ourselves in situations in which we can discharge our duty in one role only by neglecting our duty in another; but we are never justified in regarding such duties as irrelevant or of no independent weight. And this is not simply a legalistic prejudice.

It is hard to see how a society of any complexity could survive or be worth preserving if its members approached their obligations in the spirit of Fletcher's official theory. What would become of the institution of marriage if the marriage vow were taken to mean "I will remain faithful unto you until the situation appears to me to call for adultery"? Or if parental responsibility were interpreted to mean "We will care for you so long as circumstances seem to justify the policy"? The classical utilitarians with their emphasis upon "reliability, predictability, certainty" saw clearly enough that this would not do, and would not do precisely because it would be against the interests of all concerned. Hence it is an essential part of our concept of "duty" or "obligation" that we are, as we say, "bound" to act in accordance with them. This does not necessarily imply that there are no circumstances in which we may break our obligations or be freed from them, but it does imply that we are not entitled, insofar as we are bound by such obligations, to do "what love requires in the situation" if this means acting solely on a simple utilitarian calculus.

It is in this respect that moral obligations differ from rules of thumb. The baseball player sticks to the maxim "Take a pitch when the count is three balls" only when the situation is not clear enough for him to decide his policy on the facts of the case. When it *is* clear enough, he does not regard the rule of thumb as in any sense a reason for acting; and then he has, of course, no compunction whatever in disregarding it. But for the husband contemplating adultery, however well he knows the situation, his duty to his wife remains, at the very least, a consideration to be reckoned with and normally an overriding one.

[19] Cf. the description in Scholes, *Oxford Companion to Music,* of the situation at the beginning of *Figaro*: "Figaro . . . has entered the service of the Count and wants to marry Susanna, the Countess's maid. The Count, however, is running after the maid. Figaro once promised to marry another—Marcellina . . . and she appears to claim her due. . . ."

Curiously (in view of its familiarity as a theme in moral philosophy) Fletcher only once betrays any recognition that such a view of moral rules is possible and then dismisses it without argument. He asserts roundly: "If the choice is between rescuing your own father and a medical genius who has discovered a cure for a common fatal disease, you carry out the genius if you understand *agapé*. This is agapeic calculus. Sir David Ross tried to find a middle course between Kant's legalism and Mill's utility. It was not a successful effort." [20] Yet Sir David Ross, in recognizing a "special duty" to parents, was able to do justice to the fact that such a duty, although it may sometimes be overridden, may never be ignored.

The same confusion is apparent in his treatment of those more general ethical principles to which (*pace* Fletcher) all men subscribe, that one should tell the truth, keep promises, respect life, etc. They must, in his view, either be unbreakable rules or mere "maxims" which in any situation can be not only overridden but totally superseded by love. "All else, all other generalities (e.g., 'One should tell the truth' and 'One should respect life') are at most only *maxims,* never rules. For the situationist there are no rules—none at all." [21] "If a lie is told unlovingly, it is wrong, evil; if it is told in love it is good, right." [22] "For the classical moralists . . . suicide and lying are always wrong regardless of circumstances, even though loving concern might excuse such actions in the situation." [23] It is legalistic, he tells us, to ask such questions as, "Is it right to have pre-marital intercourse, gamble, steal, abort, lie, defraud, break contracts, *et cetera, ad nauseam?*" [24] In all these cases it is assumed that to say of a class of actions that actions of that class are wrong is to presuppose that there are no circumstances in which an action of that class is justified; and that, unless this is so, there is no point at all in calling such actions wrong. The fact is, surely, that "wrong" is systematically ambiguous. We say of a particular action in its full context that it is wrong if in all the circumstances of the case it ought not to be done. We also say of a type of action, such as telling a lie, that it is wrong, meaning by this, not that there are no circumstances in which it would be right, but that there is a more or less heavy burden of proof on whoever wants to justify it. It remains possible that there are certain types of action which are wrong in all circumstances, which can never in any circumstances be justified or excused, but one is not committed to this view by rejection of "situationism" as Fletcher interprets it.

[20] *Situation Ethics,* p. 115.  [21] *Ibid.,* p. 55.
[22] *Ibid.,* p. 65.  [23] *Ibid.,* p. 67.  [24] *Ibid.,* p. 124.

Fletcher constantly complains that, for the "legalist," moral decisions are "prefabricated" and he contrasts this with the spontaneity of "situationism." The "legalist," he argues, is reduced to the absurdity of framing "rules for breaking rules." Perhaps some systems of casuistry are not unfairly characterized in this way, but the *epikeia* of the ancients, which Fletcher commends, was essentially a means of correcting the law where it did not fit the facts of the particular case—"to say what the legislator himself would have said had he been present, and would have put into his law if he had known." [25] It does not dispense with law, but presupposes it. The agonizing dilemmas which, as Fletcher constantly reminds us, love may sometimes be faced with *are* dilemmas precisely because there is no solution which does not involve an action that is objectively wrong. Fletcher's failure to see this involves him at times in moral obtuseness of a quite frightening order. Thus he writes, "A situationist might or might not agree on particular exceptions like capital punishment, but he would be sure to protest that, in principle, even killing 'innocent' people might be right. Mother Maria, for example, who killed herself. What of Bonhoeffer's own decision that Hitler was not innocent and should be assassinated? Would he actually have turned his back on a man caught hopelessly on the burning wreckage of a plane, who begged to be shot?" [26] Here Fletcher is challenging the principle that one ought not to kill innocent people. As usual it is not clear whether he is claiming that the victim's innocence is irrelevant or that it may be overridden. On the simple act-utilitarianism which he seems to be advocating, whether or not Mother Maria ought to have offered her life for another's turns on the question whether her life was more valuable than that of the unremarkable girl for whose sake she sacrificed it. We may be sure that this is not how she saw it. It was a spontaneous expression of self-sacrificial love and it is surely as such that Fletcher admires it, whatever his "official" theory. Though it would be a matter of some complexity to draw the necessary distinctions, it seems intuitively clear that it is not a case of suicide, so that Mother Maria's act does not in any way illustrate the principle in dispute. How are we intended to take the reference to Bonhoeffer? It looks as if he is being criticized for wishing to settle the question of Hitler's guilt before assenting to his assassination; and, given Fletcher's act-utilitarianism, the criticism stands, for, if Hitler's assassination would have ended the war, what difference could it have made whether or not he was innocent? But, supposing he had

[25] Aristotle, *Nicomachean Ethics* 1137$^b$ 22 (trans. Ross).
[26] *Situation Ethics*, p. 75.

good reason to believe that the assassination of Churchill would have ended the war, would Churchill's innocence have been irrelevant?

Bonhoeffer, Fletcher apparently goes on to argue, is committed, if he allows innocence to count, to refusing the trapped airman's plea for a merciful death. Manifestly this is not so. He may regard his principle as being capable of being overridden and this case as one in which it should be overridden. There is no *point,* he may judge, in letting this man live, when a painful death is inevitable and there is no way, short of killing him, by which his sufferings can be relieved. Even if he believes that it is an absolute principle that one should not kill the innocent, he can question whether he is obliged to prolong the act of dying.

Fletcher's approach, in spite of his constant emphasis upon the uniqueness and complexity of the particular case, seems to lead him in practice to obliterate the morally relevant features of these different situations. It is not surprising, therefore, that he fails to distinguish also between admitting a rule to which there are exceptions (as self-defense and military service are exceptions to the rule against killing), and allowing a rule to be overridden or, to put it differently, justifying the breaking of it. If, for example, we allow with A. C. Ewing[27] that judicial punishment of the innocent may sometimes be permissible (e.g., a minor penalty imposed to placate a tyrant), this is not to say that the rule has exceptions. Where there is an exception, the rule does not apply; where breaking it is justified, the rule applies, but is overridden. The latter case, but not the former, calls for compunction and, perhaps, recompense.

Professor Fletcher insists that moral decisions cannot be "prefabricated" and that there cannot be "rules for breaking rules." He is right in stressing the irreducible element of judgment in moral decision. We must be sensitive to all the morally relevant features of the situation, and love bids us cultivate this judgment. Nevertheless there is a sense in which moral rules are and ought to be prefabricated, even if particular moral decisions cannot be. The metaphor is tolerably exact. Just as sections of a building are prefabricated in order to guarantee an acceptable standard of workmanship and obviate the waste of time and thought on designing similar parts for similar positions, so moral rules enable us to cope with innumerable recurring situations without the labor of deliberation and the likelihood of error. This is true even of Fletcher's rules of thumb. It is no accident

---

[27] *Second Thoughts in Moral Philosophy* (London: Routledge and Kegan Paul, 1959), p. 126.

that in the eighteenth century, when local builders were content to copy the design books of the leading architects, the resulting townscapes were aesthetically more pleasing than they have become since every architect sees each commission as an opportunity to express his own authentic vision. Successful moral innovations are even rarer. There is, of course, a danger that concern for our manifold duties and obligations may decline into an inflexible moralism, which blinds us to the human needs which in the end morality exists to serve; but there is the equal and opposite danger that by a myopic preoccupation with "the situation" we may overlook the entire social context which alone makes "the situation" intelligible.

I have been concerned to argue that in ethics love is not enough; it requires not only thought (which Fletcher concedes), but specifically moral thought; and not only that, but some decision as to what human ends are or are not worth seeking. Love of itself cannot guarantee a right answer to the question "What in this situation will help most and hurt least those persons involved?" There is a pervasive assumption throughout Fletcher's book that the "facts of the case" in themselves are always unproblematic and that there will, among reasonable men, be no difficulty in determining what will help or harm people, what is fair or unfair to them. The truth is, surely, that in many fields these are matters of deep controversy to which people's attitudes are influenced by their religious and metaphysical beliefs; so that there is little prospect of discussing moral questions fruitfully without a careful and sympathetic endeavor to understand the different forms of thought in terms of which they are interpreted. Thus Fletcher asks, "Is adultery wrong? To ask this is to ask a mare's nest question. . . . One can only respond 'I don't know. Maybe. Give me a case. Describe a real situation.' " [28] Presumably in any real situation involving the possibility of adultery, at least one of the parties is married. This is a fact, but it is a *different* fact for someone who holds that marriage is a sacrament and for one who sees marriage as a purely contractual relationship; different again according to varying interpretations of the obligations it imposes. So too when Fletcher asserts, "If people do not believe it is wrong to have sex relations outside marriage, it isn't unless they hurt themselves, their partners or others," [29] this apparently simple criterion is far from easy to apply. One's assessment of the extent, degree, and character of hurt will be radically affected by one's whole conception of the nature and purpose of the institution of marriage. If this is so,

[28] *Situation Ethics*, pp. 142–143.  [29] *Ibid.*, p. 140.

the further question arises as to whether there are any specifically Christian answers to moral questions or not. Is there any distinctively Christian ethic? In his chapter "The End of Ideology," in *Situation Ethics,* Professor Fletcher makes it clear that, in his own view, Christianity has nothing distinctive to say about the *content* of ethics (although there is, he thinks, something special about the quality of Christian love as a motive). This is much too large a question to take up at the end of this chapter, but it is perhaps worth suggesting that Fletcher's conception of theology predisposes him to a negative answer. Like many Protestant theologians he is overfond of dichotomies and we are not surprised to be told that

> When we get right down to it there are really only two ways to approach "religious knowledge" or belief—two kinds of theological epistemology. One is theological *naturalism*, in which reason adduces or deduces faith propositions from human experience and natural phenomena; nature yields the evidences, natural reason grasps them. Natural theology, so-called, and "natural law" ethics are examples of this method. The other approach is theological positivism (or "positive theology") in which faith propositions are "posited" or affirmed voluntaristically rather than rationalistically. . . . Thus Christian ethics "posits" faith in God and *reasons* out what obedience to his commandment to love requires in any situation.[30]

If there *are* only these two approaches, it would seem to follow that the Christian revelation can in no way contribute to our understanding of the world, for the "naturalist" seeks to derive morality from the world as apprehended by "reason" and the "positivist" has to apply a revealed morality of love to the world as scientifically understood. Such traditional Christian conceptions as the doctrine of marriage as a sacrament or as an "order of creation" can be accommodated in neither scheme. These are theological concepts which cannot be discovered in "nature" (unless "nature" is thought of as divinely ordered) and which cannot be derived from the law of love alone. They presuppose a whole theology—to use an old-fashioned term, a *"revealed* theology." But such a theology is not something that we can "posit" or not as we choose. It is a complex conceptual scheme which can, to some extent at least, be judged by its internal consistency and explanatory force. To talk, as Christians commonly do, of "the purpose of marriage" or "the function of sex" is to invoke a teleological theory of ethics based upon a theistic metaphysic, which is not shared by the humanist. This way of thinking cannot be

---

[30] *Ibid.,* pp. 46–47.

maintained in complete independence of the observed facts of human life as studied by psychologists and sociologists nor, on its own terms, is there any reason why it should be. For the God of revelation is also the God of creation.

All this Professor Fletcher would dismiss as "ideology," and he does indeed extrude it pretty thoroughly from his account of Christian ethics. Into the room thus swept and garnished there enters, not unexpectedly, "the genius or ethos or style of life of American culture and of the techno-scientific era" (interpreted in a way that, one feels, does less than justice to the influence of orthodox Christianity in the United States). As so easily happens, Professor Fletcher, in the act of banning ideology, accepts uncritically the current ideology of his time and place. It is perhaps wiser not to try to escape ideology altogether but to recognize the ideology one has and submit it critically to the test of reason and experience, prepared, if necessary, to revise or even reject it. Fletcher's virtues, his humanity, his directness, his vivid evocation of the particular, would be so much more effectively exercised if he were more sensitive to the moral and metaphysical complexities of "the situation." He is right to warn us of the danger of Pharisaism in our attitude to moral rules in case we forget the needs of people; but, if there are rules which the needs of people require us to observe, we are, in love, required to take account of them. Of this the "legalist" reminds us. Let us take care, when we go up into the temple, lest we find ourselves praying, "Thank God I am not as other men are . . . or even as this Pharisee."

# 14

# Love, Situations, and Rules

## DONALD EVANS

This essay takes as its starting point the first major book by an exponent of the so-called "new morality." In *Situation Ethics: The New Morality*[1] Joseph Fletcher attacks legalism and advocates a "situational" method for making moral decisions. He claims that there are no unbreakable moral rules and that a legalistic casuistry of complex rules and exceptions is not required for moral decision-making in particular situations. He vigorously criticizes specific decisions which legalists have made and he applauds people who have broken traditional moral rules in order to do good. Positively, he expounds his own ethic of love: Love is the only intrinsic good and the only moral norm, and love decides what is best for persons in each particular situation.

Unlike some of his critics, I am in basic sympathy with his attacks on legalism, and I agree with most of his controversial judgments concerning particular cases. Like him, I think that much Catholic and fundamentalist legalism is morally repugnant. It is refreshing to find a Christian who does not soft-peddle his denunciations and who is willing to take his stand with humane secularists against inhumane versions of Christianity. His own alternative to legalism, however, is inadequate. He says that the reader will find a method for decision-making (p. 11),[2] yet his only clear advice is a prohibition: Don't allow

[1] Philadelphia: Westminster Press, 1966.
[2] All page references in parentheses in the text of this chapter refer to pages in Fletcher's book.

rules any veto power. Apart from this advice, the rest of what he proposes is too confused to be called a method.

This is a serious charge. I should say at once that I am attacking Fletcher's ethical theory, not his particular moral judgments, and still less his personal moral practice. I agree with most of his judgments, and my guess is that he is personally a moral exemplar. But his theory or method is not much help to anyone except those who need liberation from legalism. After liberation, what then? His answer is unhelpful. Nevertheless his book does provide a useful starting point for a discussion of issues in modern ethics. The moral values and broad moral viewpoint which are implicit in much of his book are shared by many morally serious people today, both Christian and non-Christian. They deserve a much more careful and searching analysis, a better theoretical framework, than he has given.

As a Christian, I deplore the fact that the ethics which he proposes for Christians lacks many elements which I believe to be essential in a Christian ethic. This is not because I think that a Christian moral perspective is always superior to a secular one. Many of the best moral insights today are secular, and there are Christian perspectives which are very narrow and superficial. Rather, my concern arises because I think that the Christian faith has important and distinctive elements of its own which ought not to be lost in an attempt to find a common ethic for all men. In this essay, however, I shall not write specifically as a Christian theologian but as an analytic philosopher. A discussion of Fletcher and *Christian* ethics must await another time and place.

My study has four sections. The first two are critical studies of Fletcher. The last two, which are longer and more technical, begin with references to Fletcher and then pursue various issues independently. Section I deals with Fletcher's claim that love is the only intrinsic good and the only norm in ethics. His account of love is, unfortunately, a muddle. I shall try to sort out some of the many meanings which he gives for "love" and to challenge his love-monism. In Section II, I shall consider his personalism, which he presents by referring to nominalism, Buber and Kant. I shall outline these three elements and discuss the conflict between the latter two and his impersonal utilitarianism. Section III begins with a consideration of his "situational" method of decision-making. He insists that we should consider only the consequences of each particular action in each particular situation. He rejects all moral rules except those which are viewed as maxims concerning what actions usually produce the best consequences. For Fletcher, these maxims are morally relevant in only one way: they may indicate what action is most likely to produce the best consequences in the particular situation. I shall argue that there are other kinds of moral rules which rightly introduce additional considerations, and which sometimes override considerations concerning the consequences of *this* particular action. The analysis of various types of moral rules will carry us beyond an examination of Fletcher to an independent investigation of some basic problems in modern ethics. Finally, in Section IV, I shall try to fill the most important gap in Fletcher's argument. Although he asks us to reject legalism, he fails to show *why* there cannot be exceptionless moral rules and he fails to show *why* a detailed casuistical system of moral rules is not required. I shall try to show why.

Although I shall be criticizing Fletcher's theory, I shall also be trying to sketch an alternative theory. Like him, I cannot propound an ethical system. But I have a different reason for this. His position seems to be that although the facts to which ethics is applied are extremely complex and extremely varied, ethics itself is simple: it consists of love. My position is that ethics itself is extremely complex, since there are so many different kinds of value to be considered and weighed. The job of ethics is to distinguish these values, or morally relevant considerations, and to ponder their interrelations. Calling them all "love" is like painting a rainbow white.[3]

## I. *Love*

Fletcher's ethic is an ethic of love. He says that only love is intrinsically good and that love is the one and only norm. Unfortunately, he gives a confusing account of what love is, and how it operates as a norm. Indeed, he gives four conflicting accounts. First, love is an attitude of good will. The one moral test of an action is whether or not it *increases* love. Second, love is an attitude of good will, but the one moral test of an action is whether or not it *expresses* love. Third, love is not an attitude; it is what an agent *does*. The one moral test of an action is whether or not it produces good consequences (or the best consequences). Fourth, love is a *faculty* by means of which a moral agent discerns what he ought to do. We shall consider each account in turn.

1. *Increase of love as the goal of action.* Fletcher says, "Our task is to act so that more good (i.e. loving-kindness) will occur than

[3] I am indebted to several colleagues for helpful criticisms of arguments propounded in earlier versions of this chapter: William Dray, Douglas Dryer, Lorenne Gordon, David Gauthier, and John Hunter.

any possible alternatives; we are to be 'optimific,' to seek an optimum of loving-kindness" (p. 61). He also says, "Nothing is intrinsically good but the highest good, the *summum bonum,* the end or purpose of all ends—love" (p. 129). It is not clear whether the love or loving-kindness is to be maximized in the recipient of the action or in the agent or in both of them. At any rate it seems that the one moral test of an action is whether or not it increases love. And love is an attitude of good will (pp. 63–64). Apparently the only consequences that matter morally are the moral changes in the agent or recipient. Specifically, what matters is the increase or decrease in love.

This is probably not Fletcher's basic position, however. One cannot be sure, because he has not made any distinction between moral consequences and other consequences and then discussed their relative importance. By "moral consequences" I mean the consequences on people's moral character and motives, or the influence on them toward performing morally good or morally evil actions. By "other consequences" I mean other effects which are good or evil, such as health, happiness, increased knowledge, increased human creativity, or aesthetic satisfaction—and their opposites. A distinction between consequences of a moral nature and consequences of a nonmoral but morally relevant nature is important in ethics and illuminating in many particular situations of moral choice.[4] Apparently Fletcher is inclined to stress nonmoral consequences, in spite of the passages cited above. For example, he vehemently rejects Newman's judgment that the agony of millions is better than the commission of one venial sin (p. 20). I agree with Fletcher in this case. But where does he stand more generally? Should moral consequences ever have any weight?

Consider, for example, the case of the promiscuous teenagers who know nothing about contraception (p. 127). Fletcher seems to hold that in this specific case the encouragement of more promiscuity by providing information about contraceptives is either irrelevant, or of low importance, or of insufficient importance as compared with the overriding need to reduce the unhappiness produced by unwanted pregnancies and venereal disease. In a specific case I might well agree with him concerning the overriding need. But it is important to reflect concerning such a decision, and to realize that in another situation the negative encouragement-of-promiscuity consideration might well be overriding. Fletcher and I agree in rejecting "One should *never* do anything that increases promiscuity"; but this is

---

[4] See, for example, William K. Frankena, *Ethics* (Englewood Cliffs, N.J.: Prentice-Hall, 1963), chaps. 4–5.

merely the beginning of ethical reflection concerning the issue. Time and again Fletcher deals with a case merely by rejecting the unbreakable-rule approach and by making his own *implicit*[5] judgments concerning relevance, importance, and limits. Every moral decision involves implicit or explicit judgments concerning what facts or considerations are relevant, what is their relative importance or weight, and what is the limit at which one consideration becomes overriding in relation to another. Where the judgments are entirely implicit, the moral decision sheds little light for anyone else. Ethical reflection should shed light on moral decisions. But even the sheer *relevance* of moral consequences cannot be noted in ethical theory and practice unless these consequences are distinguished from other good or evil consequences. For example, one may have to consider the moral consequences of a fund-raising campaign which appeals mainly to morally dubious motives and weigh these consequences against the possibly great funds which could be raised for overseas relief. Or one may have to decide between a political action which will reduce poverty considerably while increasing class or race hatred and one which will reduce poverty less but not increase hatred. In many contexts, considerations concerning moral or immoral influence have to be weighed alongside or against considerations concerning other good or evil consequences. This weighing cannot be done by rule, but this need not mean that one should either ignore the moral consequences or leave it all to intuition. Fletcher is unhelpful because some of his theoretical statements seem to suggest that only the moral consequences (increase or decrease of love) matter, while some of his comments on examples make one wonder whether moral consequences matter at all.

2. *The agent's love as the test of actions.* Fletcher says, "Nothing makes a thing good except *agapeic* (loving) expedience; nothing *can* justify an act except a loving purpose" (p. 125). He also says, "What makes the lie right is its loving purpose. . . . If a lie is told unlovingly it is wrong, evil; if it is told in love it is good, right" (p. 65). For Fletcher, an *agapeic* ethic is an ethic of altruism, singling out the "selfless, calculating concern for others" which a Father Damien and a

---

[5] The notion of "implicit judgments" raises difficult philosophical issues. It is a hybrid notion, combining the *logical* (what the speaker must judge if he is to have a consistent and reasonable basis for his explicit judgment) and the *psychological* (what the speaker probably believes or would accept, since he is a reasonable man and has made the explicit judgment). I do not claim to be able to establish with certainty what Fletcher's implicit judgments are. If I could, there would be less point in asking him to be more explicit himself concerning the bases for his specific and explicit moral judgments.

kamikaze pilot share in common (p. 110). He explains that love is "an attitude, a disposition . . . a purpose" (p. 61) and that his ethic is "attitudinal" (p. 79). In these and other places he seems to be expounding an ethic in which an action is to be judged, not by its consequences, but solely by reference to the attitude, disposition, or purpose of the agent. All that matters morally is whether the agent is loving or unloving. "Whatever is benevolent is right; whatever is malevolent or indifferent is wrong" (p. 64).

This is a tenable theory. Various versions of it have appeared in the history of theological and nontheological ethics. Even if one does not accept it, and insists on the importance of the actual consequences of an action, it does raise problems concerning relevance, relative importance, and limits. When, and to what extent, does the "spirit" of an action matter? If our inner attitudes are very important morally, should we spend time on private spiritual or moral disciplines at the expense of doing good? Or are there many occasions when one's private attitudes are utterly irrelevant morally? More generally, how important is it to *be* a person who has such-and-such inner attitudes (e.g., attitudes at least remotely analogous to those of Christ) as compared with actually producing various good consequences in society? Are there any virtues that have a moral value which is not to be appraised solely in terms of their consequences? What about cheerfulness, loyalty to friends, honesty to oneself (so important in both Freudian and existentialist ethics), compassion, patience, honesty to others, humility, or openness to new truth? Is morality a matter of *being* as well as of *doing?* The terms "attitude" and "disposition" seem to be very similar in meaning. But we should note that although some attitudes are mainly or entirely dispositions, others have an internal dimension and are not primarily dispositions.[6] Some attitudes are mainly dispositions to act in such-and-such a way in such-and-such a situation. They consist mainly of the actions which have been instances of the disposition, or which would be instances. A purely dispositional attitude could be understood entirely in terms of external actions. Most attitudes, however, have an internal dimension, an internal way of viewing things and people which may or may not be *revealed* in actions, but which is not merely instantiated or exemplified in actions. Insofar as love has this internal dimension it is not reducible to "doing." The value of the attitude cannot be appraised solely in terms of doing, unless we deliberately exclude the internal dimension from morals. If love were a purely dispositional attitude, an evaluation of the attitude

[6] For a more detailed analysis of attitudes, see Donald Evans, *The Logic of Self-Involvement* (London: SCM Press, 1963), chap. 3.

would be an evaluation of the *actions* which the loving agent performs and tends to perform. Since descriptions of actions always include some of their consequences, an ethic of love as a pure disposition could be consistently developed into an ethic of consequences.

Although, as we shall see, Fletcher does include an ethic of consequences which is linked with "love," the passages which I cited to illustrate his "attitudinal" ethic do not seem to involve a purely dispositional account of love as an attitude. The internal dimension seems to be important, especially where he stresses the loving *purpose* of the agent. Elsewhere, however, he does not seem to maintain a rigorously attitudinal ethic. He says, for example, "It [love] is for the sake of people and it is not a good-in-itself" (p. 61). He goes on to link love, not with *being* unselfish, but with *doing* what we can (pp. 61–62). Indeed, throughout his book there is much stress on doing rather than being, on consequences rather than attitudes. In fact, he uses the term "love" with reference to good consequences of actions, as we shall see. What is the relative importance of the loving attitudes of an agent in comparison with the goodness of the consequences of his action? No light is shed on this question by Fletcher. The question does not arise, because he uses the one word "love" to cover both considerations.

3. *Love as doing good.* It is possible to distinguish a third account of love in Fletcher's book. In this account "love" is not an attitude-word at all, but a value-predicate like "good" which is applied to what one *does*. In one crucial passage (pp. 60–61), Fletcher insists that love is not a property of a person; love is not something a person has; love is not a virtue; love is what one *does*. There is no such thing as love, but there are *loving actions*. Fletcher says that love is a "predicate" of an action in a particular situation, or it is a "formal" or "regulative" principle. Thus Fletcher links love, not with good will, but with good *deeds*. His exhortation to "do love" is an exhortation to do good, to do whatever maximizes good consequences.

Some philosophers may object to talk about "doing love," but the ordinary-language impropriety does not worry me any more than it does in talk about "doing the truth." Such expressions have a point and a meaning. The problem with Fletcher, however, is that his account is so uninformative. How do we tell whether the consequences of an action are "good"? Fletcher's answers to this question are confused. We have already considered one answer: good consequences are good insofar as they include an increase in love-attitude within the agent or the recipient of the action. But this answer presupposes that "love" is an attitude-word, not a value-predicate. And Fletcher does give other answers. He accepts "the greatest *good* of the greatest number" from the utilitarians and notes that his own "good" is "neighbor welfare" rather than "pleasure" (pp. 95–96). He does not explain what this "welfare" consists of except that it is "good on the widest possible scale." He seems to imply that this includes pleasure, self-realization, and the Christian situationist's "happiness in doing God's will," but this is not clear. Certainly there is no attempt to discuss the relative importance of these varied goods. He quotes Stephen Neill's definition of love as "the steady directing of the human will towards the eternal well-being of another" (p. 104) without relating this to the love which is concerned with temporal or physical well-being. He notes that love does not necessarily satisfy the *wants* of others and cites the example of not giving heroin to a drug addict except as part of a cure (p. 117) but he does not pursue the matter further. He says that love is ultimately concerned with the neighbor for *God's* sake, but for him this is a point about motivation rather than about norms. His "personalism" might have helped to clarify what he wants to include and to stress as "good" or as "welfare"; but, as we shall see, it is too muddled to be of much use.

4. *Love as an ability to discern what to do*. One other possible interpretation of Fletcher is that love is neither a disposition (of agent or recipient of action) nor what a moral agent does, but rather an ability or acquired faculty by which an agent discerns what to do. "Love, in the imperative mood of neighbor-concern, examining the relative facts of the situation in the indicative mood, discovers what it is obliged to do" (p. 151). It is true that Fletcher rejects the idea of an innate or inspired conscience providing an intuitive, radarlike faculty (p. 53, cf. p. 23). He insists that love requires *reason* in examining the facts of the situation and in choosing efficient means. But he does seem to rely on love as an ability to make right valuations of alternatives. "Love with care and *then* what you will, do" (p. 79) seems to make love an ability or faculty. Love enables men to discern what features of a situation are morally relevant, what their relative importance is, and what considerations, if any, are overriding. Now it is possible to think of love as an ability to discern what one ought to do. Indeed, it is possible to think of loving as an *art* which a mature moral agent practices spontaneously, recognizing what he ought to do in accordance with an implicit moral perspective which is firm but flexible, sharp but sensitive. Yet in ethics it is not enough to point to such an agent; one should fill in the implicit framework of values, the complex moral perspective which underlies the discernments and

decisions of love. Fletcher's explicit "personalism" might have helped to fill in his account of love, but unfortunately it does not.

## II. *Personalism*

Fletcher explains that one of his ethical presuppositions is "personalism." His initial account of personalism (pp. 50–52, 57–59) has three main elements. First, he says that his view is "nominalistic." For him this means that there are no intrinsic values. Instead, he holds that persons ascribe value to objects, or that actions are valuable only in relation to persons. Second, he follows Martin Buber in stressing the value of "I-Thou" relations between persons. Third, he follows Kant in holding that persons differ radically from things; persons are to be treated as ends in themselves.

1. *Nominalistic personalism.* Fletcher's "nominalistic" attack on intrinsic value (pp. 57–59) has two facets. On the one hand, he holds that an object or an action is valuable because a person judges it to be so; it is not judged to be valuable because it has a property called "value" alongside its other properties. On the other hand, the property which it has in the particular situation and on the basis of which it should be judged valuable is its property of being helpful to persons. The two facets come together, for if something is "helpful" to a person, it either is valued by him (he wants it) or ought to be valued by him (he "really" needs it). But what *is* valued by an agent or by the recipient of his action is not always what *ought* to be valued; so the nominalistic element in Fletcher's personalism does not by itself "fill in" his ethic with any content concerning what values are important or overriding.

Indeed, his assertion that there are no intrinsic values (p. 58) seems to conflict with his assertion that only love is intrinsically good (p. 57). But although his language is confusing, the two assertions can be reconciled. We can interpret "There are no intrinsic values" to mean "There are no values existing apart from personal judgments of value and apart from what helps persons." And we can interpret "Only love is intrinsically good" to mean "Only love, of those things which are helpful to persons, ought to be judged by persons as being valuable *whatever else may be the case.*" Then someone else could disagree with Fletcher, while accepting Fletcher's nominalism, by saying, "Only the reduction of human suffering is intrinsically good." A nominalistic personalism need not be an ethic of love. Perhaps many other things ought to be valued because they help persons.

Fletcher's personalism thus does not receive any specific content by virtue of being nominalistic. It might have been made more specific if he had developed and sustained the elements which he introduces from Buber and Kant. But, as we shall see, he fails to do this in each case.

2. *Buberian personalism.* Fletcher refers to Buber's conviction that "true existence lies in personal relationships" (p. 50) and that these personal relationships are "I-Thou" dialogues. He seems to endorse this conviction, which implies that the main thing which makes something valuable is whether or not it promotes I-Thou dialogue or encounter between persons. For Buber, love is a *relation* between persons who meet each other with openness and concern.[7] This relation, which is of supreme value, is possible only if people actually meet. And people actually meet only in one-to-one encounter or in small fellowships where dialogue is possible.

Although Fletcher initially seems to endorse Buber's personalism, later on he seems to reject Buber. He insists that love *"always* confronts many neighbors" (p. 94, cf. p. 89) and that it must not be "sentimentalized and individualized, reduced to a merely one-to-one relationship" (p. 91). He aims his attack at Tolstoy, but it would surely hit Buber as well. Buber's "love" is one-to-one, though it is an openness to *anyone.* It is neither sentimental nor individual, but it is not a love to everyone at once.

In an amazing attack on the story of Jesus being anointed at Bethany (p. 97) he supports the disciples' utilitarian view that benefits should always be spread as much as possible and he rejects the view attributed to Jesus. Against Fletcher I would argue that Jesus' judgment is actually very "situational." Jesus is not propounding a universal rule against the reduction of poverty or the spreading of benefits as widely as possible, but he *is* implying a priority-scale of values which he applies to the specific situation. The specific personal relation between this woman and himself, expressed in her action, matters more than the alternative specific increase in goods for the poor. Would Fletcher never splurge on a luxury gift to a friend facing a crisis, since the money could go to overseas relief?

In his discussion of the Bethany incident and his insistence that neighbor-love is equal to love for *all* the neighbors (not merely for *any* neighbor) Fletcher implicitly downgrades Buber's personalism. In its stead he seems to suggest an impersonal utilitarian ethic which attaches

---

[7] This is an additional possible meaning for "love": not an attitude, not what a moral agent does, not a faculty for discerning what to do, but an I-Thou relation between two persons. For Buber, love exists "between" persons.

no special value to personal-relation love, whether in two-person dialogue or in small-group fellowship. He tends to ignore the differences between what I can "do" for someone whom I meet so that I can respond to him in an I-Thou way and what I can do for someone whom I never meet but whom I help through impersonal action. There is an important distinction between the kinds of value to be discerned in an I-Thou encounter and in a reduction of suffering produced by a charitable gift or a political lobby.

On the whole, Fletcher seems to turn from a personal-relation personalism to a basic-need utilitarianism. That is, he seems to stress the value of satisfying the minimal and basic wants of as many people as possible and to minimize the value of intimate personal relations. But since he wants to call everything that is valuable "love," he does not explicitly distinguish between the two values, so we do not have any adequate ethical reflection concerning the issue. Both emphases can be found in the New Testament. On the one hand, Dives and the indifferent nondoers of Matthew 25 are condemned for indifference to the suffering of outsiders, although they may well have been loving in their family and circle of friends. On the other hand, the love which is given supreme value in 1 Corinthians 13 is not a generalized good will toward all men; Paul specifically singles out those qualities of personality which contribute to harmony and fellowship in a face-to-face group. Both emphases can be found in contemporary secular ethics as well; even admirers of Buber find that his personalism needs to be supplemented by a dose of Karl Marx or John Stuart Mill. Responsible moral agents wrestle with questions of priority in specific situations of moral decision: If I do X, I'll be subordinating personal relations to political reform; if I do Y, I'll be doing the reverse. Which should I do?

No unexceptionable priority-rule should be expected. But a book on ethics should (a) recognize and distinguish between the kinds of values involved, that is, the kinds of consideration which are morally relevant, (b) indicate roughly what weight should usually be given to each consideration in various kinds of situation, and (c) indicate roughly the kind of circumstances in which one consideration overrides another. It may be true that this can be done only by means of a very detailed examination of particular cases. Even so, ethics should provide an explicit framework of values and a clear conceptual apparatus to apply to these cases.[8]

[8] Fletcher's *Morals and Medicine* (Princeton, N.J.: Princeton University Press, 1954) was a much more illuminating book, both in its handling of particular cases and in its theoretical framework.

3. *Kantian personalism.* When he first introduces his personalism, Fletcher says, "Kant's second maxim holds: Treat persons as ends, never as means" (p. 51). This is a misrepresentation of Kant, who said that we are never to treat persons *merely* or *only* as means.[9] I note this, not to score a scholarly point, but because Fletcher's mistake draws attention to a basic inconsistency in his whole approach to issues concerning means and ends. His pseudo-Kantian maxim implies that it is always wrong, always unloving, to treat any man even partially as a means. Yet in case after case he supports decisions in which men *are* treated partly, or even entirely, as means. And he even insists that what is done in these cases is not in any way evil, not a "lesser of two evils," but unambiguously and positively good (pp. 64–65). If you kill Jones or do not rescue him from death because you thereby can prevent the deaths of Smith and Brown, then you are treating Jones entirely as a means. I agree with Fletcher that the action may be *right;* but it is a choice between the lesser of two evils, and the action does involve evil. The *right* thing to do may sometimes be to do *evil.* Fletcher, with his characteristic urge to equate all moral concepts, protests (p. 65) against any such divorce between what is right and what is good. But the distinction is important, not merely for conceptual tidiness, but for sensitivity in moral decision-making. In some happy situations of moral choice, we can choose between a lesser and a greater *good.* The difference between such cases and the lesser-of-two-*evils* cases involves a difference between good and evil. This ought not to be blurred or ignored.

In everyday life, we are constantly using some people partially as a means in order to achieve an end for others. It is impossible to avoid this. In many cases, the lesser evil involved is so trivial, as compared with the greater evil averted, that no serious moral issue arises. For example, a man tells a lie in order to divert some "protection" racketeers from their victims (p. 64). But in most of the cases which Fletcher considers, the "lesser" evil is a very serious one; it is often the taking of a human life. He seems to think that only a legalist who believes in absolutely unbreakable moral rules will insist that the agent is doing evil. This is false. Only a thoroughly confused ethical theorist would deny that the agent is doing *evil.* This is not to deny that he may be doing the *right* thing in the circumstances.

Legalistic morality receives some well-deserved blows from Fletcher, but one thing can be said in its favor. Some of the supposedly unbreakable moral rules do point out kinds of actions which usually

---

[9] *Fundamental Principles of the Metaphysic of Morals* (London: Longmans, Green, 1946), pp. 55–56.

or always require *special justification* if they are to be right or even permissible. The rules which I have in mind deal with such matters as stealing, lying, cheating, promise-breaking, rape, maiming, and killing; also, perhaps, wanton neglect. That is, they refer to behavior where the negative version of the Golden Rule is broken (stealing, etc.) or perhaps the positive version (wanton neglect). Such behavior is not always wrong. In some cases it is *right* to steal, etc. But it is nevertheless evil—usually, and perhaps always. The degree of evil varies, of course, and sometimes it may be trivial; not all cases of stealing, lying, cheating, or promise-breaking are serious matters. But usually there is an important evil which *may or may not* be justifiable by reference to the end.

This brings us to Fletcher's discussion of "The end does not justify the means." If this slogan is a way of saying that the end *never* justifies the means, Fletcher is correct in rejecting it. But a legalist can reject it too, unless he holds that absolutely all evil is prohibited by unbreakable moral rules. Where a means is not prohibited by an unbreakable moral rule, a specific end may justify a specific means. What if there are no unbreakable moral rules? Fletcher correctly rejects any universal claim that the end *always* justifies the means. But he does not seem willing to acknowledge—in theory, at any rate—that if the particular means is very evil, then only a very special end will justify it. That is, any great evil involved in the means is not only a *relevant* consideration, but one which has great weight and which may be *overriding*. Here, as in the discussion of positive value or good, there are implicit and explicit judgments concerning relevance, weight, and limits.

We must acknowledge the complexity of moral choice. It is misleading to say that only one thing is good (love) and that only its negation or opposite is evil. There are many goods and many evils. A moral perspective, whether Christian or non-Christian, involves an implicit framework of value, according to which various considerations have relevance, relative weight, and limits or overridingness. Not even the *relevance* of various goods or evils will be clearly recognized unless the goods or evils are recognized as such. When Fletcher insists that an agent who does the right thing does no evil, and when he implies that only unbreakable-rule legalists deny this, he may mislead us. We may forget that if a means is evil it requires justification, and that often an evil means cannot be justified in a particular situation, and that even when it is justified it is still evil rather than good. Another danger arises from his quantitative way of solving problems where the interests of a number of people are involved. It is true that a moral decision *sometimes* must depend mainly on a hard-headed calculation of how much woe or welfare each course of action will probably produce to how many people. But when Fletcher *equates* love with his overly quantitative justice (pp. 87–99, 114–119), his initial Kantian personalism is largely replaced by the computer calculations of social engineering or battle strategy.

We have seen that Fletcher's personalism, whether drawn from Buber or from Kant, is overshadowed by his utilitarianism. Earlier we saw that his ethic of love as an attitude is similarly overshadowed by a utilitarian ethic of love as a doing-of-good. His "situationalism" gives rise to somewhat different difficulties, which we shall now consider. These have to do with the nature and function of *rules*.

## III. *Rules and Situations*

Fletcher's position concerning rules and situations involves two main claims. First, he accepts only those moral rules which are viewed as *maxims* concerning what actions usually produce the best consequences, and he regards these maxims as merely guides concerning what action is likely to produce the best consequences *in the particular situation*. Second, he rejects all allegedly *exceptionless* moral rules.

The second claim is one with which I agree. It will be considered in Section IV. The first claim, concerning moral maxims and particular consequences in particular situations, will be considered now.

1. *Fletcher on moral maxims and consequences.* Fletcher is inconsistent in what he has to say about rules. He says in one place (p. 55) that for a situationist there are no rules at all, but elsewhere he seems to accept rules and principles if they are understood and used in the way appropriate to moral maxims (p. 31). He seems to prefer the term "maxim" (p. 26). The main point is that a maxim— or a rule or principle viewed as a maxim—should illuminate rather than direct; it should arise from a "cautious generalization" (p. 32) and be based inductively (p. 158) on cases (p. 55). Its validity in relation to a particular situation of moral decision depends on what best serves love in *that* situation. In other words, the validity of the maxim, rule, or principle depends in each case on whether an action which is in accord with it will actually maximize good in the particular situation.

Fletcher's book begins with a quotation from G. E. Moore: "All moral laws, I wish to shew, are merely statements that certain kinds of actions will have good effects." According to Fletcher, we are obliged to tell the truth only if the situation calls for it (p. 27). He compares a moral rule concerning truth-telling with a rule of strategy or skill in a game, e.g., "Second hand low" in bridge (p. 28). That is, a moral rule is like a rule recommending a procedure which usually works to achieve an end, such as winning a game. Note that he does not compare a moral rule with a rule of the game such as "Trump cards take all other cards." Such rules of the game, as contrasted with rules of strategy, are required if one is to play the game at all. We shall consider the comparison between moral rules and such rules of the game later on. It is not Fletcher's comparison. For him a moral rule, properly viewed as a maxim, is not like such a rule of a game; it is like a rule of strategy or skill. He advocates a "full and respectful use of principles" if they are treated as maxims, that is, as advisers or illuminators rather than directors (p. 31). He disclaims antinomianism, the rejection of all rules, principles, or maxims. But he conceives of rules, principles, or maxims in a thoroughly inductive and pragmatic way. They indicate what sorts of actions have produced good results in the past and which are thus likely to work in the future.

He says that antinomians or "existentialists" rely on the situation itself, there and then, to provide its own ethical solution (p. 22). He disagrees with this view, insisting that moral maxims can be used as guides, and that reason, rather than an alleged intuitive faculty, is required. He also makes it clear that remote as well as immediate consequences should be considered. But he does seem to maintain a position which contemporary philosophers call "act-utilitarianism":[10] only the particular consequences of the particular act are to be considered. For Fletcher these consequences include the means to be used, the desired end to be achieved, and the other incidental consequences (pp. 127-128). (Fletcher also mentions motives, but not, apparently, as reasons for doing $X$ rather than $Y$.) Act-utilitarianism is implied in his treatment of moral rules as maxims concerning what actions usually produce the best consequences. It is also implied when he makes the following of a moral rule entirely contingent on "love's need" (p. 26), or on whether or not "the situation calls for it" (p. 27).

Fletcher's account of moral rules as moral maxims gives us a rough idea of what he means, but it is useful to proceed with an independent analysis of the expression "moral maxim." The Shorter Oxford English Dictionary defines "maxim" as "proposition expressing some general truth of science or of experience" or "rule or principle

---

[10] For a further explanation of this term, see Frankena, *op. cit.*, pp. 30-32.

of conduct." The use of "maxim" which is relevant for our purposes is one which somehow tries to combine both these meanings. The term "maxim" is better than "summary rule" [11] because a maxim is a *general* truth, a generalization. It is *based* on past cases which can be summarized, but it is not itself merely a summary of those cases. A moral maxim tells us what kind of action usually produces the best consequences.

A moral maxim is not the same as a causal proposition of the form "Doing $X$ in situation $S$ usually ('as a rule') causes consequences $C$." An example of such a proposition would be, "Being cheerful during a crisis usually evokes courage in others." A moral maxim is like such a proposition, but it includes an evaluative element: "Doing $X$ in situation $S$ usually produces consequences $C$, which are the best." (Similarly an "egoistic" or "prudential" maxim is not "Doing $X$ in situation $S$ causes $C$" but "Doing $X$ in $S$ causes $C$, which is what I want".)

Causal propositions such as "Doing $X$ in $S$ usually causes $C$," or simply "$X$ usually causes $C$," are what H. L. A. Hart and A. M. Honoré call "causal apothegms." [12] Hart and Honoré point out that "A short circuit very frequently causes fire" does not establish or justify any particular causal proposition, since it itself is based on particular causal propositions whose truth is established on other grounds. A causal apothegm is merely a guide in looking for a cause or in producing or averting an effect. Similarly a moral maxim, which is merely a causal apothegm plus a moral judgment concerning an effect, does not itself establish any particular causal proposition plus moral judgment, since it itself is based on such. The causal apothegm "$X$ usually causes $Y$" is not a premise from which one can conclude "$X1$ is the cause of $Y1$"; it is only a reason for giving initial consideration to $X1$ as possibly being the cause of $Y1$. Similarly a moral maxim, "$X$ is usually the best thing to do in situation $S$" is not a premise from which

---

[11] Paul Ramsey uses this expression in "Two Concepts of General Rules in Christian Ethics," *Ethics*, Vol. LXXVI, No. 3 (April, 1966), pp. 192–207; and throughout his recent volume *Deeds and Rules in Christian Ethics* (New York: Charles Scribner's Sons, 1967). He derived it from John Rawls's discussion of a "summary view" of moral rules in "Two Concepts of Rules," *Philosophical Review*, Vol. LXIV, No. 1 (January, 1955), pp. 3–32.

[12] *Causation in the Law* (Oxford: Clarendon Press, 1959), p. 45. Hart and Honoré say that "X usually causes Y" can be paraphrased to read, "It has been very often found that X was the cause of Y." This is inaccurate. The causal apothegm is based on a summary of past findings, but it is not itself a summary. It refers not only to past findings but also to unobserved past cases of X and Y, and to future cases of X and Y. It is a generalization.

one can conclude, "*X1* is the best thing to do in *S1*," but only a reason for giving initial consideration to *X1* in situation *S1*.[13]

If I am correct in thinking that Fletcher is asking us to treat all moral rules as moral maxims, then he is advocating a view which runs counter to both common sense and the views of many philosophers. Not all moral rules are merely maxims, though some may be. Consider, for example, the moral rule "Keep your promises." I have an obligation to do X because I promised to do X. This moral obligation provides a reason for doing X which may have to be weighed *against* a reason derived from noting the particular effects of doing X in the particular situation; it is not the same as the latter reason. Nor is the point merely that the consequences of not doing X when X has been promised are different from the consequences where X has not been promised. No. The fact that one has promised to do X is in itself a moral reason for doing X; it is a reason distinct from the fact that breaking one's promise in this situation will have such-and-such consequences.

Against Fletcher I would maintain that not all moral rules are moral maxims. Other rules refer us to reasons or considerations in *addition* to considerations concerning the particular consequences of the specific action in the particular situation. Such rules are of two main types, which are distinguishable though not mutually exclusive. I shall call them "promissory rules" and "rule-utilitarian rules." We shall consider each in turn.

2. *Promissory rules.* Promising is a linguistic act which takes place according to various conventions. The utterance (or writing) of such-and-such words in such-and-such a context constitutes a promise, or one of the more specific forms of promise: pledge, contract, covenant, marriage vow, etc. An utterance which is a promise has the meaning or performative force of a promise.[14] In saying, "I promise to do X," I create a moral obligation to do X. This moral obligation does not always override all other moral considerations, but promise-making does create *a* moral obligation. Even when the moral obligation is minimal, so that it is easily overridden, its existence cannot be denied unless one rejects the whole institution of promise-making.

The utterance of the words, "I promise . . ." is not always a

[13] In Section IV I shall consider the possibility of *universal* moral maxims ("X *always* produces the best consequences") based on universal causal apothegms.

[14] For a more detailed discussion of promises in terms of "performative force" see Donald Evans, *op. cit.,* chap. 1. The notation of "performative force" is derived from J. L. Austin's "illocutionary force" in *How to Do Things with Words* (Oxford: Clarendon Press, 1962).

promise. A speaker might, for example, be acting in a play, or joking, or testing a microphone. Or he might be learning English, and not yet understand the meaning of the words. Usually, however, the context makes it clear that a promise is undeniably being made. Where this is so, a speaker cannot later deny that he made a promise, even if he made it insincerely. An insincere promise is nevertheless a promise, just as a false statement is nevertheless a statement. Of course promises do have explicit or implicit exception-clauses: "I promise to do X *unless* such-and-such conditions obtain." The moral obligation created by a promise is similarly restricted. Some promises entail no moral obligation because they were not freely made. If a promise was made under such duress that the agent was not responsible for his promise-making, he is not under any moral obligation to fulfill his promise.

In most contexts, if I freely say, "I promise to do X" I freely promise to do X. And if I freely promise to do X I create a moral obligation to do X. There is an entailment-connection between (free) promises and moral obligations. Where a proposition $p$ entails a proposition $q$, then if someone accepts $p$ he cannot consistently deny $q$ and if he denies $q$ he cannot consistently accept $p$. Consider these propositions:

$p$: "He freely promised to do X unless . . ."
$q$: "He has a moral obligation to do X unless . . ."

Note that the truth or falsity of $p$ can be established independently of whether or not he accepts $q$. If he freely said, "I promise to do X unless . . . ," and if the context was such as to make it clear that he was making a promise, then he did freely promise to do X. Sometimes the truth of $p$ cannot be established, but usually it can. And where it can, this is done *without reference to whether or not he now accepts q*.[15] If the truth of $p$ is established, he cannot consistently deny $q$, unless he rejects the whole institution of promise-making. This is not surprising, for the whole point of the institution of promise-making is that promising is an action in which an agent creates a moral obligation to do X, an obligation whose existence he cannot later deny whenever he decides it would be convenient. It is true that most

[15] This distinguishes the entailment-connection between "He promised" and "He has a moral obligation" from that between "X was a murder" and "X was wrong." Whether or not X was a murder depends on whether it was a killing and whether it was wrong; for "murder" means "wrong killing." So if I deny that X was wrong I can *thereby* deny that X was a murder; and I cannot be logically compelled to agree that X was a murder *unless* I agree that X was wrong. But unless I reject the whole institution of promise-making, I *can* be compelled to agree that I have an obligation, if it is a fact that I did promise.

promises in everyday life have loopholes. The exception-clause in a promise is usually both vague and implicit, and so is the corresponding clause in the statement of moral obligation; but this sort of openness obtains for most entailment-connections in everyday language.

A man who makes a promise to do X commits himself in advance *not* to decide whether to do X *solely* on the basis of his judgment concerning the probable consequences of doing X in the particular situation of decision. He already has one moral reason for doing it: "because I promised." When he has to decide, this reason may be overridden by reasons arising from a consideration of consequences. Or it may be supported by other reasons which arise from a consideration of consequences, namely, the bad effects on personal relations where a trust has been breached. But the reason does have a distinctive weight of its own, which depends on the obligation created by a promise. Promises entail obligations.

The moral rule "Keep your promises" is partly justified by reference to the meaning of "promise." This justification must not be misunderstood. It is not that we can derive "Promises *ought always* to be kept" from the meaning of "promise," as one can derive "Murder is always wrong" from the meaning of "murder" ("wrong killing"). From the meaning of "promise" what follows is that if anyone promised (freely) to do X he has *a* moral obligation to do X. And although "He promised to do X" entails "He has a moral obligation to do X," it does so only if we do not deny the whole institution of promise-making. Such a denial would not involve any logical contradiction. Nor need it involve the mistake of denying the empirical fact that, according to the linguistic conventions of society, promises do entail obligations; to deny this would be to show that one did not understand the meaning of "promise." But a promise-skeptic can deny that moral obligations are ever "really" created by promises; or, to put it another way, he can refuse to acknowledge any of the alleged moral obligations allegedly created by promises. He might declare his views openly, or he might hold them secretly, taking advantage of others.

The possibility of a promise-skeptic reminds us that when we accept the linguistic conventions by which promises entail obligations we commit ourselves not only to a way of talking about other people ("He promised, so he has a moral obligation") but also to an acknowledgment—in general and in advance—of moral obligations created by our own promises. To accept the entailment is to accept the institution of promise-making, and this involves a general *moral* commitment. This differentiates the entailment from most entailments, but once the difference is recognized, it does not seem to me to be misleading to go on calling it an "entailment." To *deny* that promises entail obligations may be misleading, for unless the institution as a whole is rejected, the fact that Jones (freely) promised to do X does entail that he has a moral obligation to do X. Unless one is a promise-skeptic, one cannot consistently affirm the fact and deny the obligation. One does not *decide in each case* whether or not the obligation follows from the fact.[16]

Perhaps I should note a possible objection. What if someone makes a promise to do X, and X is something very wrong (e.g., lying, rape, or murder)? Some philosophers might hold that since such a promise ought not to be made, it is null and void with respect to moral obligation; the agent has no obligation at all to fulfill his promise. On such a view, "Jones promised" does not entail "Jones has a moral obligation" in such a case, even if Jones and most people think that it does. It seems to me, however, that such a case is more felicitously viewed as one where he has *an* obligation to do what he promised, but the obligation is easily overridden by the obligation not to lie or rape or murder. Nevertheless the objection is useful in reminding us that acceptance of the entailment-connection between someone else's promise and his obligation involves moral commitments on *our* part. If I fully agree that Jones's promise entails a moral obligation, however minimal, then I agree that in a relevantly similar situation *I* would also have one. Sometimes, of course, "He has a moral obligation" may be spoken in a neutral, noncommittal way (say, by an anthropologist), so that it is roughly equivalent to "He thinks that he has a moral obligation." But usually, "He has a moral obligation" entails "*I* would have a moral obligation . . . ." So the distinction which I made in the last paragraph, between talking about other people's obligations and creating our own, breaks down when it is pressed.

But let us turn to consider a different issue concerning promises. The promise-skeptic's position reminds us of a further question which needs to be asked about the institution of promise-making, with its basic promissory rule "Keep your promises," and its entailment-connection between promises and obligations: What *justification* is there for the institution? The answer is obvious. If most people, most of the time, broke the basic promissory rule, there would not be sufficient assurance concerning the future behavior of others in society. Without the existence of some form of promissory rule, observed by most peo-

---

[16] Concerning promises and entailments, see John Searle, "How to Derive 'Ought' from 'Is,' " *The Philosophical Review* (January, 1964); R. M. Hare, "The Promising Game," *Revue Internationale de Philosophie*, Fasc. 4 (1964); also essays by various authors in *Analysis* (1964–1966).

ple most of the time, there would be no society at all. This is true in two ways, which need to be distinguished. (Analogous justifications can be given for "Tell the truth," but I will not give them here.)

First, a society can be partially defined as a group in which mutual expectations depend partly on promise-keeping rather than entirely on mere regularities of behavior. If the institution of promise-keeping disappeared because fewer and fewer people kept their promises, whatever remained could not be called a "society" at all. An analysis of the notion of a "society" shows that conventions concerning promising *must* exist in a group if it is to be a society; and if conventions are to exist, they must be generally accepted and acted upon.

Second, it is an empirical fact that human societies depend on promise-keeping for their existence as groups in which basic needs (e.g., food and shelter) are satisfied. If few people were to keep promises, mutual expectations which have depended on usual promise-fulfillment would become so unreliable that the group would disintegrate and people would suffer greatly.

The second justification is, in an obvious sense, "utilitarian." The basic promissory rule is justified by reference to the adverse consequences of its being usually violated, and these consequences are not appraised in a way which presupposes any intrinsic value in promise-keeping as an institution. (We shall consider utilitarian justifications of rules in Section IV.) The first justification, however, is misleadingly called "utilitarian." Nor is the main point that the word "society" has an analytic connection with "promise-keeping," but that society, so defined, has an *intrinsic value*. The "usefulness" of the institution of promise-keeping depends on an assumption that mutual human relations based on the moral obligation created by promise-making have an intrinsic value; a society based morally on mutual trust and mutual commitment is better than a "pack" based nonmorally on mutual expectations concerning regularities of behavior. Since promise-keeping is not being justified by reference to anything other than itself, this justification is not aptly called "utilitarian." We should note, however, that it is not the intrinsic value of each *particular act* of promise-keeping that is here cited but, rather, the over-all intrinsic value of the *institution* of promise-keeping.

Promises are important because of the kinds of personal relation and of personal virtue which they make possible. Making a promise to someone is a way of committing oneself to him. An inner attitude of commitment is not possible unless the institution of promise-making exists. The content of a commitment depends on the content of the specific promise which one makes or is willing to make. A commitment is not a preverbal or nonverbal disposition. It is either a linguistic act, or an attitude which has to be defined by reference to that act: the attitude which one has if one performs the linguistic act sincerely. Insofar as *love* for someone includes commitment or loyalty, it cannot be understood without reference to specific promises which someone either makes or is willing to make, and it cannot exist unless some form of promise-making convention or institution exists.

So far we have been considering the basic promissory rule, "Keep your promises." There are, however, a great many partially promissory rules which govern the duties involved in a man's *status* or *role* within family, corporation, club, army, church, or other social institution. Sometimes a status or role is explicitly accepted, as when a man agrees to be treasurer of the tennis club or applies for Canadian citizenship. Sometimes the status or role already exists in the eyes of others by virtue of some fact. I am a citizen of Canada or the son of Ira Evans by birth. If I explicitly accept a new status or role, or if I acknowledge a status or role which a social group claims that I have, then I accept various moral obligations. The status or role may carry very specific and legally defined obligations or very general and vaguely indicated obligations. (What, today, are the moral obligations of a *son*?) The importance of the moral obligations varies enormously. Nevertheless the very *meaning* of the status or role usually involves some reference to moral obligation. It is self-contradictory to say, "I accept my job as treasurer of the tennis club, but I am under no moral obligation to do anything concerning its finances." In some cases, the purely descriptive meaning of the key term can be invoked: "I am his son, but I am under no moral obligation to him." Here the term "son" must mean something like "biological procreation"; one is refusing to acknowledge any of the status-and-role meaning of "son." Many statements involving status-and-role terms are not indefeasibly moral in meaning.[17] My main point, however, is that in accepting or acknowledging a status or role within a social group one is *often* thereby accepting or acknowledging a moral obligation to behave in accordance with that status or role; one cannot logically deny that the duties of the status or role indicate morally relevant considerations. The acceptance or acknowledgment is a form of promise-making. For example, it is the duty of a priest-confessor to observe the seal of the confessional. In accepting the role of confessor, he accepts a moral obligation to fulfill this duty; he has made, in effect, a *promise* to do

---

[17] For a more detailed discussion of status-and-role terms and of "Indefeasible" versus "Prima-facie" commitments, see Donald Evans, *op. cit.,* especially chaps. 1 and 4.

so. Fletcher rightly attacks a particular decision made by a confessor: not to reveal that an innocent man is about to die for the penitent's crime (p. 132). Sometimes the moral obligation to keep a promise by doing the duty arising out of one's role should be overridden. (Indeed, I would maintain that no promise ought to be unconditionally binding.) Yet it is obvious that there would be no possibility of a confessional if the confessor's decision as to whether or not to divulge secrets depended *solely* on the probable consequences in each particular case. Even if he were to consider in each case the adverse consequences for the confessional as an institution, this would provide only an additional reason alongside, "I accepted the office and so I have a moral obligation to fulfill its duties."

I am not advocating an ethic of "my station and its duties." Too often an appeal to one's duty as a father or a soldier or a company director is a way of evading responsibility for consequences to people *outside* the family, army, or business. Too often the moral obligations of one's role or office are grossly inflated in comparison with other considerations. In particular, the duty of a citizen to support the decisions of his government (say, concerning Vietnam) can become demonic in its demands. Institutions need to be challenged and changed. But insofar as an institution is good, the obligations which one has because of one's place in that institution are *moral* obligations which provide moral reasons in their own right. Sometimes these obligations conflict among themselves: duty to family versus duty to country. Sometimes they conflict with the obligation to tell the truth: duty to the State Department versus duty not to deceive the public. Sometimes they conflict with considerations concerning consequences: duty to obey a superior officer versus concern about civilian casualties. Sometimes the obligations are only of minor importance. Nevertheless they are *moral* obligations. And the moral rules which are invoked ("If you are a such-and-such, perform the duties of a such-and-such") are not merely moral maxims. They provide reasons for doing $X$ even where a calculation of the good and evil consequences of doing $X$ in a specific situation would lead one *not* to do $X$.

Appeal to these moral rules may be backed either by reference to a man's implicit or explicit acceptance of a role (and hence by reference to his *promise*) or by reference to the over-all good of society which is furthered if most people in similar situations usually observe the rule. This second kind of appeal, to the utilitarian justification of the rule, will be considered in detail later on. Here we should merely note that it, too, is not an appeal simply to the particular consequences of a man's obeying the rule in the particular situation.

3. *Moral rules and rules of a game.* Sometimes moral rules, especially those which are not moral maxims, are compared with rules of a game.[18] This comparison can be useful in showing some of the inadequacy of Fletcher's moral-maxim account of morality, but it can be misleading. In making the comparison we should note that games may involve at least four different kinds of rules. A rule may sometimes belong to more than one of these kinds, or dwell on a borderline between them; but the distinctions are nevertheless real and important.

*a) Constitutive rules of the game.* These determine, for example, what *counts* as a "move" in chess or a "goal" in soccer. Apart from such rules there is no such action as a "chess move" or a "soccer goal." If my action fails to conform to the relevant rule, it is not a chess move or a soccer goal, although I have pushed a round piece of wood or kicked a ball into a net. In the context of the game, my action is null and void; it doesn't count. Constitutive rules of a game are analogous to the rules which determine what linguistic acts count as a promise.

*b) Regulative rules of the game.* These prohibit or require specific actions in specific situations and often prescribe penalties for violations. The actions may be described in everyday terms drawn from outside the game ("trip") or in technical terms defined by constitutive rules of the game ("roughing"). Examples: no tripping in hockey, no roughing the passer in football. Where a penalty is attached to a regulative rule, it is not to the effect that a particular action fails to *count* in the game (like the "penalty" of not scoring if one shoots the puck after the whistle blows); this would make the rule a constitutive rule. Regulative rules of a game are very similar to many *laws* in society. For example, a traffic law prohibits my stopping my car in some circumstances and requires me to stop it in others. A subclause of the law may or may not be required in order to define what constitutes "stopping." If such a clause is required, it (though not the whole law) is a *constitutive* rule, similar to laws which set forth what constitutes a legal contract. But such a clause may not be required. The traffic-regulation law concerning stopping may make use of an everyday meaning of "stopping" which existed long before there were *any* traffic regulations.[19] This everyday meaning depends on rules of

[18] E.g., Paul Ramsey, *op. cit.*, and John Rawls, *op. cit.*

[19] Rawls (*op. cit.*, p. 22) fails to realize that this can occur in the case of *regulative* rules, and not merely in the case of rules pictured as *summaries:* his account suffers from a failure to distinguish between constitutive and regulative rules. Max Black notes that I can "park" my car even if there are no laws govern-

everyday language which might well be called "constitutive." Every regulative rule, like every meaningful utterance, depends on the existence of rules of language. But this does not mean that every regulative game-rule or law describes actions in terms whose meaning depends on *special* constitutive rules of the *game* or the *law*.

c) *Rules of skill or strategy in a game*. These are the prudential maxims of a game. Usually, if I follow such a rule, I will increase the likelihood that I or my team will win the game. Example: "For a backhand shot in tennis, shift your grip to put your knuckles on top." Whenever following the rule would not help me toward winning the game, it is prudent for me to break the rule. As a prudential maxim, a rule of skill or strategy is analogous to a moral maxim. The latter differs in that it involves a judgment of consequences in terms which go beyond the winning of a game. Some rules of skill or strategy, such as "Second hand low" in bridge, have a secondary feature which should be noted. If my partner *expects* me to follow this rule, an additional consequence of my breaking it may be that I mislead him, thus reducing the likelihood of winning. This does not usually mean that such rules are promissory rules, since the partner's expectation usually provides a consideration only in terms of its relevance to probable effects on winning the game. But someone might view "Second hand low" as a promissory rule which ought to be followed by anyone accepting the "role" of second player in a game of bridge; some people play games very seriously. And more generally, a failure to follow *any* rule of skill *may* involve letting someone else down in a *morally* culpable way, because there has been some form of implicit promise to follow the rule. But I think it is clear that, *qua* rule of skill or strategy, this sort of rule is not a moral promissory rule and that it is analogous to a moral *maxim*.

d) *Moral rules applied to the game*. Although part of the point of some games is to provide a special context in which some kinds of deceit are *not* morally blameworthy (a good quarterback is a master of deceit), moral rules against deceit *are* applied to games. Cheating, or feigned conformity with constitutive or regulative rules, is usually morally wrong. So is "throwing" a game; one ought to try to win, since one's participation implies some sort of promise to try. Such rules are not *analogous* to moral rules; they *are* moral rules. They are like "Don't tell lies" or "Keep your promises."

---

ing parking in a remote village which I visit; but for me to have the concept of "parking," there must be constitutive *traffic* laws *somewhere;* this is not true of "stopping." For Black, see "The Analysis of Rules," *Models and Metaphors* (Ithaca: Cornell University Press, 1962), pp. 124–125.

This digression concerning rules of a game is useful if we are pointing out defects in Fletcher's view that all moral rules are to be understood as moral maxims. Where a moral rule is a moral maxim, it is analogous to rules of skill or strategy in a game. But we can point out that there are other kinds of rules involved in a game. Moral rules are also analogous to regulative rules of a game. Moreover, moral rules themselves may form part of the rules of a game. What about *constitutive* rules of a game? Are moral rules analogous to these? My own answer is No, but an extreme legalist might press such an analogy. In a game, as in a court of law, my aim is to win, and I cannot win except by conforming to the constitutive rules. According to a legalistic theory which I reject, my aim in the moral game or courtroom of life would be to produce as much good as possible according to the constitutive rules, and what would *count* as good would be entirely dependent on these rules. Just as my shooting the puck into the net does not count at all in the game if I move offside in order to shoot it, so my saving a human life would not count morally if I lied in order to do it. The only actions that would count as moves in the moral chess game of life would be those which conform to the moral rules.

If moral rules are analogous to *regulative* rules of a game, no such legalistic conclusion follows. A regulative rule of hockey has for its purpose the general interests of the game of hockey; a good rule is one which makes hockey a satisfying game to play and to watch. But a player sometimes prudently breaks such a rule in order to achieve his own purpose, which is to win the game. Some moral rules —namely the rule-utilitarian rules which we shall consider next—are analogous in that their purpose is to further the general interests of society. A man sometimes rightly breaks such a rule in order to achieve his own moral purpose, which is to bring about the best consequences for others in the particular situation. He breaks the moral rule, however, for a moral reason, whereas a player breaks a regulative rule of hockey for a prudential reason.

To summarize: Some moral rules are maxims which are analogous to rules of skill or strategy in a game. Second, some moral rules (e.g., against deception) are themselves applied in a game. Third, some moral rules are analogous to regulative rules in a game. To these we now turn.

---

[20] For other discussions of issues in this section, see Frankena, *op. cit.*, chap. 3; Kurt Baier, *The Moral Point of View* (New York: Random House, paperback,

4. *Rule-utilitarian rules.*[20] A rule-utilitarian rule is one which is justified by considering the consequences of its being followed by most people or by everyone, as compared with the consequences of its being broken by most people or by everyone. In contrast with this, an act-utilitarian rule is a moral maxim which tells us what acts usually produce the best consequences, that is, what acts have highest utility. Rule-utilitarian rules, however, are not based on summaries of particular judgments concerning the utility of particular acts. Rule-utilitarian rules are not established by showing that observance of the rule usually produces good consequences in each case, though this *might* be so. A rule-utilitarian rule is established by considering the *compound* effects of many people, or all people, observing the rule in comparison with the *compound* effects of their violating it. One considers the over-all utility of the rule, not the utility of each separate act.

As Kurt Baier says, "No harm is done if one person walks across the lawn. But the lawn is ruined if everyone does." [21] Similarly, little or no harm is done if one person throws a cigarette carton on the public beach, but the beach is ruined if many do. Little or no harm is done if one person buys a can of meat on the black market during wartime; but much harm is done if many do or everyone does. Similar justifications underlie parking regulations, speed limits, conventions concerning queuing, deadlines for submission of theses or annual reports, rules against advertising by medical doctors, laws restricting divorce, and a host of other regulative rules. When a man faces a moral decision, one of these rules may point to a consideration which is morally relevant and which is nevertheless not the same as a consideration arising from the particular case itself. Indeed, the particular consequences may be morally irrelevant—for example, when I walk on the grass. And if the particular consequences of an action *are* morally relevant, they provide a different sort of consideration from that provided by a rule-utilitarian rule. It is one thing for a man to consider the consequences of his breaking the speed limit right now in this situation, and another for him to consider the consequences of many drivers or all drivers breaking the speed limit in similar situations. It is one thing to consider the particular consequences, in

---

1965), pp. 132–137; R. M. Hare, *Freedom and Reason* (Oxford: Clarendon Press, 1963), chap. 7; Marcus Singer, *Generalization in Ethics* (New York: Alfred A. Knopf, 1961); I. M. Crombie, "Moral Principles," in *Christian Ethics and Contemporary Philosophy*, ed. Ian T. Ramsey (London: SCM Press, 1966); Dorothy Emmet, *Rules, Roles and Relations*, (London: Macmillan & Co., 1966), especially chaps. 4, 7, 8, 9.
[21] *Op. cit.*, p. 132.

situation *S1,* of his breaking a moral rule against premarital intercourse, and another to consider the over-all consequences of all or many people doing so in situations of type *S.*

The justification of rule-utilitarian rules is a very complex matter. I can here give only an initial analysis which begs many questions and ignores many distinctions, but it may be possible to clarify a few important theoretical issues. One step is to distinguish five different possibilities concerning the observance of a rule.

*a*) General observance: all people follow the rule all of the time

*b*) Usual observance: most people follow the rule all or most of the time; or all people follow the rule most of the time

*c*) Mixed observance: many people follow the rule but many do not

*d*) Usual nonobservance: most people break the rule all or most of the time; or all people break the rule most of the time

*e*) General nonobservance: all people break the rule all of the time

Very roughly speaking, a rule is justified by comparing the consequences in (*a*) or (*b*) with the consequences in (*d*) or (*e*) [or, sometimes, (*c*)]. Sometimes the comparison is between two hypothetical sets of consequences, since in each case we are considering what the consequences *would be*; perhaps the rule is being proposed for the first time. More frequently the comparison is between actual consequences and hypothetical consequences. Where a rule is usually observed, we can try to estimate the actual consequences of its usual observance; then the comparison is with what the consequences would be if nonobservance were to become usual or general. There is always at least one hypothetical element in the comparison. This hypothetical element has to do with the over-all consequences if a large number of people were to behave differently from the way in which they do in fact behave. We ask, "What if people were to follow the rule generally or usually?" or "What if people were to break the rule generally or usually?" These questions are obviously of a different type from the question, "What if *I* were to follow (or to break) the rule in this particular situation?"

Rule-utilitarian rules are closely associated with the so-called "generalization argument," which tests a moral decision to do X in situation S by asking, "What if *everyone* were to do X in situation S?" Fletcher pours scorn on this argument (p. 131) and implies that it is never cogent. He is mistaken. The generalization-argument question is often a legitimate way of appealing to a rule-utilitarian rule, or of testing it. We should note, however, that the question is limited in its applicability. It implies that it is *not* the case that everybody actually does X in situation S. In most contexts the question also implies that the consequences would be bad rather than good. Hence the question applies where general observance or general nonobservance of a rule would produce bad consequences for society. If general observance of a rule would produce bad consequences, then if the rule exists it should be revised or abolished, and if the rule is being proposed, it should be rejected. If general nonobservance of a rule would produce bad consequences, then a partial justification of the rule has been indicated.

One point is crucial for our understanding of the generalization argument. We must realize that the argument is relevant only where a rule exists or is proposed, and where this rule is a regulation concerning what everyone within a designated class ought to do or not to do in situations of type S. That is, someone is either citing or proposing a regulative rule for *society*, a rule which requires a rule-utilitarian justification. The generalization-argument question does two jobs. Like the question, "What if *most* people did X?" it may form part of a rule-utilitarian justification of a rule. But it also refers us to considerations concerning *fairness* or *rights*. Only when a special reason can be given is it fair or right for one man to make an exception in his own case, if general (or usual) observance of a rule is in the best interests of society. The special reason might in some cases be act-utilitarian: "If I don't break the rule in this particular situation, the particular consequences will be very bad." Such a reason overrides the generalization-argument reason in some cases, but not in all.

Fletcher seems to have two main objections to the generalization argument (pp. 130–131). First, he notes that the argument is not used against such things as celibacy, although if everyone were celibate the human race would perish. I agree that the argument is irrelevant here, but there is a reason for this, and the reason does not apply in other cases. The argument is irrelevant here because no regulative rule exists to prohibit celibacy for all mankind. Moreover, no such rule need be proposed, for there is no danger that many people will become celibate. Second, Fletcher denies that a rule can be devised which can cover a number of particular situations and yet eliminate the possibility that its observance in any particular situation may produce evil. But this is precisely the point at issue. A rule-utilitarian insists on the possibility that in some cases a man rightly observes the rule even though, in the particular situation, this produces more evil than good. General observance of the rule produces the best consequences over-all. It is possible that this consideration, plus the restriction on the individual's right to make his own exceptions to the rule, may sometimes rightly override considerations concerning the particular consequences in the particular situation.

The generalization argument, which is linked with rule-utilitarian rules, needs to be distinguished from the "wedge argument," which is a special case of act-utilitarianism. Fletcher attacks both, and seems to equate them (pp. 130–131). In the one case, we ask, "What *would* be the over-all consequences if *everyone* were to do $X$?" In the other case, we ask, "What *will* be the over-all consequences if $I$ do $X$? Will I actually influence many others to do the same? If so, what will be the over-all consequences of this? Will my action be the thin edge of the wedge?" The generalization-argument question may be relevant when the wedge argument is irrelevant, for example, when I am sure that my action will influence nobody, since it is done in safe secrecy. Conversely, where the generalization argument is irrelevant since no regulative rule is involved, my concern about influence on others may make the wedge argument relevant. Often, however, both arguments are involved, though they may not be clearly distinguished.

Against Fletcher I have maintained that the generalization argument has a legitimate place in moral reasoning. This does not mean that I agree with philosophers who make it a necessary test for all moral judgments. At first sight, however, one is inclined to think that it is a necessary test. Consider the following:

(i) If $I$ ought (ought not) to do $X$ in situation $S1$, then *anyone* ought (ought not) to do $X$ in situations of type $S$.
(ii) If *anyone* ought (ought not) to do $X$ in situations of type $S$, then *everyone* ought to (ought not to).
(iii) As a matter of fact, if everyone were to do (or not do) $X$ in situations of type $S$, the over-all consequences would be bad.
(iv) Hence I ought not to do (ought to do) $X$ in situations of type $S$, including $S1$.

Note that "anyone" and "everyone" may refer to an unlimited class of human beings or to a restricted class, e.g., doctors or divorcées.

Step (*i*) is sound, if the "ought" is a moral one. Any moral judgment is in principle universalizable. If I ought to do $X$ in this particular situation *S1*, then anyone ought to do X in any situation S which resembles *S1* in the morally relevant respects. My moral judgment commits me to an implicit or explicit moral rule. But from this it does not follow that I must test my rule ("Anyone ought to do X in S") by asking what would happen if *everyone* actually observed it. For there is a difference between what is included in "situation S" where only a few people do X and what is to be included in "situation S" where everyone does X. The consequences of each person's doing X if few people are doing X are different from the consequences if everyone is doing X. What if the actual situation is that only a few people are likely to do X, and that the over-all consequences of a few people doing X are not bad, but perhaps good? Is it *always* the case that I ought not to do X if the over-all consequences of everyone doing X would be bad? Surely not. Yet steps (*ii*) and (*iii*) seem to require us always to test our moral judgments by considering the consequences of everyone doing likewise. For these steps seem to mean that whenever I make a moral judgment concerning what *anyone* ought to do, I am "legislating" for society, propounding or endorsing a regulative moral rule for *everyone* to follow. Obviously if this *is* what I am doing, then I must consider what would be the over-all consequences if everyone were to observe the rule, for I am calling on everyone to observe the rule. In requesting or exhorting everyone to do X, I would be acting irresponsibly if I believed that the over-all consequences of everyone doing X would be bad.

We have seen that where there already exists a regulative rule which passes rule-utilitarian tests, the generalization-argument question is relevant. But where my moral judgment does not involve citation of such a regulative rule for society, must I always be *proposing* such a rule? Does the requirement that a moral judgment be universalizable (applicable in principle to any similar person in a similar situation) mean that a moral judgment always implies a regulative rule for society, a rule which must be given rule-utilitarian tests including the generalization-argument question? Can the generalization argument be derived from the universalizability requirement (plus utilitarian considerations) so that it provides a necessary test for all moral judgments?

My answer is No. In order to defend this position, I propose that we make a broad distinction between two kinds of moral rules: "societal" and "personal." A societal moral rule is a regulative rule which sets forth what everyone within a designated class ought to do or not to do. It is backed by a sanction of moral disapproval which is inflicted on violators by most of those within a social group. When, as sometimes happens, it has been enacted as a law, there are legal penalties as well. Some societal moral rules are explicitly promulgated by nameable moral authorities within the society (e.g., the Pope), but others have no known promulgators. Many are implicit, while nevertheless operative as part of the moral context in which people make decisions. (Whether or not a societal rule "exists" becomes a complicated issue once we allow for the possibility of implicit rules; I am ignoring this complication.) If a societal rule is to have its desired result in social utility, individuals must curb their inclinations to be their own legislators and casuists, judging when to make exceptions so as either to break or to revise the societal rule. The individual's right to do this must be restricted to some extent, for the over-all good of society. It is not fair for him to break a societal rule whose general or usual observance is required to promote such good, unless there is some special reason.

There are many different ways in which a moral rule may be *non*societal and hence "personal," though universalizable. Sometimes a rule is personal because it is unformulated. Any moral judgment must be universalizable, and so it implies a moral rule. But, as I shall show in Section IV, it need not be explicitly universal*ized*. A man can concede that if anyone were in a "similar" situation, he ought to do $X$, though he is unable to pin down all the morally relevant similarities so as to set forth an explicit rule. Yet only an explicit rule can be proposed as a societal rule so as to be tested by the generalization-argument question, "What if everyone did $X$?" Sometimes the rule implied by a moral judgment might be formulated, but in such a way that its only practical application is to the one situation from which it arose. The situation is described in such complex detail that although a repetition is not logically impossible, it is so unlikely as to be irrelevant. This is because the agent's moral reasoning has involved a great many diverse factors in the particular situation, including some which are very unusual or distinctive. Having considered these factors, he has made his moral decision. Since a philosopher has asked him to formulate a rule, he obliges, but his rule has the form, "Whenever anyone who has characteristics $C1 \ldots C25$ is in a situation which has features $F1 \ldots F99$, he ought to do $X$." Since in practice the rule is applicable to only one case, it is useless as a societal rule. The more a moral judgment resembles an artistic judgment in its subtle sensitivity and creativity, the more likely it is that the moral rule which is implied either cannot be formulated or is formulated so that it applies only to the one case.

The unformulated and uniquely applicable moral rules which we have considered are not *regulative* rules. There are, however, some regulative rules which are not societal. A man may formulate an explicit moral rule to regulate his own actions, and disapprove of anyone whom he observes breaking the rule, and yet not advocate it publicly so as to press for its adoption as a societal rule. That is, he may commit himself to a rule which is applicable to anyone within a designated class, and yet not actively "legislate" it for everyone within that class. There are at least four different sorts of reasons which may be given for such a position.

First, a man may refrain from actively "legislating" his personal moral rule because he cannot make even a rough estimate of what the consequences would be if everyone followed it. Ignorance is not bliss, but a reason for caution. Perhaps he believes that any father should put his teenage daughter on the pill unless there are medical reasons to the contrary. He disapproves of his acquaintances when they neglect this precaution. But he does not initiate "legislation" by a letter-to-the-editor about it, mainly because of the need to protect his daughter from publicity, but partly because he does not know what the over-all consequences would be if *all* fathers did likewise; they might be good, or they might be bad; who knows? In other cases a man has a personal moral rule that anyone who thinks such-and-such ought to do X, but he has little idea of how many people this would involve if it were generally practiced, or what the over-all consequences would probably be; so he does not actively promote his personal rule as a societal rule.

Second, a man may refrain from actively "legislating" his personal moral rule because if everyone did likewise, the over-all consequences would probably be more bad than good. He is reasonably sure that his own doing X in situation S produces good consequences, and that if a few more people did likewise the over-all consequences would be good, but there may be "too much of a good thing." He expresses moral disapproval when he happens to observe violations occasionally in his daily life, but he does not press for societal acknowledgment of the rule. Most of the generosity-examples which philosophers cite against the generalization argument are relevant here. Few people in our society are lavishly generous to others, but everyone ought to be. Yet if everyone were, the results would be either absurd (like a children's game in which one is "out" if caught in possession of the object being passed around) or tragic (like the "potlatch" culture of some Indian tribes, which was destroyed by its own societal rules on competitive generosity).

Third, a man may have a personal moral rule which, he believes, ought to be constantly open to revision in relation to new social conditions. If his rule were to become a societal rule, both he and others would lose this flexibility, since a societal rule requires restrictions on revisions being made by individuals. The resulting rigidity of the rule and the sacrifice of moral autonomy for individuals are dangers which may outweigh any advantages of a societal rule. Another consideration, closely related to this concern for flexibility and freedom, is caution in invoking massive social disapproval as a deterrent of wrongdoing. A man may be reluctant to "legislate" his personal moral rule as a societal rule because this involves calling for massive social disapproval of violations. Such disapproval is a weapon which is not to be handled lightly; it may get out of hand. Sometimes such disapproval would be disproportionate to the wrongdoing. Sometimes the over-all effects of such disapproval are bad (e.g., perhaps, the effects of massive social disapproval of homosexuality). Although a societal moral rule is not usually a *law* as well, some of the reservations which we have about extending the range of activities covered by the law apply as well to societal rules. The threat of moral disapproval by one's social group, like the threat of legal punishment, is a deterrent to be used with caution. I may disapprove of anyone's doing X, but this does not necessarily mean that I call for societal *enforcement* of my personal moral rule.

Fourth, a man may be concerned about hypocrisy in society. If a rule is to exist as a societal rule it must be generally or usually acknowledged in word if not in deed. What if it is unlikely that more than a few people will actually observe the rule, since the prohibited behavior is too tempting or the enjoined behavior too demanding? Either it will not become a societal rule in spite of a man's efforts to make it such, or it will become a hypocritical societal rule, contributing to the moral corruption of society. So it is either impractical or immoral to try to "legislate" the personal moral rule.

If a man proposes (or endorses) a societal rule, he assumes a responsibility for the consequences of his own advocacy and also for the over-all consequences if everyone were to follow the rule. The ethics of societal-rule advocacy deserves an independent and careful study, particularly by people who are especially involved in this activity, such as church leaders. Obviously the findings of social scientists may be very important in such deliberations, but there are also distinctive ethical issues. For example, what if a church advocates a societal rule permitting premarital sex under certain specific conditions? Suppose that this is a good rule in that its particular and over-all consequences would be good if *everyone followed it,* but that one actual effect of the church's advocacy is likely to be an undesirable increase in premarital sex under many *other* conditions. Which consideration should have most weight?

My main point, however, is that a moral rule which is theoretically applicable to anyone (because of the universalizability requirement) need not always be "legislated" as a societal rule for everyone. The generalization-argument question, "What if everyone did it?" is not a necessary test for all moral rules. I should emphasize that this conclusion does not rest on an assumption that "everyone" must refer to all mankind. Some moral rules apply to a restricted class of agents, and some of these are societal, for example, those which specify the duties which go with an office or role. It is also true that some of the reasons against legislating a moral rule may be less powerful where the class of agents is severely restricted. But these reasons are not always eliminated. And where a moral rule has the form, "Whenever an agent who has characteristics $C1 \ldots C5$ is in a situation having features $F1 \ldots F10$, he ought to do $X$," it is often too limited in scope and bewildering in detail to be of any use as a societal rule (except perhaps as a *law*, in some cases), even though it could have several applications in practice.

There is a tension between societal rules and other moral considerations. For the general good of society, it may be best if all people or most people follow a societal rule, making few or no exceptions in the light of their own judgments of particular situations. But in particular situations, this may mean that sometimes individuals do great harm or fail to do great good in relation to those most immediately concerned. At the very least, the remote general good of society may be grossly overweighted in comparison with the personal happiness of individuals. Moreover, the primacy of societal rules over personal moral judgment may prevent people from developing their own capacity for making independent, mature, and responsible moral decisions. Fletcher is rightly concerned about these dangers: great evil produced in particular cases, undue subordination of the happiness of individuals, perpetual moral infancy for the masses. I share much of his concern, especially where he deals with societal rules concerning such matters as divorce and abortion. But his general theoretical position seems to allow no place at all for societal rules. This is simply a mistake. Such rules have a place in any rational ethic; the real issue is how important their place should be. This issue cannot be helpfully discussed unless a distinction is made between personal rules and societal rules, and unless both are recognized as morally relevant. Against one form of legalism I have rejected the claim that all moral rules must be societal rules requiring the generalization-argument test. Against Fletcher I want to insist that societal rules can indicate moral considerations which are independent of one's judgment concerning the particular consequences of one's own action in the particular situation.

Of course a societal rule *may* satisfy both rule-utilitarian and act-utilitarian tests: if everyone follows it, it will produce the best over-all consequences; and when each person follows it, the particular consequences on each occasion are usually the best. But only if the particular consequences were *always* the best would there be *no* possibility of a conflict between the two tests in a particuar case. In Section IV I shall consider the possibility of *universal* act-utilitarian moral maxims in which "usually" is replaced by "always."

Before we move on to Section IV, I should make a few brief comments on my classification of moral rules. For one thing, the relation between moral *maxims* and *regulative* moral rules needs to be clarified. A moral maxim has the form, "Doing X in situation S usually produces consequences C, which are the best." This is not itself a regulative moral rule, but it might be used as the basis for a regulative moral rule: "Anyone ought to do X in situation S." This regulative rule might be either a societal rule or an "unlegislated" personal rule.

Early in Section III we saw that *promissory* rules are ultimately justified in a rule-utilitarian way and also by reference to the intrinsic value of personal relations based on mutual commitments. Though there may be examples of promissory rules which are personal, they are characteristically *societal*. So the class of societal rules includes both promissory rules (which have a rule-utilitarian aspect) and rule-utilitarian regulative rules.

My classification of moral rules is merely exploratory and sketchy, but I think that I have established my main point: that not all moral judgments are rightly made by reference *solely* to the particular consequences of the particular action in the particular situation, since there are rules other than moral maxims which provide additional moral considerations. This means that Fletcher's "situational" act-utilitarianism is an inadequate ethic.

I do agree with Fletcher, however, in his rejection of exceptionless moral rules. To this we now turn.

## IV. *Exceptionless Moral Rules*

Fletcher holds that the only exceptionless rule of law is "always love." He denies that any strictly universal rules can be derived from this primary rule (p. 27). The only explicit argument which he gives to support his claim is that we cannot derive universals from a universal (pp. 27, 32); but this is not much of an argument. His implicit argument seems to be that moral rules are all moral maxims, and that these rest on summaries or inductions which can never be strictly universal (p. 32). But not all moral rules are moral maxims, and perhaps even the maxims *can* be strictly universal or exceptionless. Fletcher's fundamental attack on legalism is thus in need of support. A strong defense is especially necessary in view of the formidable challenges which have recently been given to any view which rules out the possibility of exceptionless moral rules.[22] I shall try to provide such a defense. Some initial clarifications are necessary, however.

1. *Analytic rules.* First, I must set aside analytic moral rules. "Murder is always wrong" is an exceptionless moral rule. But it is exceptionless at the price of emptiness. "Murder" means "wrong killing." "Wrong killing is always wrong" is true, but it is no guide at all in making moral decisions. A moral rule of the form "Doing X is always wrong" is only applicable in decision-making if "doing X" describes a kind of action which one can identify without having judged already that it is always wrong. Otherwise the rule is merely a way of informing or reminding someone concerning how one is using a word: "I don't call a killing 'murder' unless it's *wrong* killing."

2. *Statements of basic moral obligations.* I also wish to set aside some statements which express basic kinds of moral obligation:

| | | |
|---|---|---|
| *a*) | (Promises) | I have a moral obligation to keep my promises |
| *b*) | (Nonreversibility) | I have a moral obligation not to do as I would not be done by |
| *c*) | (Benevolence) | I have a moral obligation to consider the interests of others as well as my own |
| *d*) | (Utilitarianism) | I have a moral obligation to do as much good as possible |

Another philosopher may reject one or more of these statements of obligation. There is no point in arguing the matter here. The main point is that none of the statements sets forth an exceptionless moral rule of the form, "Always do X in situation S." Rather, each indi-

---

[22] Paul Ramsey, "Two Concepts of General Rules in Christian Ethics," *Ethics*, Vol. LXXVI, No. 3 (April, 1966); *Deeds and Rules in Christian Ethics* (New York: Charles Scribner's Sons, 1967). I. M. Crombie, *op. cit.* For a powerful *attack* on exceptionless-rule ethics see Jonathan Bennett, "Whatever the Consequences," *Analysis* (January, 1966).

cates a type of basic consideration which is morally relevant in deciding whether or not to do X in situation S.

3. *Indefinite Rules.* A third class to be set aside is somewhat similar to the class which we have just considered, but differs in that its members are rules. These rules give a very indefinite description of the action which is prohibited or enjoined: "Never be indifferent to suffering," "Always be open to new truth," "Always consider the interests of others as well as your own" (cf. *c* above). Such rules may well be exceptionless, and if *they* are the only kind that a defender of exceptionless moral rules has in mind, I will accept his claim. But such rules are virtually useless as rules, for when I accept them the real issues of moral decision remain. What is to *count* as "indifference," "not being open to new truth," or "considering others' interests"? Indefinite rules are analogous to indefinite empirical claims such as "Every action produces a reaction," which only indicate a direction in which to look as one investigates a problem. Of course "definiteness" is a matter of degree. "Never deceive anyone" is more definite than "Never be indifferent to suffering" and less definite than "Never tell a lie." The examples which I shall have in mind will all be fairly definite or very definite. My arguments against exceptionless moral rules will not be circular. I will not rely on an "out" every time my legalist opponent seems to confront me with an exceptionless moral rule. I will not say, "Oh, but that's an *indefinite* moral rule." My arguments will assume that a rule is sufficiently definite for this move not to be possible.

Although I am assuming that the description of the action in a moral rule is fairly definite, I am not assuming that it is always "neutral" in Crombie's sense.[23] The description *may* be neutral. That is, in accepting it I do not imply any moral attitude toward the action or acknowledge any moral obligation in relation to it, for example, "killing," "having intercourse," "causing pain." But the description may also include words such as "lie," "lechery," or "promise," which usually do imply moral attitudes or acknowledgments of some moral obligation. The only non-neutral description that I am ruling out is one like "murder," which includes the notion "unexceptionally wrongful act" in its very meaning. If "lechery" is like "murder" in this respect, then it is ruled out. If not, not. Here again I must answer in advance a charge of circularity. I am not requiring of an exceptionless

---

[23] *Op. cit.*, pp. 245–248. His notion of "non-neutral" is similar to my "self-involving" in *The Logic of Self-Involvement*; but he fails to distinguish between a speaker-dependent *implication,* and behavior which merely provides *evidence* concerning attitudes.

moral rule that it be analytically true and at the same time refusing to consider any such rules. My argument against allegedly exceptionless moral rules will *not* be that they are nonanalytic. A rule need not be analytic in order to be exceptionless.

4. *Exceptionless rules and universalized rules.* Our next step is to clarify the notion of "exceptions" to moral rules. The issue concerning exceptionless moral rules is sometimes confused with the issue concerning the universalization-requirement for moral rules. When I do X in situation S and judge that this is morally right, I am committed to a universalized moral rule: *Anyone* in situation S ought to do X. But I am not committed to refraining from any future qualification of the moral rule. An exceptionless moral rule—in my use of the term "exceptionless"—would be one which already has all admissible exceptions or qualifications written into it.

In talking about "exceptions" to a moral rule it is important to distinguish between two possible kinds: universal and singular. The first kind of exception can be written into the rule, and once this is done, the exception disappears; it is no longer the case that I break the rule by doing such-and-such, for the rule has been revised so as to include this kind of case. For example, the rule "Never tell lies" is *broken* if I tell a lie to save my friend's life, but a new rule is *obeyed* if the old one is revised to read: "Never tell lies except when a human life is in danger." Such exceptions are analogous to exceptions to scientific laws, where these are incorporated into a revised scientific law. As Ninian Smart has pointed out, a negative instance in science is not a single event but a *repeatable* event.[24] "X always causes Y except when Z is present." If X only failed to cause Y *once* when Z was present, this would constitute a *singular* exception, a random case.

Can there be a singular or random exception to a moral rule? If I say, "Never tell lies except in this one instance" can this be a moral rule? No. I must have a reason for the exception, and it must be at least theoretically possible for this reason to apply in another case. Hence the rule is explicitly or implicitly revised so as to incorporate a universal exception: "Never tell lies except where there is such-and-such a reason for lying."

Suppose that I insist that a particular case is unique, that the complex set of features of the particular situation which make it an exception are not at all likely to occur again. If I were to formulate a moral rule to universalize from this case, incorporating my complex reason, it would be so specific, detailed, and complicated that it would

[24] *Philosophers and Religious Truth* (London: SCM Press, 1964), p. 40.

be useless; there would never be another case to which the rule would apply. Nevertheless the requirement of universalizability can and must be met: if anyone *were* to be in a situation which fits the description given in the complex rule, the rule would apply to him as well. A moral rule cannot have singular exceptions: it can only have universal exceptions which become part of the rule, either explicitly *or implicitly*. (Later we shall see that rules and their universal exceptions need not always be explicitly formulated.)

The requirement that a moral rule be universalizable thus entails that a moral rule must be "exceptionless," in the sense that no *singular* exceptions are allowed. The issue with which we are concerned, however, is whether or not a moral rule can be "exceptionless," in the sense that no (further) universal exceptions are allowed. From the fact that no singular exceptions are possible we cannot infer anything concerning the possibility of what I am calling "exceptionless" moral rules. The universalizability requirement does not show that universal exceptions are impossible; it only shows that any exceptions must be universal ones.

Nor does the requirement rightly lead to the conclusion that morality not only can but *must* consist of a complex casuistry of moral rules, each rule being explicitly formulated with all its exceptions. Such a conclusion arises from a failure to recognize that the requirement of universalizability is a purely *formal* one. An agent need not be able to *formulate* the rule, specifying all the universal exceptions. He can maintain that his decision is a moral one merely by acknowledging that if anyone else were in a similar situation, he ought to do X too. By "a similar situation," he would mean a situation which is similar in the morally relevant respects. He may have considered a great many morally relevant features of the situation and of the consequences of doing X, giving varying weight to each of them, and perhaps being unable to articulate many of them at all clearly. He cannot fill out all the "material" so as to universalize his moral rule in detail. How could he include any clear reference to the weight given to various factors? His moral rule cannot form part of a detailed system of casuistry. Only in a *formal* way does he satisfy the requirement of universalizability.

The setting forth of one's reason or reasons for a moral decision is related to an implicit formal requirement of universalizability in a way which is similar to the relation between everyday *causal* judgments and the formal requirement of determinism as this is discussed by Hart and Honoré.

There is nothing absurd in combining with the assertion that this [the dropping of a lighted cigarette] was the cause of the fire a refusal to formulate or assent to any given generalization specifying conditions of invariable sequence, though we do not and could not deny the formal claim of (unspecified) *ceteris paribus*, i.e., that there are some factors in the present case which, if they recurred, would always be followed by fire.[25]

Similarly there is nothing absurd in doing the following: I set forth a reason for doing X, e.g., "I have a moral obligation to help a stranger." I refuse to formulate or assent to any specific universalized moral rule concerning doing X. Yet I agree that some universalized moral rule is implied. Many moral decisions are backed by a *single* reason which is linked to a nonuniversalized personal or societal rule: "Help strangers." It is nonuniversalized in that its universal exceptions are not written into it. On the other hand, some highly complex and difficult moral decisions involve a complex *variety* of reasons pro and con, with various weights given to them. In neither case, but especially in the latter case, is it likely to be morally useful to try to formulate fully the universalized rule which is formally required. It is usually better to regard both societal and personal moral rules as nonuniversalized directives to consider important morally relevant factors in a situation. The consistency and continuity of one's moral life should depend on one's commitment to respond to these varying directives, and to various other kinds of consideration, in each particular situation where they are relevant. (Often it is the recognition of relevance which is the crucial factor.) Only rarely will there be any need or any point in trying to formulate a universalized rule in all the requisite detail, for moral situations rarely repeat themselves in *all* the morally relevant ways. Moral reasoning is in this respect more like common-sense investigations of causality and unlike a scientist's search for invariant laws. The formal requirement that a moral rule be universal*izable* does not mean that we must construct an intricate system of casuistry in which every rule is universal*ized*.

If universalizability is only a formal requirement, this removes a major argument in support of one of the two pillars of legalism: a morality of complex and explicit casuistry. The other pillar remains: the exceptionless moral rule. Before I try to knock it down, however, I should concede one fundamental point concerning universalizability. It *is* important as the basis of the "reversibility" test for moral rules.

[25] *Op. cit.*, p. 45.

If Jones is harming Smith, he should ask himself, "If *anyone*, including Smith, were in my shoes ought he to do X? In particular, ought he to do X if I were in his shoes and receiving the harm?" If I am doing something which is contrary to the needs or interests of another person, in the sense that *I* would not want it done to me, this fact provides a moral reason for not doing it—unless I believe that someone *ought* to do it to me in similar circumstances. This is only a very rough test, and various objections can be made against interpreting it in this way and that, but it does provide me with a type of morally relevant consideration which is important in many situations. The test is obviously appropriate in cases of killing, maiming, and stealing. It also usually provides an additional reason in cases of promise-breaking. It provides *a* reason in each case, not necessarily or exceptionlessly an overriding reason. The test depends on the formal requirement of universalizability. If my decision is to be a *moral* one, then I must admit that anyone else would have a right or an obligation to do the same thing in a similar situation, even if I were on the unpleasant receiving end of the action.

To review: Before asking whether or not there can be any exceptionless moral rules, I have set aside analytic moral rules, truisms concerning moral obligation, and indefinite moral rules. Second, I have distinguished between the claim that a moral rule must be universalizable so as to allow for no singular exceptions and the claim that it must be exceptionless, i.e., not open to any further universal exceptions. Third, I have distinguished between the formal requirement that a moral rule must be universal*izable* and the (mistaken) claim that it must be universal*ized*—i.e., explicitly formulated with all its universal exceptions.

Presumably any serious candidate for the status of exceptionless moral rule would already be universalized. The question at issue is whether any such rule can be exceptionless. That is, it may already contain within itself various precisely formulated universal exceptions; but the question at issue is whether any *further* universal exceptions are allowed. We are now in a position to consider this question.

5. *Moral maxims and exceptions.* Let us first consider moral maxims. When I discussed them earlier, I assumed that they were to be formulated in terms of "usually" rather than "always": "Doing X in situation S *usually* produces consequences which are the best." Why not "always"?

One possible reason is that the underlying causal apothegm cannot be universal. All we can know is that doing X *usually* produces C. But surely *some* causal apothegms may be universal: Doing X always

Situation Ethics 409

produces *C*. There are great practical difficulties in the way of discovering universal causal apothegms which would be serviceable as bases for moral maxims. "Doing *X*" is typically a matter of "stealing," "lying," "committing adultery," etc. That is, the description of the action is in common-sense terms rather than in the scientific terms which are usually required for strictly universal causal connections. It is true that even strict universality or invariance is not an absolute, for even a scientific law involves a *ceteris paribus* clause when it is applied—though only minimal deviations are envisaged. But there seems to be no theoretical reason why a moral maxim could not be *as* universal as a scientific law, provided only that it be based on such a law. We may be skeptical concerning maxims which are commonly proposed as universals: does adultery always produce unhappiness in the innocent party, does it *always* weaken the institution of marriage, etc.? But as social science progresses, and we rely less and less on pulpit polemics or antipulpit polemics for our empirical information, *some* exceptionless causal apothegms may emerge. So far, I have not seen any. Possible candidates turn out to be either statistical or analytic. Let us suppose, however, that we have established the following causal apothegm: "Doing *X* in situation *S*, except where *S* is *K*, produces consequences *Ca, Cb* and *Cc*." If I judge that *Ca, Cb* and *Cc* are extremely evil, I may set forth a universal moral maxim: "In situation *S*, except where *S* is *K*, anyone ought not to do *X*." If I set forth such a maxim, backed as it is by a universal causal apothegm, there is a *further* difficulty in the way of making it exceptionless. This additional difficulty is the crux of the matter.

Sometimes doing *X* produces consequence *Cd,* which is so good that doing *X* becomes the right thing to do. So I modify my maxim, qualifying it not only by "except where *S* is *K*," but also by "except where doing *X* produces *Cd*." But what about other possible exceptions of the *Cd* type? Morally relevant consequences cannot be worked into the underlying causal apothegm. There is no limit to the possible consequences of doing *X* in various possible situations. The universal causal apothegm can only provide us with a moral maxim if we rule out in advance the moral relevance of unmentioned possible consequences. As a moral agent I may refuse to do this. This refusal is a *moral* decision. If I say, "There *cannot* be any exceptionless moral maxims" my "cannot" is not a *logical* "cannot"; it is a *moral* "ought not." It is not logically impossible to base a moral maxim on a universal causal apothegm.

My discussion of moral maxims has been very theoretical and abstract. The likelihood of our actually having causal apothegms which are both strictly universal and usable as bases for moral maxims is not great. Where we *seem* to have moral maxims based on such causal apothegms, it is because a reference to such-and-such a consequence is part of the *meaning* of the word used to refer to action X. To this we now turn.

6. *Intrinsically evil actions.* Here are some examples of words used to describe actions where direct consequences of the action are built into the meaning of the word: "kill," "rape," "maim." In each case the inherent direct consequence is evil: death, unwilling intercourse, disfigurement or loss of a bodily member. There is no need or place for a causal apothegm. The word "kill" is inapplicable unless death occurs—and similarly in the other cases. The moral rule "Never kill" is not open to the objection that sometimes killing does not produce death. My objection to the moral rule as an exceptionless rule is of the same sort as my objection to a universal moral maxim as an exceptionless rule: one ought not to set aside in advance the possible moral relevance of unmentioned possible consequences. Even if I now qualify the rule "Never kill" by making it "Never kill except when it produces consequences $Cd$," I cannot fill in all the possibly-relevant consequences $Ce$, $Cf$, $Cg$, etc., for these have no limit. It is true that I can universalize my rule: "Anyone ought not to kill except when it produces consequences $Cd$, $Ce$, $Cf$ or $Cg$," but I cannot rule out the possibility of further exceptions. I may give very great weight to the direct consequences of my actions in comparison with the indirect consequences, but this does not rule out the possibility that an indirect consequence $Cx$, not now foreseen, may require an exception.

7. *Evil-motive actions.* Just as there are words for actions which include a reference to an inherent and evil consequence of the action, there are also words for actions which include a reference to an inherent and evil *motive* for the action. "Gluttony" implies greed, "revenge" implies hatred, "lechery" implies lust, "ostentation" implies vanity. Perhaps it is possible to say, "It was an act of revenge, but he was not moved by hatred." The link between act-word and motive-word may not be unbreakable. If so, instead of saying, "Revenge is always wrong" one could say, "Revenge motivated by hatred is always wrong." Indeed, someone might even claim that as an empirical fact, revenge is always motivated by hatred. I am suspicious of most such claims, e.g., that extramarital intercourse is always motivated by a desire to exploit the other person. But let us concede the possibility for purposes of argument. The central issue is whether an action which is done for such-and-such a motive is *always wrong*.

Suppose that hatred of a person is always evil. Such an assumption might be based on a conviction that hatred always issues in actions which are themselves evil, so that hatred is indirectly and dependently evil. But I am proposing that we consider a moral view in which hatred is also evil in itself. Now on such a view could it be held that an action which is motivated by hatred is always wrong? Could there be an exceptionless moral rule of this kind?

Consider a hypothetical case. I hate Jones and I am about to kill him. By killing him I will prevent him from killing a hundred women and children. I know, however, that my hatred will be my only motive, or my dominant motive, if I kill him. Should I refrain from killing him because my motive would be evil? Surely not. Even if I hold that an action which is motivated by hatred is always "wrong," I should nevertheless kill him if I believe that this is what I ought to do.[26] The term "wrong," in this case, is not used to prohibit actions. It is used to appraise actions in various ways, especially after they have been performed. My action in killing him is or was wrong *in that* I was motivated by hatred; it is or was wrong in that respect.

Does one's motive *ever* provide a morally relevant consideration when one is deciding what to do? Suppose that I am deciding whether to keep or to break a promise. In one situation I might have a morally evil motive for keeping it (lust), and in another situation a morally evil motive for breaking it (hatred). Would the recognition that such-and-such is my motive provide a morally relevant consideration alongside "I have a moral obligation to keep promises," "What if everyone else did it?" or "What will be the good and evil consequences of doing it?" Awareness of motives is relevant, of course, in estimating probable consequences and in guarding against bias in one's judgments, but are motives independently relevant considerations? In the case concerning whether I should kill Jones, I said that if I believe that this is what I ought to do, I should do it; my evil motive should not stand in the way. But is my evil motive a morally relevant consideration when I am trying to determine whether I ought to do it? Yes, I think it is. This is because I have a moral perspective in which my own moral character and integrity is in general a morally relevant

---

[26] The example involves many subtleties and problems which cannot be discussed here. If my moral conviction that I ought to kill him so as to save others is not operative (does not provide a motive), then my hatred is the only motive. If my moral conviction is operative, my hatred may nevertheless provide the most important or dominant motive. Note that we are not considering a case where my moral conviction is operative and *replaces* the hatred (which alone *would be* operative if the conviction were not operative): in such a case my actual motive in killing him is a good one, although my hatred is in itself evil. But how does one sort out motives into operative and inoperative or dominant and subordinate?

consideration. But only if it were a universally overriding consideration would I accept "Actions from motive $M$ are always wrong" as an exceptionless moral rule which governs decision-making. Such a moral perspective seems to me to be perverse and monstrous. Yet it is the moral perspective implied by New Moralists who say that love—that is, the agent's attitude or motive of love—is the *only* intrinsic good, and lack of love is the *only* intrinsic evil.

My personal position is that some consequences are always evil and that some motives are always evil, but that this does not mean that there are exceptionless moral rules, for there are other considerations which *may make it right* to perform actions involving such evil. My objection to exceptionless moral rules does not depend on an alleged impossibility of strictly universal connections between a kind of action and an evil consequence or an evil motive.[27] A description of an action may even include a reference to its direct consequence or its motive. Moreover, it is not logically impossible for there to be strictly universal connections between doing $X$ and consequence $C$ or between doing $X$ and having motive $M$. I am skeptical, however, concerning the alleged universal connections which have been propounded by moralists; so in practice I have an additional reason for rejecting the exceptionless character of moral rules which are alleged to be inherently wrong. But what about moral rules which do not purport to deal with inherently wrong actions? Why cannot a rule-utilitarian rule be exceptionless?

8. *Rule-utilitarian rules and exceptions.* Ian Crombie has argued that although rules concerning "inherently-wrong" actions cannot be exceptionless, "factitious principles" can be.[28] His "factitious principles" are roughly similar to my "rule-utilitarian rules." It may be "morally expedient," he says, that some rules be observed universally, since the over-all consequences of such conformity are better than the over-all consequences of individuals making their own modifications of the rule in relation to particular situations. He says that a judgment that this is so cannot include a claim to *know* that it is so, for no human being could know enough to be able to make a precise comparison between the alternative over-all consequences. But an omniscient God could know. And perhaps God has revealed such morally expedient rules to men. "It does not seem absurd to suppose that the creator might require his fallible creatures always to do that which it is normally best to do."[29]

---

[27] Crombie's objection seems to depend on this: *op. cit.*, pp. 260–261.
[28] *Op. cit.*, pp. 257–261.   [29] Crombie, *op. cit.*, p. 260.

Crombie's argument must not be misinterpreted. He is not claiming that any such rules have actually been revealed, but only that *if* they have been revealed, they *could* be exceptionless. And he is not claiming that such rules would show us what actions are inherently wrong. If I should break such a rule, I would not necessarily be doing something inherently wrong. The action, judged by itself in terms of its consequences and its own specific moral obligations, might be right. But I would not merely have disobeyed an *arbitrary* divine rule. I would have refused to obey a morally expedient rule: universal obedience to this rule actually promotes the best over-all results for mankind, and God has revealed this rule to men because He *knows* what actually promotes the best over-all results for mankind and because He is benevolent toward mankind.

Crombie's argument is important, but I do not think that it holds. If a hypothetical revelation of rule-utilitarian rules is plausible, then it is equally plausible that any such revelation would be accompanied by a command to look out for exceptions, and this for two reasons: (*a*) any rules which fallible *men* can understand and apply are unlikely to be infallible, and (*b*) if God is concerned about individuals as well as society, He is unlikely to subordinate individual good so completely to social good; and no pre-established harmony between the two is either assumed by Crombie or compatible with the common facts of life.

This is in no sense a refutation of Crombie. It is merely a reminder concerning other theoretical considerations. Actually, the claim that there *cannot* be any exceptionless rule-utilitarian rules depends on a *moral* decision not to let the consequences for society be an unexceptionally overriding consideration in relation to consequences for individuals. The claim that there *are* no exceptionless rule-utilitarian rules depends on a rejection of the claim that universal observance of specific societal rules always does promote the best interests of society or the best interests of the individuals concerned. Unless one accepts an inerrant-dictation view of revelation, one's judgment as to whether an alleged revelation of a rule-utilitarian rule really is a revelation depends partly on one's own empirical and moral judgments concerning the consequences of universal observance of the rule. The history of allegedly revealed and allegedly exceptionless rules seems to me to be a history of empirical error and moral evil. This does not mean, however, that I reject the possibility of rule-utilitarian rules which should *usually* be observed and which are supported partly by an appeal to revelation. It is not that revelation informs us of complex *causal* apothegms concerning the consequences of observing such rules.

Rather, revelation gives some understanding of the divine *valuation* of consequences. A Christian will usually give more moral weight to a covenant-vow than to increased pleasure because he believes that this emphasis is more in conformity with God's revelation concerning what is good and evil for men.

But this takes us well beyond the frontiers of secular ethics into the land of theological ethics. I promised not to venture there, and a promise is a promise, even if I have already broken it several times during this chapter.

# Index

Abbott, Walter M., S.J., 206, 235
Abraham, 145–146, 277
Adam, 181, 185
Albert the Great, 144
Althaus, Paul, 289–291
Ambrose, St., 153
Anselm of Laon, 144
Anshen, R. N., 186
Aoerle, D. F., 193
Aristotle, 42, 102, 116, 140–141, 144, 168, 200, 315–316, 361
Arntz, Joseph, O.P., 141, 148
Aubert, R., 170
Augustine, St., 153, 308
Austin, J. L., 383

Baier, Kurt, 46, 392–393
Barnes, Hazel, 328
Barrett, T., 227
Barth, Karl, 32, 69, 71, 105, 268, 288–291, 297, 299–302, 307, 309, 318–319, 327, 336, 341, 344
Bartocetti, V., 227
Bartsch, Hans-Werner, 297
Battles, Ford Lewis, 267
Baxter, Richard, 286–287, 289
Bayle, Pierre, 319
Bea, 326
Bell, Daniel, 328
Bender, L., 228
Bennett, John C., 140
Bennett, Jonathan, 128, 130, 403
Bentham, Jeremy, 338, 352

Berdyaev, Nikolai, 344
Bergmeier, Mrs., 83–84, 86, 88, 90
Bergson, Henri, 302
Bethge, Eberhard, 316
Biechler, James E., 162
Biéler, André, 178, 185
Black, Max, 46, 390–391
Blaine, Graham B., 117
Böckle, Franz, 236, 347
Bohr, Niels, 316
Bonaventure, St., 144
Bonhoeffer, Dietrich, 5, 268, 276, 281, 283, 291, 293, 306, 309, 316, 344–345, 361–362
Boyer, C., 230
Braithwaite, R. B., 301, 303
Brandt, Richard B., 187
Braun, Herbert, 300
Brentano, F., 208
Bring, Ragner, 304, 310
Brunner, Emil, 268, 276, 279–280, 283, 288, 291, 303, 316–317, 344
Buber, Martin, 342, 344, 368, 375–377, 380
Buddha, 325
Bultmann, Rudolf, 297, 300, 308, 312–313

Calvin, John, 62, 177–186, 190–196, 267–269, 275, 286, 289, 291, 308, 310, 314, 317, 319
Cathrein, V., 227–228, 230
Cerfaux, L., 234
Chrysippus, 141

Churchill, Winston, 362
Cicero, 143–144
Clement of Alexandria, 150
Cochrane, Arthur C., 179, 183, 185
Cogley, John, 183
Cohen, A. K., 193
Confucius, 270
Congar, Yves, O.P., 161, 165
Connery, John R., S.J., 254
Coventry, John, S.J., 169
Cox, Harvey, 251, 253, 257, 259, 282, 284, 327, 344
Crombie, I. M., 40–41, 47, 49, 95–112, 393, 403–404, 412–413
Cullmann, Oscar, 234
Curran, Charles E., 156, 168, 172

Dalmau, Iosephus M., S.L., 171
Damien, Father, 371
D'Arcy, Eric, 47–48, 50
Darwin, Charles, 170
David, 45
Davies, W. D., 236
Davis, A. K., 193
Davis, Henry, 227, 273
Delhaye, Philippe, 141
DeLugo, J., 228
Demant, V. A., 4
DeMott, Benjamin, 259–260
Denzinger, H., S.J., 170–171
Dilthey, W., 208
Döllinger, Johann Joseph Ignaz von, 170
Dray, William, 369
Dryer, Douglas, 369
Duhamel, Joseph S., S.J., 223

Ebeling, Gerhard, 276, 278
Eichmann, Adolf, 343
Eichrodt, Walther, 307
Einstein, Albert, 331
Elert, Werner, 310
Eliot, T. S., 270
Elter, E., 227
Emmet, Dorothy, 38, 329, 393
Euclid, 331
Euthyphro, 112–113
Evans, Donald, 121, 124, 372, 383, 388
Evans, Illtud, O.P., 148
Ewing, A. C., 343, 362

Farber, Leslie, 257–258
Fichte, Johann Gottlieb, 305
Fitch, Robert E., 270
Fitzpatrick, Joseph P., 273
Fletcher, Joseph, 4, 57, 83, 123, 140, 212, 215, 218, 243, 250–251, 269–270, 282–285, 311–312, 340, 351–353, 355, 357–365, 367–383, 389–390, 392, 395–396, 401–403
Fontinell, Eugene, 153
Ford, John C., S.J., 220, 225
Frankena, William K., 5, 41, 48–49, 120–122, 124–125, 186, 330–332, 370, 381, 392
Freud, Sigmund, 259, 311, 315, 318, 372
Fried, Morton H., 187
Fuchs, Josef, S.J., 140, 241
Fuller, Lon, 133, 194
Fuller, Reginald, 297

Gaius, 142
Galileo, 170
Gallup, George, 158
Gauthier, David, 369
Genicot, E., 227
George VI, 315
Gibson, A. Boyce, 118
Gilleman, Gérard, S.J., 51–53, 234
Gilson, Étienne, 155, 171
Gogarten, Friedrich, 297, 321, 344
Goldschmidt, Walter, 187
Gonzalez, I., 227–228
Gordon, Lorenne, 369
Graham, Billy, 327
Granfield, Patrick, 155
Gratian, 144
Gregory XVI, 154
Griesbach, Eberhard, 212, 344
Grimm, Harold J., 278
Grisez, Germain G., 226
Gustafson, James M., 9, 233, 235, 271

Hamel, E., S.J., 153
Hare, R. M., 38, 195, 333, 353–357, 386, 393
Häring, Bernard, C.SS.R., 82, 134, 139, 170, 334
Haroutunian, Joseph, 184
Harrison, Jonathan, 79

# Index

Hart, H. L. A., 72, 188–189, 302, 382, 406–407
Hartmann, N., 209
Heidegger, Martin, 300
Heim, Karl, 305–306, 344
Heinzel, G., S.J., 161
Henry, Carl F. H., 134, 291
Hepburn, R. W., 73, 77
Hildebrand, D. von, 209
Herberg, Will, 288
Hirsch, Emanuel, 299
Hitler, Adolf, 101, 315, 343, 361
Holmer, Paul, 293–294
Honoré, A. M., 382, 406–407
Hook, Sidney, 186
Hooker, Richard, 182
Hottinger, Mary, 317
Hume, David, 189, 226, 300–301
Hunter, John, 369
Hurley, Denis E., 151, 172

Isidore of Seville, 143, 146
Iwand, H. J., 301, 315

James, William, 347
Jaspers, Karl, 319
Jerome, St., 153
Jesus Christ, 26, 29, 125, 128, 132–133, 175, 204–205, 207, 215, 231, 234–236, 238–243, 255–256, 269, 276–278, 281–282, 284, 291, 299–316, 319–322, 335, 347, 349, 372, 376
Johann, Robert O., S.J., 149, 249
John XXIII, 165, 213
John the Baptist, 305
John, St., 234, 255–256
Johnson, F. E., 273
Johnson, Lyndon B., 3
Jullien, J., 151
Jung, C. G., 298–299
Justinian, 142
Justin Martyr, 313

Kant, Immanuel, 38, 90, 133, 209, 279, 285, 300, 303, 329, 342, 353, 360, 368, 375–376, 378, 380
Kelly, Gerald, S.J., 220, 225
Kenny, Anthony, 45
Kierkegaard, Søren, 135, 300–302, 305–306, 312–313

King, Mrs. Magda, 300
Kirk, Kenneth E., 274–275
Kluckhohn, Clyde, 186, 188–190
Kohlbrügge, H. F., 314
Kroeber, A. L., 186

Laird, John, 41
Lau, Franz, 321–322
Lazareth, William H., 290
Lehmann, Paul L., 4, 32, 140, 276, 314, 315, 318, 327, 340–341
Lemmon, John, 123
Leo XIII, 150, 154–155, 162, 165, 170–171
Lerner, Daniel, 186
Levy, M. J., 193
Liguori, Alphonsus de, 82, 212–213
Linton, Ralph, 186
Locke, John, 193, 311
Løgstrup, K. E., 312, 321
Lohmeyer, Ernst, 313
Lonergan, Bernard, 166
Lottin, Odon, 141, 144
Lotze, R. H., 208
Lowrie, Walter, 135
Luther, Martin, 14, 38, 60–65, 266–267, 269, 276–280, 289, 291, 293–294, 297–298, 304–308, 310–311, 314–315, 320–322, 335, 347
Lynch, J. J., S.J., 225
Lyons, David, 80–82, 87, 90

Mabbott, J. D., 56
Mandelbaum, Maurice, 343
Manschreck, Clyde L., 266, 278
Maria, Mother, 361
Maritain, Jacques, 147, 244
Marty, Martin E., 271
Marx, Karl, 165, 315, 318, 325, 377
Masters, William H., 258
McCormick, Richard, S.J., 102, 163, 224, 252
McKenzie, John L., S.J., 161, 235
McNeill, John T., 177, 267
Mead, Margaret, 186–187, 329
Mehl, Roger, 301
Melanchthon, Philip, 266–269, 278, 310
Melden, A. I., 55–56, 72
Michel, Ernst, 212

Milhaven, John G., S.J., 128, 149, 251, 252
Mill, John Stuart, 338, 353, 360, 377
Miller, Leonard G., 72
Möhler, Johann Adam, 160
Monden, Louis, S.J., 239
Moore, G. E., 115–116, 118, 301, 333, 380
Mortimer, R. C., 57
Moses, 212, 267
Muelder, Walter G., 341, 343
Muggeridge, Malcom, 260
Murdoch, Iris, 73
Murray, John Courtney, S.J., 148, 157–158, 166–167, 239, 241, 272–273

Neill, Stephen, 312, 374
Neumann, Erich, 298
Newman, John Henry, 218
Newton, Isaac, 331
Niebuhr, H. Richard, 29, 280, 290–291, 342–345, 347
Niebuhr, Reinhold, 313
Nielsen, Kai, 186–189, 193–195, 303
Nietzsche, Friedrich, 40, 315, 318
Noldin, H., S.J., 161, 163, 227
Noonan, John T., Jr., 35, 150, 154
Noth, Martin, 307, 314
Nygren, Anders, 304, 314

Oldham, J. H., 344
Oppenheimer, Helen, 68, 73, 123
Orme, William, 286–287
Örsy, Ladislaus, 155–156
Outka, Gene H., 41

Padberg, John W., 170
Parsons, Talcott, 186
Pascal, Blaise, 300, 331
Paul, St., 27, 36, 40, 49, 236, 239, 255 (Saul), 266, 276–277, 280, 285, 294, 299, 304, 306, 308–309, 314, 347, 349, 377
Peerman, Dean G., 271
Pelagius, 285
Pelikan, Jaroslav, 266
Peter, St., 215, 309
Pfänder, A., 209
Picasso, 19
Pike, James A., 326, 340
Pius IX, 154
Pius X, 150, 171
Pius XI, 150, 220
Pius XII, 150, 171, 220
Plantinga, Alvin, 48, 332
Plato, 103–104, 166, 200, 209, 308, 315
Poincaré, Henri, 301
Pusey, G. B., 308

Quervain, Alfred de, 314

Rad, Gerhard von, 307
Rahner, Karl, S.J., 139–140, 148, 165, 237, 246
Ramsey, Ian T., 41, 68, 71, 73, 95, 118, 123, 177, 271, 301–303, 393
Ramsey, Paul, 4, 59, 120, 130, 243, 246–248, 276, 317, 330, 382, 390, 403
Rand, Ayn, 338
Rawls, John, 330–331, 382, 390
Rembrandt, 19
Rhymes, Douglas A., 243, 282–283, 327
Richardson, Alan, 315
Rickert, H., 208
Ricoeur, Paul, 258
Riga, Peter, 160
Ritschl, Albrecht, 303, 317
Robertson, D. B., 34
Robinson, John A. T., 3, 4, 212, 243, 245–247, 253, 268, 271, 282–283, 326–327, 241
Robinson, N. H. G., 290–291
Rommen, Heinrich A., 141
Ross, W. D., 360
Russell, John L., S.J., 140–141
Ryan, Columba, O.P., 148, 248
Ryan, William, S.J., 51

Sabetti, A., 227
Sade, Marquis de, 338
Sahlins, Marshall, 187–188
Salaverri, Ioachim, 160
Salsmans, J., 227
Sarah, 146
Sartre, Jean-Paul, 328
Scheler, M., 209
Schillebeeckx, Edward, O.P., 149
Schmitt, A., S.J., 161, 227
Schmitz, Kenneth J., 148
Schnackenburg, Rudolph, 236, 243
Schöllgen, Werner, 259
Schönmetzer, A., S.J., 170–171